CURE, CARE, OR CONTROL

DATE DUE

JUL 1 9 1993	
OCT 2 7 1993	
AUG 0 8 1995	
SEP 0 4 1995	
FEB 1 9 1998	
NOV 0 7 2002	

SUNY SERIES IN NEW SOCIAL STUDIES ON ALCOHOL
AND DRUGS

HARRY G. LEVINE AND CRAIG REINARMAN, EDITORS

CURE, CARE, OR CONTROL

ALCOHOLISM TREATMENT
IN SIXTEEN COUNTRIES

EDITED BY
HARALD KLINGEMANN
JUKKA-PEKKA TAKALA
GEOFFREY HUNT

STATE UNIVERSITY OF NEW YORK PRESS

Published by
State University of New York Press, Albany

For information, address State University of New York Press,
State University Plaza, Albany, N.Y., 12246

Production by M.R. Mulholland
Marketing by Fran Keneston

Cover design by Renée-Paule Danthine

Library of Congress Cataloging–in–Publication Data

Cure, care, or control : alcoholism treatment in sixteen countries /
    edited by Harald Klingemann, Jukka-Pekka Takala, and Geoffrey Hunt.
        p.   cm. — (SUNY series in new social studies on alcohol and
    drugs)
    Includes bibliographical references and index.
    ISBN 0-7914-1059-5 (hc : acid-free). — ISBN 0-7914-1060-9 (pb :
    acid-free)
    1. Alcoholics—Rehabilitation—Cross-cultural studies.
    2. Alcoholism—Treatment—Cross-cultural studies.   I. Klingemann,
    Harald, 1948-   . II. Takala, Jukka-Pekka, 1948-   . III. Hunt,
    Geoffrey, 1947-   . IV. Series.
    HV5275.C87   1992
    362.29'28—dc20   91-21915
                                                                    CIP

10 9 8 7 6 5 4 3 2 1

CONTENTS

ACKNOWLEDGMENTS

This publication is the outcome of an interdisciplinary cross-cultural project. The Kettil-Bruun Society for Social and Epidemiological Research on Alcohol provided intellectual context, professional stimulus, and an international network for the effort. The editors have appreciated particularly the inspiring support of Robin Room and Klaus Mäkelä.

The book might not have seen the light of day were it not for the generous support of the Swiss National Research Foundation and the encouragement at the SUNY Press of Harry G. Levine, Craig Reinarman, and Rosalie Robertson. Grants from the Swiss Institute for the Prevention of Alcohol Problems and the Finnish Foundation for Alcohol Studies provided partial support. Working meetings were hosted by the Swiss Institute, the Finnish Foundation, and the Dr. Mladen Stojanovic University Hospital of Zagreb, at Selce, Yugoslavia.

One of the editors, Jukka-Pekka Takala, drew heavily on the favor and support of three institutions: the Finnish Foundation for Alcohol Studies, the Nordic Council for Alcohol and Drug Research, and Finland's National Research Institute of Legal Policy.

The editors are especially grateful to Dr. James Gallagher who revised the manuscript, painstakingly and with much consultation with authors and editors, taking care as far as possible to retain their native flavors while securing the clear expression of what they wished to convey. The cover design owes its distinctive touch to the artistry of Renée-Paule Danthine.

A special word of appreciation is due to Renée Girardet, who provided the crucial secretarial backup, always managing to identify unerringly the most recent revision of a country chapter in the light of yet another editorial update or change.

Introduction

Geoffrey Hunt, Harald Klingemann,
and *Jukka-Pekka Takala*

This book had its origin in a conference in Sweden in October 1984, convened by the late Kettil Bruun to discuss *Societal Responses to Alcohol Problems and the Development of Treatment Systems*. The discussion revealed intriguing similarities and differences in the ways in which different countries managed alcohol problems. For example, one very obvious similarity across a number of countries was the growth in treatment facilities since the end of World War II. However, this expansion was by no means uniform, and therefore other questions arose, such as: What factors had encouraged or hindered this growth? To what extent had growth been the result of factors specific to the control and treatment of alcohol problems or to similar health care systems or even similar societal development? In addition to these more general questions, discussions at the conference also raised more country-specific questions. For example, why had the alcoholism-treatment system in Austria developed in close connection with psychiatry, but in Sweden and Finland as a branch of relief or social welfare? Why had the disease concept of alcoholism so much impact on treatment in the United States but less in the United Kingdom?

These and many other sociological questions stimulated a small group of social science researchers to meet to examine more systematically the development of treatment systems in an international context.

The first step was the preparation of a description of the legal framework of alcohol treatment in six countries (Austria, Finland, Hungary, Poland, Sweden, and Switzerland). These studies were published in a thematic issue of *Contemporary Drug Problems* in spring 1987. The group then decided to extend the scope of the study and the range of countries by commissioning papers from other social scientists and from medical professionals. The resulting papers form the basis of this book. Its initial title—*International Studies in the Development of Alcohol Treatment Systems* (ISDATS)—was intended to highlight the comparative as well as the structural aspects of alcohol-treatment systems. There was no intention to discover which were the best methods of treatment.

In part, the project was seen as an extension of the International Study of Alcohol Control Experience, which had sought to explain the social dynamics of the post-war increase in alcohol consumption in seven countries, and to study the control measures in their historical context (Mäkelä et al. 1981, p. xii), but had not been concerned with the diversity of treatment systems.

For this book the editors had three aims. The first was to present an up-to-date account of treatment systems in as wide a sample of countries as possible. With few exceptions (cf. Porter, Arif, and Curran 1986), there has been a marked absence of material on the different types of treatment systems in different countries. The literature has tended to concentrate either on the evaluation of different forms of treatment or on the characteristics of clients and the etiology of their drinking behavior. The second was to trace the evolution of treatment systems over time in order to highlight the changes that had occurred since 1945, examining such issues as the shift from involuntary inpatient to voluntary outpatient treatment and the export of concepts and methods of treatment from one country to another. The third was to identify and highlight the relative impact of economic, political, legal, medical, and ideological factors on the evolution of treatment of alcohol problems in a range of countries. For example, what had given alcohol problems a high place on the political agenda in the U.S.A. and Sweden but a much lower place in Italy and France?

The initial intention of including a widely representative range of countries and cultures proved impracticable; the collection of chapters is not representative of global cultures; rather, it is heavily biased toward European and anglophone countries. The brief reports from Nigeria and China cannot redress the imbalance, but they do offer an interesting view on how alcoholism is regarded and dealt with in two countries very different from each other and from the others represented in this book. Their treatment efforts seem to differ little from the medical treatment of alcoholism elsewhere, but they are much more marginal in society than the treatment systems of the European and North American countries included.

However, despite the European bias of the countries represented, they do represent diverse types of treatment development. For example, the U.S.A., Finland, and Sweden have been strongly influenced by the temperance movement, but France and Italy much less so. The formerly designated "East European" countries had centrally planned health-care systems, whereas health care in the U.S.A. is greatly influenced by market forces. It is only relatively recently that France, Italy and the Soviet Union have recognized alcohol consumption as a major problem, but in Finland and Sweden this has been recognized since the nineteenth century. Alcoholics Anonymous has greatly influenced the treatment system in the U.S.A.; in Nigeria, however, traditional healers perform rituals to remove the curse of alcoholism, attributed to evil spirits.

The countries also represent different alcohol cultures, from the traditional high-consumption wine countries of southern Europe to the spirits-drinking north European countries; from Italy, where the main task of legislation about alcohol is to maintain the quality of wine, to Finland, where the law is used mainly to say where and when it is permitted to purchase and drink alcohol, and who is allowed to do so; in other words, from countries in which wine drinking has traditionally been regarded as a normal part of everyday life, to countries that have tried to prohibit the consumption of alcohol.

True, some stereotypes may be partly mythical (see the chapter on Italy), and differences in both beverage choice and alcohol-consumption levels have been diminishing (cf. Sulkunen 1976, Sparrow 1989). However, the trend toward homogenization is far from complete and, at any rate, during most of the period covered by the chapters in the book—roughly since World War II—the differences in alcohol culture and alcohol-control policy have been even greater than they are now.

What is "Alcoholism Treatment"?

For a study designed to produce comparable knowledge about the same topic in different countries the problem of defining the object of the study must be faced. What is meant by "alcoholism treatment"? Analytically, one could start by considering how Mäkelä and Säilä (1987) divided the management of alcohol-related problems into four components:

- the provision of material services and spiritual comfort to needy or unhappy drinkers
- the treatment of alcohol-related medical complications
- the manipulation of drinking patterns and levels of intake
- the control of disruptive behavior.

This outline encompasses all three concepts in the title of this book—*care, cure,* and *control.* Of course, one problem is that "alcoholism treatment" may mean almost any combination of the four components, and there are often ambiguous glidings from one component to another. Uncontroversially, "treatment" applies only to alcohol-related medical complications, but it is questionable whether the provision of material or spiritual comfort to drinkers can be called treatment. Then there may be agreement in theory that control of disruptive behavior should be kept conceptually separate from "treatment", but the distinction does not always hold in practice. It is also debatable whether the manipulation of drinking patterns and levels of intake can be called treatment in a strict sense, but it is just this (the third component of Mäkelä and Säilä) that is probably most often thought of when speaking of "alcoholism treatment".

We believe that a detailed analysis of the activities of various treatment organizations would be necessary for a deeper comparative study—and in such an effort Mäkelä and Säilä's four components would be useful. However, this study had a less ambitious goal—to discover what it was that societies said was "alcoholism treatment" rather than what they did to manage alcohol problems.

According to the working definition for the ISDATS studies, "alcohol-treatment systems" refer to measures and organizations that explicitly offer individuals treatment or help for alcoholism, alcohol-dependence, or alcohol-related problems in their ways of life. The definition did not include general prevention, health education of the public, or alcohol-control policy. Treatment is expected to make an improvement in the individual's condition or at least arrest its deterioration, but it was not required that the efficacy of the treatment had been scientifically established. The definition covered institutions that did little more than provide housing and some comfort in the lives of their clients, if they did so under the rubric of treating or caring for the alcoholic.

However, contributors were expected to apply critical common sense in their characterization of the alcoholism-treatment systems. The wider working definition of "alcohol treatment system" covered organizations that treated alcohol-related medical problems other than alcoholism, as well as those that handled and controlled alcohol-related problems of law and order or social discipline.

The emphasis on treatment specifically labeled alcoholism treatment risked introducing bias into the comparisons. It meant that alcohol treatment offered as part of the general health or psychiatric services would receive less emphasis than that provided by organizations set up particularly for the treatment of alcoholism. It is the treatment provided by such organizations— including those specialized in alcoholism and "other addictions"—that is referred to as specific or particular alcoholism treatment.

The word "system" in "alcohol treatment system" refers broadly to those social structures and processes that have the function of alcohol treatment, and, in a narrower sense, to the interconnection of different treatment units or agencies, chains of treatment, and referral channels. Obviously, countries vary greatly not only in the extent and efficiency of their coordination of treatment services: a mere collection of services does not constitute a system. In some countries "alcohol-treatment systems" may take in more than alcohol-related problems.

A "shopping list" was drawn up to guide data acquisition and the drafting of national chapters. It suggested an introductory section that should describe the historical background of alcoholism and alcohol-treatment activities in a country, as well as its socio-political structure and trends in alcohol-related problems. This was to be followed by an "inventory" of alcoholism-treatment institutions, which would take account of informal treatment resources; the legal division of labor between judicial, health, and social authorities; institutional treatment philosophies and specific methods; the target groups of treatment efforts; treatment acceptance and social control; institutional cooperation and financing structures; and the extent to which the treatment components functioned as a coherent or unified system. Finally, there was to be a section on alternative treatment resources, especially in the area of mutual-support (self-help) groups and unconventional methods, and their relationship to the mainstream structures. Authors were encouraged to act as key informants for their countries and to develop their own particular national themes.

Although the authors were encouraged to follow the list, the reader must realize that this collection of national reports does not constitute a strictly comparative reference work in which identical variables appear in each report. Indeed the accounts vary greatly. The differences reflect the problems that many authors experienced in their attempts to keep to the "shopping list." No one can be expected to encapsulate in a simple descriptive statement the variety and complexity of alcohol treatment in such countries as the United States and the Soviet Union. Moreover, even smaller and relatively homogeneous countries such as France and Italy lack data on such key variables as numbers of clients attending outpatient facilities.

The editors had long discussions about whether a strictly comparative handbook or reference work, or a collection of national stories, would be the ideal mode of presentation. Given the great heterogeneity of the sample of countries and the differences in the scope of the qualitative and quantitative data available (and the often inadequate information systems) it was felt that the guidelines for the authors represented a healthy pragmatism and guaranteed at least a minimum of comparative information. At the same time they were sufficiently flexible to permit the authors to point out the most significant characteristics and the particular features of their national treatment systems.

A truly comparative empirical study (e.g., using identical survey techniques and questionnaires) in a few Western countries would have made it possible to follow textbook methods of international studies. The editors had to decide between choosing only a very few countries with adequate and developed alcohol information systems or a more cross-cultural approach. In deciding in favor of the latter, their aim was to obtain new information from a wide range of countries although many had poor information systems and no tradition of survey research. These deficiencies, it was felt, should not prevent them from trying to describe those countries' treatment systems.

The choice of a cross-cultural approach also raised the difficulties of producing an "equivalence of meaning" in particular analytical expressions. For example, the authors often translated terms from legal texts in such a way that the exact connotation remained unclear. The names used for national treatment institutions and forms of treatment were in some cases difficult to translate. Therefore, it was decided, as far as possible, to retain the terminology used by authors and to list in a glossary those key words or definitions considered to be "common sense" within a country but not readily intelligible to foreigners.

However, the problem of equivalence did not arise only with regard to language, for certain dimensions of comparison proved to be "ethnocentric." One instance of this was the question of what exactly should be considered an alternative form of treatment or a genuine "self-help" group. The original definitional characteristic of "group autonomy with no professional leader or participation" was found to be too restrictive for East European countries. For Nigeria, the use of folk medicine raised the question as to whether it could be legitimately described as an alternative form of treatment. The reader will find therefore that the authors have brought to bear on the study their different professional and cultural backgrounds. Each chapter reflects to some degree an interplay of three factors. First, the authors' professional bias may influence the focus of the paper; some have a background in biological and clinical research, whereas others have been trained in the social sciences. Second, the perspectives of different chapters often reveal the major concerns of a country and the way in which alcohol problems are perceived. For instance, the Italian authors dealt with the seeming contradiction in Italy between the growth in treatment facilities and the parallel decline in consumption; and American authors concentrated on the relationship in their country between public and private treatment systems. Finally, the tone of a chapter may reflect a particular cultural framework. For example, the papers from the U.S.S.R., China, and Nigeria not only describe their treatment systems, but also, at a different level of analysis, convey a totally different way of talking about that information (e.g., alcoholics, drunkards, alcohol dependents). In their very language and style they tell us something about the way that academic discourse is (or has been) carried out in those countries and those systems. In adopting an alternative style they remind us of the ethnocentrism of Western scientific discourse.

Taken as a whole, the contributions contained in this book provide the reader, for the first time, with a compendium of comparative information on the evolution of alcohol-treatment systems. We are sure it will be useful to future researchers in enabling them not only to place the development of their own countries' treatment systems in a wider context but also to begin to examine the extent to which that development shares common structural features with that of other countries and cultures.

Spring 1990

References

Mäkelä, K. et al. 1981. Alcohol, society and the state. *A comparative study of alcohol control* 1. Toronto: Addiction Research Foundation.

Mäkelä, K., and S.-L. Säilä. 1987. The distribution of alcohol-related overnight stays among different authorities in Finland, 1960–1980. *Contemporary Drug Problems* 14(1): 125–36.

Porter, L., A.E. Arif, and W.J. Curran. 1986. *The law and the treatment of drug- and alcohol-dependent persons: A comparative study of existing legislation.* Geneva: World Health Organization.

Sparrow, M. et al. 1989. Alcoholic beverage taxation and control policies. *Brewers Association of Canada,* 7th ed. Ontario, Canada.

Sulkunen, P. 1976. Drinking patterns and the level of alcohol consumption: an international overview. *Alcohol 3.* New York: John Wiley & Sons.

Present State and Prospects of Treatment of Alcoholism in the Soviet Union

N.N. Ivanets, I.P. Anokhina, V.F. Egorov, Y.V. Valentik
and S.B. Shesterneva

More than 4.5 million alcoholics are under medical observation in the U.S.S.R. For every alcoholic, there are three to four alcohol abusers, who are included in so-called risk groups. Various treatment, rehabilitation, and preventive measures are applied to alcoholics and risk groups. There is a specialized health service for alcoholics and people with alcohol problems, called in the U.S.S.R. the "narcological" health service. This paper considers the structure and organization of this service.

History of the Special Service for Alcohol Problems

The first state edicts on measures to overcome inebriety in Russia were adopted in the middle of the seventeenth century. They concerned the sale and consumption of alcoholic beverages. They were complemented by church interdictions, social educational measures and voluntary movements to encourage sobriety. Much later, in the second half of the nineteenth century, medical measures were initiated. In the late 1880s alcohol-related problems were attracting the growing attention of physicians and other representatives of the Russian intelligentsia. In 1897 the 12th Congress of Physicians, held in Moscow, adopted a resolution to organize a special section on alcoholism. As a result several hospitals and outpatient clinics were established, supported mainly by philanthropic funds.

In 1909–1910, at the initiative of a special commission of the Health Association, the 1st All-Russian Congress on the campaign against inebriety was held. Russian psychiatrists made important contributions to the organization of antidrinking activities. At their meetings they discussed such subjects as the early diagnosis and treatment of alcoholics, the building of state hospitals, and means of enlisting the cooperation of various medical specialties.

The problems of the organization, continuity, and evaluation of the efficacy of the treatment of alcoholism were discussed at the famous Pirogov Meetings. V.M. Bekhterev founded a special institute with outpatient and inpatient divisions for the medical care of alcoholics.

During World War I, institutions for the treatment of alcoholism were closed. After the Great October Socialist Revolution, the 8th Party Congress, in 1919, adopted a program that put the campaign against alcoholism on a par with that against tuberculosis and venereal diseases. The first resolutions of the Soviet government were followed by legislative and administrative measures against drunkenness, and in 1923 specialized inpatient departments for alcohol problems ("narcological" departments) were established in psychoneurological clinics, as well as separate outpatient clinics ("narcological dispensaries"). These were timely measures. The increase in annual per capita alcohol consumption from 0.2 to 1.2 liters (in absolute alcohol), beginning in 1923, resulted immediately in the growth of alcoholism. The number of inpatients with alcohol psychoses increased by 7.6 times between 1923 and 1927 (Lisitsin and Kopyt 1983, 94). The special outpatient clinics, the dispensaries, were then included in the reorganized psychiatric services, and inpatient psychiatric clinics began to admit alcoholics. The first specialized hospital was opened for the treatment of alcoholics with acute symptoms, and an inpatient clinic for the long-term treatment of alcoholism was set up in one of the Moscow region settlements.

In the 1930s the U.S.S.R. compared favorably with many other countries with regard to alcohol problems. However, by the end of the 1940s the incidence of alcoholism had risen to an annual rate of up to 18 cases of alcoholism per 100,000 population (Lisitsin and Kopyt 1983, 94). This increase occurred although medical and social problems related to alcohol were receiving a great deal of government attention. The influence of previous administrative measures on the level of inebriety and alcoholism was carefully studied and the results of treating alcoholism in various health establishments were assessed.

After the Great Patriotic War of 1941–45 alcohol consumption resumed its increase, and from 1.9 liters per capita in 1940 reached 4.7 liters in the middle of the 1960s (Lisitsin and Kopyt 1983, 76–77). Drunkenness and alcoholism caused appreciable economic and social damage. Serious large-scale measures had to be taken. Health bodies were given important new tasks. Special outpatient and inpatient clinics were set up all over the country. The Ministry of the Interior undertook certain responsibilities for antialcohol activities and opened its first sobering-up stations. In 1964 it set up the first treatment-and-labor camp, in the Kazakh Republic (see below). At the same time, in the Moscow region, health centers were being opened at large industrial enterprises. These stations, camps, and centers are well-established components of today's developed network of specialized services for people with alcohol problems.

However, alcohol consumption continued to grow, and in 1970 reached an annual rate of 6.8 liters per capita (U.S.S.R. National Economy in 1985). The prevalence of alcoholism increased accordingly, averaging 17% of the population for 1955–68. The numbers of alcohol patients registered for observation increased from 167.1 per 100,000 population in 1965 to 425.5 in 1971 (data provided by the Department of Medical Statistics of the U.S.S.R. Ministry of Health).

In 1972 the network for compulsory treatment of alcoholics was established. Actions taken after the 1972 decree were a turning point in the medical care of alcoholics. The prerequisites were being provided for the organization of a separate specialized health service. The question was discussed at the 6th All-Union Congress of neuropathologists and psychiatrists. In 1975 the U.S.S.R. Ministry of Health Board resolved to establish such a service. In 1976 special services were organized within the system of the U.S.S.R. Ministry of Health to increase the efficacy of treatment and prevention. The institutions and divisions were listed, staff limits were laid down, and instructions for treatment were issued. The newly established health services were provided with up-to-date medicines and equipment. The special system established in 1976, with subsequent additions, is that in operation today.

The Structure and Development of the Service

The specialist service for alcohol and drug abuse problems encompasses a number of institutions, organizations, and divisions for the early diagnosis of alcoholism, drug addiction, and toxicomania, to provide medical and social assistance and to prevent these conditions. It is organized according to administrative and territorial boundaries. Within an administrative subdivision (such as a union or autonomous republic, region, city, or rural area) the service and other local treatment and preventive institutions of the U.S.S.R. Ministry of Health, commissions for the campaign against inebriety and alcoholism of the soviets of people's deputies, local bodies of the Ministry of the Interior, and other organizations officially constitute a coordinated system with common goals.

The service is based mainly on republic, territorial, regional, and town dispensaries. It includes outpatient clinics, diagnostic laboratories, health centers at industrial enterprises, and inpatient clinics at industrial, building, and agricultural enterprises, where treatment is combined with obligatory work. Patients are paid for their work according to their occupations and skills. There are also day centers with various forms of treatment, including work therapy. Rural areas have interdistrict dispensaries. Psychiatric and general health clinics also accept alcohol patients as part of the system (Fig. 1).

To coordinate the network of alcohol services, the U.S.S.R. Ministry of Health has a separate administrative department. The countrywide organization of special facilities under the Ministry of Health is complemented by the treatment-and-prevention and treatment-and-labor institutions of the Ministry of the Interior. A treatment-and-labor camp is a specialized establishment where antialcohol treatment is combined with labor. Patients

FIGURE 1

Typical Structure of Narcological Service in a Region, Territory, or Republic

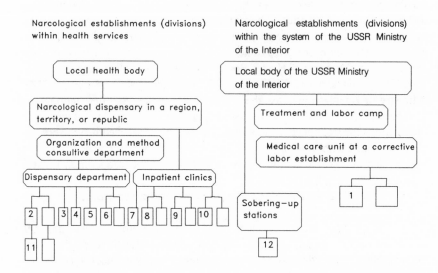

are paid for their work. A sobering-up station is an inpatient facility where acutely intoxicated persons receive medical treatment to sober them and to prevent alcohol-related complications. It also carries out antidrinking propaganda. New cases of drug addiction are discovered at these stations. The special units at the medical facilities of corrective labor camps have the same range of services as the corresponding institutions or divisions of the health services, differing from them only by a special regimen. Special institutions and departments of the Ministry of the Interior are provided under legislation that compels certain alcoholics to accept medical care; these are people with alcohol problems, who avoid medical care and violate public order and community regulations (see below).

Table 1 shows the development of the alcohol and drug abuse ("narcological") service between 1976 and 1987.

The service was markedly improved after the additional measures taken by the U.S.S.R. Ministry of Health in accordance with the 1978 decree of the U.S.S.R. Council of Ministers: "On additional measures to be taken to intensify the struggle against inebriety and alcoholism." It became more active with the expansion of its network and staff increase. This is illustrated by the figures showing the growth in the number of alcoholics registered for medical observation.

TABLE 1.A

Expanding Network of Narcological Establishments, 1976–1987

	1976	1978	1984	1985	1986	1987
Narcological dispensaries	19	73	153	215	410	509
• interdistrict narcological units and departments	1,486	2,545	3,287	3,432	3,566	3,603
• anonymous-treatment units					166	235
• antialcohol propaganda and prevention units					207	274
• outpatient treatment clinics (paying patients)					34	49
• feldsher narcological units at industrial,			5,921	6,956	7,742	8,099
building and agricultural enterprises				6,391	7,181	7,489

TABLE 1.B

Narcological Beds, 1976–1987

	1976	1978	1984	1985	1986	1987
Narcological beds at industrial, building, and agricultural enterprises	29	50	100	11	125	131
(thousands)	9	22	63	73	82	88
Beds for the compulsory treatment of alcoholics with serious concomitant diseases				1,369	2,324	2,959
Planned provision of beds (per 100,000 population)	11.3	19.0	36.3	40.1	44.5	46.0

TABLE 1.C

Narcological Staff Limits, 1976–1987

	1976	1978	1984	1985	1986	1987
Planned provision of psychiatrist-narcologists	2,024	4,096	7,313	8,468	10,815	12,046
Actual numbers of psychiatrist-narcologists	1,215	2,683	5,316	6,188	7,828	8,900
Ratio of psychiatrist-narcologists per 10,000 population	0.5	1.0	1.9	2.2	2.8	3.1

TABLE 2

Distribution of Alcoholic Patients Newly Registered for Observation
by Year and by Severity of Condition (per 100,000 Population)

	1980	1983	1984	1985	1986	1987
Total (all stages)	488.2	540.5	520.1	564.1	532.5	498.1
Stage I	71.8	88.7	86.3	102.2	135.5	145.5
Stage II	395.2	439.5	422.3	452.7	388.2	345.6
Stage III	21.2	12.3	11.5	9.2	8.8	7.0

The increase in alcoholism in subsequent years was associated with certain economic and social factors; the high, though stabilized, level of alcohol consumption in the 1980s had a significant effect. Consumption in 1984 amounted to 8.4 liters per capita (Lisitsin and Kopyt 1983, 76–77). At that time, however, the special services were beginning to show results: the numbers of alcoholic psychoses decreased and the incidence and morbidity indices of alcohol psychoses improved.

The 1985 decrees of the government and Party gave new impetus to strengthening the material and technical basis of the services and improving their activities. The numbers of physicians specialized in alcohol problems have increased by 45%, of beds for alcoholics by 25%, and of special dispensaries 2.7 times. In addition to the expanded network of centers, more divisions for the anonymous treatment of alcoholics, on a self-supporting basis, have been established. Also, differentiated bed limits have been introduced, specifying one to six beds per 10,000 population in different administrative subdivisions.

In addition to the previously opened units for teenagers, the dispensaries have several new divisions—for instance, anonymous-treatment units and units for antidrinking propaganda and preventive medical assistance. Since 1985 the network of anonymous-treatment services for paying patients has been expanded. Patients with early signs of alcoholism apply readily for anonymous treatment. Most are well-socialized persons, who include research workers, physicians, artists, drivers, and others.

Organization and method departments, developed from the corresponding units of the dispensaries, are responsible for coordination and also carry out much consultive work.

Since 1987, psychiatrist alcohol specialists are appointed to the staff of district physicians: one per 850 alcoholics and alcohol abusers without symptoms of alcoholism (the previous ratio was one per 70,000 population). Also, each rural district has at least one such specialist.

In 1985, to improve antialcohol therapy, various enterprises and organizations were given the task of producing medicines and medical equipment. As a result of these and other measures taken in 1985–87, the service is now sufficiently equipped for the successful treatment of alcoholism. Its results are shown in Figures 2 and 3. As the numbers of alcoholics registered for medical observation tended to stabilize, the annual incidence of alcoholism declined gradually. Particularly manifest has been a reduction in the incidence of alcoholic psychoses. The numbers of patients at the more serious stages (stages two and three) of alcoholism have decreased, changing the entire picture of alcoholism morbidity (Table 2). It is of interest that the diagnosis of alcoholism is now made earlier; physicians from general health services are widely involved in early recognition of alcoholics among the population.

The Legal Basis of Treatment

Health legislation in the U.S.S.R. recognizes alcoholism as an illness dangerous to the environment and therefore requiring special treatment and prevention. Alcoholics are treated in special hospitals for addicts. Numerous alcohol abusers without symptoms of alcoholism undergo preventive observation and treatment in the special alcohol and drug abuse dispensaries and in general health clinics. Most alcoholics apply for medical care voluntarily and receive it at the treatment-and-prevention institutions. A physician alcohol specialist decides in consultation with the patient and family whether the patient will be treated as an inpatient or an outpatient. Nonvoluntary patients with acute or chronic alcoholic psychoses can only be hospitalized, as they are considered to constitute a danger to themselves and to other people. Alcoholics are subject to compulsory treatment when they:

- avoid voluntary treatment and continue to drink after treatment, violating working discipline and public order despite public or administrative disciplinary measures;
- have committed a crime but lack conscious control and are, therefore, not amenable to the law;
- have committed a crime although capable of appreciating reality, but have been taken ill at the time of passing or serving the sentence;
- have committed a crime to obtain alcohol, being conscious and therefore responsible in law.

Compulsory treatment for one to two years combined with labor is prescribed for alcoholics who avoid treatment but have not committed a crime. They are treated in the specialized treatment-and-labor camps of the Ministry of the Interior.

Alcoholics who lacked conscious control at the time of the crime, or who before being sentenced show signs of severe mental disorder, receive medical treatment only. Such disorders are pathological intoxication, acute alcoholic psychosis such as delirium tremens or hallucinosis, Korsakoff's psychosis, dipsomania, and alcoholic delusion of jealousy. In exceptional cases, pronounced alcoholic deterioration of personality may be considered such a disorder.

Alcoholics who suffer from the disease while serving the sentence are obliged to take treatment as well, which is given at psychiatric facilities. The length of the treatment depends upon the course of the disease.

Alcoholics who have committed crimes to obtain alcohol are compulsorily treated at medical care units of corrective labor establishments, treatment-and-labor camps, or specialized divisions of treatment-and-prevention institutions of health organizations. The decision concerning commital to compulsory treatment in a treatment-and-labor camp is made by the court on the basis of a health certificate presented by a commission from an alcohol, psychoneurological, or other health establishment. The commission consists of a neuropathologist and internists and is headed by a specialist psychiatrist; it determines the contraindications and the diseases that excuse a patient from undergoing treatment at a treatment-and-labor camp. Decisions about the state of consciousness of the intoxicated person and about an alcoholic criminal's need of medical treatment are made on the basis of a forensic psychiatric examination in a neuropsychiatric hospital or dispensary.

The criteria for the selection of alcoholics for antialcohol and work therapy in the treatment-and-labor camps are kept under review to prevent the unjustified committal of well-socialized patients to a special regimen.

Organization of Inpatient Treatment

Alcoholic patients newly registered for observation are given at least a 45-day treatment course, which is sufficient for a gradual application of all basic methods of antialcohol therapy. Duration of treatment during repeated hospitalization, and for patients with serious concomitant diseases, depends upon the clinical condition. Patients with contraindications to being sent to a treatment-and-labor camp are placed under strict observation in special hospital wards (divisions). Because of a high incidence of somatic diseases, these patients are first treated with psychotherapy and other nonpharmacological methods.

In the units at industrial enterprises treatment lasts three to four months. Data indicate that treatment in such units is about twice as effective as that in the alcohol departments and outpatient clinics of the general health service. Daytime inpatient treatment lasts one or two months on an average.

Inpatients in treatment-and-labor camps and corrective labor institutions receive detoxification and somatic treatment in their medical care units.

The outpatient treatment of alcoholics takes three years, because of the chronic pattern of the disease, possible occurrence of psychosis, aggravation of pathological craving for alcohol, and various behavioral deviations, and for other reasons.

Intensive and frequent treatment courses are prescribed for newly diagnosed alcoholics, particularly when there are clinical symptoms of the disease and adverse social consequences of alcohol abuse. After discharge from hospital or treatment-and-labor camp, they continue with less intensive outpatient treatment. During the three-year course the patients are observed actively, and afterward passively (if no relapses occur). The number of therapeutic courses is gradually reduced, together with the number of supportive visits to control abstinence. Patients in stable remission are removed from the register (about 500 cases annually).

In the treatment-and-labor camps and corrective labor institutions of the Ministry of the Interior, alcoholics are treated mostly as outpatients. In the camps, the intensive treatment carried out after the course of inpatient detoxification and somatic therapy takes half or two-thirds of the time of their stay in the camp. The rest of the time is given to confirming the results of treatment and orienting the patients toward a sober way of life.

In the corrective labor institutions, with a two-year stay, alcoholics take a complete course of antialcohol therapy, followed by partial observation. After discharge they are observed at their local special facilities. For a short-term sentence, treatment and subsequent observation take place at their place of residence.

Principles and Methods of Treatment

The alcoholism treatment system follows well-established principles: a treatment plan based upon thorough knowledge of alcoholism pathogenesis, and therapeutic measures adapted to clinical findings, personality traits, and the particular characteristics of the environment; comprehensive treatment; orientation of the patient toward total abstinence from alcohol; and stepwise and sequential treatment. As a rule, alcoholic patients are treated in three stages (Ivanets 1983). First, the intake of alcohol is stopped, intoxication treated, and the pathological craving for alcohol and acute abstinence syndrome arrested. The patient is examined and psychotherapy instituted with both the patient and the family. Second, the patient receives intensive antialcohol treatment. Third, maintenance and rehabilitation therapy is instituted.

At the first stage, traditional detoxification agents (thiol preparations, hypertonic salt solutions, and plasma substitution solutions) combined with vitamin preparations and medication for relief of symptoms are complemented by psychotropic drugs (tranquilizers of the benzodiazepine series and neuroleptics) for the treatment of affective, psychopathic, and neurosis-like disorders and reduction of pathological craving for alcohol.

Nonmedical approaches are practiced on a large scale. For instance, surface controlled craniocerebral hypothermia and sorption detoxification methods are employed to treat the alcohol abstinence syndrome (Sosin 1987). Among nonpharmacological methods of treating the abstinence syndrome, acupuncture is widely employed, permitting rapid relief from its less severe forms.

At the second stage much more varied methods and means are used. The most common is conditioned reflexotherapy, which has been widely used since 1933, and which sets up a stable aversion to alcoholic beverages and a vomiting reaction, used as a negative unconditioned stimulus. However, this method has various shortcomings—contraindications, difficulty in choosing dosages, instability, and rapid extinction of the negative conditioned reflex— and does not enjoy wide popularity at present. Among traditional agents used are alcohol sensitizing drugs. Teturamum (disulfiram, Antabuse) is used separately or, more rarely, for teturamum-alcohol reactions.

The creation of a ''chemical barrier'' cannot solve all problems, however. It does not influence psychopathological disturbances. Various psychotropic agents have been traditionally used for alcoholism (Ivanets and Igonin 1975), primarily because of the variety of associated psychopathological disorders, ranging from light neurosis-like disorders to rudimentary, hallucinatory, and delirious reactions occurring upon withdrawal. Mild drugs are preferred since they act selectively, have no pronounced side effects, do not develop tolerance or cross-tolerance to alcohol, and do not interfere with social adaptation of alcoholic patients. Some neuroleptics and tranquilizers meet these requirements.

For affective disorders, tricyclic antidepressants are widely used, and lithium salts more rarely. Tranquilizers are used with caution because of the risk of dependency.

Neuropeptides are perhaps the most promising drugs among those in present use. Cholecystokinin, for instance, can modulate dopamine turnover and inhibit primarily the dopamine system of the brain. Patients with alcohol abstinence syndrome feel physically and psychologically better in the first minutes and hours after injection of the drug. It has proved highly effective in treating an aggravated pathological craving for alcohol in remission and in preventing relapse (Anokhina 1988; Anokhina et al. 1988).

Recent years have seen a greatly increased interest in methods of electro-stimulation of the central nervous system, which activate the endorphinergic brain systems. For instance, transcranial electrostimulation of patients with alcohol abstinence syndrome, performed by combining direct current with square pulses of alternating current of 70–80 Hz, rapidly arrests the principal symptoms of the syndrome during therapy (Grinenko et al. 1987, 47–48).

Drug therapy is frequently combined with other forms of treatment. Apart from the stable suppression of pathological craving for alcohol and the strengthening of a conditioned emotionally negative reaction to alcohol, antialcohol therapy has other important uses: in cases of anosognosia (denial), for instance, and for personality disturbances, and to orient patients toward total abstinence and a deliberate sober way of life. These tasks are complemented by psychotherapy, such as group hypnosuggestive therapy and autogenous training. A form of therapy in increasing use is nondirective psychotherapy for small groups of patients, followed by the organization of psychotherapeutic associations.

Promising new methods of psychotherapy are being used for major clinical symptoms of alcoholism. One such method is situational and psychological training, designed to suppress pathological craving. It consists of structured group discussions, the reproduction of situations and conditions that aggravate the craving, and autorelaxation. In the course of training, the patients overcome anosognosia, and learn to recognize initial signs of a growing craving for alcohol and overcome it (Ivanets and Valentik 1986, 366–68).

Studies are also being made of different forms of transcranial electric and magnetic techniques. Maintenance therapy, which continues for three years, is an obligatory stage of antialcohol therapy. It is carried out in the dispensaries by repeated courses of psychotropic drugs (for affective disorders or aggravated pathological craving for alcohol during remissions), courses of sensitizing agents, and symptomatic treatment. Maintenance therapy consists of client-centered and group therapy (if the patient had group psychotherapy while in hospital). Sometimes, short-term inpatient treatment is repeated to prevent relapse.

Conclusion

The efficacy index of alcoholism treatment in terms of annual remissions is at present about 30%. This low value reflects the tendency of most alcoholics registered for observation to avoid treatment; it reflects also their negative attitude toward treatment. For them, hospitalization is only a compromise, a concession to the pressure of the positive environment. Hence, their psychological reorientation toward sobriety and the overcoming of anosognosia can be very difficult. The development of the treatment system should be seen therefore in the framework of general policy on alcohol, especially as laid down in the "Resolution on Actions Taken to Overcome Drunkenness and Alcoholism," approved by the Soviet government and the Communist Party in 1985. This policy, with its severe restrictions, provides for a multidisciplinary approach to alcohol-related problems. It has two main thrusts toward the reduction of demand for alcoholic drinks—regulation of availability, and a change in public attitudes and value orientations. Not since before 1920 has an industrial society introduced such radical measures for regulating the production and availability of alcohol.

However, reduced availability has stimulated home production of alcoholic beverages (*samogon*) and the consumption of alcohol substitutes. Despite severe sanctions this illicit distillation has increased enormously. The rise in sugar consumption indicates that *samogon*-makers have compensated for the reduction in state production of alcohol. Reliable data on per capita consumption are necessary in order to interpret changes in the treatment system and in client groups.

Measures to decrease demand for alcohol have been found difficult to implement. Effects of informal control measures (such as the foundation in 1985 of the All-Union Temperance Promotion Society), health education, social changes, and changed public attitudes can be expected only after some time. Again, this affects public attitudes toward treatment institutions.

The increased emphasis on research and training is an interesting indicator of the high national priority accorded to the alcohol issue. Extensive training is being made available to provide the developing services with highly qualified staff. Physicians specialized in alcoholism are getting more opportunities to improve their skills at the specialized departments of advanced training institutes. The training of nurses in social and psychological methods of treatment of alcoholics and risk groups is being considered. The expansion of fundamental biomedical research on alcoholism has attracted many scientists.

Organizational measures are being taken also to develop and improve antialcohol therapy. Rural services are being improved. There are many more interdistrict alcohol and drug abuse dispensaries, as well as much larger administrative divisions. These include special regional divisions, hospitals, and consultive and diagnostic facilities at sobering-up stations.

References

Anokhina, I.P. 1988. Neirobiologicheskiye aspekty alkogolizma (Neurobiological aspects of alcoholism). *Vestnik* AMN SSSR 3:21–28.

Anokhina, I.P., et al. 1988. Primeneniye neiropeptida kholetsistokinina dlya lecheniya alkogolizma (Cholecystokinin neuropeptide used for treatment of alcoholism). *Voprosy narkoligii* 1: 14–17.

Grinenko, A.Y., et al. 1987. Ispolzovaniye activiruyushchego endorfinergicheskiye sistemy mozga transkranialnogo elektricheskogo vozdeistviya dlya lecheniya alkogolnogo abstinentnogo sindroma (The use of the transcranial electric effect activating endorphinergic brain systems for the treatment of alcohol abstinence syndrome). In *Novyi metod transkranialnogo obezbolivaniya* (A new method of transcranial anesthesia). Nauka 47–48. St. Petersburg.

Ivanets, N.N., and A.L. Igonin, comp. 1975. Primeniye psikhofarmakologicheskikh sredstv pri lechenii khronicheskogo alkogolizma. *Metodicheskiye rekomendatsii* (Psycho-pharmacological agents used in the treatment of chronic alcoholism). 21. Moscow.

Ivanets, N.N. 1983. Medikamentoznaya terapiya alkogolisma (Drug therapy of alcoholism). In *Alkogolism* (Alcoholism), Mitsina, ed. G. V. Morozov et al., 311–431. Moscow.

Ivanets N.N., and Y.V. Valentik. 1986. Mesto situatsionno-psikhologicheskogo treninga v sisteme reabilitatsii bolnykh alkogolizmom (Situation- and psychological training used as a rehabilitation means in the treatment of alcoholism). In *Reabilitatsiya bolnykh nervno-psychicheskimi zabolevaniyami i alkogolizmom* (Rehabilitation of patients with neuropsychological disorders and alcoholism). Abstr. of papers 366–68. St. Petersburg.

Lisitsin, Y.P., and N.Y. Kopyt. 1983. *Alkogolism* (Alcoholism) 76–77, 94. Moscow: Meditsina.

Provisional instructions on application; compulsory medical measures with regard to persons with psychic disorders who have commited a crime. Annex 18 to the Resolution of the U.S.S.R. Ministry of Health of March 21, 1988, no. 225 on actions to be taken to improve psychiatric services.

Regulations of the conditions and procedure of rendering psychiatric services approved by the Presidium of the Supreme Soviet of the U.S.S.R. on January 5, 1988. No. 8282-XI.

Resolution of CC CPSU and the U.S.S.R. Council of Ministers of 1958 on intensification of the struggle against inebriety and alcoholism and on regulation of sale of alcoholic beverages.

Resolution of CC CPSU and the U.S.S.R. Council of Ministers of 1972 on intensification of the struggle against inebriety and alcoholism.

Resolution of the USSR Council of Ministers of 1978 on additional measures to be taken to intensify the struggle against inebriety and alcoholism.

Sosin, I. K., comp. 1987. Ispolzovaniye poverkhnostnoi upravlyayemoi kraniotserebralnoi gipotermii i sorbtsionnykh metodov detoksikatsii v kompleksnom lechenii alkogolisma (Surface controlled craniocerebral hypthermia and sorption detoxication methods used as an ingredient of the composite treatment of alcoholism). *Metodicheskiye rekomendatsii* 21. Moscow.

U.S.S.R. national economy in 1985. 1986. 609. Moscow.

The Development of an Alcohol-Treatment System in Hungary

Zsuzsanna Elekes

Introduction

Sociopolitical Structure and Trends in Alcohol-Related Problems

After the initial period of postwar reconstruction in Hungary, lasting until 1949, three periods may be distinguished (Andorka and Harcsa 1988):

i) *The period of extensive industrialization, from 1950 to the mid-1960s.* A doubling of the numbers of nonagricultural workers resulted in a marked increase in social mobility. In 1962–64 half of the management and professional class was of worker and peasant origin and about half of the nonagricultural workers had come from agricultural-worker and peasant families. While per capita national income increased, per capita personal income declined temporarily in the first half of the 1950s—an indication of the sacrifice the population had to endure for economic growth. After 1956 important changes took place in economic and social policy. Economic growth was no longer pursued at the expense of a decline in living standards. However, the institutional conditions of economic and social development remained largely unchanged until the mid-1960s.

ii) *The period of "transition to the conditions of intensive development": Introduction of the economic reforms (the mid-1960s to 1978).* During this period, both per capita national and personal income increased rapidly, and for most Hungarians the preconditions of a modern way of life were created. Officially, working hours were reduced, but much of the consequent free time was spent at other work to supplement income. In this way most workers in the low-income bracket achieved a higher standard of living, but at the cost of less leisure and less variety of leisure activities, and a more stressful way of life. Mortality rates of middle-aged men began to rise from the mid-1960s.

iii) *The period from 1978 to 1988.* In the second half of the 1970s the world economic depression began to affect Hungary. The delayed, and in some respects inadequate, response of the economy to the changes in the world economy was an indication of the many faulty mechanisms persisting in the Hungarian economy despite economic reforms, and of the need of further reforms.

Economic growth slowed down. Between 1978 and 1985 the national income increased by only 7% and per capita real personal income by only 7-8%. Real wages per employed person declined by about 11%. The population tried to compensate for this decline by increased employment of women of the 25-54 year age-group and by more intensive efforts to increase personal income by extra work, made possible by government decisions to expand opportunities for such activities. At present about 75% of Hungarian households engage in some type of income-supplementing activity. Two groups—unskilled workers and pensioners—were not in a position to take advantage of these opportunities, and large families still could not make ends meet.

The slowdown in economic growth had other effects also—a slowing of the transformation of the social structure, and an arrest of the trend toward a rising educational level among the youngest adult groups. The undue stress of everyday life contributed also to an increase in social problems, such as a very low birth-rate, a high divorce-rate, and high mortality rates, as well as to an increase in suicides and alcoholism, and probably also in mental disorders.

The public health and social policy of the post-1945 period in Hungary was determined mainly by the illusion that alcoholism and mental and other illnesses or social problems were "remnants of capitalism" and would automatically be eliminated and disappear under socialism. This naive and now discredited notion for long influenced policy, treatment, and research. This is why Hungarian researchers had little opportunity to study social problems and deviant behavior between 1952 and 1983, despite clear signs of their rising prevalence. One indication was a doubling in the numbers of suicides. At present suicide accounts for 33 of every 1,000 deaths and for 45.3 deaths a year per 100,000 inhabitants. These are the highest rates of any country in the world, and the annual rate of suicide attempts is estimated to be five times as high.

Alcohol consumption in neat alcohol per capita increased from 5 liters in the 1950s to 11.7 by 1980, and it has remained at approximately this level since then. Consumption of wine, beer, and spirits is equally high. Wine consumption is more or less static or has declined slightly in recent years; beer consumption has risen tenfold since 1950 and by 50% since 1970. The consumption of spirits is more than six times as high as in 1950, and almost twice as high as in 1970. The death rate from cirrhosis of the liver, which was 0.39 per 10,000 inhabitants in 1931, 0.74 in 1938, 0.40 in 1948, and 0.66 at the beginning of the 1950s, is now 4.2 per 10,000.

Since the 1960s, and especially since the mid-1970s, interest has focused increasingly on these problems. Nevertheless, as a report of the Hungarian

Academy of Sciences (1986) stated, "Hungarian society was largely unprepared for the growth of the disorders of suicide, alcoholism, and the problems connected with childhood and youth...Our approach so far has been characterized by a late reaction to the existence of the problems, and when we have reacted we have done so in a way that has been ad hoc and sometimes uncoordinated."

The response to the alcohol problem has been limited to the treatment of alcohol addicts within the health care system. It is only since the mid-1970s that there has been an alcohol policy as such. Research has been similarly limited. The first sociological research on alcoholics was conducted in 1970 (Andorka, Buda, and Cseh-Szombathy 1972); this was an exception, however, and it is only since the early 1980s that such research has become possible to any significant extent.

Historical Survey

Major Changes before 1945

In Hungary the first "circle for abstemiousness" was formed in 1619. The first organization of Good Templars was formed in 1901 with, as one of its aims, that of the promotion of temperance. In 1904 the Antialcoholism Labor Union was founded. In 1905 the periodical *Alcoholism* was launched, and the Antialcohol Committee of the Medical Society established. The first and apparently only "sobering-up sanitarium" was established in 1909 and continued until World War II; it accommodated 25–30 patients.

In 1919 one of the first measures of the short-lived Hungarian Soviet Republic was to prohibit the sale of alcoholic drinks, and to establish an antialcohol committee. Antialcohol movements practically ceased with the end of the Hungarian Soviet Republic (Karpati 1969).

Alcohol Treatment in the Postwar Era

The postwar history of alcohol treatment in Hungary parallels its sociopolitical history.

i)*1950 to the mid-60s*. Two features characterize this period. First, the complete lack, and later the sparseness, of special institutions for the treatment of alcoholism. Second, the close association of treatment of alcoholism with that of neuroses and psychoses, because of, at first, the lack of an independent network of welfare centers for alcoholics, and later, the scantiness of the network and the lack of alcoholism specialists.

Shortly after the end of the war, in October 1945, the National Public Health Council discussed setting up an antialcohol council. In 1948 a paper on alcoholism was presented at the Centennial Congress of Doctors, but practically no articles or studies were published and no measures taken until

1957 in connection with alcoholism and alcohol addicts. An article by the Ministry of Health official responsible for mental health services, published in 1951 (cited by Bakonyi 1983), characterized the situation very well: "The number of mental disorders increases in imperialism, but decreases in socialism. Growing poverty of poor people results in the spread of insanity in capitalism, but socialist society enforces the decrease of mental disorders." Of course, there were mental disorders and people with alcohol problems at that time. Isolated data, for Budapest only, show that the numbers of acutely intoxicated taken to hospital by ambulance from public places increased from 2,710 in 1950 to 3,200 in 1951, 3,621 in 1953, and 8,260 in 1954. Neurological clinics treated 171 alcohol patients in 1949, 1,017 in 1954 and about 1,700 in 1954, in their mental wards (Szirtes 1958). In the absence of any special provision or system of welfare centers for alcoholics, those who consulted doctors were, and still continue to be, treated at neurological clinics or in mental wards. Also, methods of treating alcoholics and of managing alcoholism have been determined largely by developments in mental health practice.

Hungarian psychiatry still bears the imprint of the long-lasting autocracy of neurology in scientific activities and in education, and its predominance in medical practice. Hungarian neurologists had an international reputation at the beginning of the century. They controlled university education in neurology and psychiatry in common. They are no longer so well-known abroad but are still very influential in Hungary, and psychiatry is still associated with neurology in education and in scientific practice. There was no independent scientific association of psychiatrists before 1980. The subordinate role of psychiatry is also seen in the higher number of hospital places for neurology, and in the training of neurological specialists and the management of neurological and mental hospitals mostly by neurologists (Bakonyi 1983, 204–5). Neurological and mental hospitals have been separated only since the second half of the 1970s.

We have seen that official policy in the 1950s regarded alcoholism and insanity to be remnants of capitalism and that they were expected to disappear under socialism. In addition, Stalinist science policy denounced psychoanalysis as an irrational and mystical science, and a bourgeois ideology, although psychoanalysis had had a long tradition in Hungarian psychology. The world's first department of psychoanalysis had been established in Budapest.

The severe damage caused by disrupted continuity, political denouncement, and subordination to neurology in Hungarian psychology could not be quickly repaired. Its effects on the morale and standing of most psychologists are still evident in their professional activities.

Treatment methods of the 1950s were determined principally by the acceptance of Pavlov's reflexology, which displaced practically all other methods. Treatment, when it took place, was limited to reflex conditioning with apomorphine and the use of an emetic for several years.

ii) *The mid-1960s to the late 70s.* The revolution of 1956 had shown that the social problems associated with low living standards, poor living conditions, and deviant behavior could not be completely neglected. Economic reforms resulted in some moderate reforms in social policy also, and hence in a certain renewal of social sciences from the beginning of the 1960s. However, the management of alcohol problems remained limited to the treatment of alcoholics within the health care system.

The first comprehensive legislation for the care and treatment of alcoholics came into effect in 1966. It was the real beginning of an alcohol treatment system in Hungary. A network of welfare centers for alcoholics was begun and some hospitals instituted separate alcohology wards. Treatment was not to be limited to an active withdrawing cure, which was to be only the first stage of treatment, and had to be followed by well-organized health and social care.

After 1966 not only did alcohol treatment become more intensive, but also discussion about treatment, especially compulsory treatment, was given new impetus. Legal compulsion was especially criticized. Courts were sometimes said to use compulsory treatment almost as punishment. Critics complained of the lack of investigation of social circumstances of alcoholics, which they considered necessary for treatment. They complained also about the effects of having to treat voluntary patients in the same place as those who had been committed for treatment by the courts or public health authorities. These critics held that the power of courts to compel people to have treatment was not consistent with the belief that people with alcohol problems were sick people. Also, many thought it wrong that the very limited provision of welfare centers should be used for people compelled to receive treatment, generally with little effect, instead of for voluntary patients. Though the discussions mostly concerned compulsion, they included also such issues as judicial and medical determination of who was an alcoholic, and the inefficiency of treatment. Both doctors and lawyers claimed that people committed by courts should be treated in an occupational-therapeutic institution controlled by the Ministry of Justice.

In 1972 these health-related judicial problems were settled and the Public Health Act came into force. Basically, this act determines the judicial regulation of the treatment of alcoholics and is still in force, with minor modifications.

Although at the end of the 1960s the treatment of alcoholism still consisted of aversion therapy for two to three weeks at a time, specialists were, more and more, aware of its ineffectiveness. An increasing number of published studies stressed the need of completing the withdrawal cure by psychotherapy and sociotherapy. By the end of the 1970s those psychologists who were trying to adopt more modern views on the treatment of alcoholism were making some impact on the public (Kardos 1969, 1970; Levendel 1970, 1974).

iii) *The period 1978–88.* This was the period of economic depression and a growing number of social problems. Increased concern about these problems resulted in several sociological research studies and in proposals for their prevention or reduction. However, owing to lack of funds or of any commitment to fundamental change, only formal changes were made. In 1977 a government regulation expanded antialcohol activities, and the act of 1972 was slightly modified.

In accordance with a government decision, the Ministry of Health organized the Scientific Methodological Center for alcoholics, in the framework of the National Neurological and Mental Hospital. This center took the place of the national alcohol institute, which experts had long advocated. Its task was to coordinate and supervise professionally the health care network concerned with alcohol problems, and to educate and advise on methods of treatment. In 1986 it was merged with the newly established National Alcohology Institute.

A 1982 regulation instituted a new form of treatment: compulsory occupational therapy at treatment institutions. It follows a civil procedure committing a patient to occupational therapy in a closed health institution.

In 1983 the National Committee for Antialcoholism became the State Committee for Antialcoholism. The former had operated as a social committee of the Red Cross. The latter became the advisory and reporting organ of the Council of Ministers. Thus, the fight against alcoholism was admitted to be a state responsibility. The most important tasks of the state committee were stated as: to study alcoholism-related problems; to work out suggestions for decreasing the social, health, moral, and economic damage and losses caused by alcoholism; to spread information and educate the people; to report on regulations and procedures; and to require the relevant central and local organs to describe, analyze and evaluate Hungarian and international experience. The president of the state committee was the deputy president of the Council of Ministers, and its members were delegates of ministries and concerned national organs. In the spring of 1988 the committee was incorporated in the newly established Health Maintenance Committee, thus losing its direct connection with the Council of Ministers.

The replacement of the standard aversion therapy brought to light problems that had been hardly noticeable previously. Psychotherapy was unsuitable for welfare centers and hospitals, owing to the lack of trained professionals and its need to continue over a long time. Sociotherapy and after-care required social welfare centers, transitional institutions, and day sanitaria. There were almost none of these and they could hardly be established in the financial circumstances of the time. This was one reason why surveys reported only a 10–16% recovery rate in the second half of the 1970s, a rate that only just exceeded the rate of spontaneous recovery (Simek 1979). The reason was the continuing predominance of aversion during treatment, and the simplistic notion of alcoholism as drinking and cure as nondrinking.

Treatment Institutions— A Review of Alcohol-Specific and Nonspecific Services

The Legal Division of Labor between Judicial, Health, and Social Authorities

The care and treatment of alcohol patients in welfare centers or in a hospital takes place almost exclusively within the framework of the public health system. The legislative basis for the alcohol treatment system provides for the division of competence between judicial, health, and social authorities, as follows (Elekes 1987, 113–24):

1. *Voluntary treatment and care,* with no legal implications. Voluntary patients apply for treatment on their own initiative, and they are treated by health care measures alone.
2. *Compulsory treatment and care,* ordered by the local authority on the initiative of those affected, after the individual's repeated neglect of family or work, recurrent violent behavior, etc. Compulsory treatment is a matter for the local authorities and health care agencies together.
3. *Compulsory occupational therapy at a treatment institution,* which follows from a civil procedure that commits the individual to a closed institution. The court decides upon treatment.
4. *Forced cure,* which the criminal court can order if a crime is related to alcoholism. The court decides whether it is to be given at an occupational therapy institute or in prison.
5. *Forced detoxification,* which is applied by the police and local authorities to people found severely intoxicated in public places, who are transferred to a detoxification center for twenty-four hours at most.

Voluntary treatment has no legal implications; compulsory treatment and compulsory occupational therapy at institutions are civil procedures; forced cure is a criminal procedure; and detoxification is principally a matter for the police and local authorities. Despite the diversity in legal arrangements, voluntary patients, compulsory patients, and detoxification patients are treated in a common health agency framework, at the same dispensaries and hospital departments. Similarly, compulsory occupational therapy, a civil procedure, and forced cure in the form of occupational therapy, a criminal procedure, take place in the same institute, which is under the Minister of Justice.

Institutional Treatment: Philosophy and Methods

Practically all the different treatment methods are used today: somato-
therapy, psychotherapy, sociotherapy and occupational therapy. They are
applied together or separately, depending on the patient and on the specialist's
opinion. However, the current situation can be best described by a quotation
from a recently published book on mental health, which raised a heated debate:

> It becomes evident from the open superiority of biological psychiatry,
> which is derived from neurology, that all the other, different opinions
> are opposed to it in every field. Doctors do not boast of their "deviant"
> socio-psychological interest at the beginning of their career, partly
> because their superiors would not be pleased at it and partly because
> normal and honorable professional advance can only be reached through
> neurological examination and practice. And if a recognized specialist
> were to express his previously hidden views or were to change his
> opinion, he could not have done so without disadvantage and loss of
> prestige, because he would have started his career from the very
> beginning with insufficient knowledge and practice. As a result, such
> professional change hardly ever takes place. It is all the more so, because
> the majority of head physicians got a department exclusively as a
> consequence of their neurological success and not as a result of their
> development in social psychiatry, until quite recently. [Bakonyi 1983,
> 214–15]

Treatment Capacity and Other Statistics

Information about welfare centers for alcoholics has been published
annually in the Yearbook of Public Health only since 1965. Earlier data may
be found in the statistics of neurological institutes. Those that relate to welfare
centers for alcoholics are of uncertain value. Data on hospital beds are not
published and data on hospital beds of alcoholics are included with those of
psychiatric patients.

At present the daily working hours of doctors in welfare centers for
alcoholics are only three hours per 100,000 inhabitants, or 50% of the accepted
norm of the Ministry of Health. According to a 1984 estimate, welfare centers
for alcoholics had only five full-time psychiatrists and the rest were part-time
(Hungarian Academy of Sciences 1986, 89). Over twenty years, until 1980,
the work hours of doctors increased by 1.8 and of social workers by 1.6, but
between 1980 and 1985 they decreased by 20% and 24%, respectively.
Although the annual number of visits per registered patient more than doubled
during those twenty years, and now stands at 4.8 per patient, this can hardly
be considered satisfactory. Moreover, since 1980 the numbers of visits have
been decreasing.

Similarly, the proportion of those who left welfare institutions as "recovered, improved" has decreased. In 1980 it stood at 15.5% and in 1985 at only 9.9% (Yearbook of Public Health 1985, 86).

Information about the use of hospital beds by alcohol patients is available only from the cross-sectional examination of 1985 data. These show that alcohol patients occupied 1835 hospital beds at the time of the examination, which is only 57% of the Ministry of Health norm for the satisfactory treatment and care of such patients.

How Systematic is the Treatment System?

In Hungary alcohol treatment takes place almost exclusively within the public health system. Consequently, the organization and financing of the public health system determine the care of alcohol addicts.

The health system has three levels: basic health services, with panel doctors and panel pediatricians—each serving an average of 2,000 to 3,000 persons; a network of specialist consultation institutes; and hospitals and clinics. The integration of the public health system, introduced in 1974, provided for the specialist consultation institutes to supervise the panel doctors, and for hospitals, professionally and financially, to supervise their specialist consultation institutes, and the corresponding public health institutions. Of course, the Ministry of Health is the ultimate supervisor of all the public health institutions, but the medical profession has its own national specialist institutions, which provide professional supervision. In the case of alcohol treatment the first such supervisory institution was the National Neurological and Mental Hospital. Its tasks with regard to alcohol were taken over in 1977 by the Scientific Methodological Center for Alcoholics, established within the hospital. They were transferred, in turn, in 1988, to the National Alcohology Institute, which is independent of the hospital.

The problems of public health are increased in the treatment of alcoholics, since it takes place at the periphery of the public health system.

Hungarian public health is highly hospital-oriented. This results from the great influence of large organizations and their ability to promote their own interests, and from the very centralized development of the health-care system. A consequence of this hospital-centered view is that the only way that public health institutions can perform their duties is to increase the number of hospital beds. Any kind of comprehensive care that involves a multistage public health system, including examinations, care, and treatment, and aftercare, becomes very difficult to organize. Since there is a great number of people with alcohol problems and they are considered to be treatable only by increasing hospital facilities, and hence at great expense, the management of the public health services seeks to avoid the problem (Antal 1984).

There are other reasons also: the health services are free, or, more precisely, they are financed from the national budget; the means of development and maintenance are distributed centrally; and people are not free to choose their doctor. The outcome is that doctors are interested in referring patients to other specialists as soon as possible and not in curing them, as in this way they can "care for" the maximum number of patients with the least effort, within their given work time and for their given salary. The crowding of clinics and the little time that doctors can give each patient are further reasons for doctors to practice in this way. Most of these problems result from the "passing on" of patients instead of treating them immediately or directing them to the proper public health institution. People can use influence to choose both hospital and doctor, and give tips, or "gratitude money," and thereby "purchase" better care. In Hungary patients generally "express their gratitude" to the doctor after every operation performed as part of the "free" medical service. Of course, the operations have no fixed "price"; it varies by operation, by hospital, and even by surgeon. It is estimated that patients pay 50 to 100% of their monthly income for a surgical intervention, as private fees to surgeons (Antal 1987). The spread of "gratitude money," which is a significant addition to doctors' incomes (doctors' salaries are very low in Hungary, and they are therefore under some pressure to complement them in some way), adds to the disadvantage. "Gratitude money" is rather rare when people do not feel that they are sick and when they have no genuine wish to recover, and where most patients are socially disadvantaged. Also, the lack of "gratitude money" contributes further to the shortage of doctors and specialists in the field, where professional success is rare and professional prestige low.

Financing Structure

Since the end of World War II very little money has been spent on public health in Hungary. The ratio of public health expenditure is consequently low in the budget, and expenditure increases at a lower rate than that of increase of the national income. Health expenditure accounts for 5.4% of the national budget, and for 3.9% of the Gross National Product (Andorka and Harcsa 1988, 275).

In principle, the distribution of public health expenditure is determined by Ministry of Health indicators and norms (e.g., number of doctors per 10,000 inhabitants, daily cost of treatment, etc.). In practice, funds are expended through special mechanisms that promote special interests, and success in obtaining funds is closely related to personal relations, knowledge of informal channels, and the influence of large organizations. The ability of these organizations to promote their own interests is an important factor in their development, as a result of their integration with the Hungarian public health system. In other countries smaller organizations are recognized to be more effective, and even the Hungarian economy has been showing similar tendencies since the mid-1970s.

Clearly, the problems of the public health system are multiplied in the treatment of alcoholism. It is at a disadvantage in the allocation of funds, partly because indicators for allocation have not been properly established in this field, and funds are usually allocated on the basis of such indicators; and partly because the doctors, wards, and institutions concerned have too little influence to apply for funds. The lack of prestige is due partly to the previously listed reasons and partly to the prevailing public health view that deviants, and especially alcoholics, and provision for their care, must give way to "normal" patients and provision for their care. According to Antal (1987, 58–61) "there are such strong selection mechanisms under the cover of 'free and equal' medical services as would not be tolerated in any 'market' society. This is due to the distribution and utilization of the resources of the health service, which first of all serves the interests of certain physicians' groups, not those of the patients."

Alternative Treatment Resources

There are no self-help groups as such in Hungary. The first antialcoholism clubs were formed in 1965, first in Budapest and some other towns. Their original purpose was to follow the example of successful self-help groups in other countries, primarily Alcoholics Anonymous, and to establish such clubs in Hungary. It was thought that this would be one type of after-care that could increase and stabilize the results of treatment. At first, they operated within the framework of the Red Cross, but they came under the control of local councils in the mid-1970s. At present they have about 150 members, but their numbers vary. Also, their effectiveness is variable, apparently because they are not genuine self-help groups. They are organized from the top, and operate under supervision of local councils and the control of specialists. They are therefore more like public health institutions than self-assistance groups. Their aims are not clear or clearly stated, and they lack the means for achieving their original purpose (Gerevich 1985).

In 1981 the Protestant Church established a mission for people with alcohol problems, which may be considered a true anti-alcoholism self-help group. It began with 35 members. It organizes lectures, meetings, and conferences for people with alcohol problems and their families, provides social care, and calls on the professional services of psychologists and psychiatrists when necessary.

Discussion

The number of alcohol addicts has been increasing steadily in Hungary since the end of World War II. Both the death rate for cirrhosis of the liver and alcohol consumption are very high by international standards. A system of welfare centers for alcoholics was established only in the mid-1960s and still lags far behind needs in both quantity and quality. Its lack of progress may be attributed to the low status of public health, postwar attitudes toward deviant behavior, and the prevailing view that the care and treatment of deviants should have low consideration, even in public health. Hence the capacity of the welfare centers remains low and their treatment ineffective, the conditions of treatment are unsatisfactory, and there are too few specialists in alcoholism. The conditions in which treatment is carried out and the prevailing opinions about the care of alcohol addicts are not conducive to the idea that alcoholism is an illness. Also, most people with alcohol problems undertake treatment only with strong persuasion, or because they are compelled by the local authority or the court to do so. During the treatment they are conscious more of the stigma attached to their condition than of any determination to be cured. Consequently, treatment is often kept secret and the idea of illness rejected, which decreases cooperation in treatment as well as its efficacy.

Research in the last few years shows that macrosocial tendencies explain best the spread of alcohol-related problems. It follows that certain changes in those tendencies would halt or reverse this spread. At a time when alcohol consumption and alcohol-related problems are expected to increase rather than decrease or stabilize, precisely as a result of economic and social problems, when the drinking culture is likely to be changed only with great difficulty and very slowly, and when consumption can be influenced only within certain limits, the earliest possible recognition and treatment of alcohol-related problems is likely to be the most effective course of action.

Between 1980 and 1985 one of the principal research projects of the Hungarian Academy of Sciences (1986, 165–79) was devoted to revealing the conditions that conduced to, and the reasons for, social maladjustment, and to proposing measures for its prevention or reduction. The following measures, among others, were proposed for decreasing alcoholism:

1. Limiting the availability of alcoholic drinks so that the continuous increase in per capita alcohol consumption should be arrested and eventually reversed.
2. Influencing the professional attitudes and practice of specialists, and the views of the public, and changing drinking habits and the uncritical acceptance of intemperate drinking.

The following measures were proposed for the care of people with alcohol problems:

- widespread screening, and the replacement of aversion treatment by psychotherapy and sociotherapy;
- an increase in the number of special hospital beds and hospital wards;

- the complementing of outpatient and hospital treatment by treatment in transitional (rehabilitation) institutions, such as occupational therapy day sanitaria, and care in protected night hostels;
- the establishment of a separate fund for services and studies;
- the extension of education in alcohology and of training of alcohology specialists;
- much better support to antialcoholism clubs, which should be given much more independence.

These proposals are part of a total proposed plan designed to influence social macrotendencies in all possible ways and to create an institutional system for preventing social maladjustment, establishing a network of social workers, and organizing mental health services and the training of specialists.

The prospect for these proposals is uncertain. The research and the proposals have stimulated the interest of specialists and the public in social maladjustment. Public opinion tests carried out by the Research Center for the Mass Communication Media (Nagy Lajos 1985), in which respondents were asked to rank about twenty social problems according to probabilities of their occurrence by the year 2000 in Hungary, ranked the spread of alcoholism fourth in 1980, and second in 1983 and 1985. The spread of crime was ranked sixth in 1980 and 1983, and third in 1985; and the spread of mental problems seventh in 1980 and 1983, and eighth in 1985.

If social problems are ranked by the degree of change in public opinion, drug use came first, crime fourth, and suicide sixth.

However, not only did public interest in social maladjustment change. At the same time more research money was made available for social problems. The increasing amount of social maladjustment greatly increased interest in the subject. Talking about deviant behavior at the beginning of the 1980s was a means of "clearing the air." In talking about suicide, alcoholism, or drug use, it was possible to speak about several other social problems. Since then, and especially since the beginning of 1988, the situation has changed. Because of growing publicity, people have lost interest in deviant behavior. In the last two years a slight decrease in the suicide rate and in alcohol consumption has given policy makers the illusion that their policy is successful. However, the decrease is so small that it is hard to tell whether it is a real tendency or a statistical error.

Alcohol policy is influenced also by cultural traditions and by the revenue that the government derives from alcohol consumption. Also, it has to find a middle course between two poles of public opinion. On the one hand, "the state does not want to solve alcohol-related problems, it is better that people drink than that they protest because of economic and social problems." On the other hand, "the state deals too much with alcohol-related problems, for, every time it does something, it does what the Soviet Union does."

At a time when expenditure on public health and social policy must be reduced, there is an increasing tendency to shift the responsibility for protecting health from social policy to the individual. If the worsening of health indicators is attributed to the population's drinking and eating habits and an unhealthy way of life, then attention is diverted from the great inadequacy of health provision. While this applies to health care as a whole, it is especially pertinent to alcohol-related problems.

So far, only a few of the research proposals of the academy have been realized. The future is doubtful. In 1988 everybody realized that a new economic policy would take five to ten years to resolve the present crisis. The economic policy is likely to bring an increase in social problems and social conflict for several years, but it may also liberalize political life, bring fundamental changes in the organization and financing of health care and education, and stimulate a growing number of independent activities in several fields. If the political and economic changes instituted in 1988 are to continue, there is likely to be less money and more social problems. At the same time, the government will wish to avoid deeper social and political conflicts by changes in the management of social problems, and promoting independent private-sector activities. These may result in some favorable changes in social policy as well as in alcohol treatment. If the political and economic changes are not continued, the situation will certainly deteriorate.

References

Andorka, R., B. Buda, and L. Cseh-Szombathy. 1972. *Az Alkoholizmus Kifejlödésének Tényezï* (Factors in the evolution of alcoholism). KSH.

_____, and Harcsa, I. 1988. Modernisation in Hungary in the long and short run measured by social indicators. *Sociological Working Papers* 1:1-287.

Antal, Z.L. 1984. A Kórházi Kezelés Idejét Befolyásoló Té nyezök (Factors influencing the duration of hospital treatment). *Tôrsadalomkutatás* 2:54-69.

_____. 1987. A Betegek Utjanak Elemézse: Érszüküléses Betegek Orvosi Kezelésének Vizsgalata (Analysis of patient's path: Survey of the medical care of vascular stenosis patients). *Medvetanc* 1:21-42.

Bakonyi, P. 1983. *Téboly, Terapia, Stigma* (Insanity, therapy, stigma). Budapest: Szépirodalmi Kiadó.

Elekes, Zs. 1987. Legislative arrangements relevant to alcohol treatment in Hungary. *Contemporary Drug Problems* 14(1): 113-23.

Gerevich, J. 1985. Az Önsegités Elve - és Hazai Megvalósulásának Nehézségei (The principle of self-help and the difficulties of applying it in Hungary. *Alkohológia* 2:1-18.

Hungarian Academy of Sciences. 1986. *Társadalmi Beilleszkedési Zavarok Magyarországon* (Social maladjustment in Hungary: Final research report). Budapest: Kossuth.

Kardoz, G. 1969. Terápiás Irányelvek és Módszxertani Problémák a Krónikus Alkoholisták Gyógykeselésénél (Therapeutic principles and methodological problems in the treatment of chrinic alcoholics). *Referaló Szemle* 21:7–12.

Karpati, E. 1969. Az Alkoholizmus Elleni Küzdelem Magyarorszagon 1940-ig (Fight against alcoholism in Hungary until 1940). *Referalo Szemle* 21:13–25.

Levendel, L. 1970. Az Alkoholbetegek Kezelésének Rentabilitásáról (On the cost-effectiveness of the treatment of diseases caused by alcohol). *Alkohológia* 1:15–23.

Nagy Lajos, G. 1985. Aggodalmak és Várakozások (Worries and expectations). *Alkohológia* 4:5–9.

Simek, Z. 1979. Az Alkohológiai Tudományos Módszertani Központról (On the Scientific Methodological Center for Alcoholism). *Alkohológia* 4:1–4.

Szirtes, Gy. 1958. Az Alkoholizmusról (About alcoholism). *Nepegeszsegügy* 2–3.

Yearbook of Public Health. 1985. Budapest: Egészségügyi Minisztérium.

The Odyssey of the Polish Alcohol-Treatment System

Jacek Morawski

Poland is a central European country with a population of over 37 million and an average density of 119 persons per km². About 80% of the population makes its living on nonagricultural occupations. The change from an agricultural to an agricultural-industrial economy after World War II was associated with a large influx of rural dwellers to towns. Two of the country's crops, rye and potatoes, are raw materials for the production of distilled alcoholic beverages—particularly spirits and vodkas.

Poland is one of the world's principal producers of vodka, and in Poland vodka is the most highly consumed alcoholic beverage. In 1987 it accounted for 67.4% of the country's per capita consumption of 7.0 liters of pure alcohol. Wines and meads accounted for 15.1%, and beer for 17.5%.

Historical records testify to the prevalent use of vodka as early as the seventeenth and eighteenth centuries in the eastern territories and in the nineteenth century in central and western Poland. The drinking pattern in which vodka predominates, known in Poland as the northeastern or Scandinavian pattern, continues to be the most popular; it involves occasional heavy drinking bouts leading to intoxication (Morawski 1983).

Consumption is concentrated: 10% of the heaviest drinkers account for some 60% of the country's total consumption of alcohol. Drinking is still considered a male domain but the sociocultural norms that forbade women from drinking and becoming intoxicated are loosening or, in many places, disappearing.

The prevalence of spirits in the drinking pattern is generally said to be the main cause of disorderly behavior among drinkers and of mental disorders in those who abuse alcohol. Alcohol-related problems are therefore seen as primarily pertaining to social order and to psychiatry.

Historical Background

An interesting example of social attitudes to addictive behavior in Poland is found in a seventeenth century military law, *Corpus Iuris Militaris*

Polonicum, of which article 25 reminded the military "to keep clear of harlotry, drunkenness, excessive gambling, and other such follies: whoever is caught and reprimanded by the Captain of the Horse and fails to stop shall be reported to the Commander-in-Chief and punished by him." However, modern alcohol treatment has not evolved from a penal system. Church alms-houses, mental asylums, and reformatories pioneered methods of caring for alcohol-dependent persons. Some of the church-run poorhouses of the sixteenth century later became hospitals. The first mental home was opened in 1534, in Cracow.

The first reformatory for tramps and beggars was founded at Gdansk, in 1629. One of the best known of such institutions was a reformatory in Warsaw, founded in 1736, and to which inmates were sentenced by courts. They included mentally ill, prostitutes, wives left there by their husbands to undergo corrective treatment, and children left by their parents. The chief means of reform were work and moral teaching.

Work on the reform of alcoholics came to an end with the disappearance of Poland as a sovereign nation, after a series of partitions begun by Prussia, Russia, and Austria in 1772. Poland became an independent nation again only after World War I.

At the turn of the twentieth century psychiatrists began to take note of alcoholic patients and admit them to hospitals. Later, special institutions were founded for alcohol-abusing persons. Among the first were a center for alcohol-dependent persons, opened at Miechowice near Bytom, in the south of Poland in 1904, and a home for alcohol-abusing males, run by the Camiliane Brothers at Tarnowskie Gory, also in the south, established in 1907, with forty-three beds.

A widely employed procedure for the committal of alcohol-dependent persons to an inpatient center was to deprive them of legal standing. Thus, a regulation on incapacitation, valid until 1918 in the Austrian partition zone of Poland, enabled a court to order the admission of a person to an institution even before there was a ruling on whether he was fully incapacitated. The court could also make its ruling contingent on the patient's treatment in an institution for a specified period; in other words, it suspended the "incapacitation" until the results of treatment became known.

Inpatient institutions for alcohol-dependents were soon followed by outpatient clinics, of which probably the first was established at Poznan, in 1907. Their chief method was moral treatment, but certain drugs, such as emetics, laxatives, sedatives, and even aphrodisiacs, were tried as well.

Between the two World Wars the state established two inpatient centers for treatment of alcohol dependence. One, the State Inpatient Treatment Center for Nervously Exhausted Women, was founded in 1927 at Goscijewo; and the other, a corresponding center for men, was opened in 1933 at Swiacko. Antialcohol consulting centers linked to the movement for mental hygiene were also established.

Also during this period two laws were enacted on limiting the sale of alcoholic beverages. Neither included provision for treatment, but they introduced penalties for public drunkenness. These laws were strongly influenced by the theories and practices of the American temperance movement.

The moral approach to alcoholism was dominant. Alcoholics usually entered the welfare and psychiatric system as emergency cases or as the direct result of a legal procedure in connection with incapacitation. Psychiatry met the challenge of treatment by both moral and pharmacological means, moving slowly toward the disease concept of alcoholism.

Alcohol treatment centers and most psychiatric hospitals were destroyed under the German occupation between 1939 and 1945.

Introduction of a Compulsory Treatment System

Soon after the war, attempts were made to reactivate alcohol clinics. The medical profession, influenced by the works of Magnus Huss and Jellinek, recognized alcoholism as a disease and claimed that alcoholics should be cured. Early publications by these authors, who were therapists, emphasized the somatic and psychological consequences of alcohol abuse. The first article on experience with disulfiram (Antabuse) treatment appeared in 1949. This treatment was considered very promising and its introduction a turning point in alcohol treatment (Zajaczkowski 1949).

A psychiatric criminological study in the early 1950s concluded that prolonged alcohol abuse led invariably to catastrophic social consequences, including criminality. Thus every alcoholic was considered a potential criminal.

One prominent professor of psychiatry and criminology stated:

Treatment should be obligatory. The diagnosis of habitual alcoholism should result in compulsory treatment. Some cases should have continuous treatment in an alcohol clinic. The rest—alas very numerous—should be compelled to stay in a special treatment institution. Without a law compelling alcohol addicts to have treatment, the whole social action in this field will fail totally. [Batawia 1951]

Polish psychiatrists discussed for long the need to introduce compulsory treatment imposed by an administrative body. The intention was to transfer from doctors to an administrative body the responsibility for ordering or not ordering compulsory hospitalization. A psychiatric law containing the provision was drafted. However, it did not stipulate that compulsion should be the basic rule of treatment of a certain category of patients.

The political situation in Poland after World War II did not favor the systematic treatment of alcoholism. The aim of the new political order was to build a new society where social justice would be accompanied by a spontaneous decrease of all social pathology along with the development of socialism. Criminality, alcoholism, and other social relics of the past were expected simply to disappear. A 1935 law limiting the sale of alcoholic beverages had not been enforced, because the income from the state monopoly of alcohol production was the foundation for the new state budget (Wald and Moskalewicz 1987).

However, in the mid-1950s social pathology was widespread and even intensified among the working class in the newly established industrial centers, which were to be the showcases of the new social order. Alcohol then became a convenient explanation for these phenomena, and official propaganda made it a scapegoat for social problems and the source of all evil. Thus the blame was not laid on the imperfect system or on the working classes, but on ethyl alcohol, which for centuries was known to be harmful to humans. This peculiar displacement of the causes of social problems tended to obscure the causes inherent in the social system, an obvious price to be paid by any society subject to an abrupt social overhaul.

Those two trends led to two laws for combating alcoholism, in 1956 and 1959. Unlike the prewar legislation, both shifted the emphasis from alcohol to alcoholism. They instituted a treatment system based on compulsion. Its root in compulsion had its expected impact on everyday practice, which is still evident today. Treatment was provided for those alcoholics who, as well as abusing alcohol, caused the breakdown of family ties, demoralized minors, avoided work, or systematically violated public peace and order.

The alcohol treatment system was created as a separate part of psychiatric services. It consisted of sobering-up stations, commissions for compulsory treatment, and outpatient and inpatient alcohol treatment facilities. Members of the commissions were activists from antialcohol committees, other voluntary organizations, and health-service workers. They could decide whether to send an individual for compulsory treatment in an outpatient clinic or apply to the civil court for inpatient treatment in a special institution for alcoholics. Also, they could enforce their own and the court's decisions.

Compulsory treatment permitted coercive police action to remove an alcoholic to an inpatient or outpatient center. If the treatment determined was to take place in an inpatient center, the commission could also decide whether a compulsory stay of up to two years was required. Besides compulsory hospitalization or hospital visits, patients were required to work and undergo medical treatment. Evasion of compulsory treatment was liable to three months' imprisonment and a fine.

Alcoholics were moved around in a closed system. They entered the system through the sobering-up stations, socio-medical commissions, and courts. They were then sent to outpatient clinics or inpatient institutions. On conditional discharge from the inpatient institution, they were placed in the care of their local commissions and outpatient clinics.

The system proved very inefficient. The socio-medical commissions and most of the planned outpatient clinics came into operation but the sobering-up stations and inpatient institutions were developed very slowly. Less than 50% of the planned system was completed. Treatment was very ineffective. Compulsory patients were given priority but even they had to wait for admission from several months to several years. Persons who wanted to be treated voluntarily had practically no opportunity to receive voluntary treatment and could only ask for compulsory treatment. Indeed, some people did so although the commission's procedures were similar to a criminal trial and the regulations in an inpatient institution made it seem like a prison.

The staff of outpatient clinics was absorbed by watching the dates on which compulsory patients had to report to the clinics. Hence the most popular therapy was the so-called disulfiram regime: patients attended on a given day, received Antabuse diluted in a glass by the nurse, were registered, and returned home. The system helped neither the health nor the social condition of the patient. It was criticized as fulfilling neither ethical nor legal requirements. The commission often did not follow the prescribed procedure, which led to abuse of the system. The most powerful institutions were the inpatient centers, and their directors formed the elite of the alcohol treatment profession. The needs of institutional care were given priority and outpatient clinics were neglected. The main aim of alcohol-treatment services was to increase the numbers of beds. However, inpatient treatment was rather ineffective. A national survey in 1977 showed, on a one-year follow-up, a rate of 5.6% of abstainers among compulsory patients and 13% among voluntary patients. The survey found also that very few of those who appeared before the socio-medical commissions were examined for alcohol dependence, and that half of those sentences to compulsory treatment were not alcohol-dependent.

Sobering-up stations were intended as the first stage of a systematic approach to treatment that alcohol-dependent persons had to follow. They were intended as an early diagnosis point for alcohol dependents, who were then to be directed to forced treatment in alcohol centers. In practice, however, these functions were very rarely accomplished. The stations became simply "revolving-door" institutions.

Treatment Institutions

In the early 1980s a new long-term alcohol policy was initiated, of which one element was the modernization of treatment and rehabilitation programs. A 1982 act entitled "Upbringing in Sobriety and Counteracting Alcoholism" devoted one chapter to the treatment and rehabilitation of alcohol-dependent persons.

The old concept of alcoholism was "any drinking of alcoholic beverages that causes any harm to anyone." The new concept reflected the changes introduced in the Ninth Revision of the International Classification of Diseases, in 1980, as well as new concepts of alcohol-related problems and the alcohol dependency syndrome (World Health Organization 1977). The new approach led to a decrease in the proportion of antisocial drinkers entering alcohol facilities and a consequent decrease in the numbers of cases of physical alcohol-dependency. The organization of the new system was influenced by the ideas of community psychiatry in Poland. The Ninth Revision of the International Classification of Diseases became a formal basis for the control of alcohol problems by both health services and other services that provided care for people with alcohol problems.

The new treatment model is based formally on the following principles:

1. Not all alcohol-dependent patients need the specialized services of an alcohol treatment system, and the primary health care system should be given responsibility for a significant portion of the tasks in this field.
2. Priority in alcohol treatment should be given to the psychosocial approaches used widely in psychiatry (psychotherapy, family therapy, group therapy, community care).
3. Outpatient and intermediate forms of treatment should be preferred to inpatient hospitalization.
4. The same approach should be adopted for all patients entering alcohol treatment; it should not depend on whether the patient is admitted voluntarily or is ordered by the court to attend the treatment center.
5. Support should be given for the foundation of voluntary associations that offer various forms of help to alcohol-dependent persons, persons who are at risk of dependency, and their families.

The new model incorporated the elements of its predecessor, but their functions were changed. New types of institutions were provided for. The law granted also considerable freedom in the arrangement of units in treatment facilities, to take into consideration possibilities, needs, and preferences of local communities. The primary care system was made responsible for diagnosing alcohol-related health risks and for providing suitable care for both alcoholism and its related problems.

The tasks of alcohol outpatient clinics were modified. They are now expected to make available continuous consultations and improved diagnostic and treatment practices for patients from the primary care system, and specialist services in support of primary care. Psychosocial methods of treatment are stressed, especially psychotherapy and community care. At present, as a rule, physicians work only part-time as consultants in outpatient clinics. One alcohol outpatient clinic in each region is responsible for coordinating all alcohol treatment in the area.

Inpatient treatment is still carried out in the alcohol wards of psychiatric hospitals and separate alcohol treatment centers, but treatment is short and intensive, three months at most, and work is no longer an obligatory part of treatment. Sobering-up stations still operate but they are now supervised by the Ministry of Health rather than the Ministry of the Interior. However, they remain disciplinary institutions whose task is to prevent alcohol-abusing persons from harming themselves or others.

The system was to be supplemented by new institutions. It was assumed that intermediate forms of treatment, such as day wards, night wards, hostels, and patient clubs, would supplement the work of the outpatient clinics and inpatient institutions. However, these have not yet been provided. Detoxifying wards are the newest facilities for patient care. Their main task is short-term care lasting from several to twelve days. In addition to detoxification they conduct clinical observation, establish therapeutic relations with the patients and their social environment, and initiate treatment of alcoholism.

Other new facilities are industrial cooperatives with a special rehabilitation program, self-help community houses, and social care houses for alcohol-dependent persons. These became necessary because existing rehabilitation facilities, especially social-care houses, did not admit alcoholics.

Several other systems—the courts, the local commissions for counteracting alcoholism, and a system for the treatment of prisoners—also support the public health system in the treatment of alcoholics.

The social-medical commissions for compulsory treatment of alcoholics were replaced by area commissions for counteracting alcoholism, which differ in many ways from their predecessors. They are composed of representatives of the local administration and community activists, and are financed from the antialcohol fund. They operate with the local branches of the state administrations in communes, towns, and districts of larger cities. Their tasks are to initiate, coordinate, and assess the activities related to counteracting alcoholism in their catchment areas; to provide treatment and rehabilitation for persons dependent on alcohol, as well as assistance for these persons and their families; and to send people who abuse alcohol to facilities for alcohol-dependence examinations. They investigate community and family conditions, and assist court probation officers in the supervision of persons obliged by the court to take alcohol treatment. In this respect the commissions form the first link in the chain of the involuntary treatment system. This is a legacy from the previous compulsory treatment system, but it avoids many of the disadvantages of that system. Compulsory measures now consist of submitting to a medical examination in order to obtain an expert medical opinion, appearing before the court, being taken to the treatment institution, or submitting to supervision by the probation officer. These may be practiced only by the police, if ordered by the court, or by the court itself. Thus it falls completely within the justice system.

An important element of the former compulsory treatment system was an independent group of experts (physicians or clinical psychologists) who determined whether the individual was alcohol-dependent and, if so, the type of treatment indicated. If the diagnosis of alcohol dependence was confirmed, the regional court might order the individual to submit to alcohol treatment by using a civil law nontrial procedure. Today, however, patients are not compelled to attend for treatment. A patient cannot be prevented from leaving an inpatient facility. However, the civil court must be informed when a patient leaves against advice.

The obligation to undertake treatment may remain in force for up to two years. The 1982 law is not absolutely precise on this matter, and has become a source of controversy between the health sector and the courts. This is because the courts want to reserve for themselves the control of all decisions concerning discharge from hospital, the interruption of medical treatment, or any changes in type of facility, even though these are clearly medical decisions.

Alcohol-treatment centers are financed from two sources: the local communal budget, which is the main source, and the general health service fund. So far, these outlays have not been separated and it is hard to say what proportion of the local budget is earmarked for alcohol-related services. The communal budget may be supplemented by local antialcohol resources derived from the central antialcohol fund, financed by up to 3% of annual sales of alcoholic beverages. This fund can cover only specific expenditures, such as the construction, renovation, and furnishing of centers or the funding of health education. It cannot be used for staff salaries, for instance. Officially, treatment for alcohol problems is free of charge to the patient. Payment is taken for certain welfare services as well as for a stay in any sobering-up station. The cost of such a stay is calculated so that payments made by the clients are sufficient to cover the cost of running the station.

Functioning of the System

The present state of alcohol treatment may be classified as transitional. A series of new policies are being formulated and implemented, old services are being adapted to new principles, and new services are being created and developed. Over the last few years considerable funds have been allocated to the system. However, given the country's serious economic condition, neither the source nor the continuity of funds can be assured.

The 25-year-old shadow of forced treatment still disturbs the functioning of the present system of alcohol-related care. It continues to linger in the attitudes of the general population, and of the staff of treatment centers and patients, as well as in those of the administrators of the ministries of health and welfare, and other ministries.

The normative model seeks to combine all centers into one system. This would permit patients to be directed to the centers best suited to their needs.

At the same time, certain mechanisms are used to check excessive duration of patient care, to avoid dependence on treatment and hospitalization. One is a recommended limit of fourteen days of stay in a detoxification ward, and of three months in an alcohol-treatment ward. However, the staff of the centers, as well as the courts, in the case of patients obliged to submit to treatment, are pressing to have these limits lifted. They do not apply to outpatient clinics and this can result in "perennial patients," generally enrolled by abstainers' clubs operating at the clinic or even at other outpatient clinics or clubs, as voluntary patients are not bound to use their local services.

The current system of alcohol treatment was developed as a specialized part of the mental health system. It has a clearly medical character, with doctors in central roles and staffed mainly by nurses. Since the 1970s the number of psychologists has continued to grow and they now form a large and influential group.

Primary medical care is oriented mainly toward two populations: farmers and the working class, especially where access to specialized medical services is difficult. Rural medical practitioners have claimed many positive results in alcohol treatment. Industrial medical officers are less inclined to introduce alcohol treatment into their field of operation, apparently because most workers do not approve of such treatment at their place of work. A survey of a representative sample of 1,116 clients of inpatient alcohol treatment centers found that after discharge from hospital only 15.4% of patients were willing to continue treatment under the plant doctor. Of these, 47.3% would continue treatment outside the job, and 5.6% were indifferent. The remaining 30.7% had no intention of continuing treatment (Morawski and Swiatkiewicz 1987).

Although public alcohol treatment is free of charge, some patients prefer treatment in medical or psychological cooperatives, which charge for services. As a rule, people turn to cooperatives for implantation of Esperal or for certain unconventional methods such a hypnosis or acupuncture. Also, they feel that treatment is more discreet in cooperatives than in the public system.

The clubs of patients and abstainers have increased in number from 73 in March 1984 to 313 in February 1989. However, only a few of them operated regular community-oriented programs. Published reports from 1986 showed that they had about 3,000 members, of whom 2,350 had drinking problems. More recent figures are not available. Thirteen clubs have acquired legal status and five issue their own publications. Most are connected with health service centers. Fifteen are sponsored by the Social Antialcohol Committee, and four by the Commissions for Counteracting Alcoholism; some are sponsored by the Patriotic Movement for National Rebirth, the Polish Women's League, and other organizations. Most are active for two to seven days a week. Only eighteen have a positive financial balance. Forty-three have joined the Regional Board of Clubs.

Alcoholics Anonymous is also growing rapidly in Poland. At first, its activities were supervised by professionals, who tried to modify some of its ideas to adapt them to alcohol-dependent persons. However, it did not gain ground until the professionals were removed from its management; then its original program became accepted in full and was propagated by its own publications. At present, the network of AA and Al-Anon groups supports several thousand alcohol-dependent persons. The number of Al-Ateen groups has grown to 10 and of Al-Anon groups to 101.

It is known that a certain proportion of alcohol-dependent persons who stopped drinking had maintained contact exclusively with AA groups and known nothing of the official alcohol treatment services. However, this has not been documented and there are no data on rates of spontaneous remission.

One element inherited by the present system, the service provided by sobering-up stations, has not achieved its intended potential. The medical service that these stations provide may be compared to first aid in an emergency. The tendency is not to extend their services and, in particular, to reduce the use of medicines that can be dangerous in interaction with alcohol. They provide mainly health education, and, at discharge, educational talks about the prevention of alcoholism. Also, when indicated, they notify a patient to the local Commission for Counteracting Alcoholism. However, the stations can implement very little of their preventive functions. Instead, some function as holding facilities, which is reflected in the high percentage of individuals, up to 50%, who are remanded and handed over to the militia. Sometimes the only reason for going to a sobering-up station is that an individual who is only very slightly intoxicated has committed an offense. This often leads to conflict between the staff of the station and the militia. Sobering-up stations lack the equipment for rapid detection of the blood-alcohol level.

Whereas in the 1970s all sobering-up stations were fully used, today, with slight local variations, less than 40% of their beds are occupied. Their results are still very modest and they are likely to take some time yet before they achieve their intended potential.

Positive effects of the new system include an increase in the number of patients entering treatment without a court's decision; the development of alternative forms of treatment, such as AA and abstainer clubs; the more frequent employment of psychologists in alcohol clinics; and the dissemination of psychosocial therapeutic methods.

There are also some negative effects. Thus, neither doctors nor patients favor the inclusion of treatment for alcohol problems in the primary care system. There are pressures from the justice system to return to compulsory treatment, and limits have been imposed upon the services of sobering-up stations. New types of treatment facility, even those essential to the proper functioning of the system, are instituted very slowly. The number of alcohol-treatment units hardly increases, for as new centers are established old ones are closed or their functions are changed.

Statistics and Research

The Ministry of Health maintains five kinds of statistical records relating to patients treated for alcohol problems. They are: annual hospital reports and statistical sheets of inpatient alcohol clinics, statistical sheets of general hospitals, annual reports on the operation of outpatient alcohol clinics, annual reports on sobering-up stations, and annual reports on emergency service. There are also reports on the use of the antialcohol fund.

Alcohol-treatment statistics are employed first for the appraisal of the operation of treatment services and for drawing general epidemiological conclusions. Their use for more profound analysis remains limited. It is equally impossible, for instance, to calculate the cost of treating an average patient and to say which centers are expensive and which are not. Extension of the analysis is expected to follow full computerization of the data. Inpatient treatment statistics are the richest source in this respect.

Access to the statistics is relatively narrow, even for specialists. The basic information on inpatient and outpatient treatment is published annually in the statistical bulletins of the Institute of Psychiatry and Neurology. These bulletins appear irregularly, however, which thwarts any monitoring functions they might have. Also, the statistical reporting systems are changed every few years, which makes it difficult to assess long-term trends. Sometimes statistics are computed for a short time only. Thus, in 1972 and 1973 only, data on poisoning with alcohol and alcohol substitutes were collected and published. They referred to place of occurrence, rural or urban incidence, circumstances of work, association with traffic accidents and with robbery, manslaughter and other crimes, and the aid provided in the ambulance and in outpatient care. Why this was begun and then discontinued is unknown. Under these circumstances special epidemiological and evaluative studies become especially valuable.

Alternative Treatment Resources

Alternative programs, independent of the state health services, are a new element of the Polish alcohol-treatment system. They include doctors' cooperatives, self-help groups, church groups, and programs run by private organizations. Doctors' cooperatives are part of the official treatment system, but they are self-financed and their patients must pay for their services.

There are several kinds of self-help groups. They include clubs for total abstainers and Alcoholics Anonymous. The former are registered as independent associations, each with its own policies, headquarters, and personnel. As a rule, they offer an introduction to problems of temperance; to nonprofessional

counseling for persons dependent on alcohol; to medical or social assistance
for alcohol-dependent persons; and the social control of excessive drinkers.
Alcoholics Anonymous groups are established in various state, social, and
religious institutions as well as at work establishments. They have no legal
status but they form communities that cultivate temperance. They provide a
range of preventive and rehabilitative activities.

An Evaluation of Trends

The alcohol treatment system in Poland has changed considerably in the
last 90 years. However, the changes have not necessarily paralleled the level
of alcohol consumption. With regard to the resources invested in the system,
five periods may be distinguished:

1. Before World War II, alcohol consumption was low, amounting to
   less than 2 liters per capita a year. Medical treatment of alcoholism
   was in its beginning. During the war and for a short time afterwards
   no active treatment took place.
2. The years 1948 to 1956 saw a modest but steady increase in alcohol
   consumption. Political circumstances blocked attempts to set up
   alcohol treatment facilities.
3. Between 1957 and 1964 annual per capita consumption stabilized at
   4 liters. An alcohol treatment system was established and a great deal
   of money was spent on it.
4. Between 1965 and 1980 annual consumption doubled to 8 liters per
   capita. During this period the development of an alcohol treatment
   system stopped, when only one-third of the planned network had been
   established.
5. In 1981 the annual per capita rate dropped suddenly to 6.4 liters,
   and then resumed a slow growth. A modernization of the system was
   undertaken, and at first very large financial and organizational
   investments were made. However, despite the rise in alcohol
   consumption in 1985–88, the new system stagnated. Much of the
   resources were reallocated to other health programs.

Trends in approaches to alcohol treatment in Poland appear to be
connected to changing views about the nature of "alcoholism" and hence about
its "treatment," and to progress in psychiatry, rather than to actual consumption
of alcohol and the needs of patients. Three different approaches may accordingly
be distinguished: the "moral" approach, the oldest; the "alcoholism as a
disease" approach, beginning in the 1950s; and the most recent, the "alcohol-
related problems" approach, beginning in the 1980s. The second has not fully
replaced the first, nor the third the second: all three are practiced today in

the treatment system, although in different proportions. This is one reason for many of the dysfunctions of the system. Nevertheless, the changed approaches brought obvious advantages, in particular the trend from dualism (inpatient and outpatient facilities only) to diversification of services, which better meets the needs of patients.

At the same time, however, the trend in legal processes related to persons apparently in need of treatment has been from a purely civil to a compulsory procedure. Changes in the committal procedure have greatly affected the functioning of the treatment system. These trends form a circle from civil-law procedures (e.g., incapacitation) to criminal procedures (e.g., compulsory measures) and back again to civil-law procedures. The process is probably not yet completed, for, from time to time, there are demands to return to compulsory measures against "alcoholics" and these influence national lawmakers and state administrations.

Two trends are common to both the alcohol treatment system and psychiatry. One is the trend from the isolation of patients in institutions to their integration within the community. Some of its signs are the recent preference for outpatient clinics, and the growth of the self-help movement and of community-based programs. The other is the trend from purely medical to psychosocial programs, and from medical staff only to a combination of medical and supporting nonmedical staff. Provided the national economy stabilizes, these trends should culminate in an integrated holistic approach to the treatment of alcohol problems.

Conclusion

The history of Poland's alcohol treatment system has mirrored the country's historical, political, and economic instability. The industrial era ushered in the country's first efforts to treat, in one way or another, people suffering from the effects of alcohol abuse. However, the cyclical political policies that have governed the country, together with the varying policies concerned with alcohol-related problems, have produced inconsistent results. Treatment programs have ranged from voluntary, often church-sponsored, in the 1600s, to completely involuntary, determined by state-appointed commissions and overseen by the judiciary system, through the 1960s and 70s. Only in the last decade has there been a serious attempt to return to a voluntary and more client-oriented treatment basis. However, despite the most recent political changes, the present system is still tainted with the stigma of compulsion.

Like the different political systems, the various methods of treating alcoholism have not followed consistent principles, in that they have ranged from the imposition of moral reform, through treating the condition as a serious illness, to the current practice of treating the whole person from a combined medical and psycho-sociological point of view.

The current treatment system could improve greatly the lot of the alcohol-abusing individual in Poland, but the country's political and economic difficulties are likely to hamper seriously the functioning of the system. If they cannot be resolved within a reasonable time, the system may well become overloaded and allowed to deteriorate.

References

Batawia, S. 1951. *Spoleczne skutki nalogowego alkoholizmu* (Social effects of alcohol addiction), 99–100. Warsaw: PZWL (State Medical Publishers).

Morawski, J. 1983. Alcohol-related problems in Poland 1950–1981. In *Consequences of Drinking. Trends in Alcohol Problem Statistics in Seven Countries*. Ed. N. Giesbrecht. Toronto, Canada: Addiction Research Foundation.

Morawski, J., and G. Swiatkiewicz. 1987. Alcohol in employment settings in Poland. *Employee Assistance Quarterly* 3(2): 105–19.

Wald, I., and J. Moskalewicz. 1987. From compulsory treatment to the obligation to undertake treatment: A conceptual evolution in Poland. *Contemporary Drug Problems Spring:* 39–50.

World Health Organization. 1977. *Alcohol-related disabilities*. Ed. G. Edwards et al. WHO Offset Publication, No. 32. Geneva, World Health Organization.

Zajaczkowski, H.. 1949. Leczenie alkoholizmu przewleklego srodkiem uczulajacym (Treatment of habitual alcoholism with a sensitizing drug). *Polski Tygodnik Lekarski* 4(16): 3–8.

Therapeutic Communities and Aftercare Clubs in Yugoslavia

Branko Lang and *Jasna Srdar*

Yugoslavia is the part of Europe and the Mediterranean basin that was settled by Slavs between the sixth and the eighth century A.D. There they found Greek and Roman vineyards, which had been cultivated by Illyrian tribes. The land on which vine was cultivated in those ancient times is still used for the same purpose today.

Vine growing was an important economic factor for the nations and nationalities that form Yugoslavia today. The wine was of very good quality, and there is evidence of its consumption in the middle and north European countries and even at courts of some sovereigns (Hudolin 1973). Vine growing and wine production and consumption were regulated by the "Vinodol Law" from 1288. In the nineteenth century a European wine fair was organized at Zagreb. The industrial production of strong drinks began at that time. Though there is no reliable historical evidence, it seems that excessive drinking and alcoholism were less common and widespread before the industrial production of alcoholic beverages than they are today (Lang 1988).

Yugoslavia has a population of 22 million. Its per capita consumption of pure alcohol is 15 liters (Nicolic 1986); about half is consumed as wine and the remainder equally as beer and spirits. In wine consumption, Yugoslavia is below France and Italy and above Poland and other east European countries. Levels of production and consumption of alcohol vary little throughout the country (Kapetanovic 1985). Epidemiological studies have indicated that 12 to 15% of adult males can be classified as alcoholics (Hudolin et al. 1967).

Historically and culturally, the nations and nationalities that form Yugoslavia have lived between two great cultures—the Christian and the Muslim. The boundary between these two worlds was very unstable, depending on war power and temporary success in war, which led to overlapping cultural influences. In the sixteenth century the Turkish historian Chelebia notified the Sultan that the Turkish army had cut down and destroyed vineyards when it invaded the Dalmatian region, as a means of damaging its economy. Early in the present century increased production and consumption brought a noticeable increase in alcohol-related problems, made worse in the 1930s by the great economic crisis. It was then that the first social movements against drinking and alcoholism began. In some parts of the country, alcoholism prevention efforts were directed at groups of children and youth, and at the peasants. These efforts were introduced by Andrija Stampar, whose public-health philosophy led him to establish, in Zagreb, the School of Public Health and in 1948 to be one of the founders of the World Health Organization. Many educational films were shown, and educational materials published, dealing with disadvantages of alcohol consumption. Abstainers' organizations and clubs were organized.

Since before World War II, alcoholics with psychiatric problems (delirium, other psychoses, etc.) as well as somatic complications have been treated in psychiatric institutions, and in medical and surgical departments of general hospitals. However, the treatment has been concerned largely with the complications of alcoholism rather than with alcoholism.

As elsewhere, it was only after World War II that the more thorough investigation of the treatment and rehabilitation of alcoholics began. In Croatia the School of Public Health, in Zagreb, resumed its work on the prevention of alcoholism, and throughout the country health organizations and social organizations undertook preventive programs. In 1954 the Yugoslav League Against Alcoholism was founded, and similar leagues were formed in the republics. These leagues do not correspond to a temperance movement. They are societal and professional associations organized at republic level. Through the Yugoslav league, professional and paraprofessional workers can organize and conduct preventive programs, financed partly by certain government offices and partly from social and health-care funds.

Also in the 1950s, disulfiram was introduced in Yugoslavia and treatment by Antabuse (called *tetidis*) began for both inpatients and outpatients. Dispensaries, or partial hospitalization, for the treatment of alcoholism were organized in Zagreb and Belgrade. According to the model of Alcoholics Anonymous (AA) the first center, named *Preporod* (renaissance), was opened in Zagreb (Hudolin 1973).

Preporod was Yugoslavia's first self-help group of alcoholics. Owing to the very restrictive political system of those days, the twelve-step approach of AA was not officially incorporated into the program, and the law forbade the anonymity of the members of such a group. The founder of most of the primary, secondary, and tertiary preventive alcoholism programs was Vladimir Hudolin. At that time, the late 1950s, he was head of the neuropsychiatric clinic of the "Dr M. Stojanovic" Hospital in Zagreb, later renamed the Clinic for Neurology, Psychiatry, Alcoholism, and Other Dependencies of the "Dr M. Stojanovic" University Hospital. This clinic was the first specialized university department for the treatment of alcoholism in Yugoslavia and the beginning of the Zagreb School of Alcohology.

The clinic introduced Hudolin's complex sociopsychiatric procedure in the treatment and rehabilitation of alcoholics. Later a modified version of this model was used also in northern Italy. The Hudolin model consists of group psychotherapy, family therapy, education, therapeutic community, medication (*tetidis*, antidepressants, tranquilizers) when necessary, and rehabilitation—both inpatient and outpatient—in clubs of treated alcoholics. According to Hudolin, the program should continue for at least five years. Today, more and more, this comprehensive program is family-oriented, regardless of its modalities.

In this center also the Republic Register of Alcoholics Treated in In-Patient Institutions of the Socialist Republic of Croatia was founded in 1965. It collects general data on alcoholics treated as inpatients and specific data on numbers of psychoses, other health problems and complications, mortality, etc. Authorized institutions can obtain from the register various medical, social, and occupational data on registered patients.

The General Framework of Alcohol Treatment

Alcoholics are treated as inpatients and outpatients in the general medical care system and in clubs of treated alcoholics. After World War II the introduction of socialized medicine meant that no one would suffer discrimination as regards health care and health protection. Health-care institutions are financed on the basis of either numbers of patient-days in hospital, according to various illness or diagnostic categories, or outpatient services (individual sessions, group work, family treatment, counseling). Clubs of treated alcoholics are financed according to hours of work of therapists. All financing is covered by health and social insurance. New health-care regulations provide also for private treatment separate from the normal health and social insurance.

Treatment of alcoholism is regulated by the Law on Health Protection and Health Insurance, and alcoholism is treated on the same basis as any other disease. Compulsory treatment of an alcoholic convicted of a criminal act is provided for by Act No. 65 of the Yugoslav penal code. Sometimes a convicted alcoholic may choose medical treatment instead of imprisonment. Much has been written about the motivation of alcoholics for treatment and whether their apparently voluntary acceptance of treatment is genuinely voluntary. Alcoholics, under pressure from their families, or for reasons of work or health, or a court order, accept treatment, but not all are equally motivated. In general, alcoholics and their families (owing to very intensive information about treatment) fairly readily accept the available treatment and institutions, possibly because no one under treatment may be dismissed from employment for excessive drinking. This protection applies to alcoholism as to any other medical condition, under the Law on Health Protection and the Law on Relationships at Work.

Social welfare institutions admit for treatment mostly "skid row" alcoholics. Social welfare has a much smaller role in the treatment of alcoholics than the medical-care system.

Specialized Treatment Centers

Some republics and regions have specialized institutions for the treatment of alcoholism; they use family therapy, group psychotherapy, therapeutic community and education. Rehabilitation follows in clubs of treated alcoholics. The treatment centers contain special wards and intensive-care units for cases of delirium tremens, cirrhosis of the liver, and other acute disorders. In some centers (Zagreb, Ljubljana, Belgrade, Sarajevo) outpatient treatment provided after working hours has proved to be one of the most successful ways of offering treatment.

The specialized centers have a more or less uniform approach, but alcoholics in some psychiatric hospitals and departments of general hospitals receive no specific treatment except medication and, in some instances, psychotherapy. Some psychiatric hospitals have no special programs for alcoholics other than drug therapy: sedatives, Antabuse, vitamins, etc. However, more and more, the recognition of behavioral and psychological dimensions of alcohol-related problems is gradually changing treatment modalities. A family-oriented approach is increasingly favored.

In the specialized institutions drinking is considered a secondary problem. Corrective and therapeutic action is focused upon family interactions and on changing attitudes toward alcohol consumption in the patient's family and working environment. In this way treatment comprises the primary prevention of alcoholism in the family group and the immediate environment. It is considered that without abstinence an alcoholic cannot be successfully treated.

Some therapists treat alcoholics individually (predominantly psycho-analytical), but almost all have accepted group psychotherapy, group treatment, group work, and family orientation. There is no uniform treatment system, at either national or republic level. All institutions are independent in their treatment approaches. However, there is close professional collaboration based on common professional and scientific interest. In general, it is accepted that patients should be treated and rehabilitated in their local communities and work places.

Most institutions do not select their patients, but a very few indicate some problems with which they do not or cannot deal (e.g., psychotic and severe psycho-organic disorders). Nevertheless, at the Institute for Mental Health, Belgrade, for example, the whole family is taken into the day hospital (Gacic 1978).

Most specialized institutions follow the model of the Department of Alcoholism of the University Department of Neurology, Psychiatry, Alcoholism, and Other Dependences, of the "Dr M. Stojanovic" University

Hospital in Zagreb. It consists of six functional units: an inpatient unit, a day hospital, a part-time hospital, a weekend hospital, a detoxification unit, and an intensive care unit. All of the units use family therapy, group psychotherapy, education of alcoholics and their families, therapeutic community, clubs of treated alcoholics, and drug therapy.

Indications for admission to the various units depend upon the severity of patients' conditions. Less severe cases from Zagreb are admitted for part-time hospitalization (outpatient unit) or to the day hospital, while the more severe cases and patients from outside the Zagreb area and from other parts of the country are admitted to the inpatient unit.

As a rule, when patients are admitted, family members, friends, social workers, and members of clubs of treated alcoholics participate in the treatment program. They stay in the hospital part-time for three months; attend the day hospital ten times during the patient's stay of 31 days; and visit an inpatient unit five to ten times during the 45-day hospitalization period.

Therapeutic activities consist, as a rule, of open groups led by a doctor, a social worker, a psychologist, a special-education teacher, a work therapist, or a nurse. At the Department of Alcoholism eleven to sixteen therapeutic groups form three therapeutic communities sharing common problems and daily routines, duties, and responsibilities.

Each group selects its leader, who is the group's spokesperson at the therapeutic-community meeting. All therapeutic groups meet together every day to solve crises or difficulties that arise from communal living, introduce families, analyse the 24-hour activities, etc. (Lang 1984). Crisis-resolution procedures in the therapeutic community are used as a means of stimulating the dynamics of the whole community. Therapeutic groups of the part-time hospitalization unit are active three hours a day (morning and afternoon), and those of the day hospital and inpatient unit ten to twelve hours a day. The therapeutic community and its "management board" (consisting of the therapists and patients' representatives) meet daily. Family members participate in all activities of the therapeutic groups. When necessary, both patients and family members receive individual psychotherapy.

In addition, the hospital patients take part once a week in the activities of one of the clubs of treated alcoholics. There are about two hundred such clubs in the Zagreb region, staffed by physicians (125), social workers (100), nurses (40), psychologists (14), and others (8). Patients who are residents of Zagreb, with their spouses, continue as members of the same club for at least five years after discharge from hospital.

The therapeutic community is designed to realize the great therapeutic potential of patients. Their participation in its activities activates their self-confidence and self-respect and, at the same time, is a good basis for their resocialization. Up to 70% of the patients have specific roles such as president of the therapeutic community, president of the model club, group leader, referee for education, or referee for gymnastics.

An after-care program is provided as an additional service for patients in need of prolonged psychotherapy. It consists of transactional analysis, group psychotherapy (Srdar 1988), autogenic training, gestalt therapy, psychodrama (Lang 1982), music therapy (Breitenfeld 1969), and married-couples group therapy.

Each unit has a "model club" of treated alcoholics, which, at the beginning of treatment, demonstrates the activities of similar clubs functioning elsewhere in the republic and the country. Patients take part in the activities of one of these clubs, that nearest their home, and then continue this participation on discharge.

All patients write personal reports, referring especially to their alcohol-related problems, family life, and behavioral disturbances. These are read at the meetings of groups or of the therapeutic community, and this creates a certain dynamic in the group and in the therapeutic community. Also, they keep a diary, noting the personal problems occurring during treatment and commenting upon the therapeutic procedures and their experiences with the therapeutic community. The diaries provide a basis for group discussions as well as for improving treatment.

Family members also must write personal reports during the first ten days, and married patients and their spouses must pass an examination on alcoholism by the 21st day of treatment. The objectives of the therapeutic procedures with families are: change in behavior of family members from having gained insight into their own disturbed behavior; the relief of acute crisis in interpersonal relationships; and rehabilitation and psychological restructuring of the interactions of all members of the family system.

The basic principles of therapy groups are: education in alcoholism, introduction of new patients, social learning based upon insight, supportive therapeutic action, change of behavior and, most important of all, the establishment of emotional and social closeness among the members as a basis for mutual help and support in abstinence during rehabilitation.

Referees are designated to help new members adapt to the therapeutic community. They help new members individually for three days, make them aware of the problems in the therapeutic community, and help them in their crises. They present written reports on the new members, containing all the relevant data on their lives and their alcohol-related problems.

Clubs of Treated Alcoholics: The Aftercare System

It would be naive to imagine that a treated alcoholic could abstain in an environment where drinking habits are strongly established, where one is even "compelled" to drink. A treated alcoholic who can abstain in a so-called alcohol culture is an exception and must endure huge psychological pressure and sometimes even physical compulsion. Besides, long-term rehabilitation is needed because of the social, occupational, and family disintegration caused by alcoholism, and alcoholics generally need long-term support. For these reasons a treated alcoholic needs the company of people who share the same views and who create specific defense mechanisms for coping with the alcohol culture. This was the rationale of the founding of the clubs of treated alcoholics, of which in the Republic of Croatia alone there is a network of about 500 clubs, and in all of Yugoslavia 800–900.

Clubs of treated alcoholics began to be founded in large numbers in 1964. At first they were used mainly for after-care (the first phase is inpatient treatment and the second rehabilitation), but it was soon realized that alcoholics could also be treated completely in the clubs. They are, in a way, alternative programs belonging to the category of self-help and mutual help, although they employ trained therapists—physicians, social workers, special education teachers, psychologists, and nurses. They may have paraprofessional workers also, including treated alcoholics who after two to three years of abstinence can take a six-month training course in the School of Social Psychiatry, Alcoholism, and Other Addictions, and then work in the club. About 30% of the clubs are established at work places.

The club meets once a week in the local community or at the place of work. Those who join are expected to remain members for at least five years (the period recommended by the Zagreb School of Alcohology). Membership cannot exceed 20–22 (to observe the principles of work in a medium-sized group) together with the family members. Clubs have their rules and statutes, and belong to two organizations: the Association of Clubs of Treated Alcoholics, and, in the Republic of Croatia, the Association for Mental Health Protection and Promotion and the Prevention of Addictions in the Republic of Croatia. Such clubs have been founded in all the republics and autonomous regions. In some areas they are evenly distributed and available to all treated alcoholics in particular regions. Professional medicine (general practice, psychiatric departments, clinics, and hospitals) gives them substantial professional support, and they even receive financial support, from social-insurance funds.

Specialized institutions differ in their attitudes toward treatment in the clubs of treated alcoholics. More and more, however, they accept the club system as a valuable after-care resource.

At one time, people objected to these clubs, as a form of objection to alcoholics. Some working organizations do not want such clubs in their environment. Nowadays, more and more, it is recognized that health-care and health-protection services organized at the work place can improve quality of life, in the ecological sense. Epidemiological studies of Zagreb working-class youths suggest that workers expect alcohol-related problems to be treated at the work place and give clubs of treated alcoholics attached to the work place positive ratings (Srdar 1988).

Complementary Preventive and Treatment Activities

A number of social and professional organizations promote the prevention and treatment of alcoholism. They include the Red Cross; the Railwaymen's League for the Prevention and Control of Alcoholism; the Association for the Prevention and Control of Alcoholism and Other Addictions (in the Republic of Croatia, the Association for Mental Health Protection and Promotion and the Control of Addiction); the Socialist Alliance of the Working People; trade unions; and the Association of Alcohologists, which is a member of the Associations of Physicians of Yugoslavia, with sections in the different republics and autonomous regions.

As Yugoslavia has a widespread program for the treatment of alcoholics, the contribution of alternative programs to the treatment and control of alcoholism is not significant. They are formed exclusively for other purposes such as transcendental meditation, yoga, the use of medicinal herbs, and the promotion of the alternative-medicine movement. In some cases the clubs of treated alcoholics work in ways that in other countries might be regarded as experimental or alternative to the recognized treatment.

Evaluation of Therapeutic Programs

Yugoslavia has no formal system of evaluation of its alcoholism-treatment programs. Neither the social insurance nor the health authorities require any such systematic evaluation. The treatment institutions evaluate their own work separately, which can have advantages as well as disadvantages. Some programs have been evaluated by their staff, with mostly positive results. Several master and doctoral theses have been written on the subject, but there have been no objective, scientific studies on the problem as a whole.

The first consideration in evaluation is the definition of alcoholism— that is, which theory underlies the therapeutic program: whether it is an etiological or a lineal concept within the medical model, or whether it is an etiological concept within the medical model updated by modern ecological postulates. If the latter, then the criteria against which to evaluate the program's performance or effectiveness would include abstinence or cessation of abuse of alcohol or other substances, and acceptance of the corresponding lifestyle, together with all the other relevant psychological, somatic, and social criteria.

If the theoretical basis is a comprehensive, systematic, circulatory-cybernetic model, which includes also certain social, psychological, and medico-biological components, the criteria will include primarily self-satisfaction and personal relationships in the family and at work. It will also include improvements in the psychological and physical condition attributable to treatment, as well as the attainment of abstinence.

Ultimately, the question of the definition of alcoholism remains. Every definition is an abstraction. Gregori Bateson asks whether an abstraction can be treated. How can a cure of an abstraction be evaluated? Without negating Bateson's considerations, it can be said that programs can be evaluated as well as treatment outcome for some diagnostic categories, if the scope of therapeutic corrective action is clearly defined, regardless of the possible therapeutic background.

Although such considerations must not divorce us from reality or make us depreciate our work, they do force us to reexamine some of our basic postulates and procedures with a view to improving our work and offering a satisfactory health outcome. The democratization of our society and the discarding of a uniform way of reasoning in all spheres of life permit us to examine and measure our own actions, and to change and develop them without fear of being found inadequate or being punished.

Evaluation of therapeutic programs has been, and is, possible in Yugoslavia. Certain data are available that would permit such evaluation, such as, in Croatia, the register of alcoholics treated as inpatients. However, at the national level little has been done, especially in the epidemiology of alcoholism. There are almost no reliable data on the prevalence of specific kinds of behavior or of the factors that determine or are associated with excessive drinking of alcohol. Neither are there data to relate production and consumption of alcohol to economic, social, medical, or psychological variables. Undoubtedly, these deficiencies must be remedied, and program evaluation and the testing of theories must become a feature of the alcohol treatment system, in the interests of efficiency, responsibility, and freedom.

The Treatment System in Prospect

Although the capacity of treatment services and staffing seem sufficient to meet current demand, a closer look at the development of client profiles may be instructive for planning for the future. First, between 1965 and 1983 there was a substantial increase in numbers of hospital admissions for alcoholism and, especially noteworthy, in numbers of beds and staff. Since 1983 hospital admissions have fallen slightly, possibly as a result of the strengthening of the club system as a different treatment option, decreasing the need for hospitalization.

Second, between 1965 and 1985, male admissions increased almost fourfold and female almost sixfold. The age structure of females admitted remained stable (about 40% under 44 years). Third, there has been an increase of the number of persons with severe alcohol syndromes and alcohol-related work disability. The underlying societal causes need to be investigated.

The necessary adaptation of treatment approaches requires a much better assessment of needs. Regrettably, the monitoring of alcohol-related problems, and of corresponding programs, in road traffic and industry, and among such special populations as children, juveniles, and senior citizens has not been centralized or coordinated at either the federal or the republic level. Treatment professionals expect that advances in the understanding of human behavior will result in new explanations of drinking behavior, and thus probably in new concepts of treatment, which will be reflected in treatment programs. Also, cultural, political, social, and economic developments are likely to result in innovative approaches to the organization of treatment programs, based upon better empirical knowledge about the development of alcohol problems. One factor likely to influence a future treatment paradigm is the realization of the value of a preventive transgenerational strategy designed to reduce people's needs to consume alcohol.

Recent political changes are likely to result in the autonomy for the republics in their efforts to construct their treatment networks, but possibly also in a weakening of coordination of such efforts and in regional differences in quality of care and in access to adequate treatment. Rapid political, social, and economic change, and the democratization of society, are likely to result in preventive and therapeutic programs being directed toward the affirmation of personality and individuality. It is to be hoped that such programs will become the dominant type of the future, assuring the individualization of treatment and respecting fully the individual needs of all patients and their families.

References

Bilten Republickog registra alkoholicara SR Hrvatske. 1970. Radovi Centra zu proucavanje i suzbijanje alkoholizma. Zagreb.

Breitenfeld, D. 1969. Principi muzikoterapije alkoholicara. *Anali Bolnice "Dr. M. Stojanovic"* 8:213–18.

Gacic, B. 1978. *Porodicna terapija u lecenju alkoholizma.* Belgrade: Rad.

Hudolin, V., et al. 1967. *Maladaptacija—Znanstveni projekt: SR Hrvatska, SR Srbija, SR Bosna i Hercegovina.* Belgrade, Zagreb, Sarajevo.

Hudolin, V. 1973. *Alkohizam i druge ovisnosti.* Zagreb: Medicinska naklada.

Kapetanovic, E. 1985. *Alkoholizam—zivot na dva kolosjeka.* Zagreb: Globus.

Lang, B. 1982. *Psihoterapija i terapijska zajednica alkoholicara.* Zagreb: Jumena.

_____. 1984. Lijecenje alkoholicara u Centru za alkoholizam u Zagrebu. *Anali Klinicke bolnice "Dr. M. Stojanovic"* 23:62.

_____. 1988. Odabrana poglavlja iz psihoterapije i terapijske zajednice. *Anali Klinicke bolnice "Dr. M. Stojanovic"* 27 (Suppl. 55).

Lazic, N., et al. 1986. Sistemska obiteljska terapija u lijecenju alkoholizma. *Psihijatrija danas* 18(1).

Nicolic, D. 1986. *Stanje i problemi alkoholizma u SFR Jugoslaviji.* Belgrade: Savezni zavod za zdravstvenu zastitu.

Rugelj, J. 1989. Odabrani clanci. *Al-klub* 26:1–4.

Srdar, J. 1988. Kibernetsko transakcijski pristup u lijecenju alkoholicara. In *Radovi IV. kongresa alkohologa Jugoslavije.* Sarajevo.

Srdar, J., and A. Kosovac. 1988. Analiza socijalnih faktora pojave uzimanja sredstava ovisnosti mladih u radnom odnosu. *Radovi Zavoda za socijalni rad grada Zagreba.* Suppl. 1.

Dissolving the Swedish Alcohol-Treatment System

Pia Rosenqvist and *Noriko Kurube*

Sweden is among the world's richest countries and also a welfare state. According to Esping-Andersen and Korpi (1987, 47–49), the cornerstones of the modern welfare state were laid after World War II. A uniquely Scandinavian model emerged. Sweden led the way and some years later the other Scandinavian countries followed. Among the key features of the Scandinavian approach, these authors (ibid., 69–70) mention four that set it apart from the approach of other advanced capitalist countries: 1) The assumption of responsibility by public authorities has made private provision and the market mechanism marginal, and even replaced them, in more areas of society than usual; for instance, private hospital care and private education are very rare in Sweden and the extent of public responsibility in housing and employment is unmatched in most other countries; 2) the commitment of the Scandinavian countries to universalism and equality of status extends further than that of most other countries; for instance, the core programs for income maintenance have deliberately sought to eliminate differentials between population groups: it may be said that the concept of social citizenship has been taken literally; 3) benefit levels and the standards of the social services are very high; and 4) the Scandinavian welfare states provide probably stronger economic disincentives than elsewhere—the compulsion to work at any cost has been considerably relaxed.

However, it was not until the 1980s, with the passing of the new Social Services Act of Sweden, that the social laws regulating the management of problem drinkers were changed to reflect these profound changes in the social security system (Abrahamson 1989; Holgersson 1988).

Historical Review

Many of the distinctive features of the Swedish way of dealing with alcohol problems are closely linked to the country's political and economic history. Two features in particular have some bearing on this chapter. First, it has for long been part of Swedish parliamentary and administrative tradition to charge governmental commissions with research and ambitious investigations, and this has applied also to the alcohol field. The result has been that several fairly large governmental reports have been published during the postwar period (Table 1). Three deal exclusively with alcohol treatment and several with neighboring fields such as social work. Many of the data presented in this chapter have been collected by these commissions, whose reports both reflected and influenced the ways in which alcohol and alcoholism have been perceived. They have influenced the "governing images" of alcohol problems (Room 1978), especially since there has been no other independent social research in this area (Bruun 1983).

TABLE 1

Major Changes in Legislation and Major Governmental Commissions and Investigations concerning Alcohol in Sweden

Major changes in legislation	Major governmental commissions and investigations
	1944–52 *Temperance committee.* Investigated: 1) the extent and the prevalence of alcohol use in different population groups, 2) the prevalence of alcohol abuse, 3) the function and the effects, in different respects, of the restriction system, and 4) the alcohol effects of malt liquors of different strengths.
	Seven reports among which: SOU 1952:53 Principal report on temperance policies in the future. SOU 1952:54 Sales of liquor and the care of alcoholics.
	1946–48 *Commission on the care of alcoholics.* SOU 1948:23 Report including a proposal on changes of the care of alcoholics.
1954 New Temperance Act passed	
1955 Passbook abolished—new alcohol-control policy. New temperance act in effect	
	1961 *Commission on care of alcoholics,* which especially investigated inpatient care One report: SOU 1961:58.
1965 Medium strong beer introduced	1964–67 *Investigation of the care of alcoholics in 1964.* A comprehensive investigation of treatment forms and clients SOU 1967:36, 37 Status of the care of alcoholics.

TABLE 1 continued

	1963–68 *Commission on public drunkenness.* Investigated public drunkenness and proposed decriminalization SOU 1968:55,56 Cure or penalty.
	1967–74 *Commission on alcohol control policy.* Three reports: SOU 1974:90 Alcohol policy. Part 1. Background. SOU 1974:91. Part 2. Measures. SOU 1974:93. Part 3. Summary.
	1967–77 *Commission on social service.* Dealt with the reform of social acts.
1977 Medium strong beer withdrawm 1977 Public drunkenness decriminalized	Two major reports: SOU 1974:39, 40 Social service, goal and means. SOU 1977:40 Social service and the extension of social insurance—Final Report. 1978 *Care and treatment of alcoholics.* National Board of Health and Social Welfare
1980 Social Service ACT (SOL) passed	1980 *Social drafting commission* which evaluated the Social Service Act and proposed the Care of Alcoholics and Drug Abusers Act (LVM). SOU 1981:7 LVM.
1981 Care of Alcoholics and Drug Abusers Act LVM passed 1982 SOL and LVM into effect 1988 LVM revised.	SOU 1987:22 Abusers, social service and compulsion.

Second, as Miller (1986) also has pointed out, alcohol treatment in Sweden has not been "alcoholism treatment" in the sense in which the term has been used in the United States. The alcohol problem has been regarded as sometimes the consequences, and sometimes the causes or symptoms, of alcohol abuse. Thus none of the three very thorough and impressive governmental studies in the postwar period on the treatment sector considered seriously the question of drinking—that is, they were not concerned with data on how much alcoholics drank or with alcoholism as such.

Shifts in Alcohol Policy and Treatment

By international standards, Swedish alcohol consumption has always been fairly moderate. Between World Wars I and II it amounted to about 4 liters annually of pure alcohol per person aged 15 years and older, and after World

War II it rose to 6–7 liters (Lenke 1984). Swedish alcohol control policy changed substantially in the 1940s, and there were corresponding legislative changes in the 1950s. The "passbook system," often called the Bratt system, after Dr. Ivan Bratt, who was chiefly associated with its introduction in 1919, was abolished in 1955. Under it the purchase of spirits by individuals was restricted, and the state controlled the production and distribution of alcohol (Bruun and Franberg 1985). The individual purchase restrictions were revoked in 1955, but the ban on purchases by problem drinkers was retained until 1977. More general means of controlling alcohol supply, such as the monopoly of alcohol distribution, remained in effect.

Separate temperance boards (or poor-relief boards), which combined local alcohol control tasks with responsibilities for individualized measures for abusers, were another creation of the Bratt system. The legal basis for the individualized measures was the Alcoholics Act of 1913, which called for custodial care of alcoholics who met specific criteria referring to negative social and economic consequences of abuse (Rosenqvist and Takala 1987). Though alcoholics were cared for in various ways and institutions, the Alcoholics Act resulted in the establishment of a specialized sector for their care. In 1954 the Alcoholics Act was replaced by the Temperance Act, which differed little in its spirit and provisions from its predecessor (Abrahamson 1989; Holgersson 1988; Ludwig and Westlund 1982).

However, these legal changes, which took effect in 1955, together exemplify the shifting emphasis in the alcohol field, from control to treatment, from a social to a more medically oriented definition of alcohol problems. In the final document of the government commission that ended the passbook system, the costs of the system were compared with those of treatment systems (*Statens Offentliga Utredningar* [SOU] 1952, no. 53: 32). The arguments for a new, less individually oriented, alcohol control policy contrasted these two societal approaches: the alcohol control policy sector was to be diminished and the treatment sector expanded.

The elimination of the passbook had many unforeseen, almost unimaginable, consequences. From 1955 to 1956, arrests for drunkenness skyrocketed and the incidence of delirium tremens doubled (Inghe and Inghe 1970). The welfare system with its social service centers, temperance boards, asylums, and hospitals was overcrowded with alcohol cases. This, coupled with a growing conviction that alcohol problems represented disease, and the increased revenues from alcohol sales, contributed to an explosive growth of the treatment system.

Toward a Professional Treatment Response

The arguments for a reform of the legal basis of the alcohol treatment system in the postwar years were that the old law (the Alcoholics Act) had not been employed effectively or widely enough, and that when employed it seemed ineffective. Thus a report by a governmental commission (SOU 1948, no. 23) stated that a follow-up of 474 persons, who in 1936 were committed for the first time to a public institution for alcoholics, had shown that over a 10-year period (1936–46) about 67% continued to be abusers or "showed an inclination for abuse," and that only 4% had succeeded in becoming abstainers (from SOU 1967, no. 36: 16–17).

The commission found that the treatment services responded badly to the medical-care needs of the abusers, and that modern medical treatment such as insulin, electroconvulsive therapy, and hormone and aversion therapy supposed to cure alcoholism was hardly used (SOU 1948, nos. 46–49). Thus so-called summary treatment, which comprised both medical and social measures, was recommended as an adequate societal response. To respond fully to the needs of a more liberal, nonindividualized alcohol control policy, the boards were to be strengthened and medical measures developed. Ludwig and Westlund (1982, 21–22) have given a different view:

At the beginning of the 1950s it was said that in a society without unemployment and in which the social security system guarantees most of the people an acceptable standard of living, difficulties in managing must be due to individual deficiencies. In such a framework alcoholism was regarded as an illness, on which social reforms, material improvements, and alcohol control-policy measures could have little impact. . .(It was also found) that it is an obligation of society, by careful investigation of the individual alcoholic, of his background and constitution, to make a diagnosis of his condition as a basis for adequate medico-psychological treatment. [our translation]

The 1954 Temperance Act resulted in professionals, mainly medical, being more firmly drawn into the treatment of alcoholics (Abrahamson 1989). Until then the temperance boards, which consisted of local lay people, had carried the work load of "outpatient services" and referrals for inpatient treatment. The lack of medical and professional impact was a recurrent theme in the public debates of the 1960s. One of the most influential contributions to this discussion was the book *The Incomplete Welfare* (*Den ofärdiga välfärden*) published in 1967 (Inghe and Inghe 1970). In their search for the outcasts of society, the Inghes devoted one chapter to "those who have been damaged by alcohol" and claimed that although alcohol consumption had not increased so much as had been feared in the mid-1950s, and although treatment resources had been built up, something was still utterly wrong. They contended that the situation had worsened, that the alcohol problem had become more severe, and that new groups—young people, women and children—were in the risk zone. One of the messages of the book was to advocate a more treatment-oriented approach to alcohol problems. The authors stated, for instance:

Chronic alcoholics are seriously ill people, who live in difficult circumstances, outcast and despised by other people, routinely watched by social
officers but not readily given the medical care that other sick people so
obviously obtain. [p. 246, our translation]

The Commission on Public Drunkenness also stressed the need for a more
medical orientation, arguing strongly for medical care and cure of drunkenness,
rather than fining the drinker (Table 1). Public drunkenness, criminalized as
early as the eighteenth century, had been regarded largely as the major alcohol
problem, reflecting the seriousness of the alcohol question as well as the need
for societal action. It remained a punishable offense until 1977, but under the
Alcoholics Act repeated incidents of public drunkenness or fines for the offense
had been included since the 1920s among the grounds for compulsory treatment.
Thus until it was decriminalized, public drunkenness, originally viewed as a
law-and-order problem, offered one of the major routes for alcoholics to enter
the alcohol-treatment system.

The investigation also echoed the prevailing ideas of social work in the
Sweden of the 1960s. People were very optimistic about treatment and rational
action. The good society, the true welfare society, could be achieved by
planning, and in this task social workers, psychologists, physicians, and other
experts were crucial.

Yet another governmental investigation was initiated in 1964 (Table 1)
(SOU 1967, no.36). The resulting publication questioned the social composition
of those drawn into treatment. It pointed out that society's main response to
alcohol problems was still to offer care to those who were economically
dependent on the state for their livelihood, and also dependent on alcohol, the
"doubly dependent" (Ludwig and Westlund 1982). These people were found
in the uneducated working classes and thus the Temperance Act was said to
be class-biased—an idea quite unacceptable to modern welfare Sweden. Also,
the commission said, the social response, as expressed in the treatment system,
administered by the temperance boards, was nonprofessional and punitive, and
therefore the whole system of separate temperance boards should be dismantled.
Since the different social and medical causes of alcoholism could not be
separated or disentangled, the individual who sought help was to be treated
holistically. The separation of local social work into different boards—
temperance, social aid, and child welfare—prevented such total approaches
as well as concerted action.

The investigation also echoed the prevailing ideas of social work in the
Sweden of the 1960s. People were very optimistic about treatment and rational
action. The good society, the true welfare society, could be achieved by
planning, and in this task social workers, psychologists, physicians, and other
experts were crucial.

Statistics on the activities of the temperance boards show that they were
considerably more active in the first decades after World War II than they
had been earlier (Figure 1). Measures that included some kind of intervention
(supportive and supervisory or coercive measures) almost doubled between
1950 and 1960 (from 27,000 to about 51,000). However, the numbers of cases
reported to the boards in 1960 were five times as many as in 1950. In the

1960s the numbers of reported cases in which the temperance boards intervened were already reduced and the phasing out of the separate temperance boards, between the late 1960s and 1974, probably reduced their numbers even more; by 1980 they had fallen to 55,000.

FIGURE 1

Misuser Act Cases Handled by Temperance (or Social) Boards
by Type of Measure

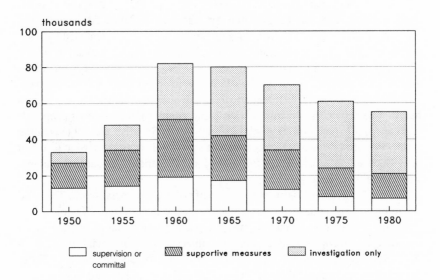

However, according to many expert opinions (for instance *Socialstyrelsen* 1978) the work load at the social offices did not diminish—cases were simply no longer being registered as temperance problems. Partly this was to avoid stigmatization. The Inghes (1970) drew attention to "misdirected measures" by social offices, which worsened the individual's plight. Earlier, Dr. Gustav Jonsson (1967), in a famous dissertation in which he launched the term *social heredity,* had argued, on the basis of data on delinquent boys, that deviant behavior not only thrived in poverty and unfortunate living conditions but also was transferred to the next generation, and then more severely. It was thus, he argued, a question of not only inferior individuals but also defective surroundings, for which remedies other than individual intervention were needed.

Ludwig and Westlund (1982) also have pointed out that the diminishing numbers of cases in which the temperance boards intervened reflected both society's increased tolerance of abusers and the availability of other measures, such as housing assistance and state-paid allowances to children. These measures did not come under the Temperance Act and therefore statistics issued under the Temperance Act were artificially low.

Treatment Institutions

Legal Framework: Coercion or Consent—The Main Issue

The goals of the social services were highly debated issues in the early 1970s. A governmental commission had been appointed to propose changes in three social acts: the Temperance Act, the Act on Public Assistance, and the Act on Child Care. The commission's work was closely watched by a so-called shadow or counter-commission initiated by the organization of the directors of Swedish social welfare offices. Many professional organizations and even the labor unions of public officials were deeply involved in the debate. Client organizations in different subareas grew strong and made their voices heard. The debate on the commission's and counter-commission's proposals was one of the most heated ideological debates in Swedish society (Svenning 1975). For instance, when the commission's proposals were referred to different authorities and professional organizations for consideration, about four hundred statements were received.

The most debated issue was the use of coercion in social work. The need for reform of the legislation was not at issue, but the question of compulsory treatment was controversial. To many, especially some unions and the social workers' organizations, coercion was unacceptable in social work in a democratic society; the client's participation had to rely on consent. Those favoring some measure of coercion maintained that society had to protect its members if they could not foresee the consequences of their actions.

The commission was itself divided on the matter, but at one point proposed legal coercion as a provision of the Mental Health Act. It did not maintain that alcohol or drug abuse was to be considered a mental illness. A 1979 bill to implement the proposal was defeated, owing mainly to the opposition of the medical profession. After much debate, with proposals and counter-proposals, the argument was finally settled by Parliament in 1981, and three new laws were enacted in 1982 to replace the 1954 Temperance Act. These were the new Social Services Act, the Care of Alcoholics and Drug Abusers Act (an act on compulsory treatment), and the Act on Child Care.

The Social Services Act. The Social Services Act, now in force, is meant to serve as a frame for public action in the field of social services in general. It spells out the broad goals, leaving it to the municipalities to achieve them, but does not specify how they are to be achieved (Pettersson 1986, 35–39). It is a loose collection of good principles: democracy, economic and social security, and equality in living conditions are goals of the social services, and the emphasis is on concerted action to serve the citizens. As an echo of the investigation of 1964 (SOU 1967, no. 36) social assistance is seen as an individual entitlement. The spirit of the law is also that nobody should be labeled an alcoholic but, rather, that each person's situation should be regarded in its totality.

The Care of Alcoholics and Drug Abusers Act. This law, which provides for compulsory treatment, also differs radically from the 1954 Temperance Act. It is intended to be applied if other means (those provided for by the Social Services Act) can not be used or would not serve a particular purpose. Originally, it could be applied only in cases of heavy drinking or drug use with risk to life. A 1987 amendment broadened the criteria for its use: since 1989 negative social consequences of abuse (together with abuse itself) are a sufficient reason for its use in individual cases. It is directed at both alcoholics and drug users. It extended the treatment period from the previous maximum of two months (with possible extension for another two months) to six months. Ideally, under this act, treatment should begin with a medical examination and continue in a special treatment unit. The act gives individuals the right to defend themselves in the administrative county court, which handles cases of possible involuntary committal.

The Act on Child Care. This act provides for the compulsory treatment of young people (under 20 years) for six months if their alcohol or drug use endangers their health or development and if voluntary measures are not applicable. It provides also for so-called intermediate coercion—that is, supervision.

Data on admissions to treatment show a fall in compulsory admissions. Inasmuch as, before 1982, other kinds of coercive measures were possible, such as supervision of heavy drinkers, the coercive elements of the alcohol-treatment system have become much weaker. However, the use of the new compulsory treatment law seems to have increased gradually, with compulsory admissions increasing from 758 in 1983 to 1,187 in 1987. Of 4,200 abusers registered and in institutions at the end of 1987, some 250 men and 80 women, or 8% of all, had been compulsorily committed. The number of women had doubled since 1982. For the vast majority (80%) of the compulsorily committed, alcohol was the main drug.

Expansion and Forms of Treatment Services

During most of the study period, Sweden has had three kinds of institution for inebriates: the state-owned and the "acknowledged," which are public, and the private. The legislation did not distinguish between the state-owned and the "acknowledged": they differed in ownership and financing. The state-owned were paid for totally, whereas the acknowledged were usually run by foundations, societies,or other bodies, but subsidized by the state. Both received

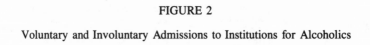

FIGURE 2

Voluntary and Involuntary Admissions to Institutions for Alcoholics

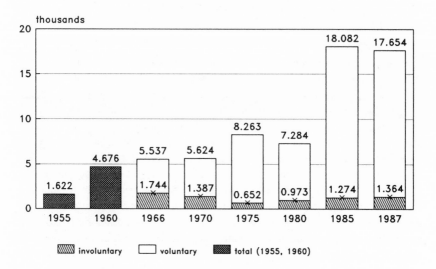

their clients through the National Board of Health and Social Welfare and had
to accept those whom the national board chose, whether they were voluntary
or compulsorily committed patients. Private institutions were also subsidized
by the state. Their clients came either directly or through temperance or other
boards, and had to be voluntary.

Figures 3 and 4 show the development of the treatment system, measured
in numbers of institutions and beds/visits. Its salient features are:

1. In the years 1955–65, after the Temperance Act of 1954 took effect,
    inpatient institutions especially grew in numbers. The emphasis was
    at first on public institutions and after the 1960s on the private, which
    could not detain patients compulsorily.
2. Between 1965 and 1975 the public institutions lost beds but custodial
    institutions (housing services) and outpatient services were being
    developed.
3. The decrease in the number of beds in public institutions continued
    evenly in the period 1975–85 and was becoming more marked in the
    late 80s. However, owing to the changed way of keeping statistics,
    it is difficult to differentiate between proper institutions for inebriates
    and residential homes (hostels) with no or little treatment for alcohol
    problems.

FIGURE 3

Beds in Public and Private Institutions for Alcoholics and in Hostels for Alcoholics

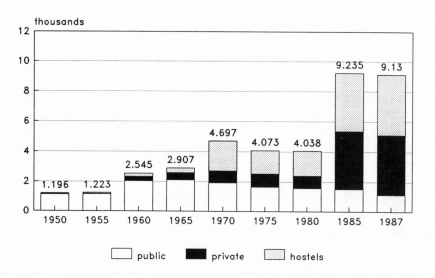

FIGURE 4

Number of Public and Private Institutions, Hostels and Counseling Clinics for Alcoholics

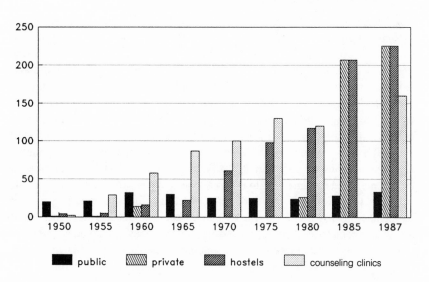

4. In recent years private institutions have gained more ground (see also
   Stenius 1988), a feature which is not unique to the alcohol treatment
   system. In the 1980s private health care centers and private pension
   schemes also have been established, though still few in numbers.
   Thus, total numbers of beds in institutions and hostels have risen again
   around the end of the decade.

The direct impact of the state on the structure of the treatment system
diminished in the 1980s. Since 1983 there are no more state-owned institutions—indeed no "institutions for alcoholics." The statistics refer only to
"treatment or residential homes." The state-centralized referral system had
been terminated earlier. Then the state subsidizing system was changed in 1986.
It was pointed out that direct subsidization of treatment institutions by the state
prevented changes in the structure of the treatment system. Short-term and
outpatient services were given as priorities. The subsidies are now being given
to the municipalities for whichever kinds of measures in the alcohol field they
prefer, whether treatment or information services. Funds for so-called
restructuring activities were earmarked in 1986–89 for the treatment sector:
the elimination of beds or inpatient institutions was state-supported. Hence
a municipality gained by providing cheaper kinds of treatment (hostels), not
only because of their lower costs but also because the municipality received
considerable sums of money (by 1987, twenty million crowns—about US$ 3.25
million). A possibly cheaper alternative might be to contract services out to
private initiatives (Stenius 1988).

Outpatient Facilities

The temperance boards constituted until the 1970s the clearest secondary-
prevention alternative and offered alcohol abusers counseling and guidance
as well as supervision and institutional care. Turning to a temperance board
had its risks—an individual who was classified as an addicted alcoholic and
caused some nuisance with drinking could eventually be involuntarily
committed. Hence, in 1946 the first alcohol counseling clinic was opened by
the City Mission (*Stadsmissionen*), explicitly as an alternative to the temperance
boards. Ironically, the need for such outpatient services had been expressed
originally by someone with long experience in matters of temperance
legislation, Professor Olof Kinberg, who had noted that certain people in need
of treatment did not dare turn to the temperance boards (*Socialstyrelsen* 1974,
no. 39: 11). Not only were these counseling clinics alternatives to the
temperance boards as facilities for voluntary treatment, but also they represented
a new approach to treatment for alcohol problems: they employed doctors and
nurses, and their use of medical treatment, especially Antabuse, attracted clients
in hope of cure. Moreover, they could offer general medical care.

In the 1940s the counseling clinics grew slowly in number, but after 1957, when the system of state subsidizing was changed and municipalities could obtain from the state up to 75% of the costs of the clinics, their numbers increased rapidly, doubling to about 140 between the mid-1960s and 1976. Most were operated by the municipalities—115 of 277 municipalities had at least one each by 1976. At first most were mainly medically oriented, but in the 1970s 66% were offering some form of individual psychotherapy, and 16% group therapy (*Socialstyrelsen* 1978).

Nonmedical measures became more common also after 1983, when it became possible to change medical and nursing posts into positions with a more social-work or psychological profile (SOU 1987, no. 22:91). Also, the Hazelden or Minnesota model had some effects on the outpatient services. Some of the private organizations running Minnesota homes are offering outpatient services as well, and in 1988 they were also trying to enter the occupational-health field.

Institutions for Alcoholics

Institutions or asylums have been the oldest and most salient feature of the Swedish treatment system. The history of separate institutions for alcoholics goes back to 1891 when the first private asylum for inebriates, called *San Souci*, opened its doors. It and other private asylums had varying degrees of success in attracting or keeping clients. The first public asylum, called *Venngarn*— today run by the Lewi Pethrus Foundation, a Pentecostal organization—which opened in 1916, could count on receiving clients on the basis of the Alcoholics Act of 1913. *Venngarn* was intended mainly for compulsorily committed clients.

> Moral persuasion means private talks between an inmate (not called "patient" as he is not considered ill in the normal meaning of that word) and one of the higher officials of the institution, usually the director or one of the assistants. The talks will deal with the patient's private matters, his attitude toward life in general and the alcohol question in particular. According to the institution, reprimands and condemnation shall be avoided if possible. Instead, one should go through "what has been" and then go over to the prospects for the future...So, work and moral persuasion! It sounds good, but I wonder if there is still not something missing! [Kassman 1939, our translation]

This description of *Venngarn* was given by a patient who had wanted more help in analyzing and changing his drinking behavior. However, in such an institution moral persuasion and so-called work therapy were then the main elements of treatment.

The investigation of 1964 (SOU 1967, No. 37: 4–14) found many varieties of work therapy: not only agricultural work but also carpentry, gardening, sewing, laundry, bookbinding, plumbing, and other kinds of work.

The postwar expansion of these inpatient institutions brought no major changes in the kinds of services offered. Some institutions offered group therapy, organized as teamwork between social workers, psychologists, and doctors, but most lacked professionals and this was a serious problem (Wiklund 1959). In 1961, for instance, of 117 established posts in the temperance offices of Sweden's three largest cities, only 35 were filled by professional social workers; 57 were filled by persons without a formal professional education, and 25 were vacant (SOU 1961, no. 58).

In the 1960s and 70s the institutions were severely criticized for providing only custody and not cure or active rehabilitation (SOU 1967, no. 36). Increasingly, the idea of combining work with cure, therapy, or rehabilitation seemed meaningless. The work that inmates were expected to do corresponded poorly to that of a developed urban society. Also, many of the clients were too old or sick for work therapy—many were on disability pension. In 1975, for instance, following a change in regulations in 1974, 23% of all those treated—not only voluntary patients in private institutions—had some kind of sickness allowance, compared with only 3% in 1965 (*Socialstyrelsen* 1978, no. 4). In addition, over the years, treatment periods had become shorter— from an average of five months in 1945 (SOU 1948, no. 23: 313) to about three in the 1960s (SOU 1967, no. 36), and two in the middle 1970s (*Socialstyrelsen* 1978).

Some institutions were influenced by the new private small homes for drug addicts, which more often used active treatment, in Sweden called milieu therapy (i.e., a collective living environment with various psychodynamic theories as a framework for interpreting deviance). When Kühlhorn (1974, 217) compared the outcome of the traditional institutions, popularly called "dryers," with that of the newer, therapeutically oriented "talk dryers," he could find no significant differences in rehabilitation rates. However, he concluded:

> If one has to take a stand for or against the therapeutic institutions one must first of all remember that the well-being of both patients and staff increased without any deterioration of the rehabilitative results. In all differentiated societies a need for treatment of specific groups will crystallize. To meet this need in agreeable circumstances is an important need in itself. [our translation]

Few institutions for alcoholics were influenced by the new trends of the 1970s in the treatment of young drug-users, the Hassela communities, which combined "tough love" and solidarity with socialist education. They were used for client groups different in many respects from the normal population. They were mostly male, unmarried, poorly educated, very poor, and either homeless or badly housed. In 1964, for instance, 40% lived on public assistance (social aid or unemployment benefits), 12% of the men lacked permanent housing, and 25% were homeless. Clearly also, quality of institution correlated with clients' social class:

> The better the quality of the services and the less compulsion, the larger the share of people from the higher ranks of society. Society's intervention has mainly been directed toward the lower ranks. [Isaksson, Norman, and Svedberg 1978, our translation]

The lower ranks in the public institutions, according to the 1964 investigation, were differentiated only by sex, difficulty of treatment, and presence of psychiatric in addition to alcohol problems (SOU 1967, no. 36). Better-off alcoholics turned to outpatient or to other medically oriented treatment. This pattern continued in the 1970s (*Socialstyrelsen* 1978) and 80s (Schubert and Krouthén 1984).

Most institutions for inebriates in the late 1960s and the 70s thus functioned more as homes for short-term recovery and help with different social and occupational problems; they claimed little or no influence on drinking behavior outside.

In the 1980s some institutions introduced new models of treatment. One trend is short-term treatment with intensive rehabilitation, inspired by the so-called Hazelden or Minnesota model. The Minnesota model has been adopted widely in Sweden; by 1988 some twenty to thirty different kinds of institution, and not only private institutions, had incorporated some of its aspects (Rosenqvist and Stenius 1988). Even one of the so-called maximum security homes run by municipalities and county councils, which can receive especially dangerous or difficult, and compulsorily committed, persons, has turned to the Minnesota model. This "new" treatment style has attracted much enthusiasm, owing in part, it seems, to its likely appeal to the middle-class, well-to-do alcoholic. However, many public officials engaged in alcohol treatment consider that the reduced availability of beds in traditional public institutions deprives chronic alcoholics of any means of dealing with their problems.

Hostels and Other Kinds of Custodial Services

Hostels provide an alternative to inpatient institutions. Originally they also were intended to have some therapeutic functions, such as to take care of individuals who were at risk, or to function as after-care facilities. However, since the 1960s these homes have been used as ordinary dwellings for lonely men, of whom 80% were homeless in the 1960s (SOU 1967, no. 36). In the 1970s only one-fifth of the inmates were employed on the open labor market and many were on disability pension (*Socialstyrelsen* 1978). In the wealthy 1970s, alcoholics could also get apartments of their own and live on disability pension (Stenberg et al. 1989, 45).

Nowadays some hostels claim that they offer therapy in addition to accommodation, but these are relatively few and have probably been responding to the incentives of the financing system to provide cheap solutions. In any case it seems that hostels favor the more socially integrated persons and this has meant, especially in the larger cities, as in Stockholm, with a new shortage of housing, that the phenomenon of homelessness has returned to the scene. The Stockholm area has 3,000–5,000 homeless men and 500–1,000 homeless women, and some cannot be offered even night shelter. The situation has been described by Agren:

Earlier one could opt for a disability pension and an apartment of one's own. Now, one could probably opt for the pension and a shelter. This could be some kind of a treatment or rehabilitation goal. Most lead a life in which they walk around the city and deteriorate. Maybe they can stay at a friend's one night, try to get by; then they might get into an institution for a turn. Or they might get too shabby and be compulsorily committed to lie in a "dryer" for some time. Maybe somebody will try to arrange for some kind of placement in a nursing home or something. Then they go out to the city again and they start to deteriorate again; maybe they'll get into the emergency clinic at the South hospital. It will be like that until they die. [from Stenberg et al. 1989, 53, our translation]

Care under a Medical Rubric

The ways in which the health sector has dealt with alcohol problems, and the extent to which it has done so, are difficult to grasp. Statistics on alcohol patients are included in psychiatry statistics or simply do not exist. Also, administrative divisions—the health sector comes under the county councils, whereas social alcohol-treatment is based on municipalities—have concrete consequences, as illustrated by Agren, who describes how they result in the homeless being deprived of medical services (Stenberg, Svanström and Åhs 1989, 52).

The ties between alcohol problems and the medical world have been many-sided. First, mental hospital statistics have portrayed enormous increases in alcoholism from the 1950s. According to Herner (in *Socialstyrelsen* 1985, no. 4) the numbers of cases with alcohol-related diagnoses in psychiatric treatment increased from 48 per 100,000 inhabitants in 1954 to 125 in 1964. This tendency became even stronger in the 1960s and 70s. Discharges per 100,000 inhabitants from mental hospitals with alcoholism as a primary diagnosis rose from 61 in 1962 to 565 in 1979. The relative share of alcohol-related illnesses of all discharges also increased. Three of the different reasons advanced to account for these increases have been:

1. decreased mean duration of stay, and also the tendency of alcohol patients to have shorter stays than others;
2. the increased willingness of the medical profession to choose an alcohol-related diagnosis;
3. a transfer of clients from the social services to the mental health sector (*Socialstyrelsen* 1987, no. 5). However, Alevard et al. (1980) found that, in regions where inpatient psychiatric care for alcohol treatment was much used, institutions for alcoholics were also used more often than in other regions.

In the 1980s discharges from mental hospitals did not increase (for instance, 429 per 100,000 inhabitants in 1983) probably because of general cutbacks in inpatient mental health care (SOU 1987, no. 22: 96).

Psychiatric wards also have been used for compulsory treatment under the Mental Health Act. For instance, in 1974, on a single day, about one thousand abusers were under compulsory treatment for alcoholism in psychiatric wards; and seven hundred and fifty persons were under compulsory detention in public institutions for inebriates (*Socialstyrelsen* 1974, no. 39: 200). Another example comes from the end of 1979, when, of 3,300 persons under psychiatric care for alcohol-related conditions, one-third had been involuntarily committed. At the same time, the social institutions contained about the same number of clients, of whom 40% had been involuntarily committed (Alevard et al. 1980).

Invariably, patients treated for alcoholism within psychiatry are socially better off than those in special facilities for alcohol treatment (SOU 1967, no. 36; *Socialstyrelsen* 1978; SOU 1987, no. 22).

Second, the medical sector seems to have been ambivalent about taking over the problem, especially in regard to allocating special resources to it. Several clinics were established for the treatment of alcoholics (four by 1965). However, most patients treated for alcoholism in psychiatric care (70% in 1974) were integrated into general wards, and this tendency has since become stronger (SOU 1987, 97–98).

The outpatient services, though clearly medical in their orientation, have remained under the municipalities and not been transferred to the county councils, which normally are responsible for the medical sector. This has been attributed to the unwillingness of the medical sector and the medical profession to take over the outpatient services (*Socialstyrelsen* 1974, no. 39).

Treatment of alcohol problems, especially their early detection, has thus been instituted within the general health and hospital services, or the occupational health services, rather than on the basis of special units. The work of Kristenson (1982), for instance, has inspired the use of short-term inexpensive interventions among people who attend health centers for other purposes.

Third, in the 1970s and early 80s physicians were strongly advocating new restrictions and possibly a new passbook system. Their motivation stemmed from the heavy workload that alcoholics imposed upon the health sector in general. In a psychiatric clinic half of all those seeking help had alcohol problems and "they seriously hampered the other patients' chances of treatment" (Ideström 1974). In a general surgical ward, 25 of 81 male patients (and five of 81 female) had suspected or obvious problems connected with abuse of alcohol (Borg et al. 1979). At a high-status seminar for researchers and politicians on alcohol control policy, in 1983, discussion on the social consequences of alcohol abuse was concerned largely with the detrimental effects of alcohol on the health-care system and on hospitals in general (Arvidsson 1984).

Division of Labor

In principle there is a clear division of labor between the medical and the social services in regard to alcohol problems. The medical sector is responsible for detoxification and acute medical and psychiatric care, and the social sector for rehabilitation. In practice this divison is by no means clear, and several other directives and laws conflict with it. For instance, since 1974, patients treated in institutions for alcoholics (which are social-service institutions) are entitled to sickness allowance (a health-care entitlement), and since 1977 can also qualify for a life-time pension (also a health-care entitlement) because of alcohol problems. Hospitals have instituted separate alcohol wards: for instance, in Stockholm the Karolinska Institute's clinic for alcohol problems was established in the early 1960s.

In the 1960s it was calculated that, of the approximately five thousand persons who were being treated for alcohol problems on one specific day in inpatient institutions, about 48% were in public institutions for inebriates, 10% in smaller private institutions, 7% in so-called hostels, and 35% in medical institutions (1.9% in alcohol clinics, 27.6% in psychiatric hospitals, 3.2% in psychiatric clinics, and 2.6% in medical clinics) (SOU 1967, no. 36).

In the 1970s the number of people in medical facilities either equaled or exceeded those in institutions for inebriates (*Socialstyrelsen* 1978; Alevard et al. 1980).

In the 1980s Schubert and Krouthén (1984), in a one-month study of alcohol cases in outpatient treatment in a community outside Stockholm, found that there were about three times more alcohol cases in social-service centers than in the psychiatric outpatient centers, but that their relative shares of the case-load in both sectors were similar, at about 20%. The two services differed clearly as regards characteristics of clients and their ways of working with them. Those of the psychiatric teams were the younger and socially better off (married and employed), and treatment was usually short-term, restricted to only a few consultations. Also, they mostly had not sought help primarily for alcohol problems, but had been found to be in the early stages of possible alcoholism.

In recent years cooperation between the social and the medical sectors has been emphasized. Legally it is the responsibility of primary health care to see to the medical needs of people with drinking problems. Ideally, primary care should also deal with early abuse and preventive measures, as it is at the primary health care centers that people make their most ready contact with the health-care system. However, there are so far only a few examples of smooth cooperation, and some groups—such as those on "skid row" or those with alcohol as well as psychiatric problems—are tossed between the two spheres.

Conclusion—Trends

Unlike the alcohol treatment systems of most countries, the Swedish system, with its roots in poor-relief, was once part of a general national alcohol-control system, but changes in the 1950s severed the close ties between the alcohol-control policy sector and the treatment system.

The prevention of alcohol problems was attempted through local temperance boards throughout the 1950s and 60s. They employed various means, from advice and guidance for individual drinkers to applications for involuntary committals. During those years the structure of the treatment system, with its emphasis on inpatient institutions, was consolidated and expanded. Involuntary committals were frequent. During the late 1960s and the early 70s the activities of the temperance boards diminished continously, and by 1974 the boards had been phased out. These years were the heyday of professionalism in treatment—in contrast to the earlier reliance on local boards consisting of lay people. Alcohol problems were increasingly seen as symptoms of other problems, whether physical, mental, or social in nature. Whereas, earlier, alcoholism had been seen as a cause of poverty, it was now regarded as a symptom of bad living conditions or of ill health. The welfare system expanded and the stigma attached to alcoholism faded: the better-off alcoholics were not easily discerned in the growing numbers of patients treated in mental or somatic clinics; and the poor among them received welfare benefits in the form of grants, apartments, pensions, and children's allowances. Hence also there was less need for involuntary committal. Especially, inpatient institutions for voluntary treatment, as well as outpatient services, grew in numbers. The boundaries of a separate alcohol treatment system had become blurred.

In the early 1980s the Temperance Act of 1954 was replaced by a general Social Services Act and supplemented by a law that included regulations on involuntary committal. This changed the basis for a separate treatment sector for alcoholics. For ideological reasons, the term "institutions for alcoholics" was replaced by a neutral term such as "treatment" or "residential" homes, and cases handled by the social welfare authorities were no longer classified according to "reasons for aid," such as alcohol abuse.

With these changes came the end also of the heavy reliance on state regulation of referral of clients and on state funding. Now, the municipalities became responsible for all kinds of treatment for alcohol problems (though medical care still comes under the county councils). To what extent these new administrative rules will eventually result in diversification of treatment remains to be seen. During the 1980s the Minnesota model was adopted widely in treatment services. Private initiatives have become not only more numerous but also more diverse in their activities. The private, but still state-regulated, homes for alcoholics, formerly run by foundations and client organizations, such as Links, a Swedish version of Alcoholics Anonymous, are being replaced by private-treatment enterprises that reach out for early problem drinkers with still intact social networks.

Heavy reliance on treatment has characterized the postwar Swedish response to alcohol problems. Although the country started out with a treatment system mostly within the social welfare sector, people with alcohol problems turned increasingly to the medical sector for help. It was not until the emergence of the Minnesota model that the social sector adopted a medical model. The optimism that surrounded its adoption was due not only to its novelty but also to the belief that the social-welfare alcohol-treatment system had finally discarded the label of poor-relief, that even well-off clients were attracted by the treatment offered. It is ironic that Sweden—*the* welfare state—is building up a new parallel system for homeless or deteriorated alcoholics by returning to the model of involuntary committal on social grounds; this is reflected in legal changes and in the subsidizing of such iniatives as the Pentecostal movement's several homes, which earlier had not been considered "treatment."

References

Abrahamson, M. 1989. Synen missbruk: 80 år diagnostisk rundgång. *Nordisk Sosialt Arbeid* 2:38–49.

Alevard R. et al. 1980. Alkoholbetingad vård och tvångsvård inom psykiatri och nykterhetsvård. *Läkartidningen* 77(5): 282–85.

Arvidsson, O. (ed.). 1984. *Alkoholpolitik och forskning.* Rapport från ett symposium om forskning och alkoholpolitik den 10 mars 1983. Uddevalla: Riksbankens jubileumsfond.

Borg S., et al. 1979. Alkohol-, narkotika- och psykofarmakabruk som orsak till sluten kirurgisk vård. *Läkartidningen* 76(44): 3897–900.

Bruun, K. 1983. Alkoholforskningens mångfald. *Sociologisk forskning* 1:3–9.

Bruun K., and P. Frånberg, ed. 1985. Den svenska supen. *En historia om brännvin, Bratt och byråkrati.* Stockholm: Prisma.

Esping-Andersen, G., and W. Korpi. 1987. From poor relief towards institutional welfare states: the development of Scandinavian social policy. In *The Scandinavian model, welfare states and welfare research*. Ed. R. Eriksson et al. New York: M. E. Sharpe, Inc.

Holgersson, L. 1988. Socialtjänst, en fråga om människosyn. En *analys av socialvårdens värderingar från medeltiden fram till socialtjänstens lagar, SOL, LVM samt SLPV*. Kristianstad: Tidens förlag.

Ideström, C.-M. 1974. Alkohol- och läkemedelsmissbrukare bland de psykiatrista fallen på KS. *Läkartidningen* no. 18.

Inghe, G., and M.-B. Inghe. 1970. *Den ofärdiga välfärden*. Stockholm: Tidens förlag.

Isaksson, K., J. Norman, and L. Svedberg. 1978. *Överlevnadsstrategier bland hemlösa och socialt utslagna*. Stockholm: Tidens förlag.

Jonsson, G. 1967. *Delinquent boys—their parents and grandparents*. Uppsala.

Kassman, G. 1939. *Jag är alkoholist*. Stockholm: Bokförlaget Natur och Kultur.

Kristenson, H. 1982. *Studies on alcohol-related disabilities in a medical intervention programme in middle-aged males*. Malmö: Dept. of Alcohol Diseases and Internal Medicine, and Section of Preventive Medicine, University of Lund.

Kühlhorn, E. 1974. Effekt av behandling. *Alkoholistbehandlingen i miljöterapeutiska och traditionella anstalter*. Mölnlycke.

Lenke, L. 1984. Alcohol in Sweden 1950–1980—An example of control policies in a deprivatized system. Paper presented at a meeting of the International Group for Comparative Alcohol Studies, October 1984. Stockholm, Sweden.

Ludwig, P., and P. Westlund. 1982. LVM Bakgrund och konsekvenser. *Meddelanden från socialhögskolan 2*. Lund: Lunds universitet.

Miller, W. R. 1986. Haunted by the Zeitgeist: reflections on contrasting treatment goals and concepts of alcoholism in Europe and the United States. In *Alcohol and culture*. Ed. T. Babor. New York: New York Academy of Sciences.

Pettersson, U. 1986. Socialtjänsten i praktiken. *Från mål till verklighet*. Angered: Skeab förlag.

Room, R. 1978. *Governing images of alcohol and drug problems*. Ph.D. Dissertation, Department of Sociology, University of California, Berkeley, U.S.A.

Rosenqvist, P., and J.-P. Takala. 1987. Two experiences with lay boards: the emergence of compulsory treatment of alcoholics in Sweden and Finland. *Contemporary Drug Problems* 15–38.

Rosenqvist, P. and K. Stenius. 1986. *Changing target groups for alcohol treatment - some points for discussion*. Paper presented at the ICAA Epidemiological Section Meetings, Dubrovnik, Yugoslavia 9–13 June 1986.

Schubert, J., and P.-J. Krouthén. 1984. Samverkan i alkoholvård mellan psykiatrisk vård och socialtjänst. *Socialmedicinsk tidskrift* 3/4:182–86.

Socialstyrelsen redovisar. 1974. *Alkoholpoliklinik-verksamheten* no. 39. Stockholm.

Socialstyrelsen redovisar. 1978. *Vården av alkoholmissbrukare. Problem och möjligheter* no. 4. Stockholm.

Socialstyrelsen redovisar. 1985. Alkoholism och narkomani inom psykiatrin. *En studie av vårdkonsumtion och dödlighet. Socialstyrelsen* no. 4. Stockholm: Modin-Tryck AB.

Socialstyrelsen redovisar. 1987. Alkohol och sjukvård. *Ett hälsopolitiskt handlingsprogram angående hälso- och sjukvårdens möjligheter att tidigt upptäckta och ta hand om patienter med hög alkoholkonsumption* no. 5. Stockholm: Modin-Tryck AB.

SOU. 1948. Betänkande med förslag till lag om nykterhetsvård. *Avgivet av 1946 års alkoholistvårdsutredning* no. 23. Stockholm: I. M. Boktryckeri-Aktiebolag.

SOU. 1952. *1944 års nykterhetskommitté V Principbetänkande* no. 53. Stockholm.

SOU. 1961. Översyn av nykterhetsvården. *Nykterhetsvårds-utredningen* no. 58. Stockholm.

SOU. 1967. Nykterhetsvårdens läge, del I. Klientel och behandlingsresurser. *Betänkande avgivet av 1964 års nykterhetsvårdsundersökning* no. 36. Stockholm.

SOU. 1987. Missbrukarna, socialtjänsten, tvånget. *Betänkande av socialberedningen* no. 22. Stockholm: Svenskt tryck.

Stenberg, L., L. Svanström, and S. Åhs. 1989. *Uteliggarna i välfärdssamhället.* Kristianstad: Tidens förlag.

Stenius, K. 1988. Market forces in a welfare society: privatizing the treatment of alcoholics, a local example. *The Drinking and Drug Practices Surveyor* 22:13–20.

Svenning, L. 1975. *Socialutredningen och framtiden.* Stockholm: Tidens förlag.

Wiklund, D. 1959. Utvecklingen av den svenska nykterhetsvården efter 1954/55. *Nykterhetsvården* no. 10: 188–194. Stockholm.

Finland: The Non-Medical Model Reconsidered

Jukka-Pekka Takala and Juhani Lehto

Finland: the non-medical approach was the title of a 1970 paper by Kettil Bruun on the alcohol treatment system of his native country (Bruun 1971). He contrasted the Finnish model with the internationally prevailing practice of treating alcohol problems in a medical framework. Bruun's message, somewhat simplified, was that alcohol problems neither could nor should be handled mainly by the medical profession: medical training was no guarantee of more successful treatment; most alcohol problems were simple and concrete problems of social life and should be dealt with accordingly.

Already E. M. Jellinek, the influential champion of the disease concept of alcoholism, had referred to the minor position of the disease model in Finland: "It cannot be said that the illness conception of alcoholism is widely spread...The lack of wider recognition is reflected in the predominating authoritarian approach toward the 'alcoholic'" (Jellinek 1960, 188).

The nonmedical approach and rejection of the disease model typify much of the Finnish alcohol treatment system.

"Medical" has many connotations. One is that there is something diseaselike in at least some cases of long-term heavy drinking, called "alcoholism". However, it is often hard to tell what people mean when they say that alcoholism is a disease. Is heavy drinking, when labeled "alcoholism", as good a reason for being excused from one's obligations as any disease, or as good a reason as a common cold or a broken leg, or measles or pneumonia? Is it a legitimate reason for drawing sickness insurance benefit? Is "alcoholism" something that doctors can treat? Or is it something that doctors do not know how to treat but that, nevertheless, should be left to the medical-care system to deal with? Is calling alcoholism a disease, without being strictly correct, a convenient way to mobilize medical treatment of the diseases caused undeniably by heavy drinking (Vaillant 1990)? Or is "alcoholism is a disease" merely a "semipropositional" statement (Sperber 1985), denoting no specific state of affairs? Or does it mean only that the drinker should be treated rather than punished or constrained for drinking or for unacceptable behavior caused by drinking?

The notion of "medical" or "nonmedical" approach has many facets. The issues and questions mentioned above have been raised in one form or another throughout the evolution of the Finnish alcohol-treatment system. Also, the system has often taken a distinctly nonmedical course, or at least one at variance with a predominantly medical orientation.

The first Alcoholics Act, passed in 1936, grafted on to the social welfare system a system of treatment, care, and control of "alcoholics" and, following Sweden's example, was not concerned with those alcoholics who were "purely medical" cases. It dealt solely with those inebriates who were a burden and a nuisance to society. The revision of the law, in 1961, followed the same basic pattern. With a few exceptions, the general health insurance, introduced in 1964, did not provide for coverage of treatment for alcoholism. Doctors were not appointed heads of alcohol treatment units, except in the particular case of the Järvenpää Social Hospital, which was founded in 1951 as the Reception Unit for Alcoholics, and renamed in 1962. A general employees' assistance program introduced in the mid-1970s was attached to the social welfare sector. As elsewhere, there has been a general shift in the handling of alcohol problems from the judicial to the socio-medical system, but mainly to the social-welfare rather than the medical sector. However, the most recent general legislation on alcohol care and treatment, the Misuser Act, which became law in 1987, stresses more expressly than earlier legislation the advantages of cooperation between the social and the health authorities in the provision of alcohol treatment services.

The structure and financing of the Finnish health services reflect the preponderance of the social welfare sector. Most of the health service agencies are public units, although the general health insurance reimburses a set amount for private treatment. Thus, a great part of alcohol treatment is financed and organized directly by both national and local government and not by health insurance. This weighs in favor of social rather than medical services, since the former tend to be the cheaper, and is consistent with the view that alcohol problems in Finland are more societal than medical in nature.

Such, then, is the viewpoint we have chosen to stress in this outline of the development of the Finnish alcohol-treatment system. This chapter first describes briefly Finnish drinking habits and the country's alcohol-problem profile and then gives a cross-section of the official alcohol treatment system at the end of the 1980s. It concludes with an account of the different types of treatment or care and their development, roughly in the order in which they became part of the system recognized by the legislation on misusers: the alcoholics' asylum, the social welfare office, the so-called A-clinics, residential services, and the health services. The order follows therefore the development of what was considered to be the care or treatment of persons with alcohol problems and not what actually happened. Hence, the health services are described last and probably with less emphasis than their actual influence on alleviating individual alcohol problems merits. Likewise, the extensive contribution of voluntary organizations has been excluded (for a description see Voipio 1986 and Niemelä 1983).

Drinking Habits and Problem Profile

Finns drink relatively little by European standards. The yearly per capita consumption of absolute alcohol remained under two liters from the beginning of the century until 1960; then it doubled by 1969 and tripled by 1975. At present, it is about 7.5 liters. The rapid increase has changed the scene somewhat, but mostly perhaps in bringing alcohol into ordinary everyday life (Simpura 1985). One outstanding feature persists, however: Finns tend to drink large amounts in a short time. Jellinek (1960, 88), in referring to the predominant authoritarian approach to alcohol treatment in Finland, suggested that it ''may be ascribed to the fact that the problem of true alcohol addiction is overshadowed by the violent manifestations of explosive occasional drinking.'' A Jellinek might find even today that problems of ''true alcohol addiction'' are overshadowed by the manifestations of explosive occasional drinking.

The profile of Finland's alcohol problems confirms this supposition. Compared with other countries, problems related to heavy bouts of drinking tend to be more pronounced than the consequences of steady heavy consumption. In 1986 the death rate for cirrhosis of the liver was 8.7 per 100,000 population compared with 26.2 and 33.6 for France and Italy, respectively, in 1981–82, and for alcohol poisoning 5.9 deaths per 100,000 (Kiianmaa and Ylikahri 1987). It has been estimated that alcohol is responsible for at least 2,000 deaths annually, or 40 deaths per 100,000 inhabitants, mostly related to heavy drinking on single occasions, resulting in intoxication, accidents, violence, suicide, and cardiac arrest (Ylikahri 1983).

Further supporting evidence is provided by data on arrests for drunkenness. In 1988 there were nearly 166,000 such arrests, or roughly one for every 25 inhabitants aged 15 years or over (1:25). The corresponding ratio for Swedes was 1:70 (1986) and for Danes—who drank markedly more than Finns—1:222 (1985) (*Nordisk alkoholstatistic* 1987). Although an arrest for drunkenness depends on police discretion and may sometimes aggravate rather than reduce disorderly behavior (Rahkonen and Sulkunen 1987), most serious observers believe that there are serious problems behind Finland's numerous arrests and that they do not result only from its citizens' low tolerance of drunkenness or from exaggerated police reaction.

While no particular type of problem profile inevitably evokes a particular type of treatment response, it appears that this sort of drinking problem is regarded as more a ''law and order'' than a medical problem.

The Alcohol Treatment System: An Overview

Table 1 provides an overview of different services for alcoholics.

Most of the services designed for the care of alcoholics are part of the social welfare system. The oldest are *institutions for alcoholics,* or asylums, usually located in the countryside, often on a farm. In 1986 there were 28, with 1,554 beds and 9,370 admissions. Most clients are voluntary, but this was not always the case. The task of social welfare offices in alcohol treatment is now largely case-management and gate-keeping; formerly they tried to influence alcoholics directly by advice and warnings. In the mid-1980s under the Misusers Act they dealt with 15,000 clients a year, most of whom were also admitted to a detoxification center or a residential facility. The so-called

TABLE 1A

Data on Cases Handled in the Finnish Alcohol Treatment
and Control System in 1988

Patients in hospitals (data from 1986, 2)	
Cirrhosis of the liver	1,343
Diseases of the pancreas	2,887
Alcohol poisoning	734
Alcohol psychosis	1,790
Disability pensions on the grounds of alcohol-related illnesses (effective at end of year, 1)	2,451
Deaths from alcohol-related illnesses (1986,1)	863
Persons with alcohol problems and using open care services of the social welfare system (2,3)	
clients at A-clinics	36,729
clients at youth clinics	2,464
clients with alcohol problems in social welfare offices	(approx.) 40,000
Clients in the residential services of the social welfare system for misusers (2)	
rehabilitation institutions	12,364
withdrawal stations	8,800
halfway homes and nursing homes	10,000
Visits related to alcohol problems to open care services (3)	
general practitioners and polyclinics	350,000–500,000
consultations with social workers	500,000
Arrests for drunkenness (1)	165,739

Sources:

(1) Alcohol Statistical Yearbook 1988; (2) Government Report 1988; (3) Lehto 1989.

TABLE 1B

Dimensions of Alcoholism Care and Treatment in
Finland's Social Welfare System 1986

Unit Type	No. of Units	No. of Beds	Clients in a Year	Treatment Days
Asylums	28	1,554	9,370	396,246
A-clinics	70		34,218	234,540
Youth clinics	11		2,895	21,356
Withdrawal stations	24	301	6,386	73,642
Halfway homes	41	929	2,500	306,695
Nursing homes	38	977	1,850	267,692
Overnight shelters	23	555	3,286	132,730

Source: Sosiaalihallitus 1989

A-clinics provide open care and treatment for people with drinking problems; they are staffed by social workers, nurses and part-time doctors. In 1986 they numbered 56, with 20 subbranches; they served 37,000 individuals in 1988. *Withdrawal clinics,* associated with 20 of the A-clinics, provide a four- to seven-day residential detoxification treatment for about 8,000 individuals a year. *Halfway houses* are meant for a short stay for people with both alcohol and housing problems; in 1987 there were 22 such houses, with 369 beds. Also in 1987, there were 76 welfare homes, with 1,930 places, which provided housing for people with alcohol problems who needed long-term care, even for routine activities of daily living, and 17 *overnight shelters,* with 583 beds (Lehto 1988b).

The role of the medical services in alcohol treatment was being reorganized in the late 1980s. Psychiatric hospitals were closing down their wards for alcoholics, as part of a plan to halve the number of beds for psychiatric inpatients and increase facilities for outpatient treatment. Psychiatric hospitals are now expected to treat only those cases and phases of alcoholism that are similar to other psychoses. In 1986 they treated 1,790 cases. General hospitals treated 4,993 cases of alcohol poisoning, cirrhosis of the liver and conditions of the pancreas (*Alcohol Statistical Yearbook* 1988). The number of "alcohol cases" treated by the general health services is very hard to determine, as what constitutes an "alcohol case" is not precisely defined. However, in the 1970s it was estimated that different "alcohol diseases" accounted for more than 1% of visits to physicians and 4% to hospital clinics, 3% of treatment days in general hospitals, and 10% in central mental hospitals (Salaspuro 1978). A "misuser case count" carried out in all health and social service facilities in 1987 indicated that the "alcohol problem caseload" in outpatient care was about the same in both types of institution (Lehto 1989).

The social welfare sector accounted for almost ten times as many inpatients as the health services (Government Report 1989).

The Inebriates' Home and the Alcoholics' Asylum

Temperance activists founded in 1888 the first inebriates' home, named *Turva,* which means "shelter" or "refuge" (Kallioniemi 1937, 18–19). Although a private organization, it received state support, and as much of the discussion that later led to direct state involvement referred to the experience of *Turva* it is discussed here. Since 1888 its regimen has remained one of the basic characteristics of Finland's alcohol-treatment system: a retreat on a country farm, total abstinence, physical work, moral education, and nonreliance on any "miracle" cure. From the beginning, work under strict discipline was regarded as an element in the strengthening of will power, and in education in general orderliness and normal living (Henrici 1900, 189). As this required much time (ibid., 193) the inmates were expected to stay one year at least. Few did so, however, and hence poor results were blamed on too short treatment. Since the commitments that patients had signed upon entry were not legally binding (ibid.,), the temperance movement soon began to demand legislation providing for compulsory committal for a sufficiently long period to produce effective results. Despite their efforts, however, such a law—the Alcoholics Act—was passed only in 1936, after the tumultuous years that led to Finland's independence (1917) and prohibition (1919–1932).

The provisions of the act were not strikingly different from those of other social welfare legislation of the era, which provided for compulsory committal to workhouses and other places. A central idea was to signal clearly that work-shyness, or living undeservedly at the expense of society, was not to be tolerated. In this respect it accorded with the penal ideology of that time, which regarded detention for the purpose of preventing crime (incapacitation) rather more favorably than did earlier or later thought in criminal law. This was the heyday of the ideology of institutional treatment in both social and criminal, as well as general health and mental health, legislation. The arguments for general prevention, individual treatment, and individual incapacitation complemented each other nicely: an individual who did not recover served as a warning to others, and while in custodial care could not be a social nuisance.

From then until well into the 1950s, the average inmate of an alcoholics' asylum had been legally committed. The 1936 Alcoholics Act laid down one year as the treatment period for first admissions. In practice, however, this norm never exceeded seven months and gradually became less. This deviation from the 12-month rule was justified at first on pragmatic grounds—there were too few beds to accommodate all who were being committed for a year.

However, the very legitimacy and effectiveness of prolonged treatment became increasingly questioned, particularly during the 1960s (Westling 1969,

55). A study in the late 60s found that the somatic health of inmates of institutions did not improve after the first four weeks (Forsberg and Hasan 1970). It is illustrative of the ideological change that had occurred that the possible benefits of moral therapy were not considered; only somatic health was measured.

Thus, the institutions for alcoholics followed the trends of the post-World War II era toward individual liberty and away from institutional care or detention, although legislation on care and treatment of alcoholics varied little between 1937 and 1987. The Misuser Act of 1961—despite claims to the contrary—was basically a new edition of the 1936 Alcoholics Act (Takala 1985a). Liberalization implied less compulsion, a shorter stay, and the easing of internal rules. The number of compulsorily committed inmates declined slowly in the 1950s and rapidly in the 1970s and 80s. Their relative number fell even more dramatically as the total number of clients grew (Figure 1).

FIGURE 1

Involuntary Admissions to Institutions for Alcoholics

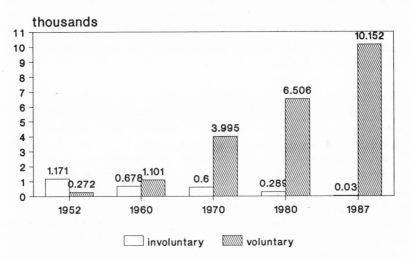

Therapeutically oriented social workers have become prominent among the staff of these institutions. The nurses' role also has changed, from granting inmates' requests for exemption from work to physical and psychological health care. Physical labor is now seen as work therapy; discussions with staff are regarded as social or group therapy, rather than training for "will power".

When the present Misuser Act became law in 1987, there were very few involuntary committals. The act reduced substantially the grounds for involuntary treatment and the legal norms for treatment periods. Only a few individuals have been committed under this law. However, this is not to say that legal coercion gave way to pure and perfect voluntariness. Since 1964 there had been an economic inducement for voluntary admission to an institution: only voluntary patients were entitled to the daily allowance granted under the general health insurance. Hence many alcoholics entered ''voluntarily'' but under the double threat of involuntary committal and loss of the sickness allowance. Economic inducements, threat of dismissal from employment, and other pressures come into play in referrals to institutional treatment (Lehto 1988a). Also, new financial arrangements have led to the founding of new, and the reform of old, institutions. This is discussed later.

Social Welfare Offices

The Alcoholics Act of 1936 had entrusted the practical implementation of the law to local welfare boards and county (provincial) governors, instead of general courts or temperance boards, which had also been suggested (Takala 1986). This decision gave the social welfare boards a central—for long *the* central—role in alcohol treatment and care. The idea was not that the welfare board would merely send drunkards to asylums. Committal to an asylum was only the ultimate of three possible steps. First, the welfare board would warn and advise the alcoholic; second, it could exercise supervision; and finally, if these two steps failed, it could use committal to an institution. In a way, then, the boards were supposed to provide a sort of outpatient treatment or counseling, but it was only under threat of committal that the milder measures were seen to be effective (Toivola 1940, 76).

In rural towns, elected members of the welfare board did most of the work with clients, while cities had specialized social workers. In the 1950s the boards seemed to believe that they could exert moral influence on drinkers through personal reprimands and supervision. Later this reliance waned, former board members recall (Takala, forthcoming). Declining faith in supervision can also explain why the number of decisions to place drinkers under supervision dropped to almost nil by 1985.

The number of clients dealt with by the social welfare offices under the Misusers Acts peaked between 1975 and 1980, and then declined. This decline did not signify fewer people with alcohol problems. A study on the characteristics of the living-allowance clients of the welfare offices (Lauronen 1988, 37) showed that forty thousand, or 20%, had misuse problems, compared with the fifteen thousand cases recorded under the Misuser Act. Also, alcohol misuse is the most common background family factor in the case of welfare measures applied under the Children's Act.

Voluntary Outpatient Treatment: The A-Clinics

Much had been expected of asylums and of committal of alcoholics when they were first proposed. In another turn of thought, however, they were seen to need correction; the ideas of voluntary care and treatment in the normal societal setting reemerged in new forms. One was the complementing of the system of asylums and social welfare boards by voluntary measures; another advocated a more radical departure—the A-clinics.

One of the champions of voluntary treatment in the community was Volmari Kanninen, who with the help of some physicians treated 30–40 heavy drinkers between the World Wars. He depicted his own model as a medical one, and he criticized the Alcoholics Act: "It has become the main goal to release society from asocial elements by means of compulsory care. The potential of curing alcoholics has been relegated to a secondary status and their handling has been regarded more as social education than treatment of the ill" (Kanninen 1938).

Kanninen's criticism had no immediate consequences, but his ideas are of interest in that they foreshadowed later developments. He recognized two basic types of alcoholic. The first, those "rather uncivilized alcoholics," Kanninen asserted, "must be treated by involuntary welfare methods"; they needed institutional treatment far away from the temptations of normal society. The other type Kanninen saw as "persons who under regular conditions impeccably discharge their social assignments, but who occasionally stray from the track and, compelled by their craving, drift into immoderate drinking. They are mostly rather highly civilized and intellectually advanced...Their use of alcohol is not only craving or vice but it has advanced into a disease, against which they are powerless. They are alcohol-ill and they need medical treatment to get well." Compulsory treatment does not suit them: "Because of their work obligations, their social status or other such reasons, they cannot take advantage of treatment in institutions implying isolation for a long period, and they are not actually in need of it, either. They must be cared for and treated in liberty; no compulsory means must be applied" (Kallioniemi 1937, 59–62; cf. Takala 1985b).

Another, somewhat later, initiative in support of voluntary treatment was a voluntary organization established in 1948 largely by persons already involved with either the official treatment or the temperance movement: the Society for the Support of Free Treatment of Alcoholics. This still active organization established a few private homes for voluntary treatment of inebriates; they were much smaller than the public institutions, and forerunners in some ways of modern therapeutic communities. It sought more beds for voluntary patients in small institutions but not a radical departure from the long-term inpatient model. Its central figure was Osmo Toivola, author of the manual on the Alcoholics Act and the principal draftsman of the 1961 Misuser Act. Although he supported voluntary treatment efforts, he often advocated involuntary means also—for instance, criticizing Jellinek's proposal in 1952 to establish a network of hospitals, clinics and asylums: "The treatment of inebriates on a voluntary basis only cannot be sufficient" (Immonen et al. 1980, 10).

A more radical line was that which came to be embodied in the A-clinics. The voluntariness of the A-clinics was different from that promoted by Toivola and his society. The A-clinics offered treatment that did not require the separation of clients from their normal environment. They rejected coercion even as an underpinning of voluntary treatment. Thus, they embodied ideas similar to Kanninen's on the "alcohol-ill," though probably adopted mostly from other sources. Much of their inspiration came from the American treatment model, developed by the proponents of the disease concept of alcoholism. However, this model was adopted selectively and only partly; it retained voluntary admission, outpatient care, and a nonmoralistic attitude, and rejected the disease concept of alcoholism and the professional medical approach to treatment in favor of a new and more therapeutic social-work model—social casework, another idea from America. Thus, although the medical model of alcoholism had some influence in the development of the idea of an A-clinic, the basic team of an A-clinic was to be one or two social workers, a nurse and a part-time physician. The director was to be a social worker, but in the early phase the director was often not professionally trained.

FIGURE 2

Clients in A-clinics and Misuser Act Clients in Welfare Offices

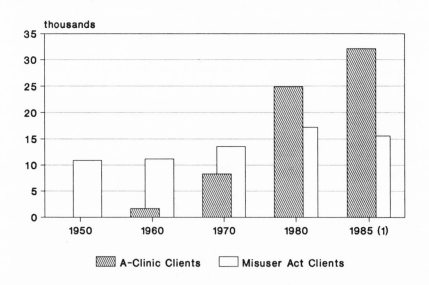

The first experimental outpatient polyclinics were established in 1953 at Vaasa and in 1954 in Helsinki. In 1955 the A-Clinic Foundation was founded and by 1970 had established twelve A-clinics. Their numbers grew rapidly.

In the 1970s they were handling more clients than were the commune social offices under the Misusers Act, and by the mid-80s twice as many as the social offices.

An important milestone for the A-clinic network was the 1974 amendment of the Misusers Act, which named the A-clinics in legislation for the first time, paved the way for their expansion under local communes, and made them eligible for normal state-budget financing. It provided also for a change in their ownership: earlier, all had been owned by the A-Clinic Foundation, but most are now owned by communes.

The treatment results of the A-clinics—as measured by abstinence and reduced drinking—proved less impressive than their advocates had hoped. An evaluation study compared an A-clinic with an alcohol unit in a psychiatric polyclinic (Bruun and Markkanen 1961; Bruun 1963). Methodologically the study was path-breaking: a relatively large number of clients, 303, were randomly assigned to either one or the other unit, and the follow-up time was relatively long. The study found that the new A-clinic "cured" no more alcoholics than did the psychiatric clinic. However, the authors preferred the ideology of the A-clinic (Bruun and Markkanen 1961, 78). Possibly also it was the more cost-effective, for it was cheaper to run. Another consideration is that the other pole of the comparison was not the traditional institution for alcoholics.

The social work of A-clinics differs in many respects from that of social welfare offices. In the latter the major tasks of the social workers were—and still in most offices are—the administration of social support, assistance with housing, gate-keeping for different residential institutions, and the administration of compulsory measures, such as committal to institutions. In the A-clinics the social workers are called social therapists. They do not administer material assistance but concentrate on counseling and various other methods of "discussion therapy"—individual, group, and family therapy. Also, these clinics accept only voluntary clients, and cannot impose on them any sort of legal or material pressure.

The presence of a nurse and a part-time physician in the basic A-clinic team enables it to offer treatment for withdrawal symptoms and minor health problems common in heavy drinkers. Mostly, new clients consult the nurse first, and in many clinics more than half of the clients see only the nurse (Murto 1988). This arrangement has given some problem drinkers access to health services which they would often find difficult to obtain at general health service units.

However, for their basic livelihood and necessary material help, poor drinkers with multiple problems have to resort to social welfare offices, where they must submit to thorough social investigation but cannot obtain even paramedical help, although often they are ill. The social welfare offices had been bypassed when, in the 1970s, the social services were expanding in the

direction of "social therapy," such as educational advice centers, family
counseling, and A-clinics.

The great expansion of the A-clinic network coincided with the
development of a political climate in which alcohol problems were recognized
as being fairly commonplace and as affecting the normal, active labor force.
In 1972, as industry was expecting a shortage of workers, the labor unions
and industry signed their first agreement on employee assistance programs,
which were job-based referral systems for workers with alcohol problems.
Briefly, it provided for employees who appeared intoxicated at work to be
offered first the chance of treatment instead of dismissal. To meet this need
was one of the weightiest arguments used for the spread of A-clinics in the
mid-70s.

A recent study of the clients of different alcohol treatment services in
the Greater Helsinki area (Kylml 1988) shows that Kanninen's two classes
are, in a way, reproduced in the two major systems: the average A-clinic client
is significantly better off than the alcohol client of the social welfare office,
as regards employment, housing, and general social status. Still, however,
little more than half of the A-clinic clients have regular employment.

TABLE 2

The Major Income Source of Misuser Clients in the A-Clinics and
Social Welfare Offices, Greater Helsinki Area 1987 (percent)

	A-Clinics	Social-welfare Offices
Regular employment	54	12
Irregular employment	10	18
Social insurance	22	25
Living allowance	7	40
Other	7	4
Total	100	99
(N)	(184)	(99)

Source: a survey of clients in alcoholism treatment services (Kylmälä 1988)

The traditional asylums for alcoholics and the new A-clinics differed
greatly, and there were certain needs that neither covered. Persons with difficult
withdrawal symptoms who needed a more stable environment than an outpatient
clinic could offer, but who would not consider long-term custodial care in a
traditional asylum, had no place to which to turn except hospitals, general or
psychiatric. A remedy was sought by establishing so-called withdrawal
treatment stations, or detoxification units, in association with A-clinics. The
first units were founded in the 1960s and were officially recognized by the

1974 amendment of the Misusers Act. Now there are 20 such units, providing a four- to seven-day residential detoxification treatment, during which also the client's social problems are discussed and follow-up treatment is arranged, if necessary.

The withdrawal clinics developed as part of the A-clinic network, and adopted the A-clinic's staffing model. The head of the clinic is usually a trained social worker, and nurses carry out much of the treatment; a physician attends only a few hours a week. As a rule, medical or professionally trained nursing staff do not attend at night or at weekends. This limited staffing makes it difficult for these clinics to treat acutely ill patients adequately.

Residential Services

Overnight shelters. A common image of the 1930s linked inebriety with vagrancy and work shyness; an equally common post-war image has been that of the homeless male alcoholic (Taipale 1982), particularly in the 1940s and 60s. Many of those who were unable to find lodging on the normal market were labeled inebriates. In the late 60s and early 70s many of the homeless alcoholics drank substitutes such as cheap cologne and industrial alcohol, particularly one infamous brand known as *T-sprii* (withdrawn from the market in 1972). Mortality was very high among them. It was at that time that new public shelters were opened, a temporary emergency measure at first. They have remained, however, and though some have moved to more adequate premises their standards are still minimal:

A hundred men or so are sleeping along the walls, many of them on bare concrete. In fact, you cannot talk about sleep, since drunks growl in the hall. In a corner, they argue over a bottle, one of them in a wheel-chair. Some of the men have grabbed a piece of cardboard or newspaper shreds to lie on [Taivalsaari 1987].

For intoxicated homeless persons who are not "ill enough" to be admitted to a hospital or "disturbing enough" to be arrested for drunkenness, the 17 overnight shelters with their 600 beds are practically the only places for sleeping indoors. Most other units for alcoholics have rules that deny admission to drunk persons: a recent survey found that 86% of welfare homes and 70% of halfway houses had such rules (Lehto 1988b, 31).

Homelessness is an important factor in arrests for drunkenness. Such arrests are the most widespread form of involuntary "treatment", accounting for more than 500 people on an average night.

Before public drunkenness was decriminalized in 1969, people could be fined for it, and this often resulted in imprisonment for those who could not pay the fine, many of them homeless, and in a heavy load for the prison system (Westling 1960; Anttila 1960). Decriminalization did not, and was not meant to, abolish arrests for drunkenness; it changed their legal grounds and did away with imprisonment as an alternative for nonpayment of fines. A recent working party of the Ministry of Social Affairs and Health has proposed that services for intoxicated persons be so developed that the number of arrests would be halved by 1993 (STM 1988a). Such a reduction would still mean one arrest per 40 adults annually, which would leave Finland still at the top of the list of comparable nations in this respect.

Halfway houses and hostels. The 1974 amendment of the Misusers Act brought normal state and municipal budget money not only to the A-clinics but also to overnight shelters, detoxification units, halfway houses, and hostels. This brought about a rapid increase in the number of different private and communal alcohol treatment units, designed partly for chronic inebriates who had dropped out of the labor market (overnight shelters, hostels), and partly for people who were employed or seriously attempting to reenter the labor market (A-clinics, detoxification units, halfway houses).

Halfway houses were meant for temporary accommodation in a therapeutic community led by a social worker. Clients would enter them after a drinking bout or possibly after a period of treatment in an institution, stay for one to three months, and move on to normal housing. However, because of the general housing shortage, it is often very difficult to return to normal housing. The first halfway house was opened in 1963, and there are now 22, with 369 beds (Lehto 1988b).

Hostels ("welfare homes") are for supported long-term housing—years rather than months—for people with alcohol problems and who cannot be expected to return to normal housing and employment. The hostels were differentiated from halfway houses in the early 1970s, as the latter were crowded with alcoholics on old-age or disability pensions. In 1987 there were 76 such hostels, with 1,930 places (Lehto 1988b).

In the 1980s housing services for alcoholics developed rapidly, almost entirely in the form of long-term hostels, while the number of halfway houses decreased. The quality of the halfway houses is variable; most are so far below present-day standards of nursing homes for old people that they resemble more the old-style communal houses for the poor elderly (Lehto 1988c, 82).

Health Services and the Treatment of Patients with Alcohol Problems

Although most of the specific official measures aimed at alcoholism were linked to social services, the health services, both general and psychiatric, could not avoid dealing with alcohol problems. General medicine was responsible for the treatment of serious somatic disorders common in heavy drinkers: cirrhosis of the liver, pancreatitis, alcohol poisoning and (earlier) tuberculosis. Also, the better-off problem drinkers and their families consulted doctors rather than social offices. Even today, it is said that the country's only private mental hospital takes charge of the detoxification of wealthy drinkers. In addition, physicians have tried to help alcoholics, mostly without wider support or recognition.

A number of psychiatric hospitals began to treat patients with alcohol problems, at first with trials of after-care for alcohol psychosis, in particular delirium tremens. Some used aversion therapy in the late 1940s, but the method soon lost popularity. Disulfiram (Antabuse) has been administered since the 1950s at least, but there are no reliable aggregate data on its use. It is the one medicine that is popularly believed to have some effect on the pattern of drinking. In many instances, mostly probably unofficial, taking disulfiram has been made a precondition for some benefits, such as social-welfare allowances or withdrawal of impending dismissal from work.

With the rapid rise of consumption of alcohol in the 1960–1975 period, many psychiatric hospitals organized special wards for alcoholics, which provided, first of all, detoxification. Follow-up care, if any, was supposed to take place in social welfare facilities.

The late 1970s saw a movement to reduce the dominance of institutional inpatient care in psychiatry—a movement significantly later and less radical than in Italy or many parts of the United States. Beds used by alcoholics not in an acute psychotic state were one of the first targets. The last wards for alcoholics in mental hospitals were closed in 1990.

Normally, cutbacks in psychiatric hospital beds have been compensated for by an expansion of psychiatric outpatient facilities, but this has not applied to the treatment of alcohol problems. At least, the staff of many A-clinics complain that regional mental health centers tend to send on to A-clinics all those who are thought to have any alcohol problems, even those with clearly psychiatric disorders. This seems to indicate a contraction of the involvement of psychiatry in alcohol treatment, a curious instance of demedicalization, or at least "depsychiatricization," of alcohol treatment in Finland (Lehto 1989).

In principle, the 1964 General Health Insurance Act could have led to better services for alcohol problems at the level of primary medical care. However, the administrative guidelines for the enforcement of the act excluded the outpatient treatment of alcoholics from the daily allowance coverage for lost income, thus frustrating attempts to care for people with alcohol problems under primary medical care. (Similarly, outpatient counseling under the social authorities was excluded.) This is one reason why Finnish alcohol treatment is relatively nonmedicalized (Lehto 1987). However, the insurance does reimburse a set amount of private medical fees for private care under a medical rubric. Thus it helps medicalize the alcohol problems of the highest social strata. Even the daily allowance can be obtained if the physician provides a different diagnosis, such as exhaustion, instead of alcoholism.

The Primary Health Care Act, which became law in 1972, implied a rapid expansion of community care services. At the same time, the demand to provide care for alcohol problems was met by expanding the A-clinic network under other legislation—that is, not under the medical care system. Hence, alcohol problems were not taken in hand seriously by the rapidly growing municipal health centers.

Since the mid-1970s the health sector has shown renewed interest in alcohol problems, and a number of treatment experiments have been conducted in the primary health-care system (Suhonen 1986; Lundholm and Sinnemäki 1987; Suhonen and Nyqvist 1988; Suokas 1988). One focus of attention has been the early detection of alcohol problems. Biochemical markers of heavy drinking (gamma glutamen transfer [GGT], and mean corpuscular volume [MCV]) have been used in combination with "mini-interventions." A few maternal and child health care stations have tried to develop methods of detecting and treating drinking problems in pregnant women. A number of communal general hospitals have begun to provide for detoxification. The first, and so far only, professorship in alcohol studies is that of "alcohol diseases", founded as a biomedical specialty at the University of Helsinki. There seems to be some basis for an extension of the care and treatment of alcohol problems within the public health sector. So far, hopes and efforts have been directed mainly at health education and the care of minor problems.

The Impact of Financing Structures

The financing arrangements for alcohol treatment may influence the nature of care and treatment in subtle ways. For instance, as mentioned above, the decline in compulsory committals in the 1960s had also an economic background: because of new financing regulations, voluntary admission to an institution for alcoholics became more rewarding than it had been for both the local community and the client. Similarly, the 1984 Act on the Planning and Financing of Social and Health Services gave local government authorities more options. They could more freely decide on the kinds of institution they would finance, and they could more easily purchase services from private institutions. This has encouraged the establishment of private alcohol treatment services, which partly occupy the same field as the more traditional institutions for alcoholics.

One effect of the 1984 Financing Act has been increased interest on the part of local authorities in setting up their own treatment centers, instead of state and regional units. In the 1980s some urban local authorities established so-called rehabilitation units by combining a former halfway house with a withdrawal clinic.

The new wave of privatization of alcohol treatment is exemplified by a number of new private clinics, notably two Minnesota-type (Cook 1988) clinics for intensive 28-day cures. Their work is based on the twelve steps of Alcoholics Anonymous, and likewise they endorse an AA-type disease-concept of alcoholism. This means that their approach is not very medical: physicians and medical methods play a minor role, in keeping with the AA emphasis on learning self-treatment methods and on group activity rather than on professional care. The Finnish Minnesota clinics market their services particularly for employee assistance programs and, in a way, have taken the place of Järvenpää as the elite institution. A recent study which compared the treatment outcome of a Minnesota clinic with that of the Järvenpää Social Hospital (Keso 1988), found that, as measured by abstinence after treatment, the new clinic had better results, at a statistically significant level. However, it is unclear whether the good results were due to the novelty of the institutions or to something more stable in their approach (Poikolainen 1989). There is also a new Rehabilitation Clinic for Women, based on the model of the Betty Ford Clinic in the United States; the AA-type disease notion is central here too.

Finally, the relatively low degree of medicalization of Finnish alcohol treatment may be explained partially by the financing structure of the health services, particularly by the balance between private and public branches. The weight of health insurance is smaller and that of public health greater than in those Western countries where alcohol treatment is most medicalized (U.S.A., Germany, Netherlands).

Finland has fewer private services, and, until recently at least, they may have had enough paying clients even without a medical model of alcoholism. In the public sector, an interest in economizing has encouraged the option of the social-work model. However, the present increase in the supply of private alcoholism treatment also implies a more frequent use of medical labels in treatment.

Division of Labor among Health, Social-Welfare and Judicial Authorities

Alcohol problems seem to fall into an area in which neither providers of health services nor social welfare authorities nor the police feel at ease. This makes division of labor among them an intricate matter, often a subject of conflict. The passing of the Alcoholics Act in 1936 can be seen as an attempt to obviate or solve this difficulty in the division of labor. Prisons, mental institutions, and workhouses wanted to get rid of inmates whose basic problem seemed to be alcoholism, and who did not seem to fit in with the true purposes of the institutions. A system of warnings, supervision, and institutional facilities for alcoholics would solve the problem, it was thought (Takala 1986, 539–42). This new system was then grafted on to the social welfare system. Similar reasoning influenced the founding of later institutions, such as the A-clinics, alcohol-specific housing services, and overnight shelters, all designed to ease the burden on the health system and housing authorities.

The question of the medical or the nonmedical nature of alcohol problems has been at issue at every stage of the development of the Finnish system of alcohol treatment. Already the first Alcoholics Act of the 1930s might have been coupled with the medical services. In 1935 the national health director, criticizing the Alcoholics Bill, said, "alcoholism proper, which subjects the alcohol consumer to social welfare measures, must be regarded as a disease, which must be treated according to the same principles as other diseases''— that is under the health authorities (Piirainen 1974, 148). Perhaps another turning point was reached in the 1950s, when AA reached Finland, the A-clinics were beginning, the Järvenpää Reception Unit for Alcoholics was set up, and the still new drug, Antabuse, boosted expectations of finding a specific medical treatment for alcoholism. While residential institutions were developing in a medical direction, the outpatient units opted for the model of social casework. In the 1960s a general criticism of "total institutions" (Goffman 1961) lent indirect support to the outpatient social casework model.

Again, the national health director, now Niilo Pesonen, argued unsuccessfully that the treatment of alcoholics should be supervised by the National Board of Health, because "alcoholism is an illness and must be handled accordingly" (Pesonen 1967).

The early 1970s were another turning point. As counseling and outpatient services seemed to be a response to the demand for services for employee assistance programs, these services could equally well have been set up within the local health centers as within the social welfare system. Similarly, as has been pointed out above, health insurance could have incorporated outpatient treatment of alcoholism, and the developing outpatient psychiatric services could have included alcoholism treatment. However, the disease perspective never prevailed when decisions were made about what the state should do about the treatment and care of heavy drinkers. For instance, the Council on Intoxicants, which laid the groundwork for the present Misuser Act, said that to regard misuse of intoxicants as a disease had in some cases hampered practical therapy and made clients more passive. "A disease is taken to be something independent of will, and also healing is supposed to depend on outside experts" (Komiteanmietint 1978, 46). Sometimes the winning argument took the form of admitting that in some cases heavy drinking might well be an illness, but that what the state could afford was to provide care or treatment to those who caused other trouble in society. With the development of the welfare state, the range of tasks that the state could legitimately undertake has gradually widened.

Physicians have always been involved in alcohol treatment, but were seldom appointed heads of alcohol-specific treatment units—often, it was said, because they were too expensive to hire. The other reason was that medical training, while helpful, was neither strictly necessary nor sufficient to cope with the problems for which these units were made responsible. Of course, the health-care system has always had substantial responsibility for the treatment of many alcohol-related disabilities and diseases.

In Finland, as in many other countries, there has been a shift from the judicial system toward the socio-medical system in the handling of alcohol problems. However, the greater weight has been given to the social rather than the medical authorities. One essential aspect of the change comes out graphically in a study by Mäkelä and Säilä (1987). They compared the numbers of "alcohol related overnight stays" in facilities of different authorities in 1960 and 1980. In 1960, 74% of the 2,200 "alcohol related stays" on an average night took place in judicial facilities, most of them in prisons by defaulters of fines imposed for public drunkenness. In 1980 the category 'drunkenness-related fines defaulters' had become insignificant, a direct consequence of the decriminalization of public drunkenness in 1969. In 1980, 71% of the 3,270 alcohol-related overnight stays occurred in social welfare institutions, which emphasized housing as much as, or more than, care or treatment. Mäkelä and Säilä excluded from their study those serving prison sentences for driving while intoxicated; their inclusion (perhaps 700 cases on an average day) would show a less dramatic shift but would not change the general contours: a clear shift from prison to social welfare. Also, stays in medical institutions have increased, but only threefold as compared with the more than fivefold increase in the social welfare sector.

Conclusion

To Kettil Bruun the "non-medical approach" implied the avoidance of groundless promises of "cures" that demanded no effort on the part of clients. To Jellinek, nonacceptance of the disease concept went with an authoritarian attitude toward the drinker. In practice, neither point of view was wholly borne out. The social-work model went together with unfounded promises of cure: an official medical belief in the efficacy of treatment was an essential element of the policy that set up an alcohol-treatment system incorporating, as an essential part, compulsory institutional care. The same model in its operation has allowed a gradual easing of authoritarian attitudes. There are today fewer official moralistic reprimands, hardly any instances of compulsory surveillance, and very few cases of compulsory committal to institutions, and all this has happened largely within the social-work model. The use of legal compulsion has declined significantly, but other forms of social pressure have taken on more structured forms (employee assistance programs, house rules for housing services, etc.). These changes, though similar to those favored by one strand of the disease ideology, did not usually take place under a medical rubric: rather, they were argued for, and regarded, as expressions of a basic humanistic attitude and the protection of civil rights.

Thus, a similar shift that took place elsewhere from "badness to sickness" (Conrad and Schneider 1980), from judicial to medical authorities, occurred in Finland as a shift from stringent social work with legal compulsion to a more amiable and therapeutically oriented social work. The municipal social welfare offices represented the disciplinary aspects of social work, whereas social therapeutic models have been rather close to a medical or disease model. The flexibility of the social-work label is evident also in that alcohol-specific social work agencies have adopted approaches that originated in a disease-concept setting or a medical environment, and were linked to sickness insurance. These include therapeutic outpatient work and the Minnesota model.

In a therapeutically oriented social-work model one talks of "treatment" and "rehabilitation" of alcoholics—the rhetoric is similar to that of the disease model. The practice, however, may be more in the nature of "care" and "support" than of "treatment." However, this again is not different from what a medically labeled agency can offer for excessive drinkers: both medicine and social work lack specific effective means to combat alcoholism.

Another disclaimer also must be made about the change in the nature of social work. It has not been merely a simple conversion from authoritarian moralism to humanitarian social therapy. We are convinced that the legal measures used by social workers in the handling of alcoholics have changed toward less coercion, and that official agencies now offer heavy drinkers more and better services (care, support, material means) than they did 30 or 40 years ago. However, this is not a result of a simple ideological conversion to social therapy. There is still control, discipline, and many-faceted coercion, while in the early days of the alcohol treatment system there was much compassion, support, and human concern about the plight of heavy drinkers.

Also, though there has been a true change toward a more voluntary and open care and treatment, there is an apparent tendency to revert to the use of institutional care: the provision of alcohol-related housing has been increasing. Society's open care has not succeeded in rehabilitating its most miserable drunkards back to normality; they still need support in their housing and daily life. Often the discipline to which they must submit and the material conditions in which they must live are little better than those of earlier institutions for alcoholics.

References

Anttila, I. 1960. Juopumussakot—kallis ja tehoton järjestelm. *Alkoholipolitiikka* 25(4): 156-157.

Bruun, K. 1963. Outcome of different types of treatment of alcoholics. *Quarterly Journal of Studies on Alcohol* 24(2): 280–288.

Bruun, K., and T. Markkanen. 1961. Onko alkoholismi parannettavissa? *Kokeellinen tutkimus nykyaikaisen alkoholisitipoliklinikan hoitotuloksista.* Helsinki: Väkijuomakysymyksen tutkimussäätiö: julkaisu 11.

Bruun, K. 1971. Finland: The non-medical approach. *29th International Congress on Alcoholism and Drug Dependence* (Melbourne Sessions) 545–555. Australia.

Conrad, P., and J. Schneider. 1980 *Deviance and medicalization, from badness to sickness.* London: C. V. Mosby.

Cook, C. 1988. The Minnesota model in the management of drug and alcohol dependency: miracle method or myth? *British Journal of Addiction* 83(7): 735–48.

Forsberg, S., and J. Hasan. 1970. *Huoltolaan toimitettujen miesalkoholistien fyysisen kuntoutumisen piirteitä neljän ensimmäisen viikon aikana.* Helsinki: Alkoholipoliittisen tutkimuslaitoksen tutkimusseloste 58.

Government Report. 1989. *Valtioneuvoston kertomus eduskunnalle päihdeolojen kehityksestä vuonna 1988* (Government report to parliament on the state of intoxicant misuse 1988). Helsinki.

Henrici v., A. 1900. Über die Trinkerheilanstalt "Turva" in Finnland. VII. *Congrès International contre l'Abus des boissons alcooliques, Session de Paris 1899.* Paris.

Immonen, E., et al. 1980. *A-klinikkasäätiö 1955-1980* (The A-Clinic Foundation 1955-1980). Helsinki: Kouvola.

Jellinek, E. M. 1960. *The disease concept of alcoholism.* New Haven, Connecticut: Hillhouse Press.

Kallioniemi, O. 1937. Alkoholistihuolto Suomessa (Historiallinen tutkimus). *Alkoholitutkimuksia* I. Helsinki: Suomen Akateeminen Raittiusliitto.

Kanninen, V. 1938. Onko alkoholismi sairautta? *Alkoholikysymys.* 6(3): 115–25.

Keso, L. 1988. *Inpatient treatment of employed alcoholics: a randomized clinical trial on Hazelden and traditional treatment.* Helsinki: Research Unit of Alcohol Diseases. Helsinki University Central Hospital.

Kiianmaa, K., and R. Ylikahri. 1987. Alkoholijuomien aiheuttamat terveyshaitat. Kulutuksen rakenteen ja juomatapojen vaikutus. *Alkoholipolitiikka 52:285—91.*

Klingemann, H., and J.-P. Takala. 1987. *Editors' introduction: International studies of the development of alcohol treatment systems—a research agenda for the future.* Contemporary Drug Problems 14(1): 1-13.

Komiteanmietintö. 1978. 40. *Päihdeasianneuvottelukunnan mietintö. Ehdotus päihdeongelmaisten huollon kehittämisestä.* Helsinki.

Kylmälä, J. 1988. Pääkaupunkiseudun päihdehuollon asiakkaat. *Pääkapunkiseudun julkaisusurja* B 15. Helsinki: YTV.

Lauronen, K. 1988. Toimeentulotukiasiakkaat ja heidän elämäntilanteensa. *Sosiaalihallituksen julkaisuja* 9. Helsinki: Valtion painatuskeskus.

Lehto, J. 1987. Juopon toimeentulo. *Sosiaalinen aikakauskirja* 81(2): 46-50.

———— 1988a. Pakkohoito päihdeongelmien ratkaisussa. *Sosiaalinen aikakauskirja* 82(2): 11-16.

———— 1988b. Vessa, vesiposti, keittokomero ja huone. *Sosiaalihallituksen raporttisarja* 6.

———— 1988c. Hoitoa, huolenpitoa vai hätäratkaisuja? *Sosiaaliviesti* 4:81-82.

———— 1989. Juoppouden säätely ammatillisena auttamistyöönä (The regulation of problematic drinking as a work of professional helpers). Licenciate Thesis, Institute of Social Policy, University of Helsinki.

Lundholm, U., and T. Sinnemäki. 1986. Päihdeongelmaiset terveysasemalla. *Lääkintöhallituksen julkaisuja 6.*

Mäkelä, K., and S.-L. Säilä. 1987. The distribution of alcohol-related overnight stays among different authorities in Finland, 1960-1980. *Contemporary Drug Problems* 14(1): 125-36.

Murto, L. 1988. *Alustus päihdehuollon terveydenhuoltopäivillä Hämeenlinnassa* 4.2. 1988 (unpublished).

Mustala, P. 1953. Alkoholistihuollon kehitys. *Sosiaalinen aikakauskirja* 9-10: 359-69.

Niemelä J. 1983. *Kääntymys ja kuntoutus.* Hämeenlinna, Finland: Uusi Toivo.

Nordisk alkoholstatistik 1981-1986. 1987. *Tabeller.* Stockholm: Socialstyrelsen.

Pesonen, N. 1967. *Haastattelu.* Huoltaja 11-12.

Piirainen, V. 1974. *Vaivaishoidosta sosiaaliturvaan.* Karisto, Hämeenlinna.

Poikolainen, K. 1989. Myllyhoidon ja tavanomaisen alkoholistihoidon tulokset puntarissa (review of Keso 1988). *Sosiaalilääketieteellinen aikakauslehti* 26(3): 202-03.

Rahkonen, K., and P. Sulkunen. 1987. Miten päihtyneiden säilöönotoilta voitaisiin välttyä. *Alkoholipoliittisen tutkimuslaitoksen tutkimusseloste* 177. Helsinki.

Salaspuro, A. 1972. Alkoholiin liittynyt terveyspalvelukäyttö Suomessa vuonna 1972. *Alkoholitutkimussäätiön julkaisuja* 29. Helsinki.

Simpura, J. (toim.). 1985. Suomalaisten juomatavat. *Alkoholitutkimussäätiön julkaisuja 34.* Helsinki.

Sosiaalihallitus. 1985. *Tilastotiedotus 2.* Helsinki.

Sosiaalihuoltotilasto. 1982. STV XXI:B:24. Sosiaalihuolto 1982. Sosiaalihallitus 1985.

Sperber, D. 1985. On anthropological knowledge. Cambridge, England: Cambridge University Press.

STM (Sosiaali- ja terveysministeriö). 1988a. Rattijuoppojen hoitoonohjaustyöryhmän muistio. *Työryhmämuistioita* 11. Helsinki.

———— (Sosiaali- ja terveysministeriö). 1988b. Säilöönottotarpeen vähentämistyöryhmän muistio. *Työryhmämuistioita* 3. Helsinki.

Suhonen, H. 1986. Alkoholihaittojen vähentäminen terveyskeskuksen työmuotona. *A-klinikkasäätiön julkaisuja* 2. Helsinki.

Suhonen, H., and L. Nyqvist. 1987. Alkoholin suurkuluttaja perusterveydenhuollon asiakkaana. *Lääkintöhallituksen julkaisuja* 9. Helsinki.

Suokas, A. 1988. Kynnyksen alentaminen terveystarkastuksilla—Hämeenlinnan kokeilun tuloksia. Päihteiden ongelmakäytön ehkäisy. *Sosiaalihallituksen raporttisarja* 21. Helsinki.

Taipale, I. 1982. Asunnottomuus ja alkoholi. *Alkoholitutkimussäätiön julkaisuja* 9. Helsinki.

Taivalsaari, E. 1987. Yö ensisuojassa. *Oma Markka* 10:8–9.

Takala, J.-P. n.d. *Treatment and care of alcoholics in two rural communities in Southern Finland, 1950-1980.*

———. 1985a. Om läkarens on medicines roll i alkoholistvården enligt den finska alkoholistlagen av år 1936. *Alkoholpolitik—Tidskrift för nordisk alkoholforsknig* 2(2): 69–75.

———. 1985b. Valtioneuvos Kannisen toiminta: vähän tunnettu episodi alkoholiongelmien hoidon historiassa. *Tiimi* 1(1): 42–45.

———. 1985c. Why was the Finnish Alcoholics Act substituted by a new law in 1961? Paper presented at the Alcohol Epidemiology Section of the International Council on Alcohol and Addictions, June 3rd-7th, 1985. Rome, Italy.

———. 1986. Ideas and Organizations: notes on the Finnish Alcoholics Act of 1936. *Contemporary Drug Problems* 3(3): 527–54.

Tirkkonen, J. 1961. Päihdyttävien aineiden huollosta annetusta laista lääkärin kannalta. *Alkoholikysymys* 29:157–68.

Toivola, O. 1940. Alkoholistihuolto nyt ja lähitulevaisuudessa. *Alkoholiliikkeen aikakauskirja* 75–78.

Vaillant, G.E. 1990. We should retain the disease concept of alcoholism. *The Harvard Medical School Mental Health Letter. 6(9):4–6.*

Voipio, M. 1986. The development of voluntary care of alcoholics. Paper presented at 32nd International Institute on the Prevention and Treatment of Alcoholism, June 1st-6th, 1986. Budapest, Hungary.

Westling, A. 1960. Förvandlingsstraffet för böter sasom kriminalpolitiskt problem. *Puheenvuoro Suomen kriminalistiyhdistyksen vuosikokouksessa* 22.4.1960. Nordisk kriminalistik årsbok.

———. 1969. Alkoholistien kuntoutusongelma Suomessa. *Alkoholipoliittisen tutkimuslaitoksen tutkimusseloste* 35. Helsinki.

Ylikahri, R. 1983. Terveysvaikutukset. In *Alkohoki ja yhteiskunta.* Ed. T. Peltoniemi, Teuvo, and M. Voipio, Marrti. Helsinki: Otava.

From Alcoholism to Problem Drinking: Alcohol Treatment in England and Wales, 1945-1990

Geoffrey Hunt, Jenny Mellor, and *Janet Turner*

In England and Wales since the latter part of the nineteenth century, concern about the treatment of alcohol-related problems has been evinced, not by the government, but by professional organizations and small groups of committed men and women. Unlike many other European governments, the British government has shown little interest in taking the lead in providing treatment facilities. Moreover, legislation has tended to concentrate on solving particular drinking problems, such as driving while intoxicated or football hooliganism, often as a result of public concern. The hidden costs of such alcohol-related problems as family break-up, child abuse and neglect, job absenteeism, and homelessness have tended to be regarded as separate social problems, and consequently have not been brought together in official thinking under any "alcohol problems" umbrella. According to a report by the Royal College of Physicians (1987), alcohol misuse is involved in a significant proportion of absenteeism from work, marital discord, divorce and family violence, as well as being associated with an increased level of child abuse. Maynard (1989) has estimated that the social costs of alcohol misuse to industry, including sickness absence, housework services, unemployment, and premature death, is 1.7 billion pounds sterling.

Several factors have contributed to this failure on the part of government. First, as in many other industrialized societies, the brewing and distilling industry is a powerful lobbying group, which ensures that any new legislation on alcohol conforms to its notions of acceptability. Hence, although it supports campaigns to eliminate driving while intoxicated or "pub violence," it opposes the establishment of any connection between social drinking and its hidden costs. Also, it wishes to maintain the viewpoint that only a tiny minority of drinkers, conveniently defined as alcoholics, are responsible for alcohol problems and that most social drinkers benefit from drinking (Baggott 1989). While it encourages campaigns to attack the fringe elements of drinking, it is totally opposed to any legislation that may curtail its freedom to advertise and sell its products, or result in any reduction in the total consumption of alcohol.

A second factor is that alcohol consumption has always been an integral part of British culture. The importance of drinking and drinking places can be seen in, for example, the idealization of the English village "pub" as a quintessential element of the English cultural landscape, along with the village church and the village pond. This romanticization is quite different from the way in which other countries view drinking and drinking places. Thus, in the United States of America, where cultural attitudes to drinking are more ambivalent, drinking, far from being associated with an idealized feature of the society, is generally associated in the public mind with prohibition, lawlessness, and social problems.

A third possible factor is the distinction made between social and disreputable drinking. Social drinking, consisting of dinner parties, cocktail parties, and Sunday lunch-time drinking at the "pub", is seen as clearly separate from the world of vagrant alcoholics and arrests for drunk and disorderly behavior. The type of drinking associated with this latter world has generally been attributed to the working class, or at least a section of the working class— namely, the disreputable poor—whereas social drinking has been associated with the middle class and the respectable working class (Price 1971; Storch 1977). This division in the drinking continuum can be connected to a clear division in treatment provision, for, although the government and public bodies have encouraged attempts to deal with the public inebriate, the state has never been convinced that social drinking presented a problem.

Consequently, the government's response to the treatment of alcohol problems has been fragmented and unsystematic. Its only contribution has been to provide limited resources to one area of alcohol treatment—that of the National Health Service (NHS), and specifically the Alcohol Treatment Units (ATUs) and hospital-based units. Consequently, other provisions have grown up as a result of private or voluntary concern as distinct from official enterprise. It is not surprising that the first comprehensive survey of alcohol treatment services was not government-inspired but was carried out by a voluntary organization, Alcohol Concern, founded in 1984 as a single organization to replace several earlier established voluntary organizations.

Today's Alcohol Treatment Services

Today, services for the treatment of alcohol problems encompass statutory facilities such as the Alcohol Treatment Units, voluntary services such as shop-fronts, advice centers, and residential facilities, self-help groups such as Alcoholics Anonymous (AA) and Drinkwatchers, and private clinics. Since little has been published about their treatment philosophies or methods, types of staff, or methods of determining success or failure, we have drawn on several sources for this information. First, there are the government circulars and memoranda issued during the period, which reflect official thinking. Second, there is the literature on alcohol research, which, with only a few notable exceptions (Orford and Edwards 1977; Ettorre 1985a), has not been concerned with surveys of services or facilities. The literature on treatment has concentrated principally on either examining the characteristics of clients or evaluating the outcome of treatment. The third source is a recent survey by Alcohol Concern, which produced a directory of all the available services (Alcohol Concern 1986), and the fourth has been our own research on alcohol treatment services (Hunt, Mellor, and Turner 1989a).

The available services can be divided into the following categories:

- The National Health Service and community and voluntary services
- Prison and probation services
- Private institutions and the military
- Self-help groups.

The National Health Service and Community and Voluntary Services

The medical profession and voluntary organizations have worked together to provide services for people with alcohol problems since the latter part of the nineteenth century and have provided the bulk of the alcohol-specific services. In 1876 the British Medical Association and the Social Science Association appointed a joint committee, which subsequently set up the *Society for Promoting Legislation for the Control and Cure of Habitual Drunkards*. Although most of those who both attended the regular meetings and contributed to the society's journal were of the medical profession (Gutzke 1984), the society also attracted a wide range of other professionals, including social researchers such as Rowntree and Sherwell, clergymen, barristers, and health inspectors, as well as former patients.

However, despite the involvement of the medical profession, it was not until the early 1960s that the health service opened its first treatment centers. As Dr. Pullar-Stretcher, then secretary of the Society for the Study of Addiction, noted in 1950:

There was in the British Isles not a single hospital which had a whole ward or unit set aside exclusively devoted to treating alcoholics [Glatt 1982, 433].

Besides the lack of treatment services, the government at the time generally believed that England and Wales was not affected by alcohol problems. This view was epitomized in 1951 in the now famous statement from the Ministry of Health informing a National Health Service consultant who had applied to attend a World Health Organization (WHO) meeting on alcoholism that "there was no alcoholism in England and Wales and that the subject hardly merited the time of a consultant psychiatrist in the National Health Service" (*British Journal of Addiction* 1950, 19).

The establishment of the first National Health Service specialist treatment unit—the Alcohol Treatment Unit at Warlingham Park Hospital—in 1952 was influenced by a number of factors (Glatt 1986). The first was the increasing international recognition, especially through the work of WHO, that alcoholism was an expanding medico-social problem requiring an official response. Jellinek, at that time a consultant in alcoholism for WHO, estimated that Great Britain had 86,000 "chronic alcoholics" and 350,000 alcoholics. Glatt (1958, 132) pointed to "an urgent need for the provision of specific clinic and hospital facilities for alcoholics." Jellinek (1960, 193) commented that an alcoholic who applied to a doctor in England "for the treatment of any of the consequences of his alcoholism will receive such treatment, but if his request is related to the treatment of his habit, the matter will not be regarded as a medical one".

The formation in 1960 of a joint committee of the British Medical Association and the Magistrates' Association to review the whole issue of alcoholism may be seen as a second factor influencing and encouraging the government to take action. It issued a memorandum recommending the setting up of specialist treatment units within the National Health Service.

Another important committee at the time was the Steering Group on Alcoholism set up by the Joseph Rowntree Social Service Trust.

Equally influential perhaps in forming government policy in this area were the new ideas about hospital care and especially the care of the mentally ill. The 1959 Mental Health Act resulted in progressively fewer admissions of psychiatric patients to large mental hospitals, and their treatment instead in either outpatient facilities or small specialist units. The idea of the small specialist unit or small hospital was further emphasized by the 1961 Working Party on Special Hospitals, which recommended treatment centers for "special patients."

In 1962 the Ministry of Health issued its first official statement on the treatment of alcoholism in a memorandum entitled *The Hospital Treatment of Alcoholism*. In it the ministry officially admitted that although hospital admissions for alcoholism had increased from 775 in 1953 to 2,044 in 1959, "few psychiatric hospitals had provision specifically for alcoholism," and that, of those admitted, over half "were scattered throughout 100 hospitals, the number admitted to each hospital varying from 1 to 19" (Orford and Edwards 1977, 7). To remedy this situation, the memorandum, following advice from the British Medical Association and the Magistrates' Association, proposed the development of specialist inpatient units with a treatment program based on group therapy. However, the National Health Service did not immediately implement the proposal. By 1968, only 13 ATUs had been created. Nevertheless, the memorandum, as Ettorre (1985a, 29) has noted, did "create the beginnings of an official policy on alcoholism treatment."

The 1962 memorandum of the Ministry of Health was followed in 1968 by a second—*Treatment of Alcoholism*. It was notable in that, besides reaffirming the need for ATUs, it introduced in an official health-department communication the notion of community care, a concept that was to play an important part not only in the official policy on alcohol treatment but also in the literature on alcohol:

> Treatment will frequently involve an initial admission to hospital as an in-patient and more than one admission to hospital may be necessary because of relapse. In-patient treatment can be best undertaken in small specialised hospital units. . . In the view of some experts, energetic out-patient care alone will sometimes give as good results. . . Out-patient treatment has the general advantage of enabling the patient to retain his job and thus remain in the community. [Orford and Edwards 1977, 8]

The idea of community care and the possibility of linking hospital and voluntary services were seen to provide a more comprehensive system of services to deal with the increasing concern about alcohol problems. The number of deaths from chronic liver disease and cirrhosis of the liver rose from 1,392 in 1970 to 1,835 in 1975. The corresponding figures for admissions to hospital for alcohol dependence were 5.17, and 8.40 per 100,000 people; and for convictions for driving while intoxicated 26,273 and 58,145 (Royal College of Psychiatrists 1986). By 1978, Health Department officials felt that the then acknowledged increasing alcohol problem demanded a community response that would make use of not only medical facilities but also voluntary and community services. As a White Paper (a government information report) noted:

> The hospital treatment services for alcoholics are at present being developed and further guidance to general practitioners on the recognition and treatment of alcoholics is in preparation. Development of treatment facilities alone will however be ineffective without a complementary development of community services. The community health and personal social services needed range across a broad front from those concerned with prevention through social work support for the alcoholic and perhaps his family to rehabilitation and if necessary resident care. [Department of Health and Social Security (DHSS) 1978, 18]

This document advocated that the health and medical services funded and organized by the central government through the National Health Service be joined with alcohol services funded wholly or partly by local government authorities. The local authorities had been called upon to support and encourage the development of voluntary agencies by offering financial aid—which would be backed up by "pump-priming" financial assistance from the DHSS. The official incorporation of the voluntary sector was further emphasized in 1974 when a DHSS initiative established the Federation of Alcoholic Residential Establishments (FARE) "to represent the interests of the growing residential care sector at a national level" (Baggott 1986, 476).

The increasing cooperation between the National Health Service and the voluntary and local authority sectors had been emphasized in a 1975 DHSS White Paper, *Better Services for the Mentally Ill*. This document stressed the crucial role of the specialist units in the community:

> These specialist units were...developed...so that they might serve as a local focus of expertise, training and research for all the services concerned with alcoholics in their region...The emphasis in provision should perhaps turn towards a more locally based treatment service with much of the work done in the community or in an out-patient or day hospital setting, supplemented by in-patient facilities whether these are specialised or part of the local psychiatric service. [Orford and Edwards 1977, 10]

Therefore, it appeared that the treatment of alcohol problems was to be a community-based endeavor encompassing all the many aspects of both statutory and voluntary sectors.

Community Alcohol Teams were another key feature of this change of strategy. These teams, developed out of a research project of the Maudsley Hospital in London in the early 1970s (Shaw et al. 1978), were seen as support teams based in the community for primary workers, such as social workers, counselors, and general medical practitioners, providing them with education and training in the recognition and treatment of alcoholism. In this scheme the ATU no longer had a central role but rather that of a center that "activates, offers advice, shows others how to help the alcoholic" and which is part of a service "with much of the work done in the community" (Orford and Edwards 1977, 11).

Various authors have suggested reasons for this shift in policy. For example, Orford and Edwards (1977), in addition to noting the attraction of the relatively low cost of community services, emphasize the increasing realization by health-policy planners that the system of alcoholism treatment centered on the specialist units was inadequate for dealing with the growing problem. Ettorre (1985a), however, stresses the importance of policy changes and health-care ideas within the health service as a whole. She argues that the incorporation of the ATUs into a more community-based strategy was merely part of a general policy to ensure that hospital services became more attuned to the needs of the community. Moreover, both she and Baggott (1986) argue that the move to community-based services reflected the realization by the health-service planners of the increasing scale and nature of the problem. Finally, writers such as Cohen (1985) and Scull (1977) have suggested that the shift from specialized treatment units to community-based services was part of a general policy of "destructuring" within the social control apparatus of the state, which involved a moving away "from the more institutionalized forms of care towards that of the community" (Bunton 1990, 606).

The final important government document in establishing health and voluntary services in the planning of alcoholism treatment services was the Kessel report, *The Pattern and Range of Services for Problem Drinkers,* issued in 1978 (Department of Health and Social Security 1978). This consultive document was notable for three reasons. First, it emphasized the notion of prevention, which was to include health education of the public, wiser presentation of alcohol in the media, "the use of fiscal powers in relation to the price of alcoholic drinks in real terms," stricter observance of the legal restrictions on availability, and the encouragement of people both to recognize their own drinking problems and to seek help. Second, it strongly advocated early intervention as a way of reducing alcohol problems, especially through the use of nonalcohol-specialist workers, such as social workers, teachers, doctors, health-education workers, and counselors. Third, it reendorsed the changing role of ATUs or specialist units from being central to the provision of services to playing a specialist backup role in the community.

Today alcohol treatment services operated by the National Health Service and the community include the following:

Alcohol treatment units. There are currently 29 ATUs. Although their central importance has declined, they remain the largest sector of the statutory alcohol treatment services. Partly as a result of their change in status, some have altered their approach. For example, instead of concentrating on inpatient care, they have become increasingly community-oriented. Indeed, according to Ettorre, they have many links with the community, including running outpatient units outside the ATU or the hospital, working with shelters for the homeless, and having regular contact with the Local Councils on Alcoholism. Moreover, they are employing more community psychiatric nurses, which suggests that increasingly the units see the needs of their patients as requiring a response "much wider than the traditional response of a psychiatric hospital setting" (Ettorre 1988, 17).

Hospital-based services. There are 12 specialist hospital-based units that are not designated ATU. Because they are part of the National Health Service, all are run by a mixture of medical and nursing staff. They offer a wide range of treatment including counseling, group work, detoxification, and social-skills training.

Community alcohol teams. Eleven community alcohol teams have been established. The central rationale of their establisment was that the "disease" notion of alcoholism had "drawn attention away from the extensiveness and variety of drinking problems" (Shaw et al. 1978, 241). Therefore the notion of a "problem drinker" as distinct from that of an "alcoholic" resulted in a much greater proportion of the population, many unaware that they had a drinking problem, being categorized as problem drinkers. To attempt to deal with this enlarged segment of the population, the community team was seen in a similar way to that outlined by the Kessel report as a support team for primary workers, providing them with education and training.

Residential facilities. This type of alcohol treatment service is probably the oldest of all alcoholism services in England and Wales. As Archard has shown (1979, 151), residential facilities developed out of the attempt of the Salvation Army in the latter part of the nineteenth century to rescue individuals from the clutches of drink:

> They established a network of common lodging houses designed to offer the "homeless poor, destitute wayfarers and incorrigible rogues" a roof to sleep under, basic material sustenance and above all an opportunity to renounce intemperance and replace it with a commitment to moral and spiritual rejuvenation.

Today there is a mixture of different types of residential facility. At one end of the spectrum there are those "whose foundations are anchored in Victorian legislation" (Archard 1979, 151), and at the other end those that are based on contemporary medical and social attitudes toward alcoholism. There are 85 in all, and according to the Alcohol Concern Directory they account for 34% of the total services.

Day centers. There are 22 day-centers, sometimes called "drop-in" centers. Most are in inner urban areas and can be divided roughly into two types: those that offer a relatively structured program, including group sessions, occupational therapy, relaxation courses, and education sessions, and the more informal, where clients are free to drop in whenever they need to and obtain help on an individual basis from counselors or social workers. Some give more general assistance also, in the form of food and medical care.

The Alcohol Advisory Services and advice and counseling services. Of the many different types of agency included under this heading, the Alcohol Advisory Services, until 1982 called Councils on Alcoholism, of which there are 49, form the largest. These began in 1962 with the setting up of the National Council on Alcoholism. According to its chairman, they were seen at first "merely as information and referral agencies" (National Council on Alcoholism

1982). Today their tasks include individual and group counseling, training in counseling, coordination of local services, and initiation of new prevention strategies.

Prisons and Probation Services

The use of prisons and criminal legislation to punish unacceptable drinking behavior began in the tenth century when, according to Shadwell, King Edgar decreed that eight pegs be inserted at regular intervals in the half-gallon drinking pot and that "whoever should drink beyond these marks at one draught should be obnoxious to a severe punishment" (Popham 1978, 256). Until late in the nineteenth century, prisons were used exclusively for incarceration and there was no attempt to treat prisoners sentenced for drinking offenses. In 1898, as a result of pressure from the Society for Promoting Legislation for the Control and Cure of Habitual Drunkards, two prisons— Warwick and Aylesbury—designated as state inebriate reformatories under the Inebriates Act of 1898 began to provide some basic rehabilitation in the form of "prayers and piecework." This experiment lasted only until the beginning of World War I. These prisons soon became overcrowded with the more "difficult" cases transferred from the Certified Inebriate Reformatories— institutions also established under the Inebriates Act and funded jointly by central government, local authorities, or charitable donations. The state reformatories found themselves having to deal not only with the more "refractory and violent" cases but also, like ordinary prisons, with "habitual" offenders. As J. J. Pitcairn, an assistant prison surgeon at Holloway prison in London, noted in 1887, in discussing female inebriates: "There are hundreds, nay thousands of Jane Cakebreads (a well-known inebriate) in existence, they go in and out of prison with monotonous regularity, turning to drink on release until they are picked up again by the police" (Hunt, Mellor, and Turner 1989b, 247).

This concern with the public drunkard was further revived or "rediscovered" (Archard 1979) nearly 100 years later, in the late 1960s, when the Criminal Justice Act 1967 was being introduced, which would both abolish the sentence of imprisonment for being "drunk and disorderly" and legislate for alcoholics to be referred to community-based hostels. As Lord Stonham noted at the time:

> The work of drying out and cleaning up these men, well knowing that they will soon be back in prison, is a stupid waste of our badly strained prison resources. . . Prison is not the place. [Report of the Detoxification Project 1985, 11]

As a result of disquiet over the inappropriateness of prison and a belief that some alternative form of treatment should be found in the community for habitual drunkenness offenders, a special committee—the Weiler Committee—

was set up in 1967. In its report, in 1972, it recommended that special arrangements be made for habitual offenders, because "repeated arrests for public drunkenness is often a symptom of the disease of alcoholism" (Report 1985, 13) and therefore the "drunks" who pass through the courts are "sick" rather than "bad." This recommendation for alternative treatment was incorporated into Section 34 of the Criminal Justice Act of 1972, which empowered the police to take people who were drunk and incapable or drunk and disorderly to a "place approved by the Secretary of State as a 'medical treatment centre for alcoholics'" (Report 1985, 13).

According to Archard (1979), there are four major reasons for this "rediscovery" of the homeless alcoholic or public drunkard: First, the creation of a new voluntary social-work movement that drew attention to this particular group; second, the development of a medical model, which defined the homeless alcoholic as someone who was sick; third, the closing of mental hospitals, an effect of the 1959 Mental Health Act, which led to the discharge of many homeless people; and fourth, a decrease in the availability of "skid-row" accommodation as a result of government closures.

The acknowledgment that habitual offenders were sick rather than criminal meant that the Home Office (the government department responsible for law and order), and specifically the prison service, was discarding its responsibility for these offenders and passing it on to the Department of Health. This shift in responsibility was then confirmed by the Home Secretary after consultation with the department.

> This brought official recognition that habitual drunkenness offenders should be taken out of the penal system and treated instead by health and social services. [Report 1985, 13]

However, although responsibility had now been handed over to the Department of Health and Social Security, this did not result in the provision of sufficient alternative services, for only five pilot detoxification centers were funded. Indeed, as Archard (1979, 16) has noted:

> The impetus to decriminalise the alcoholic on skid row has not, in practice, succeeded in removing him from the institutional reality of police cells, courts and prison. Legislation has changed the status of the public intoxicant in theory only, since detoxification facilities have not yet been implemented and the courts make little use of the limited number of rehabilitation hostels. The attempt to shift responsibility for the skid row alcoholic from an overtly punitive to an overtly therapeutic response remains therefore an ideological, as opposed to a practical issue.

Today the prison and probation services are encouraged to be aware of the problems of alcoholism. They are primarily responsible for prisoners on parole, many of whom live in hostels and halfway houses, which are designed to return them to a conventional working life. They also provide limited funding for a small number of these hostels and halfway houses.

Private Institutions and the Military

Dalrymple House, named after Donald Dalrymple, a leading campaigner for changes in dealing with inebriety, was one of the first private clinics to be set up, in 1879 (See Mellor et al. 1986; Berridge 1989). It was sponsored by the Society for Promoting Legislation for the Control and Cure of Habitual Drunkards and by the British Medical Association. The basic idea behind many of the private retreats was to provide a new environment far away from the temptations of the inebriate's previous life. This idea of creating a new environment was not new, for, as Baumohl and Room (1986) have pointed out, the inebriate institution both in the United States and in England was influenced by the model of "moral treatment," in which an important element was the creation of a curative environment. Many of these early private clinics were run by religious as well as by medical professionals. For example, Hammond Lodge was run by the Church of England Temperance Society. Most closed down after World War I and by the 1950s only a few remained, such as Caldecote Hall and Spelthorne St. Mary. These centers appeared still to operate a regimen similar to that outlined by the early reformers, which, as one historian has noted, was "little more than a religiously inclined health farm" (Berridge 1989, 29). For example, Rebecca (1970) noted that Spelthorne St. Mary had added new techniques, such as group psychotherapy, to its treatment repertoire, but that it still maintained its reliance on spiritual rejuvenation and preferred the term "therapeutic family" to "therapeutic community".

The Alcohol Concern Directory lists ten private clinics, mostly residential, with programs that last from four to eight weeks. The cost, which can be as much as 1,800 pounds a week, is met by private medical insurance or by individual patients. One or two clinics offer a few assisted places.

The three branches of the armed services—the army, the navy and the air force—have their own alcohol treatment centers. The army operates its alcohol center, run by a consultant psychiatrist and a team of nurses, in one of its hospitals in the south of England.

Self-Help Groups

Self-help groups have come to play a major part in the way in which people deal with personal problems (Peele 1989; *Newsweek* 1990). In the last ten years their number has doubled. The problems they cover range from overeating, to the need of relatives of disaster victims for support, to compulsive shopping. The reasons for this growth have included a possible increasing emphasis on the role of individuals in taking responsibility for their own lives, a disillusion with existing helping services, and the decline of traditional support systems (Robinson 1983).

Alcoholics Anonymous is still the largest of these groups. It reached England in 1946 or 1947 and held its first official meeting in London in March 1947. In 1959 its office in London issued a list of over 100 groups, and by 1983 the number had grown to 1,600 (Robinson 1979; 1983). AA is based on two seemingly contradictory notions—first, that alcoholism is an incurable disease, and second, that its symptoms do not respond to medical treatment but rather to religious belief and moral education through total abstinence.

Other self-help groups in alcohol treatment include the Lawyers Support group, the Doctors and Dentists group, and Drinkwatchers. This last group, of which there are twenty branches, is based on a philosophy similar to that of the highly successful Weightwatchers. Unlike AA, Drinkwatchers appeals to "heavy drinkers" or "mild problem drinkers" who, although concerned about the amount they drink, do not necessarily wish to give up alcohol altogether (Ruzek 1989). Each member has a screening interview, is given a Drinkwatchers Handbook and diary forms, and is encouraged to attend regular weekly group meetings for at least three months. The groups learn techniques based on the social learning model of drinking behavior (Orford 1985) to help them control their drinking, especially at social gatherings.

Who Works in the Services?

As Gutzke (1984) noted, in discussing the campaign for the provision of alcohol treatment in the latter part of the nineteenth century, the campaigners included doctors, social researchers, clergymen, barristers, health inspectors, and ex-patients. This wide range of professional background is still evident today. Although it might be assumed that most workers in the field would be either medical graduates or professional social workers and psychologists, it is clear that the qualifications required to work in an alcohol advice and treatment center are strikingly varied. For example, although many of the directors and assistant directors of the agencies possessed academic qualifications up to degree level, their past experience included such occupations as the law (there were three barristers), the navy, community work, public administration, accountancy, and education (Hunt, Mellor, and Turner 1989a).

The facilities lacking this wide range of experience have been the hospital-based units and private clinics run by doctors, either nonpsychiatrists or psychiatrists. Ettorre (1985b) noted that the directors of the ATUs were mainly consultant psychiatrists, and that 66% of the other staff were medically trained. The Councils on Alcoholism (today's Alcohol Advisory Services) have been the second exception: they have not had medical staff but most of their directors and assistant directors have had qualifications and experience in social work.

Despite the wide range of professional expertise in alcohol treatment facilities, which suggests that working with problem drinkers is a possible option for people with many types of background, neither specific training nor experience in treating alcohol problems is considered essential in the recruitment of staff. For example, in the mid 1970s the Department of Health and Social Services made funds available for the training of volunteer counselors in alcohol education and in general principles of counseling (Marshall et al. 1985; Stockwell and Clements 1987).

It is of interest that former clients are not employed as counselors. Unlike agencies in other countries, and especially the United States, where, as Miller has noted, the recovering alcoholic plays a key role in alcohol treatment, most agencies in England and Wales do not employ ex-clients except as volunteers. As one agency director remarked, "I am very wary about employing recovering alcoholics as counselors because they tend to assume that each alcohol problem is the same," whereas she regarded each case as different (personal communication). This attitude may well be related to the different ways in which the two countries regard AA and the disease notion of alcoholism (Miller 1986; Peele 1989). The notion of alcoholism as a disease is not universally accepted in alcohol treatment in England.

What Kinds of Services are Offered?

There is a wide range of services but no one unified, dominant, or overall treatment philosophy. Moreover, even a particular type of agency may use a wide range of treatment methods. For example, as Ettorre (1984, 253) noted in her work on the ATUs:

Diversity was noted in treatment objectives (i.e., whether or not units required total abstinence or used controlled drinking regime); treatment procedures (i.e., whether they use counseling by staff more than occupational therapy or vice versa); the use of drug therapy (i.e., whether or not units supported a drug-oriented regime or a drug free programme) and treatment philosophies (i.e., whether they are more influenced by eclectic ways of thinking than group work theory).

Owing to this diversity in range and types of services, the following sections summarize major trends in treatment rather than attempting to detail all the different types of service offered. The material is based largely on a survey carried out in 1987–88 (Hunt, Mellor, and Turner 1989a).

Individual and Group Counseling Techniques

There appears to be a move away from group therapy toward individual counseling. Increasingly, programs are tailored to the needs of individuals and to their specific circumstances. For example, in many of the Alcohol Advisory Services the counselor at the initial interview takes a very detailed account of the client's family, education, criminal record, and medical and psychiatric history, and on this basis attempts to make sense of the client's life, establish a good therapist/client relationship, and design a customized treatment program.

Philosophy and Goals of Treatment

Humanistic or behavioristic methods of counseling appear to be replacing psychoanalytic approaches. Both Rogerian counseling and transactional analysis were mentioned and emphasis was put on treating, or rather "helping," the whole person. The focus seemed to have shifted from the total rehabilitation of the psyche through understanding and coming to terms with the past, to the less ambitious but more manageable goal of helping the client to deal competently with immediate practical problems encountered in daily life. The general assumption behind this philosophy is that life has damaged the client and drinking is the result rather than the cause of this damage.

As a result, most of the agencies regarded controlled or decreased drinking a legitimate goal of treatment, a finding confirmed by Robertson and Heather (1982, 103), who discovered that 93% of the alcohol advice programs they surveyed regarded controlled drinking an appropriate goal of treatment:

The replies show that the majority of NHS Alcoholism Treatment Units offer controlled drinking treatment, as do a substantial proportion of Councils on Alcoholism.

The acceptance of controlled drinking methods was also borne out by Ettorre (1984), but she noted that this method was most often used as a treatment goal for outpatients, perhaps because it is more difficult to manage in a residential setting.

The private clinics and the military centers were a possible exception; they based their work on a disease model of alcoholism and advocated total abstinence. There are two possible reasons for this. First, private agencies need to be able to be clear as to exactly what they are offering clients—a solution to their drinking problem—as opposed to a rather vague notion of an improvement in their lives. Second, in the case of the military centers, the director and staff have much more effective control over the life aims and goals of clients, especially if they wish to remain in the armed services. Unlike other alcohol treatment centers, only a small percentage of the clients, 2% of army clients, attend the units as voluntary patients. Although the army may not force its personnel to have medical treatment, it is allowed to order them to attend educational classes, which are the basis of the program. Moreover, at the unit run by the navy, Antabuse was extensively used. According to the director their clients were pressed to take Antabuse because "it trivializes the whole issue of drinking'' (personal communication). He felt that abstinence was the safest path and argued that ''controlled drinking is a theoretical goal but essentially it is dismissed because it is our aim not to make people who can't stay sober total failures.''

Who Pays for the Services?

As previously noted, the government has shown little interest in setting up and funding a comprehensive continuum of care for people with alcohol problems. At the turn of the century, when the alcohol issue was high on the political agenda, the government sought to shift financial responsibility for the reformatories on to the shoulders of local government and voluntary agencies (Mellor et al. 1986). As a result of the government's unwillingness to support services, funding is a critically important issue for many of the treatment agencies.

Treatment is funded either by the statutory services, such as the health authorities, or from other sources. ATUs and hospital-based units are funded completely by the National Health Service. According to Maynard (1989) the National Health Service is estimated to expend 120.75 million pounds on the treatment of alcoholism. The Naval Hospital, and the Army and Royal Air Force facilities, are funded by the Ministry of Defence. Local advisory and counseling services and the Alcohol Advisory Services are normally funded either from joint local and health authority budgets or directly from the health or social services department. Rehabilitation homes and hostels, funded partly by local authorities, fund-raising activities, or in some cases the National Health Service, rely heavily on social security payments claimed by their residents. However, problems can arise through too great a dependence on rent paid by income support receipts—for example, a resident who decides to return to work may well lose entitlement to benefit, and the hostel will then have to deduct the rent from his wages.

In the current economic climate, and as a result of cutbacks in local government spending, many of the voluntary agencies are underfunded and increasingly employ professional fund-raisers. The struggle for funding curtails their ability to plan for the long term and restricts the range of services they can offer. Many agencies attempt to anticipate the next problem area or high-risk group to attract future funding.

Neither the ATUs nor the military agencies seemed to be affected by financial constraints, nor were private clinics affected by local-government cutbacks. However, unlike the ATUs, they had to ensure that they attracted enough patients to keep the clinics profitable. It was surprising to discover that some private clinics, in addition to their income from private patients, were partly funded from other sources, including fund-raising, the National Health Service, the Home Office, and even the resident's charge against income support.

Conclusion

The last forty years have witnessed a radical change and substantial increase in treatment facilities for problem drinkers. Whereas at first there were only a few private retreats, the remnants of a previous era, today there are about two hundred and fifty facilities. Nevertheless, there is still no unified treatment system, largely because of the government's unwillingness to develop a comprehensive system of care for people suffering from alcohol problems or to fund research into treatment and prevention.

Recent government attitudes toward alcohol are demonstrated in a booklet on the reform of the National Health Service sent to every household in Britain. The section on healthier living contains two paragraphs on alcohol. They point out:

Drinking can be enjoyable and safe as long as you don't overdo it. But too much alcohol can be bad for your heart and your liver and can cause problems at work, with family and friends. You can protect yourself by keeping count of what you drink. An easy way to do this is keep track of the units of alcohol you drink in a week.[Department of Health 1990]

These comments are followed by medical advice about the desirable quantities of intake for men and women and by pictures showing the units of alcohol contained in different measures of alcoholic drinks. The emphasis here is on the normality of moderate drinking and the responsibility of individuals for regulating their own consumption. In contrast, almost twice the amount of space is given to advice about smoking and the focus is on "kicking the habit."

Therefore, unlike such countries as the United States and Sweden, where federal or national agencies have encouraged the development of, and research into, treatment, government offers little incentive for research to practitioners or researchers in England and Wales. Moreover, many of the treatment agencies, and specifically the voluntary agencies, have funding difficulties brought about by the general economic crisis in welfare funding and by cutbacks in local-authority spending.

Other factors also are important to understanding why the system is experiencing difficulties at a time when treatment systems in other countries are expanding (see, for example, the chapters on Sweden and Switzerland in this book). First, private medicine has played a relatively minor role, compared with that of one hundred years ago. Consequently, at a time when it could take advantage of cuts in public funding, it appears unable to do so. This is in stark contrast with the situation in the United States, where according to Weisner and Morgan (in their chapter in this volume) the number of private for-profit alcohol treatment units increased by 342% between 1979 and 1987.

One obvious reason for this failure by private medicine to fill the gap is the dominant role of the National Health Service in medical care and the relative infancy of private health care and insurance in Britain. However, this in itself is an insufficient reason. To understand the failure of private medicine to capture and exploit this potentially lucrative market, we must turn to a second factor—the lack of public concern about alcohol problems. Except in relation to specific social problems, such as football hooliganism and drinking and driving, there has been little public outcry about the costs of alcohol abuse. A significant indicator of public apathy has been the relative failure of Alcoholics Anonymous either to capture the public consciousness or to dominate the treatment field, as it has done in the United States. Moreover, unlike the American experience, the self-help group movement has not incorporated to any significant extent the basic component of the AA philosophy—namely the twelve-step method.

A third factor, significant in the United States but absent in England, has been the involvement of the criminal justice system in alcohol treatment and intervention. According to NDATUS figures (1989), in 1987 the United States had 2,237 Driving Under the Influence treatment services where offenders in this category attended classes. Although in the United States the involvement of the criminal justice system has caused concern to many treatment practitioners, it has had a major impact on the treatment scene and has meant that an increasing percentage of the population has come into contact with ideas about alcohol abuse and its effects. In England and Wales, apart from a few examples of alcohol education classes for criminal offenders with alcohol problems (Baldwin and Heather 1987; Gamba et al. 1989), the criminal justice system has done little to broaden the definition of alcohol-related problem behavior or to redirect offenders into alcohol treatment programs. One suspects that the sentiments expressed in an editorial in the *Times* in 1878, which "insisted that we have never yet sanctioned the principle in this country that mere vice should entail the loss of public liberty" (MacLeod 1967, 225), might still operate today if there was any genuine attempt to expand the criminal justice system into this arena.

A fourth factor is that, despite the growing recognition by such organizations as the Confederation of British Industry of the links between alcohol abuse and job absenteeism and lost productivity, British companies have been slow to introduce employee assistance programs. This is in contrast to the United States, where most leading companies have not only introduced such programs but also institutionalized compulsory drug testing to monitor the "addictive" habits of their workers. However, it must be recognized that United States patterns of behavior are not always followed in the United Kingdom. For example, the expected "crack" epidemic in London has not occurred and the forces mobilized to deal with it have had to be disbanded.

If all these factors are combined, it is possible to begin to see that the government's lack of interest in developing a coordinated continuum of care for problem drinkers is in part a reflection of the public's lack of concern about alcohol abuse. If this analysis is correct, it would appear that, if adequate and continuous funding is to be provided, the general public as well as the government has to become convinced of the costs to society of alcohol abuse. However, it may not be easy to convince the general public, for, in general, the problem tends to be regarded as inherent in the drinker rather than in the substance. For example, an alcohol ban in Italy during the 1990 World Cup competition was acceptable because "fans" or "supporters" were already regarded as potentially disreputable, and, admittedly, alcohol makes bad behavior worse. However, the average British citizen can easily distance himself or herself from the kind of person to whom such restrictions must be applied. Equally, the homeless alcoholic is a social failure first and only secondly a drinker. These kinds of problems are characteristics of persons not "like us," and, as such, are quite different from the everyday drinking "we" enjoy as part of the fabric of social life. A great deal more information about the social and medical costs of problem drinking as it applies to all sectors of the population will have to be forced onto the public's attention if attitudes are to change.

References

Alcohol Concern. 1986. *Alcohol services: directory for England and Wales.* London.

Archard, P. 1979. *Vagrancy, alcoholism and social control.* London: McMillan.

Baggott, R. 1986. Alcohol, politics and social policy. *Journal of Social Policy* 15(4).

———. 1989. The politics of the market. In *Controlling legal addictions.* Ed. D. Robinson et al., 48–166. London: McMillan.

Baldwin, S., and N. Heather. 1987. Alcohol education courses for offenders: survey of British agencies. *Alcohol and Alcoholism* 22(1): 79–82.

Baumohl, J., and R. Room. 1986. Inebriety, doctors and the state: alcoholism treatment installations before 1940. In *Recent developments in alcoholism.* Ed. M. Galanter, vol. 5. New York: Plenum Press.

Berridge, V. 1989. History and addiction control: the case of alcohol. In *Controlling legal addictions.* Ed. D. Robinson et al., 24–42. London: McMillan.

Bunton, R. 1990. Changes in the control of alcohol misuse. *British Journal of Addiction* 85:605–15.

British Journal of Addiction. 1950. 19.

Cohen, S. 1985. *Visions of social control.* Cambridge: Polity.

Department of Health. 1990. *The national health service reforms and you.* London: Central Office of Information.

Department of Health and Social Security. 1978. The pattern and range of services for problem drinkers. *A report by the Advisory Committee on Alcoholism.* London: HMSO.

Ettorre, E. M. 1984. A Study of alcoholism units—I. Treatment activities and the institutional response. *Alcohol and Alcoholism* 19(3).

_____. 1985a. *Alcoholism treatment and social policy.* London: Addiction Research Unit.

_____. 1985b. A Study of alcoholism treatment units: some findings on units and staff. *Alcohol and Alcoholism* 20(4): 371–78.

_____. 1988. A follow-up study of alcoholism treatment units: exploring consolidation and change. *British Journal of Addiction* 83(1): 57–65.

Gamba, B. et al. 1989. Alcohol education courses for offenders: an update on U.K. services. *Alcohol and Alcoholism* 24(5): 473–78.

Glatt, M. M. 1958. The English drink problem: its rise and decline through the ages. *British Journal of Addiction* 55.

_____. 1982. *Alcoholism.* London.

_____. 1986. A study of alcoholism treatment units. *Alcohol and Alcoholism* 21(2): 225–26.

Gutzke, D. 1984. The cry of the children: the Edwardian medical campaign against maternal drinking. *British Journal of Addiction* 79:71–84.

Hunt, G., J. Mellor, and J. Turner. 1989a. Inebriates, alcoholics and problem drinkers: services in England and Wales 1879–1987. *Report.* London: Polytechnic of North London.

Hunt, G., J. Mellor, and J. Turner. 1989b. Wretched, hatless and miserably clad: women and the inebriate reformatories from 1900–1913. *British Journal of Sociology* 40(2): 244–70.

Jellinek, E. M. 1960. *The disease concept of alcoholism.* Boston: Hillhouse Press.

MacLeod, R. 1967. The edge of hope: Social policy and chronic alcoholism 1870–1900. *Journal of the History of Medecine* 215–45.

Marshall, S., et al. 1985. *Training volunteers to counsel problem drinkers and their families.* Addiction Research Centre, Universities of Hull and York, Occasional Paper.

Maynard, A. 1989. The costs of addiction and the costs of control. In *Controlling legal addictions.* Ed. D. Robinson, 84–100. London: MacMillan.

Mellor, J., et al. 1986. Prayers and piecework: inebriate reformatories in England at the end of the 19th century. *Drogalkohol* 10(3): 192–206.

Miller, W. 1986. Haunted by the Zeitgeist: reflections on contrasting treatment goals and concepts of alcoholism in Europe and the United States. In *Alcohol and culture: comparative perspectives from Europe and America.* Annals of the New York Academy of Sciences. Ed. T. Babor, 472:110–29. New York: New York Academy of Sciences.

National Council on Alcoholism Annual Report. 1982. London: National Council on Alcoholism.

Newsweek. 1990. Unite and Conquer. February 5th.

Orford, J., and G. Edwards. 1977. *Alcoholism: a comparison of treatment and advice, with a study of the influence of marriage.* London: Oxford University Press.

Orford, J. 1985. *Excessive appetites—a psychological view of addictions.* London: Wiley.

Peele, S. 1989. *Diseasing of America.* Lexington: Lexington Books.

Popham, R. E. 1978. The social history of the tavern. In *Research advances in alcohol and drug problems.* Ed. Y. Israel et al., vol. 4. New York: Plenum Press.

Price, R. N. 1971. *The working men's club movement and Victorian social ideology.* Victorian Studies XVI.

Rebecca, Sister M. 1970. Nine decades of experience in the treatment of alcoholism and drug dependence. In *Modern trends in drug dependence and alcoholism.* Ed. R. V. Phillipson, 206–22. London: Butterworths.

Report of the Detoxification Evaluation Project. 1985. *Problem drinking.* London: Bedford Square Press.

Robertson, I., and N. Heather. 1982. A survey of controlled drinking treatment in Britain. *British Journal of Alcohol and Alcoholism* 17(3): 102–5.

Robinson, D. 1979. *Talking out of alcoholism: the self-help process of alcoholics anonymous.* London: Croom Helm.

———. 1983. The growth of Alcoholics Anonymous. *Alcohol and Alcoholism* 18(2): 167–72.

Royal College of Physicians. 1987. *A great and growing evil.* London: Tavistock.

Royal College of Psychiatrists. 1986. *Alcohol: our favourite drug.* London: Tavistock.

Ruzek, J. 1989. The drinkwatchers experience: a description and progress report on services for controlled drinkers. In *Controlling legal addictions.* Ed. D. Robinson et al., 35–60. London: MacMillan.

Scull, A. 1977. *Decarceration.* Englewood Cliffs: Prentice-Hall.

Shaw, S. et al. 1978. *Responding to drinking problems.* London: Croom Helm.

Stockwell, T., and S. Clements, ed. 1987. *Helping the problem drinker.* London: Croom Helm.

Storch, R. D. 1977. The problem of working class leisure. Some roots of middle class moral reform in the industrial North. In *Social control in 19th century Britain.* Ed. A. P. Donajcrodzki. London: Croom Helm.

Treating Alcohol Problems in New Zealand: Changes in Policies, Practices, and Perspectives

Liz Stewart and *Sally Casswell*

In common with most other Western societies since World War II, New Zealand has seen an increase in consumption of absolute alcohol, deregulation of controls on alcohol availability, and a steady increase in the incidence of alcohol-related problems. Per capita consumption of absolute alcohol at age 15 and over increased by 25% between 1955 and 1985. In 1985 the rate of admission to psychiatric institutions for alcohol psychosis and alcoholism was 14 times the 1955 rate. In response to these growing problems, new approaches emerged in the treatment of people with alcohol problems. The alcohol treatment system in New Zealand largely mirrors the general medical care and public health system, consisting of private, voluntary, and government-supported institutions and structures. The general health care system has been described as "in essence a patchwork of provisions which are the result of *ad hoc*, pragmatic responses to an everchanging mix of economic, political and ideological factors" (Fraser 1984). Alcohol treatment services have followed a similar pattern, and its influence is likely to continue to complicate their future evolution.

The Historical Context: From Social Control to Cure

In the late 1800s the abuse of alcohol, manifested particularly in male public drunkenness, was considered a major public order and social problem, and gave rise to a formidable temperance movement (Bollinger 1967). The chronic drunkard was viewed as a pitiful, inadequate, and deviant citizen who had got himself into trouble with drink through lack of moral fiber and will power (King 1904). State aid to impecunious citizens excluded those who had been imprisoned, had deserted their wives, had been convicted of drunkenness or were otherwise undeserving (Oliver 1977).

Responsibility for dealing with chronic inebriates lay with the law enforcement and penal system. New Zealand was a colony of Britain and the

first Acts of Parliament (in 1882 and 1898) to deal with the problem were
therefore based on English legislation. The acts provided, upon application
to a magistrate, for voluntary, family, or court committals to treatment. New
Zealand legislation contained the additional punitive provision that habitual
drunkards could be compulsorily committed even though they had not been
convicted of drunkenness or any other similar offense. The greater number
of custodial patients in New Zealand compared with Britain was ascribed to
this provision (King 1904). Chronic inebriates were initially consigned to mental
asylums, but this practice came to be considered an unsatisfactory form of
treatment for both the inebriates and the mentally ill (Oliver 1977). An
experimental home for inebriates set up in 1902 was closed two years later,
largely because of high administrative costs and lack of success with
uncooperative and recalcitrant patients (MacGregor 1904). In 1909 the Salvation
Army provided separate homes for inebriates at the request of the colonial
government, an approach that had parallels in other countries (Baumohl and
Room 1986). Responsibility for the care of chronic inebriates was shifted from
the State Services Department, which administered the asylums, to the
Department of Justice (Oliver 1977), a shift that strengthened the social-control
aspects of the treatment system. In general, treatment was limited to enforced
abstinence, a healthy diet, and physical work for periods of up to two years
(King 1904). Inebriates who did not come to the attention of the judicial system
were cared for by voluntary welfare and charitable groups (Oliver 1977) or,
if wealthy, by their private doctors (Colquhoun 1900). In the late 1800s
rudimentary services for health care, including the treatment of alcohol
problems, were provided by local, charitable, and government resources. The
state had played a considerable part in the early development of services,
primarily for pragmatic reasons. Small scattered settlements, unable or
unwilling to provide sufficient resources to fund their own services, and the
absence of a wealthy philanthropic upper class, which helped provide voluntary
hospitals and other services in Britain, made *ad hoc* state intervention necessary
(Fraser 1984).

Formalization of the welfare state system, after the election of the first
Labour government in 1935, encouraged a change in attitudes toward the
alcoholic. The state became more active in providing and mobilizing resources
to serve socially desirable ends, including welfare policies on state housing
and social security. The ideological climate in relation to welfare and health
care changed significantly under the Labour government, with less distinction
between the deserving and the undeserving (Oliver 1977).

These changes in government policy may also have contributed to changes
in the treatment of alcoholics after World War II. Initial efforts to improve
upon the "revolving-door syndrome" (repeated hospital admissions and
discharges), thought to be due largely to inadequate treatment (Bradwell 1982),
were prompted by the concern of the Salvation Army and other voluntary

bodies. Key members of the Salvation Army introduced the biomedical disease approach from the United States of America in the late 1940s (Bradwell 1982), and in 1945 Alcoholics Anonymous was introduced and spread quickly throughout the country. These events are thought to have influenced greatly the shift from segregation and control toward cure and treatment (Caughey 1958).

In the late 1950s charitable agencies began to introduce more counseling facilities, and inpatient and outpatient programs. In 1955 the National Society on Alcohol and Drugs was established in the country's then only medical school. The society adopted a biomedical approach and was strongly influenced by Alcoholics Anonymous. This significantly influenced medical views on the nature of alcoholism, which became regarded increasingly as a disease, a view that has persisted for over two decades (Caughey 1958; Casswell and McPherson 1983).

The consequent growing medicalization of the response to alcohol-related problems had the effect that the health system accepted greater responsibility for alcohol treatment services. In 1963 hospital boards received a ministerial directive to establish specialist alcoholism treatment units in general hospitals (Wainwright 1985). Psychiatric hospitals also offered more beds and treatment for alcoholics, and more general hospitals introduced medical detoxification, counseling, and referral services.

The replacement of the 1909 Inebriates Reformatory Act by the Alcoholism and Drug Addiction Act in 1966 shifted official responsibility for the custodial care and cure of patients from the Justice Department to the Health Department. Officially the change symbolized a further orientation from social control toward care and cure, although the new act varied little from the earlier act in its provisions; the state still had a custodial role, although discharged in a more humanitarian way. However, neither voluntary admissions nor custodial committals under the act have formed a significant proportion of inpatient admissions, partly because of the trend toward outpatient care. In 1983 only 11% of all alcohol-related admissions to psychiatric hospitals and other official treatment centers came under the act (Department of Health 1984). In its first fifteen years of operation voluntary admissions exceeded custodial committals.

Despite the general orientation over the last one hundred years toward treatment and away from social control, elements of social control remain for some economically and socially disadvantaged groups, such as the Maori people, the indigenous people of New Zealand. Many Maori clients reached treatment services by referral through the legal system; most non-Maori clients have sought treatment because of pressure from families or employers (Howden-Chapman 1980). Maori people are twice as likely as non-Maori to be referred from law enforcement agencies (Social Monitoring Group 1987). A high rate of enforced observance of the law and arrests for criminal offenses among Maori, especially if alcohol is a factor, have been suggested as a partial explanation for the higher proportions of Maori people in psychiatric institutions, especially young males with alcohol dependence (Social Monitoring Group 1987; Pomare and de Boer 1988). This suggests that the treatment system has been used to a much greater extent as an agent of social control over the Maori people than over the non-Maori.

The Trend from Inpatient to Outpatient Services

The shift toward more outpatient and community-based services began in the 1970s, as part of the worldwide trend away from institutional psychiatric care (Mäkelä et al. 1981; National Health Statistics Center 1987).

The high cost of inpatient facilities was another factor, particularly in the government funded hospital system. In an era of general prosperity an expanding system of medically-oriented services could absorb an increase in alcohol problems (Mäkelä et al. 1981). New Zealand was relatively prosperous in the 1950s and 60s. The well-developed welfare structure could cope with the increase in alcohol-related problems. However, the late 1960s and the 70s brought a sustained economic crisis. Expenditure on all sectors of social welfare, which had been below the average of other countries of the Organization for Economic Cooperation and Development during the previous decade, declined further (Martin 1981). The growth of private medical insurance during the previous two decades indicated the strain on the public health sector as well as a shift from the ideology of the welfare state (Fougere 1974). By the late 1970s government planning groups, such as the New Zealand Planning Council, were calling for restraint in public-sector spending and advocating a "user pays" principle for health costs incurred by lifestyle factors. Alcohol was mentioned as an important cause of social costs, especially in relation to road accidents, crime, and social disorders (New Zealand Planning Council 1979). Also, the findings of research into the efficacy of inpatient treatment compared with other forms of care have contributed to the debate (Edwards et al. 1977; Howden-Chapman and Huygens 1988).

The government's specialist advisory organization, the Alcoholic Liquor Advisory Council (ALAC), has favored the development of outpatient services. ALAC was formed in 1977 to "encourage, promote, sponsor and cooperate in the treatment, care and rehabilitation of those adversely affected by the use of liquor, whether by themselves or others" (ALAC Act 1976). Its responsibilities include the promotion of moderation, the development of problem-prevention strategies, and the funding of research. It has influenced generally the development of treatment services in several respects, mainly by providing establishment grants or continuing funding for a number of treatment services, assistance to hospital boards to set up services, research funds, and the maintainance of a regional and national advisory and coordination service.

The establishment of ALAC was recommended by a 1973 royal commission into the sale of liquor, which investigated matters concerning the sale and distribution of alcohol. It was the first major official investigation after a 23-year period of liberalization of availability, rises in the rates of alcohol consumption and alcohol-related problems, and other social, economic and cultural changes similar to those in other Western countries since World War II (Mäkelä et al. 1981). The decision of the royal commission to investigate alcoholism (although outside its formal terms of reference) reflected public and official concern about the prevalence and effects of alcohol abuse, particularly in relation to traffic accidents and alcoholism.

In its first three years ALAC gave priority to the provision of facilities away from the main population centers, and encouraged hospital boards to establish specialist outpatient centers that would offer assessment, counseling, and referral. As a result, outpatient facilities now predominate in New Zealand, and it is mainly the nonhospital sector (church, charitable, and welfare agencies) that provides inpatient or residential care. In 1987 this sector provided approximately 550 beds, compared with around 200 beds in the hospital sector (Johnstone and Hannifin 1987). The hospital sector provides most of the outpatient services. In 1985, of approximately 10,000 new clients, 89% were outpatients, and 75% of those received hospital board services (Orchard 1987). A factor associated with the change to outpatient status is the age of the patients. From 1981 to 1986 the proportion of new outpatients under thirty years of age increased steadily from 39 to 54% (Orchard 1987). This age group is less likely than older patients to have serious medical or chronic-abuse problems requiring hospitalization or inpatient treatment.

In mid-1987, for a population of 3.3 million, New Zealand had about 60 treatment services (excluding Alcoholics Anonymous groups) for people with alcohol and other drug problems. Facilities ranged from a part-time counselor for an isolated rural area, to outpatient clinics employing several full-time staff, to a publicly funded hospital with 115 beds, devoted exclusively to alcohol treatment (Johnstone and Hannifin 1987).

The Growth of Specialization and Professionalism

As the medical and mental health system became more involved in the treatment of alcohol-related problems, the alcohol treatment system became more specialized.

The fact that alcohol treatment is not seen as a psychiatric responsibility can adversely affect some psychiatric patients who have alcohol problems (Johnstone and Hannifin 1987). Psychiatric patients discharged to the community may develop alcohol and other drug problems. Alcohol treatment services may find themselves unable to treat the psychiatric condition but may have difficulty when they try to refer such patients back to psychiatric services. The psychiatric services may consider that the condition does not warrant hospitalization, or that the symptoms are due to alcohol abuse, which they do not regard as their responsibility (Johnstone and Hannifin 1987).

Interest in professionalism, qualifications and status has increased among alcohol treatment personnel. Medicalization of treatment, arising from the disease concept of alcoholism, and the shift to mental and general health-care services during the 1960s, undermined the self-help concept of Alcoholics Anonymous and voluntarism. It resulted in a significant proportion of treatment coming into the hands of professionally trained people. Since then, but parallel to the continued strength of Alcoholics Anonymous groups, more counselor training courses have been established, and there has been more attention to accreditation, career structure, and status.

In the early 1980s ALAC, in cooperation with a tertiary education institution, established a certificate course in alcohol counseling. Regional training days coordinated by ALAC are also held, and agencies conduct their own in-service training, which varies in scope and content. In 1985 the National Federation of Alcohol and Drug Workers was formed. A loose association without any secretariat, its aims include working toward a better career structure in the field, and the accreditation of professional qualifications. ALAC also sponsors regular national and regional meetings of managers of treatment agencies. However, there is no national organization of managers.

Hospital board services in particular tend to employ professional psychologists, social workers, or counselors. Although many charitable and welfare agency services also employ such staff, it is the policy of a number of agencies to employ recovered alcoholics (Johnstone and Hannifin 1987). Often salaries, conditions of employment, and career paths of staff of such agencies are much less favorable than those in the hospital system, mainly because the voluntary bodies are much less financially secure.

The Reintroduction of Elements of Social Control

As the management of alcohol problems shifted to the health care system during the past twenty-five years, the role of the police and judicial system diminished. The transfer of official responsibility for committals from the Justice Department to the Health Department in the late 1960s, under the Alcoholism and Drug Addiction Act, was an official endorsement of this trend. However, it did not represent a major coordinated change in official thinking about the management and perception of alcohol-related problems; ALAC was under the jurisdiction of the Justice Department for its first ten years, and came under the Health Department only in 1987.

In 1982 public drunkenness was decriminalized, by an amendment to the 1966 Alcoholism and Drug Addiction Act (Mackay et al. 1986). This amendment followed submissions that criminal law, in the form of the Police Offences Act, should not be used to deal with what was increasingly seen as a welfare or health concern. Police still retained powers to take drunken persons into custody, to take them either home, or to police cells for sobering up, or to detoxification centers. A second reason was that the time of the police and the courts was being taken up by a problem that was no longer regarded as being of any significance to public order. Most attention in this alcohol-related area is now focused on the control of driving while intoxicated and violence arising from alcohol abuse.

In the last ten years some social control elements have been reintroduced into alcohol treatment. To some degree this has been imposed by the judicial system, but it also reflects an integration of the aims of treatment of alcohol abuse with the tendency of the criminal justice sector to stress rehabilitation and attention to the underlying reasons for the committing of offenses, rather than punishment. The high economic and social cost of recidivist offending, and maintaining an overburdened prison system, are major reasons behind these moves.

In 1978 a government review investigating the rehabilitation programs for drivers convicted of driving while intoxicated expressed doubt about their efficacy in reducing accidents, and recommended a pilot project for New Zealand conditions before initiating any major new scheme. This proposal was not adopted but the working party was reconvened in 1981 and other recommendations were subsequently introduced (Evans 1985). From 1983, drivers convicted twice within five years of driving while intoxicated can be ordered to have their alcohol-related problem assessed. The procedure in regaining their driving license after its mandatory loss of two years takes into account reports by an approved assessment or treatment center. In 1985 amendments to criminal legislation provided for the possible remission of half of the prison sentence, if the parole board accepted a probation officer's recommendation that offenders would benefit from entering a treatment program upon release. The justice system in the form of the probation service, courts, and prisons, has now become the largest outpatient referral source for treatment agencies, accounting in 1986 for 31% of new clients. Self-referrals were second, at 22% (Orchard 1987).

Alcohol-treatment and law-enforcement agencies indicated such dissatisfaction with aspects of the new arrangements that a number of alcohol-treatment facilities considered withdrawing their services (Davies et al. 1987), or imposed quotas on the numbers of referrals to be accepted (Johnstone and Hannifin 1987). Criticism by the treatment sector has been on the grounds of lack of consultation before the programs were introduced, inadequate recompense from the Justice Department for assessment and treatment, inconsistent posttreatment follow-up of clients by probation officers; unmotivated, disruptive, and aggressive clients (Davies et al. 1987); drivers ordered to attend an assessment center but not doing so until the minimum two-year period of loss of license was nearly completed (thereby defeating the rehabilitative aims); and a too high blood-alcohol threshold, which yielded too great a proportion of "hopeless cases'' (Ministry of Transport 1986). Reviews of legislation in both areas recommended increased funding and the development of special-needs programs; and, with regard to drivers ordered by the court to attend for assessment following sentencing, a briefer interval between the sentence and their attendance (Communications and Road Safety Committee 1987). Offenders are now required to pay assessment fees, and there have been suggestions that they may in the future be made to pay for their own treatment (*Auckland Sun* 1988).

The approaches to the problem of driving while intoxicated are similar to those in California (Speigleman 1984; Weisner 1986), and New Zealand may experience conflicts and contradictions similar to those in California, extending beyond the resolution of practical difficulties. In discussing the implications of compulsion in the Californian system, Speigleman (1984) argues that in many ways the practices implicit in such programs remain unknown, "almost an official secret." He suggests that little thought has been given to the possible consequences of integrating treatment with a punishment system or of "dumping" punishment on a treatment system. Conflict arises, he argues, when punishment, which requires no willingness or agreement on the part of the prisoner/client to attend for treatment, is made part of a treatment and social-work system, which relies on the will of the individual and agreement to have behavior examined. Possible contradictory factors include disciplinary and correctional measures for not successfully completing treatment or for failing to "participate" adequately, and threats to confidentiality if it is agreed to report on therapeutic matters to the referring justice agent (Speigleman 1984).

Despite some criticism of the arrangement and concern about the incongruity of mixing punishment and treatment (Johnstone and Hannifin 1987), the New Zealand treatment system appears to accept, in general, its involvement in a punishment/treatment regimen. For example, a survey of treatment services found that care-givers considered it entirely appropriate for clients to be referred from the criminal justice system to alcoholism treatment centers. Several expressed interest in developing prison-based programs if funds were available (Johnstone and Hannifin 1987). The combination of assessment fees and a reliable source of clients is an inducement to treatment agencies to accept referrals from the Department of Justice.

Explanations have been sought for the shift to more judicial involvement in treatment. Intractable social problems tend to induce compulsive shifts in approach from one model to the other (Room 1986). For instance, the failure of campaigns against drinking drivers over the long term led society to transfer responsibility from the criminal justice system to treatment institutions, in order to be satisfied that something was being done (Spiegleman 1984).

Treatment Institutions

Changes in Treatment Models

As in other countries, the biomedical disease-model of alcoholism predominated in New Zealand during the 1950s and 60s. During the 1970s the orthodoxy of this model (and of approaches to alcohol-related problems in general) came under increasing challenge internationally (Room 1972, 1984). This challenge was reflected in the report of the 1973 Royal Commission on the Sale of Alcohol. The National Society on Alcohol and Drugs, a strong supporter of the disease model, told the commission that total abstinence was the only possible outcome of successful treatment (Royal Commission Report 1974). The commission argued that this was too simplistic a view of a complex situation, referring to overseas evidence that, in some cases, when alcohol problems were diagnosed in time, controlled drinking was an appropriate goal. Although in some treatment circles this view is still controversial, a significant number of agencies have accepted controlled drinking, in theory at least, as a possible goal for nondependent clients (Johnstone and Hannifin 1987; ALAC 1987). There is little overt evidence of the hostile reception given to American advocates of any alternative to abstinence (Miller 1986).

The formation of ALAC, in 1977, greatly influenced treatment models and the direction which today's services have taken. It was perhaps significant that the National Society on Alcohol and Drugs (NSAD), which might have been given an advisory role, was largely bypassed. ALAC appears to steer away deliberately from embracing the disease model. It does not mention the word "disease" in either its annual reports or its policy document on the development of treatment services (ALAC 1987), other than in a discussion of a theoretical model. However, the biomedical disease model remains influential within some older agencies (Johnstone and Hannifin 1987).

Most services have been reported as operating a "holistic model" (ALAC 1987). The approach is eclectic, drawing on a range of models, disciplines, and other approaches that are considered to complement rather than exclude one another. In defining an abuse problem, it takes account of a number of factors, at least in principle. These may include the physical addiction, any psychiatric illness, stress (due to, for instance, inner conflicts, sexual abuse, and unhealthy interpersonal relationships), poverty, unemployment, social inequality and injustice, role modeling, sex-role stereotyping, and attitudes and behavior of the wider society. A combination of methods may be used, including education; skills training (in assertiveness and management of anger, for example); one-to-one counseling and psychotherapy; group, family, or network therapy; action methods; behavioral therapy; stress management; therapeutic communities; outdoor pursuits programs; physical medicine, and spiritual guidance. The holistic model aims at either abstinence or controlled drinking, improved self-esteem, and coping skills, and an understanding of the personal or social aspects of the abuse problem. Success may also be measured by improved interpersonal relations, employment stability, or clients' own views of progress made (ALAC 1987).

Although the holistic model has gained popularity in professional treatment circles, Alcoholics Anonymous, in existence in New Zealand since the late 1940s, retains a strong presence within the treatment system, with around 300 groups (including Alateen and Alanon). Its twelve-step approach is also incorporated into some agency programs, while other services may use AA groups for posttreatment referral (Johnstone and Hannifin 1987). This may be more for practical reasons than for any particular attachment to its philosophy; these services often have too few staff or too few clients to permit group therapy. However, treatment personnel generally do not consider AA particularly suitable for younger clients, and also clients seem to have become less well-disposed toward AA (Johnstone and Hannifin 1987). This may be partly because of its spiritual emphasis (Wainwright and Daley 1984) and partly because of the range of alternatives now offered.

The holistic model may owe its emergence partly to strong links within the treatment system with social work, psychotherapy, and psychology. Counselors with these backgrounds are the most common group of staff employed in treatment agencies, making up 42% of staff in outpatient centers and 30% in inpatient centers (Johnstone and Hannifin 1987).

The holistic approach has perhaps made it easier to expand methods and types of services, and to broaden the definition of what constitutes treatable alcohol problems (Weisner 1986). In New Zealand as elsewhere the terminology has changed (Weisner and Room 1984; Weisner 1986) from alcoholism *per se* to include the alcohol dependency syndrome and the concept of treatable problems associated with less serious heavy drinking (ALAC 1987).

Expanding Definitions of Target Groups

Weisner (1986) has suggested that, by broadening the definition of alcohol problems and simplifying the criteria for recognizing them, the number of people who can benefit from treatment expands to fill the supply of treatment services. Whereas a few decades ago the chronic alcoholic was the sole recipient of treatment, today the beneficiaries include even those whose lives have been affected by the drinking of other persons. There has been a growing emphasis on family programs, for example, and on "co-alcoholics" and adult children of alcoholics; and services have been developed for adolescents, women, and ethnic groups. However, an important reason for developing such services has been that treatment was originally oriented toward middle-aged Caucasian New Zealand men and was therefore often unhelpful and unsuitable for these other client groups.

The adolescent client group has been growing, although there are few specialist programs for adolescents, for a number of reasons—mainly insufficient staff and other resources for their special needs and underlying problems. Most agencies have imposed an age limit of around eighteen years but some will accept younger clients (Johnstone and Hannifin 1987).

More people are presenting with polydrug abuse, although alcohol remains the major drug of misuse (Orchard 1987). Initial resistance to treating polydrug abuse has been attributed largely to insufficient credible information on the effects of other drugs, different behavioral problems, and some reluctance to move into new fields (Johnstone and Hannifin 1987). Nevertheless the system has begun to absorb the treatment of nonalcohol drug abuse; the training course for counselors, for example, has increased substantially the nonalcohol drug component and the course title has been changed from "Alcohol" to "Addiction" Studies (ALAC 1987). Also, ALAC may take on responsibility for other drugs as well as alcohol.

The need for more specialist programs for women is receiving attention. Weisner (1986) suggests that, in general, the literature on women's paths to treatment starts from the assumption that they are underrepresented in the treatment population and that it then focuses on identifying special barriers to their treatment. This appears to be common thinking in New Zealand treatment circles also. Factors that deter women from coming to treatment include shame because of societal double standards about women's drinking, unsuitability of mixed-sex programs in dealing with such issues as sexual abuse, and the difficulty that women with children have in reaching services (Johnstone and Hannifin 1987). In response to such factors, women-only programs have been established in many services, and may be run from a feminist perspective. Other services, established in the late 1980s, include a number of "women for sobriety" self-help groups, a small residential retreat for lesbians, and two halfway posttreatment houses for women.

The broadening of the focus of the treatment system and a change in the profile of clients have had the effect that less attention is given to chronic recidivist alcoholics. This is seen as a deviation from the system's original mandate to treat and care for the public inebriate, toward treatment of people whose problems are less entrenched and more amenable to treatment (Weisner 1986).

The treater finds that work with less disabled clients provides a more satisfying client/therapist relationship. The use of therapeutic strategies taken from social work, psychology, and psychotherapy, which can engage a broader, more responsive client population, also favors this trend. Of course, with better diagnostic and referral services, people may be coming for treatment earlier than previously, before becoming too damaged, and this may be reducing the numbers of chronic recidivists.

Some inpatient services in New Zealand will not accept chronic or severely disabled clients (Johnstone and Hannifin 1987). Salvation Army services, which have traditionally cared for society's unwanted (Wainwright and Daley 1984), tend to receive a larger proportion of this population for treatment or long-term residential care (Smith et al. 1979). Psychiatric hospitals also give long-term care, or patients may live in halfway or boarding houses. One or two hospital-based services run day programs for the "revolving door" patients (Johnstone and Hannifin 1987).

Accountability and Planning

Increasing attention has been paid to the issue of accountability in treatment. An agency accreditation and review system is being introduced (ALAC 1987; Johnstone and Hannifin 1987), which will include guidelines on standards of care, a code of ethics, supervision, and peer-review mechanisms. Services wishing to become accredited will be required to provide detailed information on treatment policy, program planning, management structures and procedures for assessing needs. The scheme is to be voluntary, but accredited agencies will be more likely than others to obtain resources.

Data-collection systems are likely to be improved to obtain more complete client profiles, beyond the usual demographic variables. Some services have had no data-collection system, and internal recording methods have varied from a national computer-based system used by the Salvation Army, down to aggregated tick-sheets which some of the smaller agencies use (Report of Review Committee 1988). There has also been no check for multiple recording of individuals, either within or between agencies (apart from inpatient statistics). Referral from an assessment center to an inpatient unit could result in double recording of a case, for example, and possibly treble or quadruple recording, if the individual subsequently went to a third or fourth agency. This could lead to an overestimate of the numbers of people needing treatment. In some cases, statistics have refuted staff impressions of trends in client numbers and profiles; such impressions can influence an agency's planning and its calls for resources (Johnstone and Hannifin 1987).

Funding Structures

Treatment is generally free to the client. The publicly funded hospital system absorbs most of clients' costs. All nonhospital sector services, inpatient and outpatient, may obtain funding from various sources, including ALAC, government departments or governmental committees, private trusts, and other sources. Grants from private trusts are usually for specific capital items or special programs, rather than for long-term base funding.

Most outpatient services do not charge clients. Some charge a flexible fee or charge the Justice Department for probation assessments. Residential or inpatient services not provided by area health boards may obtain a substantial proportion of their funding from sickness benefits of means-tested patients. One small private hospital charges fees and also receives some income from sickness benefits. Sickness benefits are paid for patients, and not by the bed. This can leave agencies with empty beds short of operating funds, particularly if they are uncertain over future referrals. Referrals from doctors, the justice system or other treatment agencies are often based on the referring agent's knowledge and understanding of what the inpatient service may offer. Shortage of funds may pose difficult therapeutic choices: an aim of rehabilitation is that clients save enough from their sickness benefit to support themselves after treatment, but the agency must obtain sufficient funds to cover its costs.

There is much concern within the treatment system over funding and the consequences of restricted funding for service development and staffing levels. The funding of hospital boards (since 1983, area health boards) may traditionally have been more consistent and stable than that of the nonhospital sector, but recent budget cuts to area health boards affect various hospital services and staffing levels. The alcohol treatment system is now extremely unlikely to receive additional funds, as it is accorded low priority. Area health boards may contract some services out to other bodies, which could lead to an increase in private companies running alcohol treatment services.

In the last few years government policy on grants has tended to favor seeding or setting-up grants rather than operational funding. Also it favors innovative community-based services, and this may herald further retrenchment in inpatient services as funds are diverted into new approaches. It has been argued that this policy encourages a proliferation of small services competing for resources, with subsequent fragmentation of the system (Johnstone and Hannifin 1987).

ALAC may turn solely to seeding-funding arrangements, because of the shortfall in its own funding, which is derived from a levy on alcohol sales (ALAC 1987). In the past it took over the funding of certain services that had been faced with closure. Before 1980, the annual budgetary allocations to ALAC exceeded the rate of inflation, but since then they have been pegged to it. Existing programs tend to account for the entire budget allocated for treatment services, leaving little for the funding of new programs. Also, ALAC has reduced the proportion of its budget allocated for treatment services— from 60% in 1978/79 to 33% in 1986/87—in favor of other services, such as health promotion strategies (ALAC 1987).

A Challenge to the System: Services for the Maori Population

During the 1980s in particular, the indigenous Maori population has criticized aspects of the treatment system. Before the arrival of traders, whalers, and settlers from Britain in the early nineteenth century, the Maori had no experience of alcohol. Afterwards, unscrupulous land dealers supplied them with alcohol, free or cheaply, as a means of acquiring vast tracts of Maori land. Alcohol as a tool of colonization had a devastating impact, physically and spiritually (Awatere et al. 1984).

At present, Maori constitute around 12% of the total population. They are disproportionately represented in statistics of crime, alcohol-related treatment, morbidity, and mortality. The 1986 census found that 15% of the Maori labor force was unemployed, compared with 6% of the non-Maori. Two-thirds of Maori people are in the lower socio-economic bracket (classes 5 and 6 of the Elley-Irving class scale) (Pomare and de Boer 1988). Age-standardized rates for 1980–84 show that alcohol-related deaths were nearly three times greater in Maori than in non-Maori males (Pomare and de Boer 1988).

In the mid-1980s an investigation was made of the extent to which established treatment services were meeting the needs of the Maori, and the factors that prevented those in need from seeking help. ALAC funded a Maori coordinator to undertake the work. He found that a significant barrier to access of Maori clients to treatment services was that the treatment system was staffed predominantly by *Pakehas* (the Maori term for white New Zealanders). *Pakehas* as a group tend to reinforce prevailing attitudes and ideologies, and may also be unaware of and insensitive to Maori beliefs and values (Raerino 1985). Also, the individual casework approach is alien to many Maori people, who place primary emphasis on the extended family rather than the individual. Moreover, the Western tendency to medicalize health problems was felt to be unhelpful and inappropriate.

ALAC then provided further funding to help the Maori establish their own treatment, education and preventive programs. Their programs encompass the traditional Maori concepts of health and healing, in which Maori spiritual, environmental, familial, mental, and physical dimensions are seen as inseparable. They make use of Maori community networking and activities as a means of fostering self-esteem, knowledge of, and affinity for, things inherently Maori, and cultural identification and pride. Resources have been set aside for the training of counselors for alcohol-dependent people and for other drug and solvent abusers, assessment services, prison programs, outdoor pursuits therapy, and a retreat for extended family rehabilitation, which encompasses the belief system of the Christian-based Maori churches.

Resource centers have been established in three cities to provide training, coordination and support for individual workers, committees, and treatment agencies. In mid-1988 a Maori advisor was appointed at the national ALAC office, and 8% of the ALAC 1988 budget was allocated to Maori concerns.

The last 15 to 20 years have seen a resurgence of efforts among the Maori to ensure the survival of their language, land ownership, and culture, and to achieve greater political, social, and economic equity and self-determination. The central issue for Maori is to have the 1840 Treaty of Waitangi, signed by Maori chiefs and the colonial government, ratified and honored. In Maori eyes, the treaty allowed for the parallel development of two peoples, in other words for biculturalism, rather than the existing *Pakeha*-dominated monocultural political and economic infrastructure. Since the late 1980s some government departments have undertaken to observe biculturalism in their administration, policies, and tasks. In 1988 ALAC also adopted a bicultural policy. Its practical implication is that ALAC should consult the Maori people as to the relevance to them, and the possible impact on them, of its policies, before it makes major decisions and introduces programs, so that their values and culture are taken into account. National agency managers have determined that their agencies' policies, service plans, and staff appointments must also observe the principles of biculturalism. Some agencies have set up special programs for Maori to ensure appropriateness and sensitivity to their circumstances and needs. Counselor-training courses and treatment agencies will be expected to incorporate antiracism workshops (ALAC 1988).

Other related moves by the Maori people, such as the filing of claims for compensation for tribal land that was confiscated or illegally acquired in the last century by the colonial government, or its return to them, have met with strong opposition from many *Pakeha* New Zealanders. In essence, the dominance of *Pakeha* values, institutions, and belief systems is being challenged at societal and personal levels. The treatment system is likely to meet resistance from personnel and institutions in its attempt to apply a bicultural policy. However, its application could lead to new or modified ideas about treatment and recovery of patients with alcohol-related problems, which could be of value also for the treatment of *Pakeha* clients.

The self-help approach embodied in the Maori programs is analogous to the Alcoholics Anonymous model of alcoholics helping one another, rather than relying on professionals. Also certain elements of these programs call in question the old moralistic, victim-blaming approach to the management of alcohol-related problems. They focus, not on the individual as the locus of problems, but rather on the part played in the causation of alcohol abuse by such factors as institutional racism and alienation from Maori land, tribal and family systems, language, and customs.

Future Trends

Like most welfare states, New Zealand has had to make economies in its social services. These have included restrictions on the funding of the treatment system: cuts in the ALAC budget; a retrenchment in the spending of area health boards; and the use of seeding grants in preference to long-term funding arrangements. Funding is likely to remain tight for existing services, and alternatives must be developed. As in other countries, some services may be privatized (Morgan 1981; Weisner and Room 1984). ALAC has suggested investigating private-sector sources of funding, and persuading insurance companies to provide cover for alcohol-related health damage for clients who wish to have private care (ALAC 1987). Services may be contracted out to agencies or private companies. Also, as in other health areas, there may be more specialist counselors offering private services to individuals.

Some recent trends in the United States of America could influence the New Zealand treatment system. There, an increase in the number of private treatment agencies, as well as of elements of compulsion, has brought changes in the nature of client groups, and in treatment ideology and goals. Treatment staff find that certain information demands of the judicial system conflict with their therapeutic role, with its ethos of confidentiality (Weisner and Room 1984; Weisner 1986; Speigleman 1984). Poor or severely disabled alcoholics are less likely to reach treatment or be provided for, because of their inability to pay, or because poor prognosis is equated with low cost-effectiveness (Weisner 1986). Also, the crucial role of self-motivation and voluntarism in the success of treatment has been diluted by the increase in numbers of clients referred from the United States court system. There is greater emphasis on denial; breaking through denial is seen as an essential part of treatment (Weisner and Room 1984).

In New Zealand, however, the extension of the concept of therapy beyond the medical model of "care," "cure," and "treatment" of a patient as a passive recipient is likely to become established as the norm. This involves a mutual problem-solving, risk-reducing approach with some clients, in which therapist and client together work out a coping and living strategy that is more likely than heavy drinking to bring happiness and well-being.

As agencies compete for fewer funds, some will become more efficient and give more attention to the evaluation of service delivery. Proposals for more formal assessment and accreditation reflect a concern in common for cost-effectiveness and for ethical and professional considerations. Some agencies may find it impossible to convince funding bodies of the value of their treatment goals and concepts, and may have to close.

Note

Preparation of this chapter was made possible by grants from the Alcoholic Liquor Advisory Council and the Medical Research Council of New Zealand. The authors gratefully acknowledge the assistance of Kim Conway, John Hannifin, Gary Harrison, Jennifer Hewitt, Philippa Howden-Chapman, and Craig Johnstone, who commented on drafts of the chapter.

References

Alcoholic Liquor Advisory Council. 1987. *Living with alcohol: Managing the problems.* Wellington.

_____. 1988. *Say when newsletter* no. 43, October.

Awatere, D. et al. 1984 *Alcohol and the Maori.* Auckland: University, Alcohol Research Unit.

Auckland Star. 1988. *Drink drivers swamp clinics,* April 6th.

Auckland Sun. 1988. *Tougher drink laws 'not enough.'* May 25th.

Baumohl, J., and R. Room. 1986. Doctors and the state: alcoholism treatment institutions before 1940. In *Recent Developments in Alcoholism.* Ed. M. Galanter, 5. New York: Plenum Press.

Bollinger, C. 1967. *Grog's own country.* Auckland: Minerva.

Bradwell, C. R. 1982. *Fight the good fight: the story of the Salvation Army in New Zealand 1883-1983.* Wellington: Reed.

Casswell, S., and M. McPherson. 1983. Attitudes of New Zealand general practitioners to alcohol-related problems. *Journal of Studies on Alcohol* 44(2): 342-51.

Caughey, J. E. 1958. Alcoholism: a national public health problem. *New Zealand Medical Journal* 57:8-15.

Colquhoun, D. 1900. On the need for state institutions for the treatment of inebriety, epilepsy and consumption. *New Zealand Medical Journal* 1, August.

Communications and Road Safety Committee. 1987. *Report on intoxicant impaired driving.* Wellington: Government Printer.

Davies, P., et al. 1987. Results of a survey on difficulties being experienced by agencies with pre-sentencing assessment work in the community care and half-sentencing schemes. *Unpublished survey conducted by a task group of National Treatment Agency Managers and Co-ordinators.* Wellington.

Department of Health. 1984. *The public health: Annual Report.* Wellington: Government Printer.

Edwards, G. et al. 1977. Alcoholism: a controlled trial of "treatment" and "advice." *Journal of Studies on Alcohol* 38(5): 1004-31.

Evans, K. 1985. Education and the rehabilitation of the drinking driver. In *The Conference Papers for the 1985 National Conference on Alcohol and Road Accidents,* April 18-19, 2. Auckland: Brewers Association of New Zealand.

Fougere, G. 1974. Exit, voice and the decay of the welfare state provision of hospital care. Thesis, University of Canterbury.

Fraser, G. 1984. An examination of factors in the health system. In *The Public Interest: Health, Work and Housing in New Zealand.* Ed. C. Wilkes and I. Shirley. Wellington: Benton Ross.

Howden-Chapman, P., and I. Huygens. 1988. An evaluation of three treatment programmes for alcoholism: an experimental study with 6- and 18-month follow-ups. *British Journal of Addiction* 83(1): 67–81.

Johnstone, C., and J. Hannifin. 1987. A review of drug treatment services in NZ. *The National Drug Treatment Research Project*. Manawatu Society on Alcohol & Drug Use. Palmerston North.

King, F. T. 1904. Inebriety as a disease. *New Zealand Medical Journal* 3(23): 310–30.

MacGregor, D. 1904. Report on the Home for Inebriates. *Appendix to the Journals H.22B*. Wellington: Government Printer.

Mackay, P., et al. 1986. Legislative reform and police behaviour: the decriminalization of public drunkenness. In *Policing at the crossroads*. Ed. N. Cameron and W. Young. Wellington: Allen and Unwin.

Mäkelä, K. et al. 1981. Alcohol society and the state. *A comparative study of alcohol control* I. Toronto: Addiction Research Foundation.

Martin, J. E. 1981. The modern welfare state and expenditure in New Zealand. *State Papers*. Palmerston North: Massey University.

Miller, W. R. 1986. Haunted by the Zeitgeist: Reflections on contrasting treatment goals and concepts on alcoholism in Europe and in the United States. In *Alcohol and Culture*. Ed. T. Babor. New York Academy of Sciences. New York.

Ministry of Transport. 1986. Submission to Communication and Road Safety Select Committee, December.

Morgan, P. 1981. Systems in crisis: Social welfare and the state's management of alcohol problems. *Contemporary Drug Problems* 243–61.

National Health Statistics Centre. 1987. *Mental health data 1985*. Wellington: Department of Health.

New Zealand Planning Council. 1979. *The welfare state?* Wellington: Government Printer.

Oliver, W. H. 1977. The origins and growth of the welfare state. In *Social welfare and New Zealand society*. Ed. A.D. Trlin. Wellington: Methuen.

Orchard, H. 1987. *New Zealand alcohol/drug outpatient statistics 1986*. Wellington: Alcoholic Liquor Advisory Council.

Pomare, E., and G. de Boer. 1988. Hauora: Maori standards of health. A study of the years 1980–1984. *Special Report, Series 78*. Wellington: Department of Health and Medical Research Council.

Raerino, N. 1985. Report to the Alcoholic Liquor Advisory Council from the National Co-ordinator Maori Programmes. Auckland.

Report of the Review Committee and Working Party on the review of statistics on beverages containing alcohol. 1988. Wellington: Government Printer.

Report of the Royal Commission into the sale of liquor. 1974. Wellington: Government Printer.

Room, R. 1972. Comment on "The alcohologist's addiction." *Quarterly Journal of Studies on Alcohol* 33:1049–1059.

_____. 1984. Alcohol control and public health. *Annual Review of Public Health* 5:293–317.

_____. 1986. Alcohol treatment and society: An overview. In *Recent developments in alcoholism.* Ed. M. Galanter, 5:1–9. New York: Plenum Press.

Smith, D. A. et al. 1979. *An analysis of the characteristics of patients admitted to the Salvation Army Bridge Programme,* Christchurch 1973–1979. Christchurch: Department of Psychology, University of Canterbury.

Social Monitoring Group Care and Control. 1987. The role of institutions in New Zealand. *Report* no. 2. Wellington.

Speigleman, R. 1984. Issues in the rise of compulsion in California's drinking driver treatment system. Paper presented at International Workshop on Punishment and/or Treatment for Driving under the Influence of Alcohol and other Drugs, organized by the International Committee on Alcohol, Drugs and Traffic Safety, October 1–20. Stockholm, Sweden.

Wainwright, T. 1985. A brief history of alcoholism treatment services in New Zealand 1965–1983. *Planning and Research Series* 19. Christchurch: Health Planning and Research Unit.

Wainwright, T., and V. Daley. 1984. Are we making the best use of our alcohol treatment dollars in the Canterbury Hospital Board region? Report on a seminar for interested participants. Christchurch Women's Hospital, April 12th. *Planning and Research Series* 14. Christchurch: Health and Planning Research Unit.

Weisner, C. 1986. The social ecology of alcohol treatment in the unit. In *Recent developments in alcoholism.* Ed. M. Galanter, 5:203–243. New York: Plenum Press.

Weisner, C. and R. Room. 1984 Financing and ideology in alcohol treatment. *Social problems* 32(2): 167–84.

The Role of Alcohol Treatment in a Consensus Democracy: The Case of the Swiss Confederation

Harald Klingemann

Historical Survey

The treatment of alcoholics has a long tradition in Switzerland. In the nineteenth century, both the emerging concept of alcoholism as a disease and a strong antialcohol mass movement were significant precursors of today's alcohol-specific treatment institutions. In 1877 Rochat, a Geneva clergyman, founded the Swiss Temperance Society, later to be renamed the Blue Cross. By 1898 it had 14,358 members. Numerous initiatives followed such temperance movements and were taken up by some well-known psychiatrists of the time. One of these was Auguste Forel, of Zurich, director of the Burghölzli Insane Asylum and a pioneer of special inpatient treatment facilities. The first such Swiss facility had been established in Basel in 1855, but it was only after a congress on "Fighting the Abuse of Alcoholic Beverages," in 1877, which focused on the question of "drinker asylums", and the intensive efforts of Forel and his colleagues that the movement made a significant advance. In a relatively short period (1889–98) eight more institutions were opened, accommodating up to 165 patients. Some specialized in the treatment of alcoholic women. Special wards were reserved for better-off clients, who wanted comfort rather than moral education (Bleuler 1938, 12-13), and a private profit-making institution, *Schloss Hard,* was founded for "people from the upper social classes suffering from alcohol disease."

Two factors may have contributed to this first inpatient treatment "boom." The discussions on drinkers' asylums at the Second International Congress of the Good Templars, in 1877, showed that psychiatrists, on the ground of efficiency, favored special institutions for alcoholics, which would reduce the overcrowding of mental asylums by rather difficult patients (Bleuler 1938, 3). The other was that the public realized that the "spirits plague" called for a considerable effort to provide a special treatment service: alcohol consumption had reached its peak at that time, at an annual per capita rate of 15.8 liters of pure alcohol (Schmid and Blanchard 1986, 16).

Outpatient services also can be traced back to the late 1900s, to the activities of private temperance societies, whose members regularly visited alcoholics, to persuade them to lead a sober life and to join a temperance society (see Tecklenburg 1983, 45). Gradually, after long discussions on the desirability of specialists (Huwyler 1930, 14), some of these societies opened counseling agencies, mostly in members' private homes.

Again the Blue Cross was a pioneer in establishing such agencies—in Zurich in 1890, in Basel in 1896, and in Bern in 1899. It is difficult to estimate the extent of their activities. They were only part-time and took place often in a counselor's residence and mostly with his wife's help. However, as membership of the temperance league decreased, the Blue Cross lost its innovative role, the network of nonaffiliated agencies was extended and steps were taken to assure better professional standards. By 1920, eleven nonaffiliated and three religious agencies had been established, and over the next decade most of the new agencies appeared, 29 in all (see Lauterburg; appendix).

The interwar years saw a growth of professionalization. The first national conference on treatment issues was held in 1920 and alcohol counselors formed a professional association. It issued its first newsletter in 1933. It collected statistics on the activities of member institutions and set up training programs. After World War II the growth of the outpatient sector, especially of nonaffiliated, multipurpose institutions, continued. Alcohol clinics became more therapeutically oriented and coordinated their lobbying of the federal and cantonal legislatures for resources. Reformatories, halfway houses, and retreats were opened, particularly after 1960 (Tecklenburg 1986, 569). Alcoholics Anonymous groups became more numerous, and the formalizing of training in social work, influenced largely by American models, led to the establishment in 1975 of an intercantonal specialized school of social work (IBSA).

The Decline of Federal Statistics

An attempt to describe the Swiss treatment system is hampered by the scantiness, discontinuity, and uneven quality of official statistics. Perhaps, the extent and quality of official monitoring of social problems indicate the importance that society attaches to various problems at different times. Of course, international comparison would have to take account of other socio-economic or political factors. Thus the federal structure of Switzerland, in contrast to a centralized welfare society, combined with the dominance of liberal thinking and concern about the ethics of data collection, does not conduce to a sophisticated system of social indicators. Nevertheless, over time, interesting changes took place at the national level in the collection and presentation of statistics on treatment. By 1940 the national statistical yearbook contained data on inpatient alcohol treatment centers. The Federal Office of Statistics compiled data on individual admissions and discharges. In 1970 the monographs of the federal office contained even more detailed admission and discharge data.

The federal office began in 1950 the monitoring of the outpatient sector, and this became gradually more complex. At first its report included only the number of agencies and the total number of patients, but by 1959 it had become more detailed and was published annually (with 90% of the agencies participating) together with the official report on the inpatient sector. In 1981, officially for budgetary reasons, these reports were stopped. This stimulated the agencies to produce and improve their own statistics. The Swiss-German Association of Alcohol Clinics (i.e., inpatient facilities) set up and financed its own statistical system, which, at least since 1984, provides highly differentiated information on all nine Swiss-German facilities (including data on patients' treatment history, personal characteristics, and planned aftercare). A pilot project to set up a comparable statistical monitoring system for the outpatient sector (for the first time for both alcohol and drug counseling agencies) is under way and has set off definitional discussions ("how long can a client be counted as a patient?") and competition for access to information among the various professional associations. There are no official statistics for the specialized outpatient sector since 1981, except for the only partly comparable annual reports of the institutions. Similarly, the Association of Swiss Hospitals Statistics, the main source of information for the still important nonalcohol-specific inpatient treatment sector, has begun to develop its own statistical system.

Between 1933 and 1970 the Federal Office of Statistics coordinated and collected statistics on patients of psychiatric clinics. In 1973, after a short interruption, this task was shifted to the private sector and taken up by the Association of Swiss Hospitals. This integration into general hospital statistics affected not only the response rate (which still by 1984 was only up to 40%), but also the validity and comparability of the statistics of diagnoses.

Statistics on first admissions by age and sex were eliminated and only the statistics on discharges, according to the code of the International Classification of Diseases (ICD), were maintained (classified by age, sex, and length of care). Obviously, discharge statistics are less suitable for determining prevalence rates than first-admission statistics.

Because many patients are admitted more than once, the number of main diagnoses reflects only the number of cases treated, not the number of patients. Other factors that influence the reliability and the validity of this data-source, in common with health statistics in general, are changing medical diagnostic habits (probably influencing especially shifts between main and secondary diagnosis), varying methods of data collection (e.g., decentralization and only partial computerization), and differing preferences for particular classification modes (e.g., ICD codes with three or more digits).

This general picture of recording practices suggests that the federal authorities wanted to play down the relatively prominent role of alcohol-treatment statistics in health statistics. Also it contrasts with the current efforts in Switzerland to compile national reports on AIDS, illegal drug use, and methadone maintenance programs.

On a practical level, the researcher is hampered by the interruption of statistics for several years, by regional limitations of new statistics, affecting especially the Swiss-French and Swiss-Italian facilities, and by flaws due to selective presentation for lobbying purposes. Hence, additional data must be obtained from surveys, even though they may provide only a snapshot of the system at a given time.

Alcohol-Related and General Health-Care Elements of the Treatment System

In the following section "treatment" means measures designed to alleviate the alcohol patient's problem or at least to prevent its deterioration. The range extends from institutions that offer a differentiated medical/ psychotherapeutic program, through those that stress work and fresh air, to others that provide custodial care for chronic cases or special services as part of follow-up care.

The Business Cycles of Traditional Inpatient Treatment Centers

The specialized inpatient sector has shown unusual dynamism in recent years, although its share of the total client load seems rather small. Its history reflects society's changing perception of alcohol problems. The first founding boom at the end of the last century was followed by a long period of stagnation, up to 1960. Then, between 1960 and 1980, nine new institutions were set up (Tecklenburg 1986, 569). According to the latest published federal statistics, for 1981, 507 admissions (26% women) were reported for that year by sixteen specialized alcohol-treatment institutions.

A number of important qualitative changes occurred during this second growth period. These institutions had formerly been restricted to men and characterized by an autocratic house-father management, a dominance of agricultural work during a one-year cure, a high percentage of involuntary committals with a lower-class background, and a one-track orientation toward total abstinence. The 1970s brought increasing professionalization and institutional differentiation. Most of the institutions founded after 1960 were directed by psychiatrists and met legal requirements for health-care clinics, thus qualifying for general health insurance funds. They treated other addiction problems besides alcoholism. They admitted both sexes. First admissions of women doubled between 1970 and 1980, probably reflecting a changed societal view of alcoholism in women, but also increased intake capacity from a new alcohol clinic for women in 1974 and extensions to other institutions. Supply may have partially increased demand.

Sondheimer claims that these changes resulted in three types of treatment center, differentiated by degree of institutional medicalization and integration with the general health-care system:

- Officially recognized medical facilities with a focus on psychiatry and psychotherapy.
- Facilities offering social therapy, mainly group dynamics and therapeutic milieu, directed by social therapists and in regular cooperation with doctors.
- Facilities offering social rehabilitation, with residential accommodation and separate group quarters, directed by social therapists and with regular medical supervision (Sondheimer 1986, 51).

The third and most recent expansion phase began in the mid-1980s. It led to a further increase in treatment capacity as well as to more "custom made" treatment programs. Also, it strengthened the differentiation of treatment centers along the axis of medicalization. The more medically oriented units received federal and cantonal money for expanding treatment units, and those oriented more to social therapy and rehabilitation received more funds from other services, for purposes differently labeled.

Almost all treatment centers began to expend enormous sums on new buildings. Thus, as the most recent example, the Forel Clinic in the canton of Zurich (190 admissions in 1989) is spending US\$ 7 million—about three times its annual budget—on extensions and alterations. In only six years (1984–89) its total number of client treatment days doubled, from 10,911 in 36 beds to 21,874 in 76 beds.

At first, the Forel Clinic operated a one-year cure, which was the only accepted formula. Today it offers medium-term (12 weeks) and modified long-term (6–8 months) treatment. A six-week short term "cure," specially designed for employee assistance programs, nowadays expanding rapidly in Switzerland, was stopped in Spring 1988 because of lack of clients (Annual Report #100, Forel Clinic, 1989). The clinic has also targeted new groups: with the opening of a house for young adults with alcohol problems it expects to reach a new segment of the market.

At the same time, the Forel Clinic has downgraded or redefined as work therapy the traditional practice of work in the fields or in small on-site production units. This aspect of therapy accounts for less than 50% of the time budget of the clinic's long-term treatment. Yet most clinics own much land; it represents an important part of their property and cannot be neglected.

Institutions of the second type above also have expanded and have modified their initial focus on work and fresh air as the main element of therapy. A small institution, the Mühlhof (canton Sankt Gallen, 38 admissions in 1988), is spending the equivalent of 1.5 annual budgets on a complete restructuring. While the expansion of the Forel Clinic was completely financed by the canton, about 60% of the cost of restructuring the Mühlhof Clinic is covered by the Federal Office for Social Security, which finances only vocational rehabilitation and training. This explains why most of this money will go toward new workshops and "progressive ecological-minded gardening." Although this approach is supplemented by new therapeutic elements, such as including the family in the admission procedure (Annual Report *Heilstaette Mühlhof* 1988, 15), methods of funding have a major influence on type of treatment.

Client statistics, available for the nine Swiss German clinics only since 1984, confirm the relatively strong expansion of this sector. In 1988 these clinics alone had 525 admissions, the same number as in 1981 for all the treatment centers, and an increase of 25% over the 1984 numbers.

The client profile also changed gradually, from chronic cases from lower social strata toward middle-class patients with temporary drinking problems. The proportion of high school and university graduates rose from 4% in 1984 to 10% in 1988, while the least educated group dropped from 26% to 16% (Tecklenburg 1989).

Are General Hospitals and Psychiatric Institutions Rediscovering the Addict?

It is difficult to determine whether the increase in alcohol-specific treatment programs has been reflected in the mental and general health-care system. An unpublished survey of treatment programs conducted in 1984 by the Federal Commission for Alcohol Problems found only four general hospitals with special psychosomatic wards, with an average of 16 beds. Of the 30 psychiatric clinics in the survey, five had specialized treatment units for addicts, each of about 15 beds, and the rest reported no beds reserved for alcohol patients. Therefore, the treatment capacity of general and psychiatric hospitals may be estimated to be about 150 places. However, such estimates can be unreliable, because it is hard to determine to what extent a special permanent treatment program has been implemented, whether a ward has been only officially designated or whether addiction problems are simply being vaguely declared as a special institutional focus. Also, not too much should be made of cautious testing of the Swiss market by the private hospital chains. In 1985 *Charter Medical* bought a psychiatric clinic in Vaud canton and established a program based on the Minnesota Hazelden Model (*Journal de Genève*, 2.20.1987). However, there are no other such instances and, therefore, no grounds for predicting an import of commercial treatment models in the near future.

Most, by far, of patients with alcohol-related symptoms—about 7,700 in 1987—are still treated in general hospitals and psychiatric clinics. Estimates in the early 70s, using length of hospitalization and bed supply as rough indicators, attributed only about 10-13% of the inpatient treatment capacity to specialized institutions (Leu and Lutz 1977; Tecklenburg 1986, 580). In a list of the most frequent hospital diagnoses for 1987 (VESKA Statistics) alcoholism (no. 303) was only in 11th place (5,449 of 153,279, in the 128 hospitals reporting). Age- and sex-specific analysis, however, shows that "alcoholism," with 8 to 13% of all diagnoses for 1987, ranked first among men between 30 and 49 years, the bulk of the working population, and first among women aged 40-44 (Muster 1989, 11). Nevertheless, the relative weight of alcoholism diagnoses has decreased slightly from 1985 to 1987. Unlike the specialized inpatient sector, there is no information about the treatment methods of general hospitals and psychiatric clinics or their results.

As to psychiatric clinics, the Medical Statistics of the Association of Swiss Hospitals (VESKA) for 1987 show that alcohol-related ICD-codes (#291 "alcohol psychoses," #303 "alcoholism/alcohol dependence," and #571 "chronic liver disease and liver cirrhosis") were the most frequent causes of admission of males of 35-69 years. These diagnoses are less frequent for younger men and for women (Muster 1989, 14). Since 1973 alcohol-related main or secondary diagnoses have accounted for a fairly stable rate of about 21% of all psychiatric diagnoses.

At the same time the ratio of treated alcohol patients to drug addicts has fallen steadily, from 6:1 in 1966 to 2:1 in the early 80s through 1985 (Muster 1989, 42; VESKA Statistics 1988). The public attention being paid to drug problems and AIDS affects greatly the relative importance of client groups, although the direct costs of alcohol problems to society are still much higher than those of illegal drugs.

These statistics do not support the hypothesis of a "rediscovery" of the alcoholic client within the psychiatric and general health-care system. The stagnation of treatment efforts directed at alcohol patients contrasts with the specialization, increasing capacity, and marketing efforts of the alcohol clinic; if it continues, the still important role of the general sector may be further weakened in the alcohol treatment system of the future.

Filling the gaps: Institutions and Facilities for Difficult Clients and Varying Shades of Involuntary Treatment

The highly heterogeneous category of retreats (*Wohnheime*), halfway houses (*Übergangsheime*,) and reformatories for men (*Männerheime*) includes those institutions that admit both addicts and persons socially deviant in other respects. An updating of the telephone survey conducted by the Swiss Institute for the Prevention of Alcohol Problems in 1980 (see Tecklenburg 1983, 58) and a check of the directory of members of the Swiss Association of Professional Alcohol Counselors show a total of 33 facilities in 1987 (of which four are in the French- speaking cantons), with a supply of about 600 beds. The major categories of conditions were "alcoholism/multiple drug dependence," "psychic or mental retardation," "delinquent behavior," and "in need of general social assistance/emergency cases." On the average, about 40% of the inmates have mainly alcohol problems. Typically they are male with outside employment, their prognosis is poor, and they cause the institutions many disciplinary problems—especially those who have been involuntarily committed.

Most of these facilities do not offer therapy in the narrower sense. At most, they provide a typical social-work form of assistance, such as assistance with finding work or housing, and securing an orderly lifestyle. Especially the so-called retreats and halfway houses (*Wohn- und Übergangsheime*) pursue therapeutic goals and consider themselves to be, at least in part, follow-up care institutions (e.g., Forel-Haus/Zurich; Monbijou/Bern).

Certain civil-law measures (Civil Law Code art. 370a on involuntary committal of "inebriates" and art. 397a of Civil Law Code on interdiction of "alcohol dependent persons who . . . put themselves or their families into jeopardy") and penal-code measures (art. 44, paragraph 1, "inebriates") allow involuntary committal, which, at least theoretically, should permit the treatment and improvement of the addict (Klingemann 1986a). The Index of Correctional Institutions (1965) lists three so-called worker colonies (private associations) and three special prison wards. According to Tecklenburg and the telephone survey conducted in 1980 by the Swiss Institute for the Prevention of Alcohol Problems, these institutions could accommodate 400 alcohol-dependents (year of reference 1978). This figure is difficult to interpret, because no room is reserved in the worker colonies for specific categories of clients, and prisons are usually designated for the complete range of punishable offenses. Only one prison (that at St. Johannsen in the canton of Bern) has a separate section for alcoholics and drug addicts, with a 30-bed capacity, according to the prison survey in 1984.

The four worker colonies still in existence are private associations, mostly subsidized by the Federal Office for Social Security. They hardly correspond any more, formally, to Tecklenburg's classification (1983) as repressive institutions housing predominantly persons committed involuntarily by the judicial or administrative authorities; they increasingly resemble "permanent retreats" (*Dauerheime*) and serve for the most part as a last resort for chronic addicts or people "in need of guidance."

Other treatment institutions exclude clients who do not match their increasingly sophisticated treatment programs. In 1986 only 6% of those in alcohol treatment centers were judicial referrals (1970, 10%, Klingemann 1984a, 138), and involuntary referrals by administrative bodies reached an absolute minimum of 3.6% in 1988, from 50% in 1970, according to the federal statistics.

Even though revised legislation still provides many possibilities for compulsory treatment, there has been a substantial decrease in formal involuntary treatment. However, it may have been replaced by subtler forms of informal pressure. This is suggested by a distinct shift in the referral structure: the role of the spouse and family members in motivating treatment has increased considerably, from about 8% in 1984 to 19% in 1988, in the experience of the specialized alcohol clinics (Tecklenburg 1989).

This kind of informal social control together with the trend toward more sophisticated treatment programs may explain also the remarkable growth and modernization of halfway homes, retreats, and worker colonies. Most halfway homes and retreats have been established only recently: about 60% were first opened after 1960. Even if they now have fewer formal referrals from the judicial sector, this is more than compensated for by the growing number of traditional clients, whom the specialized residential treatment centers no longer accept. The worker colonies, which also seemed to be outdated, are needed more than ever to accommodate people being "screened out." One of the four colonies, Murimoos (canton Aargau, founded in 1933, 100 residents), launched in 1983 the most expensive building program in its history with a planned expenditure of US$ 10 million, redefined its role partially as an aftercare institution, modernized the concept of protected workshops, and negotiated successfully for funding from the state and the Federal Social Security Office (Burren et al. 1983). This program was completed in 1987.

Independent Outpatient Services

Regrettably, statistics on outpatient counseling agencies are out of date owing to the changes in recording practices at the federal level. Nevertheless it is possible to extrapolate the trend prior to 1982, when the last tables were published, and to complete the picture with surveys and insider opinions. Most striking has been the growth of the nonaffiliated outpatient sector since World War II. The number of agencies has grown from 65 in 1956 to about 146 specialized outpatient facilities in 1988, mostly organized as private associations. Most are relatively small institutions, employing in 1983 only 270 staff, of which only 14% were women. This small proportion of women is atypical for social work.

The official report for 1981, based on responses of 127 counseling services, indicated that 21,396 persons had received counseling, and that 3,230 new and repeat admissions had taken place.

Over time, changing client profiles become apparent, especially a marked shift in the percentage of women, similar to that in specialized clinics. Whereas in 1961 the ratio of women to men was 1:11, it increased to 1:8 by 1971 and to a remarkable 1:4 by 1981. However, the increase in female clients did not approach the one-third decline in male clients between 1970 and 1981 (from 3,870 new admissions and re-admissions to 2,581, or from 26,403 registered cases to 18,411). According to the 1983 mail survey, about 12,000 patients were considered as active cases (Spinatsch 1987, 21). This could signify a true decline in the relative position of alcohol counseling agencies despite their growing number during the last twenty years. However, it may imply a stricter application of professional standards, resulting in lower numbers in client statistics. Today's better trained counselors probably rely no longer on numbers of telephone calls, distances covered for visits, and numbers of clients ever registered (but not necessarily contacted any more) as evidence of their efficiency.

Empirically we can test only the first part of the hypothesis of an increasing staff and institutional professionalization. Owing to the lack of detailed longitudinal data we can only speculate about the impact on client profiles.

Indeed, an increasing professionalization can be noted. According to a mail survey among staff members of specialized agencies in 1983 (with a response rate of 71% or 193 staff members), personal abstinence as a requirement for appointment, with its obvious impact upon treatment goals, had lost most of its significance. Whereas it was a central requirement for appointment between 1950 and 1970, only 19% of the supervisors appointed between 1973 and 1983 were required to be abstinent (Klingemann 1986b, 16). Most counselors (58%) take alcohol themselves (Klingemann 1984b, Table 7). Many institutions have changed their names during the last ten years, eliminating moral connotations and broadening their institutional goals to include prevention and substance abuse. Also, today's counselors have higher professional qualifications than did the earlier voluntary workers: 25% have a diploma in social work, 18% have completed an equivalent work/study training program, and 16% (including medical consultants) are university graduates. Still, more than a third are not formally qualified. This may reflect the still low prestige of working with alcohol problems among social workers in general; the frequent employment of foreign physicians in alcohol clinics seems to point in the same direction. Nevertheless, the trend toward higher qualifications is definite: the percentage of staff members without formal training has declined from 77% of those over 50 years old to 28% of those under 30 (Klingemann 1984b; Spinatsch 1987, 22).

With a certain time lag, the activities and programs of these institutions also tend to change as a result of better staff qualifications. According to the federal statistics in 1981—which were only rudimentary in monitoring treatment measures—most discharged cases (59%; n=3152) had received neither medical care nor psychotherapy. Only 11% were treated with drugs (Antabuse/Dipsan), and a mere 2% had psychotherapy (Federal Office of Statistics 1982, 42). The annual reports of the agencies for the same year showed that more than half described as important activities the distribution of Antabuse, the exercise of legal tutorial functions, and control of clients' household budgets. The 1983 survey showed that 42% of counselors conducted group therapy, 72% couple and family counseling, and almost all (97%) individual counseling (see Spinatsch 1985, 23). They felt that the time given to administration and legal cases should be halved. They recognized the importance of employee assistance programs and their insufficient outreach to young people. The dense network of drug-counseling services is probably much more attractive to young alcoholics than the traditional alcohol agencies. (The annual report of the cantons for 1984 "Drugs in Switzerland" lists 318 such institutions [1985, 30].) Treatment experts estimate that 80% of young clients would not consider contacting an alcohol treatment agency.

These findings so far suggest a trend toward better treatment for fewer patients in the specialized outpatient sector.

What happened to the client groups that these agencies lost in the course of their "modernization"? What treatments serve as functional substitutes? A look at how general social service agencies and drug counseling services operate could be instructive in this regard. However, it is hard to judge how these agencies and services regard client groups with alcohol problems or what roles they see for themselves vis-à-vis these groups. Whereas sociomedical services still have task-specific units under one roof (advice for young mothers and families, as well as counseling units for alcohol and drug problems), many social services address only the needs of specific groups (e.g., homeless, women, foreign workers). Thus, in the sociomedical services, whether a client with a drinking problem ends up in the unit for general family aid or is sent to the addiction counseling unit will depend upon how staff members define the major problem. A social-service agency will focus on social work assistance for such categories as the handicapped or the foreign worker; normally, it will not consider alcohol problems.

The only available data on this point were provided by a regional survey of 215 general social service agencies in the canton of Zurich in 1984. It was specially designed to provide information on the relative importance of various alcohol treatment resources in the canton. Given its focus on alcohol, the relatively low response rate of 33% in itself supported the assumption that the group-specific agencies in particular defined alcohol problems in their target groups as unimportant or of secondary relevance. Initial client contacts are concerned primarily with problems at work or elsewhere (see Spinatsch 1986, 29–31, 93–121).

The agencies' estimates of the numbers of their clients treated for alcohol problems during the previous year were exceeded only by the numbers treated by general medical practitioners and internists. For the reference year of 1984 the agencies' estimates were 18% (n=8000) of the total number of alcohol patients reported by the Zurich cantonal institutions. Almost two-thirds of the client load were from the lower social strata (Spinatsch 1987, 58, 61). The specialized alcohol outpatient agencies accounted for only 7% of the reported total outreach for alcohol patients, but of whom about two-fifths were lower-class clients. This suggests that alcohol counselors are increasingly selective in their caseloads.

Private Practice and Outpatient Care in Hospitals

The percentage of patients being treated in outpatient psychiatric clinics for "alcoholism as a main or secondary diagnosis" was stable, at around 7%

between 1982 and 1985 (i.e., between 855 and 903 of 11,232 to 12,324 diagnoses), but rose to 7.6% (n=1052) in 1987 (see Muster 1989, 14). Outpatient units of general hospitals report only a very low percentage of alcohol-related conditions (about 1% of all main and secondary diagnoses [VESKA Statistics 1984, 182, 193]).

By far the major outpatient treatment resource identified by the Zurich survey was the general practitioner and internist, accounting for 39% of all treatment contacts (Spinatsch 1987, 58). A survey in the cantons of Bern and Vaud confirmed the preponderance of general practitioners, especially in the early detection of alcohol problems (Ackermann 1984): their estimates of the prevalence in their practices of patients with alcohol problems average around 8% (Mueller and Weiss 1985). They rarely employed specific treatment strategies for these patients and indeed had none at their disposal. When they diagnose or suspect alcohol dependence, they only hold "supportive talks" with the patients (see Weiss 1986). However, recent experiences with testing a medical method of controlling drinking behavior (Noschis 1988a,b; Weiss 1988) show that most participating doctors had great difficulty in finding patients for the experiment (Noschis 1989, 5,6); also they seemed unwilling to detect and confront cases in the early stages of addiction development. Hence, general practitioners' estimates of the frequency with which they see such cases are unlikely to be true estimates of the numbers of patients they treat. So far there is no reliable evidence that they play the crucial role that other treatment agents attribute to them. This is discussed again in relation to referral patterns within the treatment system.

Nonpaid and Nonprofessional Treatment Services

The connotation of "alternative treatment resources" obviously depends on the contemporary point of view. At the beginning of the century, when the temperance movement was in full bloom, it would have meant paid semiprofessional help, a high-risk or new or unusual alternative to the usual part-time visiting commissions. In the present review, "alternative" means "nonpaid" and "nonprofessional" types of intervention.

Lay help, especially self-help, has developed dramatically since World War II. The temperance societies at the beginning of the century relied above all on lay help. As they lost members and failed to attract younger people, lay help was increasingly replaced by paid counseling. This could have been the end of the story. However, since 1978, with the growth of skepticism about experts in general, the Blue Cross has been running a training program for volunteers in various cantons, in an effort to revive the practice of lay help. The training is based on a model designed and used by the German Blue Cross at the beginning of the 1970s. The lay helper is trained to detect, at an early problem stage, persons or groups at risk in their communities or work place and to refer them to suitable agencies. About three hundred volunteers have been trained, a figure that clearly surpasses that of professional counselors. However, the feared threat of "cheap social workers" to professional counselor's jobs has not materialized, and, so far, the program has had only a very modest impact (Spinatsch 1985).

By contrast, the rise of Alcoholics Anonymous in Switzerland has been spectacular. It had no links with the temperance movement. After the founding of the first AA group in Geneva in 1956, numerous groups were set up in the germanophone part of Switzerland, spreading mainly from the Zurich region. Between 1960 and 1982, their numbers grew rapidly from three to almost a hundred. A 1983 survey found that the germanophone region had 96 groups and the remaining regions about 30, with a total membership of about twenty-four hundred. With this increase in numbers, average membership of groups had risen from 14 to 19 (Spinatsch 1986, 53), which may indicate a need for more groups in the future.

Compared with a 1969 survey (Chollet 1972) the 1983 survey showed a higher proportion of women in the groups. The increasing visibility and awareness of women's alcohol problems, already discussed in the context of specialized inpatient and outpatient treatment, show up once more in this context. Also, more and more, AA is seen to attract middle-class clients (Spinatsch 1987, 82).

Linking the Treatment Providers: Does Switzerland Have a Treatment System?

The notion of a "system" implies at least two related elements; in the case of a treatment system these are treatment providers or organizations that know of each other and influence each other's behavior. This means that the degree to which a "system" can be considered a true system must be judged on empirical grounds. The interrelatedness may vary from partial agreement on desirable types of cooperation, with few or no operational consequences, to a comprehensive client-oriented master plan that harmonizes organizational goals and provides for their achievement.

We have seen that the Swiss treatment supply for alcohol problems is highly differentiated. In theory, it permits numerous links. Such a linkage may be compared to a treatment chain with four linked functions: the identification of problems in an outpatient setting, preliminary treatment, inpatient intervention, and outpatient follow-up care. Ideally, patients would be assigned by diagnosis to the appropriate type of clinic and treatment (Tecklenburg 1983, 57; Sondheimer 1986). In this perfect treatment world the lay-help and self-help sector would supplement professional treatment, or at least fill gaps and remedy shortcomings. The reality is different, however, as shown by medical rates of referral to AA groups and specialized alcohol-clinics.

The attitude of Swiss health care professionals toward lay help and self-help can be characterized as integrative, rather than competitive. A study of self-help groups of patients with chronic disease or disability has shown that most had been founded with some support from professionals, who appreciated the auxiliary role of lay help (Wieltschnig et al. 1983, 109, 132). Moreover, only 25% of group members would resent any kind of professional help, although two-thirds reported negative experiences with "conventional therapy." Alcoholics Anonymous has an undisputed role in follow-up and aftercare; there is less agreement that it has a role in the treatment phase (mostly, ex-addicts are not regarded as suitable to be therapists). In any case, the linkage of professional and informal support seems to fit the ideal model. In practice, AA "has overcome its initial marginal position within the treatment network and has established itself as an independent, rather middle-class-oriented, alternative treatment resource, within the treatment system" (Spinatsch 1986, 53). Those chairpersons of AA groups who have joined the organization since 1980 are older and much better educated than the pioneers during the important founding years. Above all, they have had much less previous experience with other types of treatment. Most AA members have come directly to the groups, without any professional referral; the most that AA groups do in this regard is to recommend members to consult doctors (Spinatsch 1986, 71,74,75). This apparent lack of concern with other treatment providers is not surprising, given the AA principles of individual self-responsibility and basic incurability. However, this "splendid isolation" in Switzerland is hard to understand in view of the infiltration of AA into other countries' treatment systems.

Patterns of referral of patients to the specialized clinics have changed significantly during the recent "boom" years. The reorientation of the clinics away from chronic lower-class to "easier" middle-class patients is reflected in shifts in referral sources: increasing referrals from doctors (1984:24%; 1988:34%) and employers (12% vs. 19%; 1989 survey of the Association of Swiss German Alcohol Clinics) and a gradual decrease from counseling agencies (from 42% to 36%) and legal authorities (from 6% to 4%). The most remarkable change, however, is the growing role of informal social ties: referrals from spouses and other family members have increased from 8% to 19%. Organizational changes in the clinics as well as changes in public opinion have diminished the stigma attached to the treatment of alcoholism and made it more acceptable. Also, most clinics now do their own screening and aftercare. All of these changes indicate an increasing autonomy of the specialized clinics and a declining role for traditional treatment agencies.

In the outpatient sector, doctors refer to the clinics very many fewer patients than most other treatment providers thought they should (Spinatsch 1986, 121). A survey of doctors in the cantons of Vaud and Bern found that a remarkable 46% were treating most diagnosed alcoholics alone. Only 17% had recommended that patients join a self-help group, and a mere 13% used the services of a psychosocial counseling agency (Weiss 1986). This relatively isolated position of doctors was reconfirmed in a study in the canton of Zurich

(Spinatsch 1986). By contrast, 39% of the alcohol counselors in the 1984 survey referred their clients "often" or "very often" to a doctor (Klingemann 1986b, 271).

The behavior of AA groups, doctors, and alcohol-clinics, in contrast to the social services, which generally are unwilling to send clients to facilities that treat only alcohol patients, indicates a segmentation in the alcohol-treatment field. Traditional ties, such as those between the specialized outpatient counselors and the alcohol clinics, are gradually weakened; the cooperation of the counselors with general hospitals and psychiatric clinics appears to be the only practice that conforms to the division of labor often proposed (Spinatsch 1986).

The segmentation is not neutral: it discriminates against traditional target groups of older, chronic alcoholics with poor insurance coverage, who cannot qualify for treatment in the narrower sense. The expansion of the institutional facilities for these groups has already been mentioned. These worker colonies and halfway houses see themselves as a link in the invisible treatment chain (between the inpatient sector and return to employment), but in reality they do not serve this purpose. Communal welfare authorities use them for "hopeless cases" under guardianship, sending them these cases direct without prior treatment (Burren et al. 1983). The discussion about the ideal treatment chain that will function one day for the benefit equally of all citizens is thus pure ideology, far removed from reality. The structural causes of this situation are discussed below.

The Changing Environment of the Swiss Alcohol Treatment System

Before discussing the possible influences of socioeconomic conditions or of ideology on the professional behavior of treatment providers, it may be helpful to summarize the conclusions reached so far.

The Swiss treatment field has undergone two important quantitative and qualitative changes. The quantitative changes have been:

- a general growth in treatment capacity—indicated by the boom in specialized alcohol clinics in the 1970s and again since the mid-1980s (almost parallel with higher capacities of rehabilitation retreats, homes and halfway houses) and the striking increase of non-affiliated outpatient treatment since World War II;
- a new role of informal support systems—with the rise of AA groups since 1956 and of Blue Cross lay-help programs.

The qualitative changes have been:

- more professionalization and diversity in alcohol treatment—correlated with a steep decline of formal involuntary treatment since 1970, and more selective or discriminating institutional screening policies, complemented by the higher acceptance of alcohol treatment programs in general (including AA) by women and the middle class;

- a shift of institutional and public attention toward other social problems—exemplified by the allocation of resources, especially in psychiatric clinics, to treatment of illicit-drug users and the privatization of alcohol-treatment statistics.

Finally, there is a trend toward segmentation and autonomy, and an associated exclusion of chronic, difficult cases from the core of "new" alcohol therapy.

A useful way to explain these changes in a subsystem of societal control and health care is to interpret them as active or passive adaptations to a new environment on the part of those who provide the treatment. A more direct explanation is to link the expansion of treatment capacities to changing drinking patterns, and rising consumption and problem rates.

With a per capita consumption of 11.0 liters of pure alcohol in 1987, Switzerland is a high-consumption country. Although it ranks fourth in wine consumption among the traditional wine-producing countries, it cannot be said to be typical with regard to the consumption of wine, beer, or spirits. Its geographical and cultural diversity (of its population of 6.5 million, including 16% foreigners, 74% speak Swiss German, 20% French, 4% Italian, and 1% Romansh) also reflects different drinking patterns. This partially explains the slower development of the treatment network in the more permissive Catholic and francophone parts compared with the germanophone, Protestant areas (Tecklenburg 1986, 566). Sales data of alcoholic beverages show an increase in consumption after World War II and up to the mid-1970s, but in the early 1980s a slight decrease, especially of spirits (Klingemann 1989). Compared with these largely stable figures, survey data point to a much stronger change in drinking habits and eventually the eve of a new sobriety. A comparison of national surveys in 1975 and 1987 shows that more Swiss people than ever in the postwar period consume no or very little alcohol (Fahrenkrug 1989). Deaths from liver cirrhosis and traffic accidents, two alcohol-related problems, show a slight decline in the former and a leveling off at a high rate in the latter (Klingemann 1989) since the beginning of the 1980s.

The recent boom in alcohol-related treatment in Switzerland cannot therefore be directly linked to increasing problem rates, unlike the time of the spirits plague. Did the growth of treatment capacity simply follow after a time lag the increase in consumption during the 60s and 70s? There is no clear answer: survey data indicate that the recent treatment boom coincided with falling consumption. The distinct increase in sales figures occurred after World War II, and therefore only the recent expansion of treatment might be interpreted as a deferred societal learning process. The growth of, for example, outpatient treatment, which has been progressive since World War II, cannot be so interpreted. The most plausible assumption is that an increased public awareness and introspectiveness about the relation of alcohol consumption to social problems (see Fahrenkrug 1989) has indirectly influenced the demand for treatment. The demand in turn affects future expectations and the current investment in treatment facilities by potential care providers.

The question of the financing of treatment is a powerful explanatory variable. Strong abstinence and temperance movements brought about basic legislation on the production, trade and consumption of alcoholic beverages in the Swiss federation at the end of the nineteenth century. In 1887 the Swiss voted to accept the first Federal Alcohol Legislation (Tanner 1986), which granted federal authorities the monopoly of producing and importing, mainly potato, spirits. The partial monopoly for all distilled spirits was ratified by the adoption of Constitutional Article 32 (sub) in 1930 (Klingemann 1989). Most interesting in this context, and unique in the world, is the provision that 10% of the net proceeds received by the cantons from the Alcohol Board be earmarked for "combating the causes and effects of alcoholism." This success of the temperance movement could be achieved only in the typical Swiss spirit of amicable consent, by granting concessions to other societal groups: the federation would take up the farmers' surplus production of distilled spirits, cantons would be compensated, and restrictions would be imposed on the restaurant business to satisfy commercial interests (see Wieser 1987, 27). Since that time (1930) the alcohol tithe has guaranteed a sound financial basis for the treatment system, varying, by definition, with the varying revenues of national spirit sales.

Alcohol counseling services, as a rule formally set up as private associations, are still financed mainly by the alcohol tithe, transferred through cantonal channels; deficits are made good by local communities or private donations. Another factor favoring the expansion of treatment facilities was the partial recognition of alcoholism as a disease by cantonal insurance courts in the 1960s. This entitled patients to insurance coverage if treated by doctors and thus favored medically directed alcohol clinics and psychiatric and general hospitals.

The remarkable growth of specialized inpatient care can be attributed, at least partially, to the tendency of health insurance companies in recent years to differentiate between alcohol treatment costs of "purely medical" treatment and those "exclusively for rehabilitation." The latter, for the benefit of the cantonal health insurance companies affected by soaring health-care costs, are taken up by the better-off federal social and disability insurance system. This arrangement permits also, for the first time, mixed federal and cantonal financing for socio-therapeutic institutions and has enabled them to build and modernize facilities. Thus the varying proportions of cantonal subsidies, health insurance payments, and contributions from federal disability funds determine the type of therapy (work therapy, group psychotherapy, medical treatment) and enable these institutions to attract new clients and expand capacity (Sondheimer 1986, 51). Ideologically, of course, treatment diversity reflects a less rigid interpretation of the disease concept; in practice it is convenient for purposes of health insurance to label alcoholism as a disease. The possibility of controlled drinking as a realistic treatment goal was already discussed by leading clinic directors as early as 1978 (Sondheimer 1978). With increasing professionalization, the dogmatic view that abstinence could be the only goal of treatment is largely superseded, and the medicalization of treatment (Mueller and Tecklenburg 1978) has been replaced in practice by a more eclectic approach. Even a Blue Cross fund-raising campaign in 1988 emphasized temperance more than abstinence and lacked any missionary zeal.

The integration of alcohol treatment with the general health-care system, which in turn is affected by political changes, may be a more valid reason for the expansion of outpatient care, the new role of self-help groups, and the increasing segmentation of the treatment field.

The growth of institutional care and lay help has coincided with a new federalism and increasing concern about "exploding" health care costs.

Since the foundation of Switzerland as a federation, there has been an increase in the economic interdependence of federal agencies and cantonal governments, so much so in the 1960s that various political forces complained about an excessive weakening of federalism. The early 1970s brought growing budget deficits and federal cutbacks. The slogan "more freedom—more individual responsibility—less state" concealed a general reduction of federal subsidies, affecting such areas as cultural and health policies, and programs for marginal groups (aid to refugees, the correctional system [Voyame 1983]). Of course this emphasis on local-level solutions provides a favorable climate for community programs, lay help, self-help, and "small networks" (Gebert and Latzel 1983, 5). While this may be seen as a positive development, fueling the growth of the outpatient, lay help, and self-help alcohol treatment sector, it probably also has contributed to the segmentation of the treatment system. There are strong tendencies toward the creation of autonomous cantonal treatment systems, which increase the imbalances in treatment supply between the better-off and the less well-off cantons. The lack of intercantonal agreements and the fruitless efforts to revise the Social Health Insurance Act ("KMVG, KUVG-Revision": see Gutzwiller 1987) have contributed to this situation.

Rising health-care costs add to the attraction of cheaper outpatient care and self-help. Between 1960 and 1984 the share of the gross national product spent on national health care rose from 3.3% to 7.6%; the increase was due mainly to hospital medicine and the spread of prestigious high-technology equipment (Gutzwiller 1987, 7; Spuhler 1988, 279; Waldner 1987, 76; Frey 1976, 2). This discussion has reached also the specialized alcohol clinics, which close their ranks in the face of increasing pressure to legitimize the differences in treatment costs between them. Signs of this development are the foundation of a formal association of alcohol clinics (SAKRAM) in 1989, the publication of treatment statistics, coordinated lobbying on the cantonal level, and experiments with short-term treatment programs. A future challenge for the alcohol treatment sector will be to incorporate alternative health insurance models or elements such as, in the U.S.A., health maintenance organizations, preferred care providers, and diagnostic-related groups. This would limit individual choice of treatment and eventually weaken the principle of solidarity in social health insurance. However, its positive effects would include lower costs, the strengthening of preventive care, and a clearer explanation of the different costs of different treatment programs.

It may be concluded that the development of alcohol treatment efforts in Switzerland is much more closely linked to changes within the general health-care system and to the political culture of compromise than to problem-specific factors. A strong temperance movement, which fought successfully for the alcohol tithe, the stable political climate in general, and neutrality during the World Wars guaranteed a certain continuity in the development of the treatment system. At the same time the system underwent dynamic transformation. A hypothesis of a connection between increased federalism and the growth of self-help may be plausible but hardly valid; and it would probably be simplistic to postulate an interaction between changes in financing procedures, professionalization, and treatment ideologies. Future studies of the political bargaining process between those who determine policy, such as state and local authorities, health and welfare agencies, enterprises, and political parties, as well as a thorough analysis of the specific features of alcohol policy in federal states, may shed more light on this issue.

References

Ackermann, G. 1984. Die Alkoholkarriere der Patienten: Die Behandlung durch den Hausarzt. In *Alkoholismus als Karriere.* Ed. F. Matakas et al. Berlin.

Bleuler, E. 1938. *5 Jahre Trinkerheilstätte Ellikon.*

Burren, E., et al. 1983. *Orientierungsschrift "Aarg. Arbeitskolonie Murimoos."* Wohlen: Kasimir Meyer's Söhne.

Chollet, C. 1972. Die Gemeinschaft der Anonymen Alkoholiker. Diplomarbeit, Schule für Sozialarbeit, Bern.

Fahrenkrug, H. 1989 : Swiss drinking habits. Results from surveys held in 1975, 1981 and 1987. *Contemporary Drug Problems* 16:201–25.

Frey, U. 1976. Aktuelle Probleme des Gesundheitswesens in der Schweiz. *Schweizerische Ärztezeitung* 76(1): 2–4.

170 *Klingemann*

Gebert, A. J., and G. Latzel. 1983. Perspektiven in der Sozialpolitik. *Sozialpolitisches Forum* 4.

Gutzwiller, F. 1987. 10 Jahre schweizerische Gesundheitspolitik: Bilanz und Ausblick. In *Schweiz-Gesellschaft-Gesundheit-Politik*, Schriftenreihe der SGGP. Ed. F. Gutzwiller and G. Kocher, 12:5–16. Horgen.

Huwyler, S. 1930. Die Behandlung der Trunksüchtigen in der Sprechstunde. In *Über Trunksüchtige und ihre Behandlung.* Vorträge vom 1. schweiz. Lehrkurs über Behandlung alkoholkranker Menschen, Bern, 3.–5. Nov. 1929. Bern.

Klingemann, H. 1984a. Die Rolle der Fachklinik für Alkoholkranke im System innerorganisatorischer Zuweisungsprozesse. In *Drogen und Alkohol,* 3:129–147. Ed. D. Ladewig. Basel: Karger.

_____. 1984b. Voluntarism and professional intervention in alcohol problems as interdependent problem-solving potentials: the case of Switzerland. Paper presented at the IGCAS meeting, "Societal Responses to Alcohol Problems and Development of Treatment Systems." Lindgoe, Sweden.

_____. 1986a. Von der Kontrolle liederlichen Lebenswandels zur kontrollierten therapeutischen Massnahme: Veränderte schweizerische Rechtsnormen zur Zwangsunterbringung. *Kriminologisches Journal* 18(3): 182–201.

_____. 1986b. Kontrolle oder Kooperation? Laienhilfe und professionelle Intervention bei Alkoholproblemen in der Schweiz. *Zeitschrift für Soziologie* 15(4): 259–77.

_____. 1989. Supply and demand oriented measures of alcohol policy in Switzerland— current trends and drawbacks. *Health Promotion* 4(4).

Lauterburg, F. n.d. *Die Geschichte einer Helferschaft 1920-1945.*

Leu, R., and P. Lutz. 1977. *Ökonomische Aspekte des Alkoholismus in der Schweiz.* Zürich: Schulthess.

Marthaler. 1900. *Die Trinkerheilanstalten der Schweiz.* Zürich: Leemann.

Müller, R., and U. Tecklenburg. 1978. Die Medikalisierung des Alkoholismus. *Drogalkohol* 2:15–27.

Müller, R., and W. Weiss. 1985. *Sekundäre Intervention bei Alkoholproblemen: Implementation und Evaluation eines Instrumentes für den praktischen Arzt.* National Research Foundation: research proposal.

Muster, E. 1989. *Données sur l'alcool et les drogues en Suisse 1989.* Lausanne: Swiss Institute for the Prevention of Alcohol Problems.

Noschis, K. 1988a. Questions psychologiques autour de l'introduction d'un nouvel instrument thérapeutique pour buveurs excessifs. *Bulletin Suisse des Psychologues* 9(5): 182–87.

———. 1988b. Testing a self-help instrument with early risk-consumers in general practice: a progress report. *Contemporary Drug Problems* 15(3): 365-382.

———. 1989. *Sekundärpräventive Intervention bei Alkoholproblemen: Implementation und Evaluation eines Instrumentes für den praktischen Arzt.* National Research Foundation: final research report.

Schmid, E., and N. Blanchard. 1986. *Der Verbrauch alkoholischer Getränke in der Schweiz und im Ausland in den Jahren 1981-1985 und in früheren Zeitabschnitten.* Bern: Eidgenössische Alkoholverwaltung.

Sondheimer, G. 1978. Kontrolliertes Trinken—eine Alternative zur Vollabstinenz für Alkoholiker. *Drogalkohol* 1:3-15.

———. 1986. Die Behandlung in Fachkliniken für Alkoholkranke. *Schweizerische Medizinische Wochenschrift* 8 (3b).

Spinatsch, M. 1985. *Ergebnisse aus der Untersuchung "Selbstverständnis gemeindenaher Alkoholfürsorge und -beratung."* Lausanne: Swiss Institute for the Prevention of Alcohol Problems.

———. 1986. Kommunale Laienhilfe und professionalisierte Intervention als interdependente Problemlösungspotentiale. *Schlussbericht eines Forschungsprojektes im Rahmen des Schwerpunktprogramms "Gesellschaftliche Bedingungen sozial-politischer Intervention: Staat, intermediäre Instanzen und Selbsthilfe" der Deutschen Forschungsgemeinschaft.* Lausanne: Swiss Institute for the Prevention of Alcohol Problems.

———. 1987. Ambulante Hilfe bei Alkoholproblemen. Professionelle Beratung, private Laienhilfe und Selbsthilfe im Spannungsfeld von Kooperation und Kompetition. *Arbeitsberichte der Forschungsabteilung* 18/87. Lausanne: Swiss Institute for the Prevention of Alcohol Problems.

Spuhler, T. 1988. Les indicateurs de santé en Suisse: état de la question. In *Service de la santé publique et de la planification sanitaire du canton de Vaud,* Cahiers d'études de l'ISH, 39:263-85. Aarau.

Tanner, J. 1986. Die "Alkoholfrage" in der Schweiz im 19. und 20. Jahrhundert. *Drogalkohol* 1/86.

Tecklenburg, U. 1983. Abstinenzbewegung und Entwicklung des Behandlungssystems für Alkoholabhängige in der Schweiz. *Arbeitsberichte der Forschungsabteilung* 12. Lausanne: Swiss Institute for the Prevention of Alcohol Problems.

———. 1986. The present-day alcohol treatment system in Switzerland: a historical perspective. *Contemporary Drug Problems* 13(3): 555-83.

———. 1989. Patientenstatistik der Arbeitsgemeinschaft der Heilstätten der Deutschen Schweiz. *Unveröffentlichte Teilergebnisse.* Lausanne: Swiss Institute for the Prevention of Alcohol Problems.

VESKA. 1988. Medizinische Statistik. *Gesamtstatistik 1987.* Aarau.

Voyame J. 1983. Repartition des tâches entre la Confédération et les cantons. *Social* 3: 3–6.

Waldner, R. 1987. 10 Jahre Gesundheitswesen—Positives und Negatives. In *Schweiz-Gesellschaft-Gesundheit-Politik,* Schriftenreihe der SGGP. Ed. F. Gutzwiller and G. Kocher, 12:71–78. Horgen.

Weiss, W. 1986. *Sekundärpräventive Intervention bei Alkoholproblemen: Implementation und Evaluation eines Instrumentes für den praktischen Arzt.* Lausanne: National Research Foundation, intermediate Report.

————. 1988. Determinanten ärztlicher Aufmerksamkeit gegenüber Patienten mit problematischem Alkoholkonsum. *Bulletin des Psychologues* 9(5): 175–181.

Wieltschnig, E,. et al. 1983. *Die Rolle von Selbsthilfegruppen von Chronischkranken im Gesundheitswesen der deutschen Schweiz.* Bern: Institut für Soziologie der Universität.

Wieser, M. 1987. Verhütung von Alkoholproblemen. In *1887-1987, 100 Jahre Alkoholgesetz.* Bern: Eidgenössische Alkoholverwaltung.

Treatment-Seeking and Treatment-Reluctant Alcoholics: A Two-Class Alcohol-Treatment System in Austria

Irmgard Eisenbach-Stangl

Traditionally, Austria has been characterized by both high production and high consumption of alcohol. Per capita consumption of pure alcohol, which in 1986 was 10.3 liters, has not increased since the early 1970s. Since the end of the nineteenth century half is consumed as beer, one-third as wine, and the rest as spirits. Austria can therefore be said to be a beer and wine country.

Drinking is part of daily life. At the end of the 1970s few Austrians (about 6% of those aged 16 and more) were abstainers; about one in four drank daily. There are only slightly more abstainers among women, but sex-specific drinking habits are quite distinct and have been so throughout the post-1945 era.

Few efforts have been made to study and record alcohol-related problems. The available information indicates that physical and mental diseases are the principal consequences of overconsumption, followed by problems of security at the work place and in road traffic.

In politics the Socialist Party has always been the main advocate of state control of alcohol consumption and drinking problems, particularly the establishment of a special treatment system for alcoholics. However, as after World War I the Socialists held office for only a short period, the state took little action in this field before World War II. During World War I the previous regime had passed the "incapacitation law," which provided for restricted guardianship for "inebriates," or for courts to persuade inebriates, under threat of "restricted incapacitation," to submit to inpatient treatment for at least six months. In 1922 the on-premises sale of alcoholic drinks to people aged under 16 years was prohibited. Eventually, several of the states founded institutions for the care and treatment of alcoholics, and these can be considered as the first elements of a special treatment system.

After 1945 the Conservatives and the Socialists shared power, and as a result a specialized public treatment network was established and action was taken to counter the risks associated with alcohol consumption, especially in road traffic. The Penal Law of 1952 increased the penalties for intoxicated drivers; the Road Traffic Law of 1960 introduced the 0.8g-per-liter limit; and the Administrative Law of 1960 provided for relatively severe sanctions for violations of the Road Traffic Law.

Thus, after 1945, the state increasingly took over the control of alcohol-related problems, by means of both psychiatry and penal and administrative law. Which of the two systems—the medical or the legal—at present plays the larger part is not clear. However, so far, neither the general medical system nor the social welfare system has been explicitly assigned responsibility for alcohol-related problems, although both are confronted with a remarkable number of such problems.

Historical Survey

The Beginnings of the Special Treatment System during the First Republic (1918-1934)

Already toward the end of the nineteenth century well-known lawyers and physicians were pressing for the establishment of a special public treatment system for alcoholism. However, up to 1914, facilities consisted of only one private "abstinence sanitarium" and some homes for socially deprived inebriates (Gerényi 1902; Standard Encyclopedia 1926). These were closed between 1914 and 1918.

The year 1922 marked the beginning of the public system of professional and special treatment of alcoholism, with the establishment, in Vienna, of the first public treatment institution. This was a "sanitarium" placed within Austria's largest mental asylum. It provided for sixty inpatients. Its founder and head was the physician, Rudolf Wlassak, founding member of the Socialist Workers' Abstainers Union and author of a frequently reprinted book on the alcohol question (Wlassak 1929). He regarded alcoholism as a unique form of mental disease: a disease of will and of reason, which manifested itself through the nervous system. He was strictly against drug treatment, believing in the influence of mental processes and of education for an alcohol-free life, without reference to moral conduct.

The sanitarium was open to voluntary patients and it attracted them increasingly, but most of its patients were alcoholics who had been committed to the mental asylum by the police, or by the courts, or hospitals. However, their treatment also depended to a high extent on voluntariness: they could count on being released after detoxification, after a few days. Long-term detention required a court decision, and this assured payment for the six-month period of institutional treatment. Since the health insurance system did not recognize addiction to alcohol as a disease, voluntary patients had to pay for treatment, while the treatment of involuntary patients was covered by the community welfare budget.

Legally, a more favorable system for alcoholics was possible: the Hospital Act of 1920 had recognized institutions for the cure of alcoholics, but not mental asylums, as hospitals. The establishment of the Vienna alcohol sanitarium as part of the asylum rather than as an independent public hospital was due mainly to the poor financial condition of Vienna and the refusal of the Austrian government to allocate funds for sanitaria for alcoholics.

Outpatient treatment of alcoholics was also instituted in the interwar period. The Socialist administration of the state of Vienna, the only Austrian state to be governed continuously by Socialists between 1918 and 1934, initiated a public, professional outpatient treatment system in 1925, to supplement the "salvation of drunkards," practiced by volunteers of diverse private welfare and temperance organizations. The new system was based on a community welfare center for alcoholics, which employed trained, abstinent welfare workers full-time. The effort to professionalize outpatient care and treatment of alcoholics was manifest also in the foundation of the Working Group for the Care of Alcoholics at the end of the 1920s, as well as in the establishment of special training courses for doctors and welfare workers organized by the community of Vienna (Dreikurs 1929).

Under the same administration in Vienna the police authorities established counseling and welfare services for drinkers in twenty district offices. There, people who had violated the police law under the influence of alcohol were treated instead of punished (Brandl 1930). This police practice was extended beyond Vienna to other states (Fischer 1931). Also, at the end of the 1920s, the outpatient care system for "endangered drinkers" was extended to the other states and increasingly professionalized. Thus, for instance, Caritas, a Roman Catholic charitable organization operating in all the states, joined those private and church-related welfare organizations trying to help endangered drinkers (Obrist 1982); and abstainers' organizations, which had not previously been concerned with drinkers, initiated some services for "drinkers' salvation" (Haberschreck 1931). At the same time, in the late 1920s and early 30s, discussions began on effective methods of outpatient care that would draw upon the services of doctors, abstainers' organizations, former drinkers, and, when funds permitted, full-time welfare workers. In at least one other state besides Vienna, the government employed a full-time welfare worker, specialized in alcoholism (Zechenter 1931).

The alcohol sanitarium of Vienna remained unique, however. Three other states established small homes for homeless and disabled chronic alcoholics, two of them within a mental asylum, but they offered no professional treatment. Inpatient care outside Vienna, therefore, was almost exclusively carried out in mental asylums, to which those alcoholics whose condition was considered equivalent to mental illness could be compulsorily committed and detained legally on a court order. The asylums were characterized by a high degree of repression and lack of resources, and provided only isolation and custody (Forster 1987).

Already in the nineteenth century alcoholics had formed a substantial proportion of the inmates of the asylums (Tilkowsky 1902). After 1918 they reached a similar proportion, even in Vienna after the establishment of the special inpatient and outpatient services for alcoholics. In the second half of the 1920s about one-fourth of all admissions to the Vienna asylum—or more than 40% of the men admitted—were alcoholics (Berner and Solms 1953).

The development of the public special treatment network in Vienna was disrupted in 1934, when the Austro-Fascists seized power and prohibited the Social Democratic Party. In effect, the Nazis destroyed the treatment system by closing almost all the institutions. It was only after 1945 that the inpatient treatment of alcoholics could be separated from the welfare system, which at that time included psychiatry, and established as part of the medical system, as the legislature had planned in 1920.

The Initiative of the Psychiatric-Neurological Clinic of the University of Vienna

Already in the 1940s there were demands for the reestablishment of a sanitarium for the treatment of alcoholics. When eventually in 1961 one was established, it was under the auspices of the psychiatric-neurological clinic of the University of Vienna—again not of the state mental asylums, which had to deal with most of the officially recognized alcohol-related problems. Now, however, unlike the interwar period, the initiative was taken by doctors who were not members of temperance organizations. Indeed, they took a decisively different position from these organizations and their demands for control of supply (Hoff 1954). The institution established in 1961 was supported by the health insurance agencies and the Ministry for Social Affairs, which at that time administered also health affairs. It differed markedly from the alcohol sanitarium of the First Republic. It was exclusively for voluntary patients and could therefore be called an open institution. It had no connection with the mental asylum; until the mid-1970s it remained part of the university psychiatric clinic. Its emancipation from the mental asylum owed much to the recognition of alcoholism as a disease on the part of the health insurance agencies in 1953, and to their assumption of almost complete coverage of treatment costs. Notwithstanding the many differences between the first open institution of the Second Republic and the alcohol sanitarium of the First Republic, both had in common that their principal founders were members of the Socialist Party.

The professional context in which the psychiatric initiative was set may be better understood in the light of the diverse public positions of its most prominent representative, the psychiatrist Hans Hoff. Hoff had worked and taught in the U.S.A. during and after the war and had become acquainted with special treatment institutions for alcoholics as well as with Alcoholics Anonymous. In 1950 he was appointed head of the psychiatric-neurological clinic of the university, and in 1951 elected president of the Austrian Society for Mental Hygiene, an organization dedicated to the reform of psychiatry by making it more scientific and bringing it closer to general medicine. Hoff held other influential positions also: he was the first psychiatrist to head an important commission of physicians advising the Minister of Social Affairs; and he was vice-president of the Advisory Board for Alcohol Issues, a body within the Ministry of Social Affairs, established in 1955 mainly on his initiative.

The establishment of the first open institution in 1961, therefore, was also a result of the first efforts to reform psychiatry. Legislators had finally recognized psychiatry as part of the medical system—mental asylums had been recognized as hospitals in 1956—to the benefit of both patients and psychiatrists. Alcoholics seemed the most suitable category of patients with which to initiate such a reform, from isolation and custody to treatment. Already at the end of the nineteenth century alcoholism was considered curable on the grounds that one main source of the disturbance was separate from the person, and that cure, therefore, could be sought by separating the patient from this exterior source (Finzen 1980; Springer 1986). It was hoped that the establishment of a special treatment network would eliminate a category of clients whose problems still carried moral overtones and could not be completely defined in medical terms.

The form in which Hoff and his team defined alcoholism and the methods of treatment that they applied illustrate the efforts to establish alcoholism as a medical or medical-psychiatric problem. They regarded it as a symptom of a psychiatric "basic disease" (Hoff 1956). Consequently, the treatment methods they advocated comprised drug treatment of the primary mental disease, and of the secondary disturbance (with Antabuse), together with different kinds of psychotherapy and social care.

The first open institution of Vienna employed doctors, psychologists, nurses, and social workers—a multiprofessional team—and they cooperated with vocational advisers of the labor exchange office. For minor services the patients themselves were mobilized within the framework of a therapeutic community (Kryspin-Exner 1967). The treatment team stressed the length of time that full recovery took, the many risks involved, and the need for aftercare for several years under medical supervision. The abstinence of the staff—an indispensable principle for Wlassak—was of no concern to them.

The Decline of the Temperance Organizations and of Social Welfare
for Alcoholics

The temperance organizations welcomed the treatment initiative, although the physicians were not temperance-oriented, and the disease model and the treatment methods removed alcohol and drinking from the focus of attention. After World War II the temperance movement, whose importance had generally declined, largely withdrew from the care of alcoholics. In contrast, Caritas, which had secretly continued its work with alcoholics during the war and had intensified it after 1945, had never subscribed to the abstinence ideology of staff. It now increasingly sought cooperation with physicians, psychiatrists, and the health administrations. Finally, the health authorities of the states began gradually to undertake responsibility for the treatment of alcoholics, at first hesitantly, and significantly only in the 1960s and 70s. The change of organizations responsible for the care of alcoholics, as well as the changed understanding of alcoholism and its treatment on the part of the temperance organizations, resulted in the psychiatric initiative being met with appreciation and cooperation instead of rejection and competition.

In the long run this development led to the subordination of social welfare to medical-psychiatric treatment, which was promoted by training courses of the Society for Mental Hygiene and by others. It led also to a marginalization of those voluntary organizations that did not become involved in the new treatment system—in follow-up care, for example.

Psychiatrists who were not oriented toward temperance took over not only expertise in the treatment of alcoholics, but also alcohol issues in general. This may be observed in the records of the discussions of the Advisory Board for Alcohol Issues in its first period (1955–60): the demands of the temperance organizations for supply controls were overshadowed by those of the psychiatrists and physicians for the extension of the treatment system. The political battle against alcohol was thus largely replaced by the medical-professional battle against alcoholism (Eisenbach-Stangl 1988).

The Extension of Inpatient Treatment

Hoff (1967) celebrated the first open institution for alcoholics in Vienna as "the mother of new life." It comprised sixty-five beds, exclusively for men. The publications of the first director make clear the kind of patient for which the voluntary six-week treatment had been conceived. To Hoff's original criteria—voluntariness and an acceptable physical and mental condition—he added the expectation of regaining working capacity. This excluded therefore retired persons as well as those liable to a legal penalty (Kryspin-Exner 1967). Thus, it was not only with respect to voluntariness and financing that the treatment of alcoholics became more like that of physical diseases but also in its choice of patients. The Austrian medical system generally is marked by its preference of curable patients and its neglect of unproductive, chronically ill, and handicapped persons (Karner 1978).

As the institution's reputation grew, its admissions increased. Although readmissions increased also, the numbers treated in the institution and its outpatient facilities expanded remarkably during the 1960s. The same was true of outpatient centers in other states (Kryspin-Exner and Weigl 1969; Bitschnau 1979; Braun 1980). The Vienna institution was extended in 1966, 1974, and 1981, and today has two hundred and ten beds. Six similar open institutions were established in the 1970s and 80s, bringing the number of beds in open institutions up to about 470 in the mid 1980s, or 6.2 beds per 100,000 inhabitants. Taking into account the alcoholic station at the mental hospital at Graz, founded in 1969 and similar to the Vienna alcoholic sanitarium of the interwar period, the number of beds amounts to 522, or 6.9 beds per 100,000.

In the 1970s inpatient treatment was extended also to women. For example, the Vienna open institution added a special women's department. Also, two of the open institutions added departments for illegal-drug addicts.

The Expansion and the Separate Status of Outpatient Treatment

In the 1970s also, the special outpatient treatment system was substantially expanded: the number of organizations providing such services increased from ten in the early 1970s to eighteen in 1980 and nineteen in 1984. These numbers reflect the extension incompletely, since most of the organizations have more than one service office, and also the number of service offices has increased. Most of the new organizations were established by health or welfare authorities.

Outpatient services were expanded or established primarily for the aftercare of inpatients (Pramer 1987; Sebastian 1988). However, already during the 1970s, outpatient services began to function independently of inpatient care and a growing number of patients were treated exclusively in outpatient centers (see, e.g., Heber and Mader 1983). For instance, in 1979, in the largest outpatient center attached to Vienna's open institution, 84% of patients attending for the first time (19% of all patients during that year) were treated exclusively as outpatients (Marx et al. 1982).

The expanded outpatient and inpatient treatment system attracted patients who were socially less privileged than those of the 1960s. For one reason, the open institutions had less strict admission criteria, and, for another, the insurance agencies were more willing to finance treatment for more severe cases. Also, welfare authorities began to finance treatment, thus making people who received public assistance eligible. This development was reflected in the decreasing educational level of the patients of the Vienna open institution, as well as their increasingly unstable vocational, financial, and family circumstances (Springer 1983).

At the same time, the extension of treatment attracted the socially more privileged and also women. As in other countries they were attracted especially by the exclusively outpatient treatment, with its relative anonymity and freedom from institutional restrictions (Room 1980; Otto 1981).

The expansion of inpatient and outpatient treatment in the 1970s and 80s occurred in states that, with one exception, had been governed traditionally by the Conservative Party. In the 1970s this party also had come to accept that it was a responsibility of the state to offer alcoholics professional treatment.

Reduced Compulsion

As the special treatment system expanded, its quality changed. Only indirect indicators of this change can be cited, as it has not been otherwise documented. There are three such indicators.

The first, at the end of the 1960s, was the cessation of the discussion on special legal compulsory measures for alcoholics, which had continued since the end of the nineteenth century. The core of the discussion had been compulsory admission and treatment, and long-term detention, of alcoholics. The law provided only for the compulsory admission and short-term detention of those alcoholics who could be considered as mentally ill. Temperance organizations and psychiatrists, among them Wlassak and Hoff, strongly criticized this practice: many alcoholics were compulsorily admitted to asylums, for while intoxicated they were regarded as mentally disordered, but as soon as they were sober, they were discharged. The demand for extended compulsory measures had no effect, and neither did the demand for closed and half-closed special institutions, which the director of the first open institution had advocated (Kryspin-Exner 1967a, 1968). The cessation of the demand for more legal compulsory measures reflected the general change in psychiatry.

The second indicator was a change in judicial viewpoints. This was reflected in the continuous fall since 1961 in the number and proportion of "restricted incapacitations" due to alcoholism (Lehner 1983; Eisenbach-Stangl 1987). New regulations on incapacitation enforced in 1983, designed for the greater legal protection of the mentally ill (Hopf 1983), made no mention of alcoholics. Since the mid-1960s the courts had declared only forty-three persons a year, on average, restricted incapacitated, compared with average annual figures of seventy-eight between 1949 and 1963, and one hundred and twenty-two during the First Republic. It cannot be assumed, therefore, that the merging of alcoholism with mental illnesses, under the new law on custody of mentally impaired persons, led to increased restrictions on the legal status of alcoholics.

The third indicator, changes in methods of treatment, showed first in the decreased use of Antabuse. Before the establishment of the first open institution, it had been used extensively as a new and promising medicine by the psychiatric-neurological clinic of the University of Vienna (Hoff and Solms 1956), but during the 1970s its use fell off. If necessary, similar but more moderate drugs are now prescribed, and patients are less pressed to take them. Apomorphine has more or less disappeared from medication. Also, changes in psychotherapeutic methods indicate increasing reliance in treatment on "internal controls" of patients and lack of reliance on "external controls." Aversion therapy, common in the 1960s, has disappeared, and its place is taken by a variety of conversation and group therapies (Lentner 1988, personal communication).

The Treatment of Alcoholics in Psychiatry

The Prereform Stage

In 1971 psychiatric hospitals, including the three small university psychiatric clinics, were admitting relatively more alcoholics than in the interwar period. "Chronic alcoholism" was the most frequent diagnosis, accounting for over 25% of admissions. In addition, 7% were admitted for "acute intoxication." Most admissions for alcoholism were of men: about 47% of male admissions but only 13% of female admissions (Katschnig et al. 1975).

The relative increase in admissions of alcoholics in the postwar period was remarkable, but absolute numbers were much higher. Total admissions of psychiatric patients had increased greatly—doubling between 1960 and 1970, for instance. The increase in both cases was due not so much to increased incidence of psychiatric conditions or alcoholism as to the greater capacity of psychiatric services (Forster 1987).

Patients admitted for alcohol-related problems were discharged quickly (one-fourth of the chronic alcoholics after one week, and about two-thirds after four weeks). Hence, as a 1974 study of a sample day showed, patients with alcohol-related diagnoses in psychiatric hospitals constituted only 10% of all psychiatric inpatients (Katschnig et al. 1975).

The 1971 and 1974 studies found also that 71% of all psychiatric admissions were involuntary and that 94% of all patients on the sample day were detained compulsorily. Separate data on alcoholics are not available, but it may be assumed that their proportions did not differ from those of total admissions.

Compared with other European countries, Austria has had a substantially lower ratio of psychiatric beds to population (Pelikan 1979), but the numbers of alcoholics treated in psychiatric hospitals have exceeded by far those treated in open institutions. By contrast, until the mid-1970s, outpatient care was carried out mainly by the special outpatient centers for alcoholics; this was because there were only a few psychiatric outpatient centers and relatively few private psychiatrists and neurologists (Pelikan 1979), and these were reluctant to treat alcoholics.

The Post-Reform Stage

The reform of psychiatry began in law in 1956 when mental asylums were officially recognized as hospitals and therefore part of the medical system. However, it took some twenty years before they actually began to function like medical hospitals (Pelikan 1984). In the second half of the 1970s also, a growing number of multiprofessional outpatient centers ("socio-psychiatric" service centers) came into operation. Since then the number of psychiatric hospital beds has fallen considerably, while admissions have increased continuously. As the proportion of compulsory admissions declines slowly and that of detained persons faster, it is to be assumed that both the new outpatient centers and the psychiatric hospitals increasingly attract voluntary patients.

After the reform the proportion of "alcohol ill" among all psychiatric inpatient admissions and of beds occupied by such patients did not change. This was shown by a countrywide study of a sample day in 1983 (Laburda et al. 1984) as well as by two minor studies of psychiatric hospitals in Vienna (Gabriel 1980 and personal communication). The outpatient service centers treat about the same numbers of persons with alcohol-related problems as do the reformed inpatient institutions (Katschnig 1981; Wiener Psychiatriebericht 1983). Hence today's psychiatric services treat more alcoholics than ever before, and consistently many more than the alcohol-specific treatment system, despite the view of many reform-oriented psychiatrists that alcohol and drug addicts should be treated mainly, if not exclusively, in special institutions (Marksteiner 1985). As always, those admitted to the general psychiatric institutions are those who are unwilling to be treated, the socially deprived and the isolated, the unemployed, and those who are mentally as well as physically most afflicted (König et al. 1980; 1983).

FIGURE 1

Beds Occupied by Alcoholics in Psychiatric Hospitals and Alcohol Sanitaria

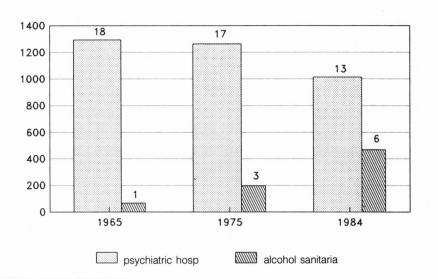

An unforeseen consequence of the reform, which was accompanied by changed public attitudes toward the mentally ill and a decreasing readiness to get rid of them by detention (Danziger 1982), has been a gap in the care of a traditional category of psychiatric patients: homeless and unemployed alcoholics. Before the reform they were admitted involuntarily. Now they enter voluntarily for one or more days to get a free bed and a free hot meal. They do not fit into the treatment pattern of the psychiatric hospitals. Consequently, reform-oriented psychiatrists especially call for the reestablishment of welfare institutions that would provide a "roof over the head, a bed under the body, and a meal on the plate" (Gabriel 1983).

Alcohol Treatment and the Penal System

The pre–World War II welfare-centers for alcoholics established by the police were not reestablished after 1945. However, a 1975 reform of the penal law introduced a "treatment-penalty" for offenders with alcohol-related problems (Eisenbach-Stangl and Stangl 1984). Lawyers, psychiatrists, and some temperance organizations had been calling for such a measure since the end of the nineteenth century. Offenders who committed a crime while under the influence of alcohol or in connection with alcohol-related problems can now be sent to a special prison where they receive treatment, provided they behave responsibly, that their imprisonment is not intended to exceed two years, and shows promising results. The special prison, which has eighty beds, receives also drug-addict offenders.

Recently it has become customary to treat offenders with alcohol-related problems, after a short imprisonment, in Vienna's open institution. They are then discharged on probation. The treatment is financed by the Ministry of Justice (Lentner and Werdenich 1985). Since 1975, alcohol-dependent offenders who, because of mental illness, cannot be considered responsible for their behavior are committed to another special-treatment prison for an indeterminate time. Previously they had been detained in mental hospitals.

The Penal Law of 1975 uses, not Hans Hoff's psychiatric definition of alcohol dependence, but a more extensive, nonmedical-psychiatric definition: all persons can be subjected to a "treatment penalty" who "are devoted. . .to the abuse of an intoxicating substance."

Since the 1969 reform of the prison law, offenders imprisoned for an offense by negligence are kept in a special prison. Many such prisoners have been sentenced for driving while intoxicated and causing an accident resulting in serious or fatal injury, or for committing a crime under "full intoxication" (until 1975 this meant 2.5g per liter blood-alcohol content and since then 3.0g per liter). These offenders can be given educational courses in the prevention of accidents, as well as six-week courses in improved driving. Since 1979 these courses are offered also to persons sentenced in an administrative proceeding or to persons who have had their driving license withdrawn (Michalke 1982).

This so-called psychological rehabilitation (Foregger 1980) resembles more the moral training of Wlassak than today's medical-psychiatric treatment. However, it is also an attempt to alter the drinking habits of persons with alcohol-related problems, and thus deserves mention.

Alternative Treatment Resources

New Trends in Social Work, Self-Help Groups, and Lay Help

The 1970s and 80s have seen a number of social-work initiatives in alcohol treatment. The social authorities have established a few scattered outpatient counseling services, staffed exclusively by social workers, and offering advice and help rather than psychiatric or medical treatment (Dorner 1984, personal communication; Marinell 1984, personal communication). Also, voluntary organizations with independent traditions in providing care, such as Caritas, have become critical of the dominance of medical-psychiatric treatment, claiming that it raises exaggerated and unrealistic expectations (Caritas Linz 1984, personal communication). However, it is not clear whether these organizations have had any influence on concepts of care and treatment. In the 1980s also, social workers began to set up "juice bars." The alcohol-free sociability offered in these bars (Frassine and Liebl 1982) resembles that of the old temperance organizations, whose traditions receded into oblivion after 1945.

Another development of the last two decades has been the growth of self-help groups. Thus, by 1988, the number of Alcoholics Anonymous groups had reached eighty-seven, or twelve groups per 100,000 inhabitants. Apart from AA, most self-help groups have been initiated by professionals and operate under their more or less extensive supervision. These professionals include those of the special treatment system, doctors, and social workers of the health and welfare authorities, general practitioners, and psychiatrists. Their aim has been either to build up decentralized aftercare or to organize alcohol-free leisure activities in addition to professional aftercare.

Alcoholics Anonymous has little association with the special treatment system for alcoholics or with the general psychiatric or medical system. Although it seeks to rid itself of its reputation of hostility to doctors and even to associate with professionals, it still sees itself as an independent alternative to professional psycho-medical treatment.

Austria has almost no tradition of lay help. Of the lay organizations of the interwar period, only the Blue Cross remains noticeably active. During the last fifteen years it has become linked to both the special treatment system and the new self-help organizations. No new special lay welfare organizations were founded after 1945, and lay help within the professional system has remained unusual.

The Two-Class System—Change and Continuity

Already in the early years of the century there were demands for a public special-treatment system for alcoholics who sought treatment voluntarily. The legal basis of a system was formulated during the First Republic, but only very few treatment institutions were established. The post-1945 initiatives were more effective, with the establishment of an outpatient and inpatient treatment system. This system was extended to all the states after 1970. In recent years demand seems more than satisfied, as judged by signs of saturation, such as increased advertising of open institutions and sometimes a lack of patients.

One reason for the increasing saturation has been the reform of general psychiatry. Previously, psychiatric institutions were characterized by repression and lack of resources, and alcoholics were compulsorily admitted. The reform, with its provision of an outpatient psychiatric treatment system, made psychiatry more attractive for voluntary patients.

The partition of the treatment of alcoholics continues, however. Voluntary patients, whose treatment is more likely to be successful, can attend special inpatient and outpatient institutions, separated physically and administratively from general psychiatry, better staffed and equipped, and also providing aftercare. Those who are compulsorily admitted as well as those whose prognosis is less favorable (chronic and acute cases) come under the general psychiatric services, whose resources and staffing still compare unfavorably with those of the general medical system. Because the special treatment system attracts alcohol patients who are less impaired, physically, mentally, and socially, than those who enter the general psychiatric system, and who also come from the socially more privileged classes, the label "two-class-system of treatment" is doubly justified.

During the 1970s when the treatment service for alcoholics was extended by the improvement of the special treatment system and the reform of psychiatry, treatment began to be offered also to criminals with alcohol-related problems. The primary reason for the extension of treatment facilities, at a time when neither alcohol consumption nor the incidence of alcohol-related problems was no longer rising, was that the Conservative Party recognized the consequences of alcohol consumption as a health problem and consequently supported the extension of treatment. Recognition was not only political, however. Therapists were emphasizing the importance of voluntariness and of insight into their condition on the part of patients. Alcoholics were themselves acknowledging their disease in public and experiencing little rejection; neighborhoods did not protest against self-help clubs, for instance.

Exclusively professional treatment is increasingly perceived as insufficient. Professionals themselves are calling for the reestablishment of welfare centers for alcoholics, and social authorities and social workers have begun to establish such centers.

How far self-help groups and welfare services will develop from complementing psychiatric treatment to providing an independent alternative will depend on, inter alia, the continuation of the "two-class system." If the reform advances and the standard of treatment in psychiatric hospitals approaches that of the special system, welfare groups as well as self-help and lay-help groups are likely to grow in importance. This trend will be accentuated if psychiatric services, in order to increase their insufficient funding, begin to treat not only voluntary patients but also involuntary patients considered likely to benefit from treatment. However, the direction of the reform will be determined by political decisions, and can therefore be only a matter of speculation at present.

References

Berner, P., and W. Solms. 1953. Alkoholismus bei Frauen. *Wiener Zeitschrift für Nervenheilkunde* 6(4): 275-301.

Bitschnau, R. 1979. Aufbau der Sozialarbeit durch den sozialmedizinischen Dienst der Caritas der Diözese Feldkirch. In *Festschrift zur Eröffnung des Krankenhauses Stiftung Maria Ebene,* Behandlungszentrum für Suchtkranke. Ed. Stiftung Maria Ebene. Franstanz: Vorarlberger Graphische Anstalt.

Brandl, F. 1930. Polizeiliche Trinkerfürsorge. *Volksgesundheit. Zeitschrift für soziale Hygiene* 4:93-99.

Braun, K. 1980. Langzeitergebnisse einer gemeindenahen Psychiatrie im Burgenland. *Wiener Zeitschrift für Suchtforschung* 1:39-41.

Danziger, R. 1982. *Psychiatrie in der Steiermark.* Graz: Amt der Steiermärkischen Landesregierung.

Dreikurs, R. 1929. Der gegenwärtige Stand der psychischen Hygiene in Wien. *Volksgesundheit. Zeitschrift für soziale Hygiene* 10:211-22.

Eisenbach-Stangl, I., and W. Stangl. 1984. Ist die Zwangsjacke repressiv? Über die Widersprüche psychiatrisch-medizinischer Kontrollen. In *Grenzen der Behandlung.* Ed. I. Eisenbach-Stangl, and W. Stangl, 7-26. Opladen: Westdeutscher Verlag.

Eisenbach-Stangl, I. 1987. Inebriety and rationality: the modernization of state controls of alcohol-related problems in Austria. *Contemporary Drug Problems* 79-112.

———. 1988. *Zum Bedeutungswandel eines Konsumgutes.* Die Geschichte des Alkohols in der Republik Österreich 1911-1984. Frankfurt am Main: Campus.

Finzen, C. 1980. *Alkohol, Alkoholismus und Medizin.* Ein Beitrag zur Sozialgeschichte der Psychiatrie. Rehburg-Locuum: Psychiatrie Verlag.

Fischer, G. 1931. Trinkerfürsorge und Polizei in der Landstadt. In *Almanach des Hilfsvereins für Trinkgefährdete "Enthaltsam und frei"*. Ed. E. Walkhoff, 55–62. Vienna: Wedl.

Foregger, E. 1980. Über die Behandlung von Alkoholtätern im österreichischen Strafvollzug. *Blutalkohol* 17:189–98.

Forster, R. 1987. Trends in mental health care in Western Europe in the past 25 years. *International Journal of Mental Health* 16:21-41.

Frassine, I., and A. Liebl. 1982. Ein Jahr Saftbeisl. *Forschungsbericht*. Vienna.

Gabriel, E. 1980. *Das psychiatrische Krankenhaus der StadtWien*, Baumgartner Höhe: Auf dem Weg zu einer integrierten Einrichtung psychiatrischer Vorsorge in der Stadt. *Österreichische Krankenhaus-Zeitung* 9:1-8.

_____. 1983. Psychiatrische Folgezustände bei langandauerndem Alkoholmissbrauch. In *Enquete über Alkoholkonsum—Krankheit und Folgen*. Ed. Magistrat der Stadt Wien, 28-34. Vienna.

Gerényi. 1902. Die Bewegung gegen den Alkoholismus in Niederösterreich. In *Bericht über den VIII. Internationalen Kongress gegen den Alkoholismus*. Ed. Kongress - Bureau, 369-83. Leipzig and Vienna: F. Deuticke.

Haberschreck, H. 1931. Die Trinkerfürsorge in der Deutschen Gemeinschaft für alkoholfreie Kultur. In *Almanach des Hilfsvereins für Trinkgefährdete "Enthaltsam und frei"*. Ed. E. Walkhoff, 63–64 . Vienna: Wedl.

Heber, G., and R. Mader. 1983. Das Anton Proksch-Institut, Stiftung Genesungsheim Kalksburg. Gründung, Entwicklung, Behandlungskonzept. In *Alkohol- und Drogenabhängigkeit. Neue Ergebnisse aus Theorie und Praxis*. Ed. R. Mader, 1-14. Vienna: Brüder Hollinek.

Hoff, H. 1954. Der akute und der chronische Alkoholismus. *Medizinische Klinik. Wochenschrift für Klinik und Praxis* 36:1425-29 and 37:1461-66.

_____. 1956. *Lehrbuch der Psychiatrie*, vol.1. Basel: Benno Schwabe und Co.

_____. 1967. Foreword. In *Die offene Anstalt für Alkoholkranke in Wien-Kalksburg*. Ed. K. Kryspin-Exner, 9-10. Vienna: Brüder Hollinek.

Hoff, H., and W. Solms. 1956. Die Errichtung einer Trinkerheilstätte. *Wiener Medizinische Wochenschrift* 18/19: 405-8.

Hopf, G. 1983. Von der Entmündigung und Anhaltung zur Rechtsfürsorge für psychisch Kranke. In *Justiz und Zeitgeschichte: Schutz der Persönlichkeitsrechte am Beispiel der Behandlung von Geisteskranken, 1780-1982*. Ed. E. Weinzierl and K. S. Stadler, 293-304. Vienna: BMfJ.

Karner, W. 1978. Das österreichische System der sozialen Sicherheit, besonders der Sicherung im Krankheitsfall. In *Systemanalyse des Gesundheitswesens in Österreich*. Ed. E. Berger et al., 2:61-77. Vienna: Montan Verlag.

Katschnig, H. 1981. Typen ambulanter Hilfen bei psychischen Krankheiten. In *Ambulante Psychiatrische Versorgung. Aktion Psychisch Kranke.* Ed. M. Bauer and H. K. Rose. Cologne: Rheinland-Verlag.

Katschnig, H., I. Grumüller, and R. Strobl. 1975. *Daten zur stationären psychiatrischen Versorgung Österreichs,* vol.1, Inzidenz and vol.2, Prävalenz. Vienna: Österreichisches Institut für Gesundheitswesen.

König, P., R. Haller, and W. Stangassinger. 1980 and 1983. Zur Epidemiologie des Alkoholismus in Vorarlberg. *Mitteilungen der österreichischen Sanitätsverwaltung* 81(9): 149-57 and 84(5): 105-12.

Kryspin-Exner, K. 1967a. Das therapeutische Milieu. In *Die offene Anstalt für Alkoholkranke in Wien-Kalksburg.* Ed. K. Kryspin-Exner, 55-61. Vienna: Brüder Hollinek.

———. 1967b. Die Auswahl des Krankengutes. In *Die offene Anstalt für Alkoholkranke in Wien-Kalksburg.* Ed. K. Kryspin-Exner, 17-26. Vienna: Brüder Hollinek.

———. 1968. Die Stellung der sozialtherapeutischen Anstalt im Gesamtkonzept der Alkoholismusbekämpfung. In *Klinik und Therapie des Alkoholismus.* Ed. K. Kryspin-Exner and T. Olteanu, 13-21. Vienna: Verlag der Wiener Medizinischen Akademie.

Kryspin-Exner, K., and A. Weigl. 1969. Der Ausbau der Anstalt. In *Theorie und Praxis der Therapie der Alkoholabhängigkeit.* Ed. K. Kryspin-Exner, 34-38. Vienna: Brüder Hollinek.

Laburda, E., J. M. Pelikan, and H. Strotza. 1983. *Bericht über die psychiatrische Versorgung in Österreich.* Vienna: Ludwig Boltzman-Institut für Medizinsoziologie.

Laburda, E., J. M. Pelikan, and H. Strotza. 1984. *Stationäre Psychiatrische Patienten. Stichtagprävalenz* 6.21.1983. Vienna: Ludwig Boltzman-Institut für Medizinsoziologie.

Lehner, O. 1983. Entstehung, Absicht und Wirkung der Entmündigungsordnung 1916. In *Justiz und Zeitgeschichte: Schutz der Persönlichkeitsrechte am Beispiel der Behandlung von Geisteskranken.* Ed. E. Weinzierl and K. S. Stadler, 149-86. Vienna: BMfJ.

Lentner, S., and W. Werdenich. 1985. *Neues Modell der Behandlung Alkoholkranker im Strafvollzug.*

Marksteiner, A. 1985. Leitlinien einer Reform. Die Veränderung der psychiatrischen Versorgung Ostösterreichs 1975 bis 1985. In *Gugging. Versuch einer Reform.* Ed. A. Marksteiner and R. Danzinger, 14-18. Salzburg: AVM-Verlag.

Marx, B., J. Jahoda, and R. Marx. 1982. Behandlung von Alkoholabhängigen in einer Fachambulanz. *Wiener Zeitschrift für Suchtforschung* 4:3-12.

Michalke, H. 1982. Driver-Improvement in Österreich—Konzept, Realisierung und Zukunftsperspektiven. Paper presented at the Conference on "Führerscheiner-ziehung, Bewährung, Nachschulung aus verkehrspsychologischer Sicht," Vienna: 9.22.1982.

Obrist, E. 1982. Beratungsstelle für Suchtgefahren. In *Helfen im Wandel der Zeit*. 60 Jahre Kärnter Caritasverband 1921-1981. Ed. Kärnter Caritasverband, 132-35. Klagenfurt: Hermagores-Druckerei.

Otto, S. 1981. Women, Alcohol and Social Control. In *Controlling Women. The Normal and the Deviant*. Ed. B. Hutter and G. Williams, 154-67. London: Croom Helm.

Pelikan, J. M. 1979. Anmerkungen zur Psychiatriereform—am Beispiel Österreich. In *Sozialarbeit und soziale Demokratie*. Ed. H. Keller et al., 127-49. Vienna: Jugend und Volk.

_____. 1984. Besonderer Rechts- und Persönlichkeitsschutz für psychisch Kranke. In *Grenzen der Behandlung*. Ed. I. Eisenbach-Stangl and W. Stangl, 43-50. Opladen: Westdeutscher Verlag.

Pramer, J. 1985. Beginn und Aufbau der Alkoholkrankenbetreuung in Oberösterreich. In *10 Jahre Club für Alkoholkranke*. Bezirk Vöcklabruck. Ed. H. Türk and E. Zimmerhackl. Vöcklabruck: Lenzing AG.

Room, R. 1980. Treatment-seeking population and larger realities. In *Alcoholism Treatment in Transition*. Ed. G. Edwards, and M. Grant, 205-24. London: Croom Helm.

Sebastian, H. 1988. *Zur Situation der Behandlung und Betreuung von Sucht- und Abhängigkeitskranken in der Steiermark*. Graz.

Springer, A. 1983. Das Krankengut der Stiftung "Genesungsheim Kalksburg". In *Alkohol- und Drogenabhängigkeit. Neue Ergebnisse aus Theorie und Praxis*. Ed. R. Mader, 15-32. Vienna: Brüder Hollinek.

_____. 1986. "Wie die junge Psychiatrie den Teufel Alkohol austreiben wollte. . ." *Kriminalsoziologische Bibliographie* 50–51:39–59.

Standard Encyclopedia of the Alcohol Problem. 1926. vol. 3. Ed. E. A. Charington. Ohio: Westernville

Tilkowsky, A. 1902. Über den gegenwärtigen Stand der Alkoholiker in den niederösterreichischen Irrenanstalten. In *Bericht über den VIII. Internationalen Kongress gegen den Alkoholismus*. Ed. Congress-Bureau, 202-9. Leipzig and Vienna: F. Deuticke.

Wiener Psychiatriebericht. 1983. Ed. Kuratorium für psychosoziale Dienste. Wien.

Wlassak, R. 1929. *Grundrisse der Alkoholfrage*. 2. Auflage. Leipzig: Verlag von S. Hirzel.

Zechenter, K. 1931. Die Entwicklung der Trinkerfürsorge in Oberösterreich. In *Almanach des Hilfsvereins für Trinkgefährdete "Enthaltsam und frei"*. Ed. E. Walkhoff, 67-71. Vienna: Wedl.

The Italian Paradox: Treatment Initiatives and Falling Alcohol Consumption

Flavio Poldrugo and *Roberto Urizzi*

Italy is a peninsula of 301,276 km^2, which projects into the Mediterranean Sea and has a population of approximately 56 million. Since the end of World War II it has been organized as a democratic republic in which the sovereignty of the people is assured by the direct election of representatives to Parliament, and executive authority is delegated to the government. Italy is a signatory to a number of international treaties and agreements, including the Treaty of Rome, which established the European Economic Community.

Since 1953 the government has delegated administrative and legislative duties to twenty local regions. In 1963, five of the regions—Valley of Aosta, Trentino-Upper Adige, Friuli-Venezia Giulia, and the two islands, Sardinia and Sicily—were given autonomous status, and therefore increased legislative freedom, because of their geographical and cultural peculiarities.

Italy, along with France and Spain, is among the world's chief wine-producing countries (Powell 1987), and consequently the alcohol industry is vital to the Italian economy. Approximately two million Italians earn their living from the production and sale of wine (Favaretti 1983) and about 10% of all arable land is set aside for viticulture (Bianchi Loconte et al. 1982). However, regional alcohol consumption does not reflect alcohol production (Figure 1). Thus, in the southern regions wine is produced mainly for export and hence consumption is comparatively low. Alcohol consumption is highest in the northern and central regions (Poldrugo et al. 1985).

Alcohol consumption increased in the 1950s and 60s, but has since leveled off, and today, on average, Italians drink less than they did thirty years ago. Also, the proportions of different forms of alcohol consumed have changed. Wine consumption decreased from a high of 116 liters per capita in 1968 to 93 liters in 1980. In 1981 distilled spirits accounted for 12.5% and beer for 6.2% of total consumption of absolute ethanol (Modonutti et al. 1987). However, the consumption of spirits and beer has increased in recent years, as demonstrated by increased imports (Figure 1).

As in other south European countries, alcohol is part of day-to-day Italian life. Alcohol, especially in the form of wine, has been traditionally regarded

FIGURE 1

Yearly Consumption of Alcoholic Beverages in Italy Before and After World War II
(Liters of Absolute Alcohol/Per Capita/Per Year)

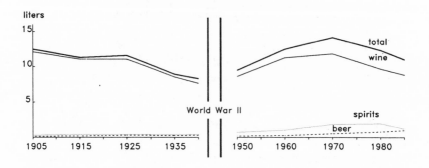

as a basic element of the Italian diet (Lolli et al. 1952), and approximately
10% of Italian family expenditure on food has been on alcohol (CENSIS 1983).
Although this assimilation of alcohol into everyday life has controlled possible
social problems (Jellinek 1976), there are still alcohol-related problems. Indeed
there is a marked contrast between the stereotype of Italians as moderate and
controlled drinkers, and the picture given by recent statistics on alcohol-related
problems. Indirect data obtained from official statistics (ISTAT 1983-1985;
Poldrugo et al. 1985) indicate that Italy may have five million heavy drinkers.
Alcohol-related mortality is considered responsible for 20,000 deaths a year.
This mortality is attributed mainly to liver cirrhosis (10,000 a year), but alcohol
has been implicated in lethal traffic accidents (3,100), in 35% of suicides (700),
and in lethal accidents on the work site (500) (ISPES 1985). Deaths attributed
to alcohol are thirty times more numerous than those attributed to drug
dependence.

Historical Survey

Major Changes before 1945

The question of alcoholism was tackled first at the turn of the century
in monarchic Italy. Three factors were responsible: 1) the newly developed
awareness of diseases of "public concern," which was highly influenced by
the positivist school of thought of Lombroso, which associated alcohol with
crime; 2) the rise of an industrial proletariat as the vector of alcohol abuse;
and 3) the founding of the first temperance societies (Morgan 1984). These
societies were influential in the introduction in 1909 and 1912 of the first
legislative norms concerning alcohol distribution.

During the Fascist period the "alcohol question" was concerned more with control over productivity and public order than with its public health aspects. The regime, in the interests of economic self-sufficiency, was determined to prevent absenteeism in industry due to alcohol misuse. In 1931 it introduced legislative norms of public drunkenness and made provision for obligatory treatment of individuals who committed crimes under the influence of alcohol. "Habitual drinkers" were obliged to take psychiatric treatment in mental asylums for at least six months. Offenders whose judgment was considered to be impaired from "chronic alcohol intoxication" had to be hospitalized for the rest of their lives in "judiciary asylums."

Reduction of wine production and Fascist policies on alcohol (Morgan 1984) resulted in a decrease in ethanol consumption from 110.5 liters of wine per person in 1925 to 87.5 liters in 1935.

Postwar History of Treatment

After the war, wine consumption increased greatly, for various reasons (Figure 1)—the accelerated economic development of the 1960s, bringing changes in living conditions (e.g., the migration of southerners to the larger industrial settlements of the north, the net increase in the national productivity index, and the individual's economic independence, contrasting with the traditional interdependence of family members) and the expansion of the alcohol market (Terzian 1982).

In the 1950s two types of drinkers could be recognized—the "traditional" and the "rejected." Traditional drinkers were heavy wine-drinkers, predominantly men, who drank in particular social contexts. For example, they tended to drink heavily at family meals, in taverns (osterie) where they met their friends to play cards or bowls, or at family or religious celebrations. Their social or family group maintained some control over their drinking, and hence resulting alcohol problems tended to go unnoticed unless medical or psychological problems arose. Rejected drinkers were also predominantly male, but instead of drinking in formal and structured social and group settings they tended to drink alone and at unsocial hours during the day. Because their drinking behavior often led to family and work disruption, they tended to live off social welfare. This group of drinkers had high suicide rates and many had mental disorders. They corresponded to traditional "skid row" alcoholics.

During this period alcohol treatment was available only for related medical problems. There was no specific treatment for the more general social and behavioral problems. Psychiatric hospitals and the neurological divisions of general hospitals offered short-stay admission and detoxification as the only treatment. A few doctors, mostly on a personal basis, were prescribing disulfiram or apomorphine after detoxification, or offering short-term psychotherapy. Chronic alcoholics with psychiatric disturbances were confined to mental health institutions. The better off preferred to be hospitalized in private clinics, which were abundant during this period (Prina 1984).

Medical debate was concerned more with the physiological mechanisms of action of ethanol in humans than with the organization of care. Federal agencies also promoted research into alcohol as a productivity risk factor (Mangano and Mangano 1969). Unconnected with this, regulations were introduced to prevent work-related injuries associated with alcohol consumption and drunken driving.

Today new and traditional drinking patterns have merged. Derossi et al. (1986) distinguish two new categories of drinkers—the modern and the emerging. Modern drinkers consume beer or distilled spirits in the form of whisky, vodka, and cocktails. They drink in bars at any time of the day. They drink heavily to cope with feelings of dissatisfaction with their lives. They are normally to be found in the industrial north. They are younger than traditional or rejected drinkers and can be either male or female. So far, because they are a relatively new category, they receive little attention.

The emerging drinkers, a recent phenomenon, are young men and women who meet and drink beer in discos, bars, and fast-food outlets. Drinking is associated not only with socializing but also with fashion and other consumer symbols. They often drink excessively, and at times take drugs as well. Their behavior is thought to be a form of rebellion against the dominant social norms of Italian society.

Since the 1970s public concern has focused on drug problems among young people, and new legislation has been introduced to deal with drug dependence. However, this concern has not extended to alcohol problems, and there are only few public alcohol-specific treatment programs. They are found either in large urban mental hospitals, as in Milan (Madeddu 1969) or Rome (Bonfiglio et al. 1977), or among voluntary organizations that deal indirectly with people with alcoholism and alcohol-related problems. Wealthier people seek private treatment abroad, especially in Switzerland.

At the end of the 1970s, administrative reorganization of the whole public health sector, including the mental health sector, heralded the beginning of treatment services. The last two decades are discussed in detail in the following sections.

Treatment Institutions—Alcohol-Specific and Nonspecific Services

Development of Alcohol Treatment Systems in Response to Health-Care Legislation

Italian legislation deals with alcohol under three different rubrics. The first, and the most important, is the quality control of alcoholic beverages, and their distribution and taxation. The second concerns law, order, and safety.

Legislative norms introduced in the early 1930s for controlling public order are outdated. Existing legislative norms on drunken driving, introduced in 1959, take account of alcohol intoxication but do not provide the criteria and methods necessary for its evaluation. This example may suggest that legislation in Italy is not meant to be implemented (Alberoni 1987). The third, and the least important, has been treatment. Recent legislation has favored its expansion, however. Although legislation is not specific to alcohol treatment, it affects it directly by the Act on Drug Abuse and the National Health Service Act, and indirectly by the Mental Health Act.

The Act on Drug Abuse and the National Health Service Act. In the late 1960s drug dependence gained much more recognition as a disorder with important social implications than alcohol dependence. It was a new phenomenon, which attracted the interest of the media as a cause of death of youth and especially because of its spread to the upper social classes, for no apparent cultural reason. In 1975 the government introduced the Act on Drug Abuse, concerned with the prevention, treatment, and rehabilitation of drug addicts (Calcaterra 1986). The different regions of Italy, under their newly acquired responsibilities for public health planning, were authorized to create medical centers for social assistance, whose functions included the prevention and treatment of alcoholism. For the first time, an Italian law had made explicit provision for the treatment of alcoholism. Drug addicts were referred exclusively to these centers and to "therapeutic communities." This showed the continuing distinction as regards treatment opportunities between drug addicts and alcoholics in need of specific treatment.

A most powerful impetus to treatment development was the introduction, in 1978, of the National Health Service, which represented a major change in the concept of health care. Alcoholism became officially regarded as an illness, and any alcoholic could choose to be treated free of charge in any Italian hospital. Previously, alcoholics who could not afford private care, especially "traditional" and "rejected" alcoholics, had to avoid public institutions. Physicians often underreported alcoholism to avoid a diagnosis that would exclude patients from insurance coverage.

The Mental Health Act. The reform in mental health care, introduced in 1978 (Mosher 1982), also contributed indirectly to the increase of public awareness of alcohol problems. All mental hospitals were closed, and this deprived alcoholics of their traditional refuge. Since then, the new community mental health centers have been unable to cope with alcoholism. Involuntary medical committal is rarely used and alcoholics have returned home in increasing numbers, thus placing a heavy burden on their families.

Current legislation lacks homogeneity among its various components. Several regions (10 out of 20) have provided for alcohol treatment in their

FIGURE 2

Registered Admissions for Alcoholism in General and Private Hospitals
in Italy between 1960 and 1979. Annual Intake per 100,000 Inhabitants.

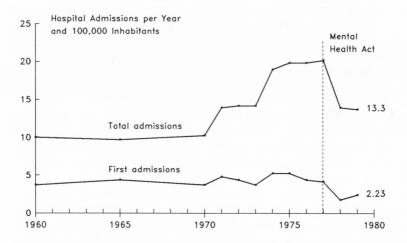

legislation. Some, especially in northern Italy (such as Veneto and Friuli-
Venezia Giulia), have formulated specific public treatment programs.

The state's attitude toward alcohol problems is still one of minimal
intervention. Thus, a national legislative proposal on prevention, treatment,
and rehabilitation of alcoholism, and designed to coordinate the entire alcohol
field (including alternative treatment for driving while intoxicated), has been
awaiting recognition by the Italian Parliament since 1984 (Calcaterra 1986).
Future developments will be associated with the need to harmonize Italian
legislation with that of the other members of the European Economic
Community by 1992. The Ministry of Transport has recently proposed to
Parliament punitive and rehabilitative measures aimed at drivers with blood-
alcohol levels above 0.8g/liter, and the suspension of renewal of driving licenses
of alcoholics.

Treatment Institutions

The organization of the alcohol treatment system in Italy is the
responsibility of the local health units. As Figure 3 shows, alcoholic patients
have multiple contacts with the health system, mostly with family doctors of
the national health service. The doctor may arrange consultation with a specialist
or referral to the public health system. Usually, alcoholics are hospitalized
in divisions of internal medicine or neurology. Otherwise they are referred
to the other outpatient facilities—the community mental health centers and the

medical centers for social assistance—that deal with mental disorders and drug dependency, which include alcoholism and alcohol-related problems. Some regions have special alcohol units.

Referral to hospital may be direct, especially in the case of acute medical consequences of alcoholism or alcohol intoxication, or of previous hospital treatment with frequent relapses. Judicial referrals apply to multiple-drug users, which include alcoholics, but they account for less than 1% of referrals. Job-based referrals are negligible as there is no special provision for dealing with alcohol problems of workers.

Figure 3 also shows possible forms of cooperation between organizations concerned with alcoholism. Rarely, an alcoholic may be treated outside the health care system.

FIGURE 3

Pathways Offered to Alcoholic Patients in the Italian System

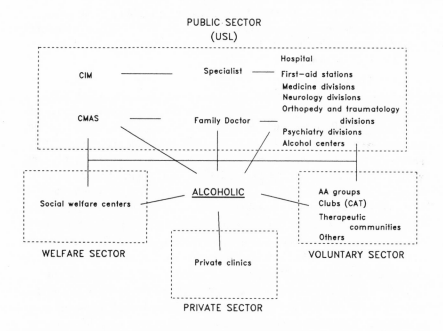

The impact of private clinics on the treatment of alcoholism is difficult to evaluate. They provide, under contract, space and services to the regions for public care. However, private institutions account for only 16% of hospital beds (ISTAT 1988). "Rejected" alcoholics may find their way to municipal social welfare centers.

In Italy, both the distribution of the alcohol treatment system and the expansion of services have been haphazard. In 1987, for example, only eight regions had alcohol units, and they were mainly in the northeast, and in Tuscany, Latium, and Apulia. More regions have medical centers for social assistance, especially those (such as Emilia-Romagna, Liguria, Marches, Umbria, Basilicata, and Sardinia) that have no alcohol units. This recent rapid expansion in the public sector has been exceeded in the voluntary sector. It is anomalous that the public health system has fewer facilities, in view of the magnitude of the alcohol problem. Medical centers and alcohol units that directly or indirectly offer alcohol treatment number 139 (12.7%) out of 1,096 public hospitals, a relatively high number compared with the few doctors who specialize in this treatment (no more than 700 out of 72,000, or less than 1%).

Treatment Rationales, and Treatment Demand and Acceptance

Owing to cultural influences, older family doctors often suggest to their alcoholic patients that they maintain moderate drinking. Specific alcohol-treatment programs, including all public treatment programs for alcoholics in the different regions, aim at strict abstinence. The treatment rationale is that alcoholism requires a multidisciplinary approach, including medical, psychological and social aspects.

One fairly standard method of treatment (known as the Hudolin method) in wide and increasing use, especially in northeast Italy, has been introduced by a group of Italian doctors who collaborate with the socio-medical programs of Zagreb, Yugoslavia (Poldrugo et al. 1980a). It consists of active psychosocial intervention, including education and prevention of alcoholism, through reality-oriented group sessions. It involves large groups extending to family and community members, assisted by members of different professions (doctors, psychologists, social workers, nurses, teachers, etc.). It includes prolonged follow-up directed to the reestablishment of social functions (Bennett 1985).

The question has been asked whether a model developed in Yugoslavia can be applied successfully in a different cultural context (Galanter 1981). However, there has been a diffusion of inpatient (alcohol units and services) and outpatient (day hospitals and dispensaries) facilities for alcohol treatment. Alcohol units are organized as separate units of departments of internal medicine, and services are provided mostly within these departments or in psychiatric wards. Dispensaries, being simple and economical, have enjoyed the greatest growth (Colusso 1988).

Major expansion and achievements have occurred in the rural areas. Moreover, the club system (discussed in the next section) has given families of alcoholics a community structure in which they feel accepted and reintegrated into society. This is because, in a society that sustains family unity, families can bear the burden of a problem drinker.

Evaluation studies are still lacking. Preliminary findings demonstrate clearly that these programs are more effective than the traditional medical management. Positive outcome rates are around 28%, compared with a previous 4%, a substantial result given that they accept all alcohol patients who present themselves for treatment (Poldrugo et al. 1980b; Fiore et al. 1989).

General data on treatment demand, or on the number of judicial or job-based referrals, are not available. This reflects a low awareness of alcohol problems, but, more generally, the undeveloped state of social research in Italy (Depretis and Donini 1980). Demand may be concentrated in certain areas, as in Friuli-Venezia Giulia, where the alcohol units are still burdened by alcoholics from areas that lack their own treatment facilities (in some cases alcoholics from other regions occupy more than 50% of beds and there are long waiting-lists).

There are also no data to indicate how physicians regard the treatment system. Medicine still reflects the cultural stigma attached to alcoholism. For example, among 351 randomly chosen patients in general hospitals (emergency units, divisions of medicine, surgery, neurology, etc.), in only one of every three cases of alcoholism and alcohol-related diseases did the diagnosis mention alcohol (De Maria et al. 1986). Medical education in Italy neglects alcoholism. Also, family doctors resist transferring patients to specific programs, because of the risk of losing their traditional patients. It is common for alcoholics entering the system of the alcohol units and of the voluntary organizations to attend only those doctors accredited to these facilities.

Alternative Treatment Resources as a Response to System Dysfunction

Institutional Experiments and Unconventional Methods

The medical sector has been responsible for only few institutional experiments or unconventional methods. Experimentation has depended mainly upon the professional experience and background of directors of psychiatric hospitals, and they have not been concerned particularly with alternative treatment resources. An interesting experience, with strong ideological influences, has been reported from the mental hospital of Gorizia, near the Yugoslav border (Casagrande 1968). It was there, in 1966, and with alcoholics, that the first Italian therapeutic community was introduced, following the model of Maxwell Jones (Jones 1953). It consisted of a self-organized community of alcoholics and members of the therapeutic team, which met daily. It began casually, owing to restoration works in the buildings. The alcoholics, who made up one-fourth of the psychiatric population, instituted an autonomous community, as they were unable to integrate themselves with the other patients. Alcoholics, doctors, and nurses shared the organization of the activities of the unit, which were directed toward demedicalization of social problems and resuming contacts with the outside world.

The experience with alcoholics was very successful. Friends and family members became associated with the community in an organized way, expanding its activities. A few years later, however, the alcohol unit was abolished on the grounds that it sought to perpetuate itself because of the alcoholics' need of interdependence, and this did not conform to the theory of Basaglia, which was influential at that time. The Basaglia school of thought denied the value of exclusive groups and held that psychiatric institutions should be closed down. Hence, all the patients were forced to leave the hospital (Mosher 1982). This theory influenced strongly the reform of psychiatric services, and its effects can be recognized in the Mental Health Act, which makes no reference to alcoholism or its treatment (Basaglia 1968).

Another therapeutic approach, which has been confined to the province of Vercelli (northwest Italy), is the hypnotic treatment of alcoholics, used for decades in the psychiatric hospital. Thousands of alcoholics have had the treatment, with positive results in 40% of cases (Granone 1971). It is an example of how a treatment program can become established without adequate consideration of the influences of social variables.

Self-Help Groups

Private and voluntary treatment facilities were established well in advance of public treatment systems. Owing to a lack of consistent official recognition of social problems, a network of "solidarity centers" was instituted in 1968, as a voluntary self-help organization. It was run by enterprising Catholic priests, to care for groups living on the margin of society. Such groups included people with mental disorders and alcohol problems, but mainly drug-dependence. Solidarity centers are now found in several of the principal cities of Italy.

Specific alcohol-treatment services were also organized privately. Alcoholics Anonymous was the first association to establish itself independently, in 1974 (Editoriale 1984). It began in the larger cities with American communities (Rome, Florence) and then spread throughout the country. Today there are about two hundred and forty active groups, in all the Italian regions. They cooperate with public health services, receiving alcoholics after discharge from hospital, and even organizing groups in hospital. They operate in the same way as in other countries, and include Al-Anon and Al-Teen groups.

The Clubs for Treated Alcoholics were organized later, in 1979. They began away from the center, at Trieste (Poldrugo et al. 1980a), near the Yugoslav border. They were "cross-fertilized" by a previous experience in Yugoslavia (Hudolin 1976). They are voluntary, nonprofit, self-help groups, with a close relationship with the public health system, and were established at the same time as the regional alcohol-treatment system (Buttolo et al. 1984). They number about six hundred and work with hospitals and health professionals; they undertake the care of alcoholics for five years after hospital discharge and operate under professional supervision. Originally the clubs were organized as autonomous bodies, but at present the public health sector tends to control their activities strictly and to merge them with public institutions. In some regions, as in Friuli-Venezia Giulia, they have received preferential recognition over other organizations in plans for alcohol treatment. There are about one hundred therapeutic communities.

Figure 5 shows the distribution of the principal organizations (Alcoholics Anonymous, Clubs for Treated Alcoholics, and Therapeutic Communities). The clubs, though more numerous than the Alcoholics Anonymous groups, are less dispersed, being found mostly in Friuli-Venezia Giulia and in the adjacent regions of Veneto and Trentino-Upper Adige. They serve mainly rural areas, whereas AA groups are found mostly in cities.

Discussion

General Summary

The history of the development of the alcohol treatment system may be divided into three periods. The first, comprising the 1950s and 60s, was characterized by a rapid increase in alcohol consumption and a complete lack of recognition of alcohol problems and specialized long-term care for alcoholics. The second period, encompassing the 1970s, saw stabilization of alcohol consumption and, especially among youth, the setting of new drinking patterns (Poldrugo, forthcoming). Drug dependence became a matter of growing concern, and new laws on alcohol treatment were enacted. The third period, beginning in the early 1980s, coincides with a downward trend in alcohol consumption, the beginning of public alcohol-treatment programs, in the spirit of the newly introduced national health service, and the growth of voluntary self-help organizations.

It is paradoxical that the expansion of the treatment system coincides with the tendency of alcohol consumption (Prina 1984) and alcohol-related mortality (Sponza et al. 1988) to decrease, for the first time.

Social policies are frequently only improvised, delegated to voluntary bodies, or complicated by bureaucracy. The decrease in alcohol consumption has resulted not from a strong national policy on alcohol control or from programs of prevention, but rather from fluctuations in the alcohol market.

The Future?

In Italy, several initiatives are flourishing in a field that was long neglected. Many others are likely to follow in the near future in the same haphazard way, especially in places where the public health sector is unwilling to take an initiative and where the demand for help is high.

The expansion of different treatment components will guarantee freedom of choice of alternative forms of treatment, which is not available today. At the same time it will introduce strong competition between the private and the public sector, and between voluntary organizations, for "good" alcoholic clients, and for preventive, educational, and rehabilitative roles. There are already signs of such competition.

A change in the state's official recognition and response to alcohol problems is expected with the introduction of measures to coordinate activities at the national level. This will be related to the introduction in the European Economic Community of common regulations for several problem areas (e.g., driving while intoxicated, and the prevention of job-related accidents).

International cooperation, comparing alcoholism and alcohol-related problems in different cultures, will contribute also to increasing awareness by the media and to the development of the Italian alcohol-treatment system.

References

Alberoni, F. 1987. *Pubblico e Privato*. Milan: Garzanti

Basaglia, F. 1968. Le istituzioni della violenza. In *L'Istituzione Negata*. Ed. F. Basaglia, 111–51. Turin: Einaudi.

Bennett, L. 1985. Treating alcoholics in a Yugoslav fashion. *Eastern European Quarterly* 18:495–519.

Bianchi Loconte et al. 1982. Social and cultural aspects of alcoholism. *Alcoholism* 18:80–93.

Bonfiglio, G., Falli, S. and Pacini, A. 1977. Alcoholism in Italy: an outline highlighting some special features. *British Journal of Addiction* 72:3–12.

Buttolo, R., G. B. Modonutti, and G. Lezzi. 1984. Un programma psico-medico-sociale per la prevenzione e il controllo dell'alcolismo in Friuli-Venezia Giulia. *Federazione Medica* 37:730–34.

Calcaterra, A. 1986. La legislazione sull'alcool in Italia. In *Giovani e Alcool*. Ed. A. Noventa and E. Zordan, 155–78. Turin: Edizioni Gruppo Abele.

Casagrande, D. 1968. Il reparto alcolisti. In *L'Istituzione Negata*. Ed. F. Basaglia, 136–46. Turin: Einaudi.

CENSIS (Centro Studi Interventi Sociali). 1983. *Consumi Italiani '83: Tradizione e Politeismo*. Milan: Angeli.

Colusso, G. 1988. Veneto: una realtà in divenire. In *Alcolismo*. Ed. V. Hudolin, 153–62. Bologna: Episteme.

De Maria, F., et al. 1986. *Alcolismo*. Problemi diagnostici e prognostici. Trieste: Edizioni Lint.

Depretis L., and G. Donini. 1980. Analisi del problema dell'acolismo giovanile. *Rivesta di Psichiatria* 15:515–28.

Derossi, L., A. R. Favretto, and A. Rolli. 1986. Immagini ed esperienze dei problemi alcool correlati in un'indagine pilota in Piemonte. *Antropologia Medica* 2:37–47.

Editoriale. 1984. 1200 punti di riferimento per dire stop all'alcool. *Il Defino* 12:21–40.

FAO (Food and Agriculture Organization). 1965–1982. Trade Yearbook 25–36. Rome: Food and Agriculture Organization.

Favaretti, G. 1983. Importanza economica delle bevande alcoliche. *Rivista Italiana di Alcologia* 2:33–35.

Fiore, A., C. Milievich, and F. Poldrugo. 1989. Evaluation of an Italian program for the treatment of alcoholism. *Alcoholism* 25:57–61.

Galanter M. 1981. Alcoholism programs in the USSR and Yugoslavia: effects of the social context on treatment. In *Current in Alcoholism.* Ed. M. Galanter, 8:183–94. New York: Grune and Stratton.

Granone, F. 1971. L'Ipnositerapia nel divezzamento degli alcolisti. *Alcoholism* 7:121–47.

Hudolin, V. 1976. The control of alcoholism. *The International Journal of Mental Health* 5:85–105.

ISPES (Istituto Studi Politici Economici e Sociali). 1985. *I rapporto sull'alcolismo in Italia.* Rome: ISPES.

ISTAT (Istituto Centrale di Statistica). 1955–1982. *Statistica Annuale del Commercio con l'Estero.* Rome: ISTAT.

———. 1983–1985. *Annuario di Statistiche Sanitarie.* Rome: ISTAT.

———. 1988. *Le Regioni in Cifre.* Rome: ISTAT.

Jellinek, E. M. 1976. Italy. In *Jellinek Working Papers on Drinking Patterns and Alcohol Problems.* Ed. R. E. Popham, monograph no. 804. Toronto: Addiction Research Foundation.

Jones, M. 1953. *The therapeutic community: A new treatment method in psychiatry.* New York: Basic Books.

Lolli, G., et al. 1952. The use of wine and other alcoholic beverages by a group of Italians and Americans of Italian extraction. *Quarterly Journal of Studies on Alcohol* 13:27-48.

Madeddu, A. 1969. Aspetti clinici, statistche e terapie dell'alcolismo. Pp. 229–246 In *Proceedings of the 14th International Institute on the Prevention and Treatment of Alcoholism.* Milan.

Mangano, M., and M. G. Mangano. 1969. *L'Alcolismo e i suoi Riflessi sul Lavoro.* Rome: Istituto Italiano di Medicina Sociale.

Modonutti, G. B., R. Buttolo, and E. Crevatin. 1987. L'Alcolismo in Friuli-Venezia Giulia. *Bolletino per le Farmacodipendenze e l'Alcolismo* 10:347–67.

Morgan, P. 1984. Industrialization, urbanization, and the attack on Italian drinking culture. *Contemporary Drug Problems,* 1984.

Mosher, L. R. 1982. Italy's revolutionary mental health law. An assessment. *American Journal of Psychiatry* 139:199–203.

Poldrugo, F., et al. 1980a. A catamnestic one year duration report on a group of alcoholics treated by the Psychiatric Clinic of the University of Trieste. *Alcoholism* 16:52–55.

Poldrugo, F., et al. 1980b. Treating a group of alcoholics: preliminary remarks after a six month experience. *Mediterranean Journal of Social Psychiatry* 1:106–111.

Poldrugo, F., G. B. Modonutti, and R. Buttolo. 1985. Alcoholism and alcohol-related problems in Italy today. *Alkoholpolitik* 2:163–72.

Poldrugo, F., and E. Aguglia. n.d. Evaluation of alcohol treatment programs. *The Alabama Journal of Medical Sciences.*

Powell, M. 1987. Data note. 8. Alcohol data in the European Community. *British Journal of Addiction* 82:559–66.

Prina, F. 1984. Alcool, società e stato in Italia. In *Alcool, Società e Stato,* Ed. Gruppe Abele, 129–79. Turin.

Sponza, S., et al. 1988. Statistical recording systems and monitoring of alcoholism in Friuli-Venezia Giulia, Italy. In *System Science in Health Care, 1, Information in Health Care Systems.* Ed. G. Duru et al., 133–36. Paris: Masson.

Terzian, H. 1982. La cultura della vigna e del vino. In *Patologia e Problemi Connessi all'Uso Inadeguato di Alcolici* 17–30. Venezia: Giunta Regionale del Veneto.

The Rise of Alcohology in France:
A Monopolistic Competition

Philippe Mossé

France has always shown a certain ambivalence toward alcoholism. Its rates of production and consumption are among the world's highest. Although the trend is decreasing—from 22 liters per adult per year in 1970 to 17 liters in 1986—alcohol-related mortality and morbidity are still high. At the same time, prevention and treatment policies are weak. Most observers consider that the French treatment system, while offering many possibilities for treatment, lacks coherent or rational organization.

The growth and apparently arbitrary development of treatment networks, which began just after World War II, owe nothing to government policy but much to professional interests. Previously, alcoholism was considered not a medical problem but almost exclusively a matter of direct social control. Of course, there were establishments and institutions that sheltered alcoholics or hid them from public view, but alcoholism was not recognized as a disease or even as a separate entity. It was placed in a gray area of marginality somewhere between degeneracy and perversion. Moreover, only some alcoholics were viewed in this way. Those whose behavior led to drunkenness rather than to antisocial conduct were not often excluded from social life; they even contributed to the strengthening of social bonds and traditions. For the others, "degeneration" and "repression" were the key words, and there was a total lack of treatment. Leveille's book *Histoire de la Folie des Ivrognes,* published in 1830, reflects well the medical thought of the period: the effects of excessive consumption of alcoholic beverages were not a medical concern (Sournia 1987). Villerme's observations on the role and place of alcohol among the masses were limited to moral questions and had no implications for treatment (Villerme 1840). Only several years later, with the rise of the idea of alcoholism as a disease, could the structuring of a system of treatment begin.

Institutions: A Segmentation Process

France like most Western countries has always tended toward ever greater integration of the health-care system—a tendency to create and control networks of health-care institutions, largely separate from, but informally connected and interacting with, general health care. However, this tendency has not extended to the financing of the system, since its evolution has been influenced mainly by professional interests. The alcohol treatment system has followed this pattern. The state has played a major role in this process, begun in the late 1960s by an active sector of the medical profession eager for recognition and specialization.

To describe the treatment institutions is to describe the achievements of a profession in constant change, affected by oversupply of manpower and increasing specialization and segmentation, gradually becoming aware of the potential of alcoholism as a medical specialty.

Until 1954 the administrative authorities regulated almost all forms of patient placement, in accordance with the 1838 law on mental patients. This law is still applied in certain cases of compulsory confinement of psychiatric patients. The 1954 law on "dangerous alcoholics" provided for the transfer of this role to a health official, who would carry out a medical examination and decide whether a social inquiry should be made to assess the extent to which alcoholic behavior represented a danger to the family or community.

Institutions for "Dangerous Alcoholics"

Until about 1950, intervention mostly meant confinement, with no prospect of treatment, since the confinement system of the time lacked any treatment methods or facilities. Custodial care was used instead of a rehabilitation system for alcoholics and mental patients until the beginning of the twentieth century. The 1954 law provided for the intervention of specialized clinics and, under Article 1, for all "dangerous alcoholics" to be placed under the supervision of health care authorities, thus according the alcoholic the status of a patient.

However, this statute created more obligations than rights. Under Article 8, any patient who refused treatment or interrupted it "by leaving the hospital without permission" could be fined or imprisoned. The alcoholic, once diagnosed and recognized as such (and whether or not he had committed a crime), was totally "cared for" by the community.

The effect of the 1954 law, supplemented by decrees in July 1955 and March 1956, was to turn over to psychiatrists the task of treating alcoholics. Today, alcoholics diagnosed under the provisions of the 1954 law account for little more than 1% of the patients treated in the specialized units created specially for them under Article 5; these units were "centers of specialized reeducation" responsible for the detoxification and reeducation of alcoholics. This failure to establish the planned number of those specialized units can be explained by the lack of financial means, but it was due mainly to the largely outdated concept of alcoholism upon which the law was based (Ropert and Collin 1975).

In 1965 some 550 beds were available in thirteen centers, all attached to already existing psychiatric hospitals, although legislators estimated that 13,000 were needed. In February 1982 the registers of the Ministry of Health counted only nineteen centers, of which only twelve were in psychiatric hospitals (or 400 of 732 beds). Thus the specialized centers created by the 1954 law still exist but their clientele has changed. Dangerous alcoholics, as defined in the law, have practically disappeared.

Facilities for Early Treatment

The recognition of the failure to provide the planned number of specialized units changed fundamentally the conditions for admission into psychiatric hospitals, and therefore into their specialized centers. This led the Ministry of Health to issue a directive in November 1970, making a new facility, the Centre d'Hygiène Alimentaire (CHA), responsible for screening and diagnosis. This directive was inspired largely by the theories of Professor Le Go, a physician in the national railway system who developed and tested a clinical screening test known as *grille de Le Go*. The aim of the Ministry of Health was to reduce the predominance of psychiatry in the treatment of alcoholism and to open it up to the various health and social professions, who would support physicians in their work. These centers were not neutral in their conception, but reflected the greater part of medical thought. They saw their role as assisting in the screening and diagnostic functions of facilities that lacked certain essential skills.

Though the creation of these centers may not have been a turning point, it represented at least an important phase in the evolution of legislators' attitudes toward the diagnosis and treatment of alcoholics. In a directive of July 31, 1975, once again recommending the creation of CHAs and specifying how to create them, the Ministry of Health again emphasized the need to reduce the role of psychiatrists and to avoid giving the public the impression that the treatment of alcoholism was part of the campaign against mental illness.

The notion of alcoholism is not reflected in the name of the center, for the theoretical reasons that Le Go explained: "If one highly positive test almost certainly leads to the positive diagnosis of alcoholic impregnation, the test must be repeated frequently in order to confirm addiction." Under these conditions "it is preferable not to inform the patient prematurely of one's suspicions. On the contrary, one must await the certainty of a positive diagnosis."

With the development of alcohology and the effort to have it recognized as a medical specialty, the need arose to establish clearly the actual or desired qualifications of the professional teams who worked in the CHAs. Thus it became necessary to change the name of the centers.

Integrated Institutions

In 1982 Professor Barrucand wrote:

The idea that the role of the CHA is first of all to diagnose heavy drinkers,
notorious alcoholics, being too weighty for that institution, seems to have
become a thing of the past in most cases. . .the time seems to have come
(or soon will), while allowing those institutions which so desire to retain
the name Centre d'Hygiène Alimentaire (CHA), to change it to Centre
d'Hygiène Alimentaire et d'Alcoologie (CHAA) or even to Centre
d'Alcoologie (CA) (Barrucand 1982, 225).

Thus, in less than twenty years, the designation of the centers changed from
Centre d'Hygiène Mentale to Centre d'Hygiène Alimentaire, to today's Centre
d'Alcoologie.

At the same time, greater coordination of screening and treatment
facilities seemed theoretically justified. Once again, a ministerial directive was
issued, reinforcing, confirming, and activating this evolution, and using the
same terms as alcohologists. A 1983 directive of the Ministry of Health
announced the transformation of the CHAs to reflect the changes they had
undergone: "a good number of CHAs provide other services for their
patients. . .Originally conceived as facilities for the prevention of alcohol abuse,
CHAs have become prevention and treatment facilities. . .these
changes. . .reduce the need for a nutritional hygiene approach. . .It is preferable
to change the name Centre d'Hygiène Alimentaire to Centre d'Hygiène
Alimentaire et d'Alcoologie". The directive also stated that those institutions
wishing to call themselves Centres d'Alcoologie might do so. In accordance
with the obvious dominance of the idea of specialization, almost all of the one
hundred and fifty or so CHAs in the country have added the term *d'Alcoologie*
to their names. Moreover, most are run by hospital physicians; many are located
in general hospitals, although their personnel is often multidisciplinary (doctors,
nurses, social workers, etc.).

As early as 1969, the National Committee of Defense against Alcoholism
(CNDA) strongly recommended that screening in CHAs be followed up by
treatment in general hospitals; hence the establishment of specialized services
in each hospital. However, the 1970 directive, supplemented in 1975, made
no mention of this point; it even favored the placing of CHAs outside hospitals
to permit closer contact with the population.

It was only in 1978 that legislators decided to encourage systematic
treatment in general hospitals. The arguments successfully used twenty years
earlier to justify a quasi-monopoly for specialized centers were now evoked
to condemn the ghetto that that solution represented for alcoholics. Specialized
beds (and no longer services or establishments) were conceived of as a means

of mixing alcoholic patients with other patients; they would accommodate all alcoholics who had previously been dispersed among various hospital services. The therapeutic objective was clear: that of allowing a specific though multidisciplinary approach to the disease of alcoholism and to alcoholic patients hospitalized for nonalcoholic conditions.

It is still too early to evaluate the implementation of the 1978 directive. However, it accords with both the evolution of medical thought, increasingly in favor of the medical treatment of alcoholism, and the rapid development of CHAs directly linked to nonpsychiatric hospital services (mainly general medicine and gastroenterology). It corresponds with the efforts of the medical profession to link screening and treatment facilities in one institution. In this way, unlike the 1954 law, the directives of 1970 and 1978 satisfied a need.

As a conclusion to this brief overview, it may be said that today's screening and treatment facilities represent a series of historical layers, all of which now coexist. Each has its historical background, its corresponding following in the profession, and sometimes even its historical leader. They include, along with the few specialized detoxification units, psychiatric services in specialized hospitals and in general hospitals, the various Centres—d'Hygiène Mentale, d'Hygiène Alimentaire, d'Hygiène Alimentaire et d'Alcoologie, and d'Alcoologie. It might be concluded from this structure that each type of facility corresponds to a certain type of therapy. However, seemingly similar institutions differ in their treatment systems, programs, and methods. Different medical teams use varieties of methods.

Methods and Practices

Screening Methods

In the past decade, two reliable screening methods have become available to practitioners. The older of the two, the *grille de Le Go,* was developed in the 1960s; it consists of a questionnaire based on clinical observation. Thanks to a series of well-balanced criteria, it permits the classification of individuals into various categories of drinkers, and the identification of "heavy drinkers" in need of treatment. More recently, in the early 1970s, a biological test—gamma GT—was developed. It measures the blood level of an enzyme (gamma glutamyltransferase) that appears in response to ethyl alcohol.

The first method depends clearly and almost exclusively upon the clinical sense and to a certain extent the subjective judgment of the physician. The second is an objective measure, expressed as a biological variable, of a given level of chronic alcoholism (Gauteret and Bourmis 1983). Certain comparative studies of the two methods have concluded that in most cases both should be used (Playoust 1979). In practice, however, they are rarely used together: "For early diagnosis it was customary to use the *grille de Le Go,* which takes into account several variables: facial features, trembling, personal problems, each being given a quantitative value: unfortunately, the score is subjective. . . Today we generally use. . . the gamma GT test, which is particularly reliable" (Aron 1981).

The acceptance of the gamma GT test in France, supported mainly by gastroenterologists in teaching hospitals, is clearly in line with the growing domination of biology over traditional medical techniques.

Although the *grille de Le Go* is used less and less, it still has followers in the old-style Centres d'Hygiène Alimentaires, among general practitioners and in occupational medicine.

Treatment Methods

As for treatment, there seems to be general agreement that "a good rehabilitation technique should be a happy medium of two therapies, one with an antitoxic aim, the other with a psychological aim" (Duflot 1971). The problem is one of the degree of complementarity or incompatibility between these two aims, as well as of determining a practical, quantitative balance between the components of a global therapy. Traditionally, therapy is considered as having three main components, which may be presented as a progression.

Medical therapy. The rationale of medical therapy is that people take alcohol because they suffer from depression or anxiety. Therapy is directed to the reduction of these conditions with antidepressants or tranquilizers. Once the symptoms have disappeared, the desire to drink disappears, without requiring more sophisticated treatment. This method is generally used in ambulatory practice and in general hospitals.

Psychotherapy. Psychotherapy assumes that alcoholism is often the result of neurosis. For certain psychiatrists, this is a modern concept of alcoholism, regarding alcohol abuse and alcoholism as symptoms, not a disease. Irrespective of etiology, all physicians consider that at least some psychotherapy is indispensable. The degree of intensity of the psychotherapeutic support varies with the practice and the specialties of doctors; it may be supplemented by medication or placebos. In some cases it is merely a matter of simple counseling; in others it may take the form of regular sessions of deep psychotherapy or even psychoanalysis.

Aversion therapy. Aversion therapy is justified by a simple assertion: "without alcohol, no alcoholism". Apparently, it is because aversion therapy is associated directly with the old concept of alcoholism as a vice and treatment as punishment that it is no longer used alone. Modern techniques tend to reduce the alcoholic's suffering; in this context the evolution of the techniques can be seen as favorable. It extends from the use of apomorphine ("the patient must be forced to drink and must not be considered as cured until vomiting and disgust are provoked by the sight of a glass"), to Professor Champeau's technique, which, while respecting the Pavlovian process, associates thirst with the thirst-quenching impression given by water, without using excessively sadistic methods.

The difficulty of producing a cure, rather than strengthening empirical or even haphazard medical practices, has the effect that doctors must have the assurance of a theoretical justification for their methods. However, no published reports of studies permit a strict comparison of different methods of treatment in different places, nor do they support definitively any specific form of treatment (most success rates run around 30%) (Svoboda 1984). Also, no study permits a strict comparison of the methods, clienteles, and results of different facilities. However, research along these lines is currently being done under the auspices of the Société Française d'Alcoologie, a recently created society of over four hundred members, of whom 70% are physicians (Favre et al. 1988).

The Division of Labor

The profusion of treatment facilities and the wide range of therapeutic techniques are usually perceived as a wealth of treatment resources at the disposal of alcoholic patients. For practitioners, there will never be too many medical teams to care for alcoholics. From this profusion, it can be concluded that "hundreds of thousands of alcoholics owe to chance their orientation toward one treatment institution or another" (Svoboda 1984) and that therefore there is no treatment system as such. This is a simplistic observation at best; it would be more correct to say that something other than medical reasoning is at work in the organization of the treatment system.

The alcoholism market and the "consumers" population that consists of alcoholics at any given moment remain limited, although they may seem extensible when considered as a function of the potential of supply services. Moreover, only relatively few institutions control the essential resources, the facilities, and even the policy behind the creation or development of screening or treatment facilities. Any increase on the part of other individuals or professional groups would only be to the detriment of those already involved. Thus what M. Foucault (1972) might have called the "problematization" of alcoholism in medical thought takes two forms: competition among physicians, leading to specialization, and recognition of specialists on the part of their peers and the state.

Since at least the 1960s, when alcohology became an independent discipline, the political and economic stakes in the debates and interventions on the subject have been, along with the question of how to regulate the alcoholic, those of the definition and choice of those on whom society and public authorities confer the right to provide care. Professor H. Pequignot, explaining the viewpoint of a hospital physician, said in 1973: "the treatment of the alcoholic would pose many fewer problems if all the hospital services and social services were to accept the patient and organize themselves . . . Thus it should be the 'specialists' who come to the patients and not the patients who should be moved about from place to place: this implies teamwork, a close collaboration between doctors within a medical service'' (Pequignot 1973).

The theoretical geography of the treatment system, particularly where hospitals are concerned, is based on the anatomy of the human body. Therapeutic reasoning would have, for example, decompensating cirrhosis patients placed in the gastroenterology unit and polyneuritis patients in neurology, or treated by the corresponding specialists. However, there are many exceptions to this rule (Mossé 1987).

For alcoholics, the problem is posed in the same way as for the mentally ill: it is a question of giving society the means to use both the penal and the civil levels, depending on the evolution of the family and the social environment, as well as on the course of the disease of alcoholism itself. This implies the existence of a network of diagnostic, rehabilitation, and supervisory or follow-up services organized around one or several hospital services. The regulations do no more than apply in practice this modern concept of psychiatric illness.

Developed mainly with the aim of maintaining psychiatric patients close to their social environment, and a direct product of antipsychiatry theories, "sectorization" became official policy in 1970. Patients are allocated to particular psychiatric units according to their place of residence, and alcoholic patients in mental hospitals may be treated in nonspecialized units, depending on the availability of the nearest hospital.

Some alcohologists advocate the application of the same principle to improve even further the treatment of alcoholics by the designation of *intersecteurs* (equivalent to catchment areas) in alcohology, as in child psychiatry. The *intersecteur* and its treatment unit would be responsible for treating all alcoholics living in a given area and would render more efficient and continuous the system designed for their diagnosis, treatment, and follow-up. For reasons of economy of scale the *intersecteur* may be larger than the areas defined by sectorization.

Financing

The financial regulations of alcohol treatment institutions are the same as those for the health-care system in general. Anyone may enter the system to attend a specialist or a generalist, without major restriction. In most cases health insurance coverage is sufficient to avoid any economic discrimination. However, in view of the multifaceted nature of the illness, most of the different kinds of treatment agency are liable to treat the alcoholic at some point in the course of the disease. These agencies may be financed in different ways and hence variety is the rule in the domain of financing of treatment of alcoholism.

The national health system covers about 98% of the French population. It is funded mainly by contributions of workers and employers. Health-care costs are covered in a wide variety of ways, depending on patient and treatment categories. On the average, the system covers about 70% of the costs, the rest being covered by private insurance or by the patient. Thus, consultations and visits to private practitioners are reimbursed at a rate of 75% of the fixed fees. These fees are negotiated between medical unions and public authorities. The system is more complex for hospitalization, which depends on the status of the patient and the establishment vis-à-vis the national health system. Usually, the patient must pay a considerable share of the costs, in the form of a *ticket modérateur*—a part of the costs of care that the patient must pay. This can be waived in the case of mental illness and also, in exceptional cases, if the consulting physician, an employee of the national social security system, so decides. In the latter case, the consulting physician makes a decision upon examination of a request from the patient's doctor. The first condition is fulfilled when the patient is hospitalized in a psychiatric service.

Recently, the High Committee for Studies and Information on Alcoholism (HCEIA) stated the conditions in the following terms: "The patient is covered by Social Security at 80% and pays the *ticket modérateur,* that is, 20%. At the request of the hospital physician, the detoxification treatment can be covered at 100% in two cases:

1. If treatment requires long and costly therapy. In this case, however, the regional consulting physician must consent, as alcoholism is not included in the list of twenty-five diseases for which total reimbursement is officially sanctioned.
2. If the treatment given enters into the framework of the treatment of mental illness" (HCEIA 1986).

Exceptionally, alcoholic cirrhosis being one of the twenty-six "long and costly" diseases, its treatment is reimbursed at 100%, whatever form it takes (visits, medication, paramedical care, etc.).

Ultimately, hospitals take up about 50% of the cost of the treatment of alcoholic patients in the French system.

Research carried out in 1980 on a sample of alcoholics hospitalized in southern France found that, over a three-year period, each patient had, on an average, sixty-four contacts with the health-care system (of which four were hospitalizations), incurring an average total cost of 70,000 francs (about US $12,000) to the national health system (Mossé 1987). It showed also that the marked differences observed in treatment costs were due mainly to differences in how physicians distributed their patients within the health care system, which was not related to patients' social or economic status. Reforms in hospital financing have not changed this distribution or the costs charged to patients.

However, two anomalies have arisen that may impair the coherence of the coverage system. The first is a change in the financing of the public system from a cost-per-day system to a global annual budget fixed in advance. It was meant to rationalize treatment costs by avoiding longer periods of hospitalization than the state of health of patients warranted. However, as private establishments continue to be financed on a cost-per-day basis, the effect has been that the public sector tends to emphasize acute care and early discharge, and the private sector continuing postcure care. However, there is so far no evidence that this anomaly is affecting the way people are treated.

The second anomaly is the artificial separation of inpatient and outpatient psychiatric care, by the different ways in which they are financed. Social Security covers inpatient costs, in accordance with the new global budgeting procedure. Outpatients, however, come under the "sectorization" system, whereby the state finances the treatment and prevention activities of decentralized clinics in a totally different way. An attempt in 1985–87 at harmonizing the financing of the two lasted only a short time. There is a risk that the coherence of treatment policies and the provision of coverage for alcoholic patients will be undermined by the inconsistent behavior of the medical profession and the conflict between interests of economy and those of financial gain.

Statistics on Alcoholism

The Ministry of Health is responsible for maintaining and updating statistics on the numbers and characteristics of people treated for alcoholism, as part of its general responsibility for morbidity and mortality statistics. It also monitors the reliability and coherence of the data collected from various sources. Despite repeated efforts to improve the system, the statistics concerning morbidity in general and alcohol-related morbidity in particular remain of poor quality. It is common to find large discrepancies between officially published data and those quoted in the literature. There is a great temptation to rely more on monographic studies than on exhaustive investigations. The former show alcoholism to be a widespread problem, accounting for up to 40% of admissions to departments of general medicine, while the latter give it a marginal role in morbidity or hospitalization. This inconsistency shows that it is not enough merely to list the principal sources: the validity and quality of the data must be assessed.

The multiplicity of treatment facilities increases the difficulty of obtaining precise statistics. Moreover, like most other patients with long-term diseases, alcoholics come in contact with a wide variety of facilities during their illness, and this can lead to confusion.

Statistics on Treated Populations

Hospital statistics. There are two main systems of hospital statistics, based on fairly different concepts. The more reliable and exhaustive system concerns psychiatric institutions and, more recently, psychiatric services in general hospitals. It refers to alcoholism under two headings: alcoholic psychosis and chronic alcoholism. These statistics, gathered by the National Institute of Health and Medical Research (INSERM) over more than twenty years, present difficulties owing to the change that took place in 1968 in the nomenclature of mental illnesses. The term "alcoholic psychosis" was retained but "chronic alcoholism" was replaced by the term "alcoholism," which includes acute intoxication. However, this change had less effect than might be expected on the feasibility of studies over a long period.

Hospital data from the second source are of much poorer quality. They consist of morbidity statistics collected by general, not psychiatric, hospitals and maintained by the Ministry of Health. For many reasons—but mainly the lack of feedback to the originating units—these statistics are no longer used. Moreover, the ministry's hospital management section has initiated an overhaul of the hospital information system, known as Projet de Médicalisation du Système d'Information. This system, inspired directly by the American Diagnostic Related Groups (DRG) system, will not fill the gap between the actual prevalence of alcohol-related problems in hospital patients and their poor representation in hospital morbidity statistics. However, it is planned to collect information on secondary diagnoses (up to five per patient discharged); thus the notion of "risk factor" will be better accounted for. The main advantage of this new system is that doctors themselves will be involved in the coding. It will take several years, however, before all French general hospitals routinely adopt this procedure.

This applies only to public hospitals; data on the activities and clienteles of private establishments come to light only rarely, as a result of occasional, probably unrepresentative, surveys.

Statistics on ambulatory treatment. Since 1963 the Institute for Documentation and Research on Diseases (IDREM) has carried out annual inquiries into the diagnoses made by a sample of fifteen hundred family practitioners. The findings are then extrapolated to represent all of private medical practice over a year. An analysis of the results for the period 1966–1980 reveals the evolution of the diagnosis "alcoholism" in private practice. The first finding is that the frequency of this diagnosis is low and has diminished progressively over the period, from 0.57% to 0.35% (Figure 1).

The very low incidence and prevalence rates of alcoholism indicated by these statistics cannot be considered a reliable or true representation of alcoholism in the private sector of medicine, but this type of information helps in understanding stigmatizing behavior and any changes that might occur in such behavior.

FIGURE 1

Visits for Alcoholism in Ambulatory Medicine

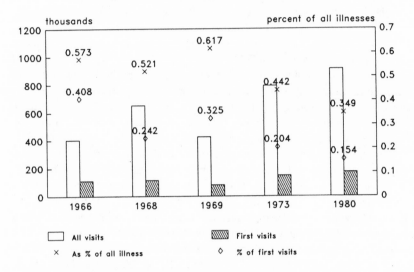

☐	All visits		▨	First visits
×	As % of all illness		◇	% of first visits

Attempts at synthesis. On the whole, we can thus conclude that available statistics, whether from hospitals or from ambulatory practice, are not sufficient for a proper assessment of the prevalence of alcohol-related illnesses. To fill the information gap, several public and private research bodies have tried to collect or obtain original information. Thus, true to one of the missions assigned to it upon its foundation in 1954, HCEIA published a study covering the period 1970–76, a regrettably short period, and covering only part of the country's hospital treatment facilities (Table 1) (HCEIA 1981).

Another study, covering a longer period (1961–1977), undertaken by two researchers of the INED (Mejle and Vallin 1981) found that, though the ratio of patients in psychiatric hospitals to the general population diminished appreciably, that of patients with alcoholism did not. Rather, the percentage of admissions into psychiatric hospitals for alcoholism increased from 41 to 45% for men, while decreasing from 10.6 to 10.2% for women. The authors of this study, which only touched on hospitalization in psychiatric hospitals, considered the relative growth in hospitalizations for alcoholism to be due either to a real increase in the problem or to the failure to integrate alcoholism into the sectorization policy. The HCEIA study suggests that the medicalization of alcoholism is a general phenomenon, not specific to psychiatric hospitalization.

The increase in absolute numbers of patients hospitalized for alcoholism has not been equally distributed among the different units meant to treat them.

TABLE 1

Distribution and Evolution of Discharges:
Alcoholism and Mental Illnesses, 1970–1976

	Distribution of hospitalized alcoholics by facility		Growth rate		Percentage of alcoholics among psychiatric patients	
	1970	1976	All mental	Alcoholism	1970	1976
General services in general hospitals	67.2%	75.9%	60%	75.9%	37.8%	41.4%
Psychiatric hospitals and psychiatric patients in general hospitals	32.8%	24.1%	72.4%	69.3%	23.4%	22.9%
TOTAL	100	100	65.9%	73.7%	31.4%	32.9%

In 1970, two-thirds of the alcoholic patients discharged had been in general hospitals; in 1976, this proportion, already high, grew to more than three-fourths. At the same time, the percentage of alcoholics among mental patients rose from 37.8 to 41.4% in general hospitals but decreased somewhat in psychiatric hospitals. Thus from 1970 to 1976 there was a relative diminution of the role of psychiatry in the treatment of alcoholism, but this role is still substantial.

Mortality Statistics

In principle, the obligation to certify cause of death should result in reliable statistics on deaths caused by alcoholism (whether as the immediate, the initial, or even an associated cause). In practice, these statistics must be treated with caution. Doctors are commonly reluctant to certify death as due to cirrhosis of the liver. Hence gross statistics attribute only 60% of cases of cirrhosis to alcohol, although an INSERM study has shown the proportion to be 80–90%. The same applies to the other two conditions—alcoholic psychosis and alcoholism—officially listed as due to alcohol.

At the same time it must be remembered that a number of certificates do not specify cause of death or define it badly or attribute it to senility. These statistics are available and often published by HCEIA according to age, sex, and geographic region. Certain studies provide also mortality rates by cause and by major occupational categories. For more precise data, specific studies are needed. The most recent date from 1982.

A recent series of studies by Damiani and Masse deal with illnesses in which alcohol plays a causal role. They set out to determine the influence of alcoholism on differences in mortality rates. After S. Ledermann, they were able to show that alcohol contributed significantly to the higher level of male mortality around age fifty as well to the high mortality rates in northeastern and western France.

Various Other Sources

Other sources of data are the social security and the judiciary systems. The former need certain data for purposes of reimbursing the costs of treatment of several illnesses linked to alcohol and covered 100%. The latter use data to identify individuals who have committed offenses while under the influence of alcohol and of whom some are in need of medical treatment. Another source, available since 1986, is a data bank called Alco Info, containing a limited number of very general figures, and which any citizen can consult by telephone. It is kept up to date by Dr. Barrucand's team at Nancy.

Alternative Treatment Resources

Along with medical treatment, both inpatients and outpatients can take part in group therapy, organized and directed by associations of former alcoholics. The great diversity of these associations permits patients to join groups of their own choice, as compatible as possible with their occupational or sociocultural background. They often counsel alcoholics to seek treatment, and refer patients to specialized establishments, which the associations run themselves. Their principal function is to recruit new members on their discharge from treatment, especially from hospital. The members undertake to play an active part in the association and, in turn, the association assists in their reinsertion into society and in consolidating their abstinence. They are not considered passive patients: the psychotherapeutic support they receive is designed to enable them to care for themselves. Such groups help reduce the alienation often associated with alcoholism. Patients compare their experience with that of recovered patients and no longer feel isolated and different.

Self-Help Groups

France has a large number of associations of former alcoholics, probably more than a hundred. Most have a corporate basis, such as *Joie et Santé* and *Amitiés,* which are associated with large companies, usually state-owned, such as the railway and airlines systems and the national electricity and gas companies. In these associations the key role is often that of the occupational physician, who establishes the connection between the company and the health-care system, without having the right to treat employees. Others are smaller associations concerned with distinct groups sometimes organized around sects or religious movements considered as marginal in France. However, the four principal such associations are the national branches of international groups: *La Croix Bleue* (the Blue Cross), a Protestant group founded in Switzerland at the end of the nineteenth century; *Vie Libre* (Free Life) a more recent lay organization; *la Croix d'Or* (the Gold Cross), which is Catholic in origin; and Alcoholics Anonymous, probably the largest, with some two hundred groups throughout the country, particularly in the cities.

Relations with Official Structures

At one time the temperance associations strongly distrusted the medical profession, but recently a rapprochement between the two has resulted in the temperance associations being recognized as one of the means by which the health care system can maintain contact with the alcoholics. Their members inform hospital patients about the temperance movement, thus attracting new members. Not only is this of therapeutic value to the patients but also it permits the associations, through the medical staff of the hospitals, to maintain contact with the entire treatment system (Laharpe and Blicke 1985). Nevertheless there is a certain element of competition as well as cooperation with the official health care system. They run many postcure centers, or halfway houses, and are thus more than simple back-up groups for the medical profession. Their recruitment networks are based on personal contact more than on any administrative or geographic division, to which official facilities, especially psychiatric institutions, are confined.

In his *Histoire de l'Alcoolisme,* Sournia (1987) points out that these associations, "by devoting themselves to alcoholics, leave nonalcoholics in peace, in no longer trying to put society on the straight and narrow." This brusque observation is no doubt valid; above all it reflects the relatively medicalized character of the associations. Sournia's comments throw more light on what might be called the French strategy for dealing with alcoholism, considered less often as a preventive or public-health approach than one geared to treatment of individual alcoholics.

Conclusion

Today, in France many years after the recognition of alcoholism as a disease, its treatment is the object of strong competition within the medical profession. What is as stake is control of the treatment network, from the screening phase to follow-up care, although such control would not conform to the fragmentation of the French health-care delivery system. Nonetheless, a part of the profession, recently grouped under the banner of "Alcohology," advocates such controls, but even this group has its divisions. The arms used in this competition are usually symbolic in nature, with the state playing the role of referee. To do so, it issues laws and decrees, turning leadership over to clinicians, psychiatrists, biologists, or other professionals.

The state's direct field of activity is concerned especially with managing and improving the quality of the statistics it collects on morbidity and mortality. It has made much progress in this respect, but much remains to be done to make prevention and treatment policies coherent and consistent. It can be done only by an enlightened state.

Note

This chapter was prepared with the support of the Haut Comité d'Etude et d'Information sur l'Alcoolisme.

References

Aron, E. 1981. Le clinicien face au buveur excessif. *Institut de Recherches Scientifiques Economiques et Sociales sur les Boissons*, 14–27. Paris.

Barrucand, D. 1982. Alcoologie. Riom: Laboratoires Riom.

Damiani, P., and H. Masse. 1988. *L'alcoolisme en chiffre.* HCEIA:143.

Duflot, M. 1971. La cure de désintoxication. Thèse Amiens: 120 pp.

Favre, J. D., C. Gillet, and A. Patris. 1988. Au terme de l'intrusion dans l'étude EVA. *Bulletin de la SFA,* 01.01.1988.

Foucault M. 1972. *Histoire de la folie à l'âge classique.* Paris: Gallimard.

Gauteret, J., and B. Bourmis. 1983. Lutte contre l'alcoolisme, les chercheurs n'ont pas chômé. *Le Quotidien du Médecin,* 01.01.1983.

Haut Comité d'Etude et d'Information sur l'Alcoolisme (HCEIA). 1981. La politique des soins en psychiatrie. *Bulletin du HCEIA* 146:10-20.

———. 1986. *Informations* 2:15–22.

Laharpe, F., and J. F. Blicke. 1985. Mouvements d'abstinents et thérapie des malades alcooliques. *Bulletin du HCEIA:* 4.

Ledermann, S. 1956. *Alcool, alcoolisme, alcoolisation.* vol. 1, INED.

———. 1964. *Alcool, alcoolisme, alcoolisation.* vol. 2, INED.

Mejle, F., and J. Vallin. 1981. La population des établissements psychiatriques. *Population* 36:1035-68.

Mossé, P. 1987. Les logiques du système de soins; le cas de l'alcoolisme. Thèse Aix-Marseille: 534 pp.

Pequignot, H. 1973. L'alcoolisme. *Journées du Groupe Médical d'Etudes sur l'Alcoolisme* 1–10.

Playoust, D. 1979. Gamma G.T. et grille de Le GO. *Bulletin du HCEIA supplément,* juin:7–38.

Ropert, R., and Y. Collin. 1975. L'application de la loi de 1954. *Informations Psychiatriques* 51:537–49.

Sournia, J. C. 1987. *L'histoire de l'alcoolisme.* Paris: Presses universitaires de France.

Svoboda, E. 1984. Quelle évaluation de l'alcoolisme? *Gestions Hospitalières* 240:715–19.

Villerme, L. R. 1840. *Tableau de l'état physique et mental des ouvriers.* Paris: EDHIS.

Rapid Growth and Bifurcation: Public and Private Alcohol Treatment in the United States

Constance Weisner and *Patricia Morgan*

Political and economic changes in health care and a heightened concern about alcohol problems over the past twenty years have shaped the course of alcohol treatment in the United States of America as much as, if not more than, changes in drinking patterns or problems. While there is growing concern about the relationship between alcohol and many health and social problems such as cirrhosis of the liver, fetal alcohol syndrome, crime, and homelessness, several measures of alcohol-related problems have remained stable or declined. For example, the National Health Discharge Survey reported alcohol-related morbidity not to have increased between 1979 and 1984, and alcohol-related traffic fatalities to have decreased since 1979 (United States National Institute on Alcohol Abuse and Alcoholism [USNIAAA] 1987). At the same time per capita consumption of alcohol, while increasing during the 1960s and 1970s, has been gradually decreasing since 1981 (USNIAAA 1987).

The consolidation of the disease model of alcoholism, changing forms of federal intervention, and economic policies affecting for-profit treatment provision have all influenced the development of alcohol treatment institutions. A country that has had a number of conflicting sentiments about the nature of alcohol problems—as stemming from moral weakness, crime, or disease— and a highly individualistic population composed of many different ethnocultural groups, and with a constitution putting a premium on state and regional differences, is likely to have many inconsistencies in how drinking problems are treated (Cahalan 1987). In less than two decades, alcohol treatment has grown from a predominantly public, nonalcohol-specific set of services within mental hospitals, general hospitals and a few voluntary agencies to a compli- cated public and private assortment of alcohol programs serving over 350,000 people on a given day (USNIAAA 1989). It is largely undocumented. Its complexity is seen in the problems involved even in attempts to determine its size. The federal-sponsored national survey of facilities in 1987 counted almost six thousand treatment units (USNIAAA 1989), and other estimates are much larger. Alcohol treatment takes place in a decentralized rather than a federal system, larger and more structurally and financially complex than most other countries' systems.

Public treatment of alcohol problems today is organized at the state rather than the federal level; it varies from state to state, and even within states. Private treatment agencies are less organized as a system. Treatment programs in both sectors are often financed from three or more levels of government, and from health insurance payments and clients' fees. However, alcohol treatment can be divided into two general organizational categories, private and public, distinguished by different funding mechanisms and most often serving different clienteles and providing different services. This division reflects the organization of general health-care services in the United States. Indeed, treatment of alcohol problems in the United States can be understood only in the context of the structure and financing of health services in general.

Financing of Health Care in the United States

The United States has several distinct categories of health-care financing. Many employed individuals and their families receive health insurance coverage as an employment benefit. These benefits can differ significantly. Some cover basic health maintenance and acute care, as well as major hospital services; others provide only partial coverage. However, only 71% of Americans under age sixty-five have private health insurance: 64% as an employment benefit and 7% as a privately purchased benefit (Institute of Medicine 1990).

Those without work-place or private coverage fall into several different systems of care. Medicare is a social insurance system that covers many of those over age sixty-five, some categories of the disabled, and 1% of those under sixty-five. The Department of Defense and the Veterans Administration provide health care to 3% of the under-65 population. Medicaid is an entitlement program jointly financed by federal and state governments, and pays for health services for the 7% of the population receiving federally supported welfare income maintenance. Medicare or private insurance covers 99% of those over age sixty-five, giving this age group more extensive coverage than others for some types of benefit. These programs and their relationship to alcohol treatment are discussed later; not all make provisions for the same types of treatment. However, an estimated 38 million Americans have neither public nor private health insurance: 72% of them are employed, 28% full-time and full-year, and 44% part-time or part-year (U.S. General Accounting Office 1986; Institute of Medicine 1990).

Financing of Alcohol Treatment

The financing of treatment for alcohol problems follows largely the same pattern as that described for general health care, although coverage under each category is less complete. For example, health insurance covers alcohol treatment for only 53 % of insured federal employees and only 68 % of insured private-sector employees (U.S. General Accounting Office 1986; Institute of Medicine 1990).

The public alcohol-specific treatment system (essentially those programs financed from state and federal funds administered by the state and some local funds) provides services predominantly to the uninsured—that is, unemployed or low-paid uninsured employees who cannot afford private treatment (Institute of Medicine 1990), and individuals referred by the courts. The system is relatively young. Almost all nineteenth-century institutions for inebriates had closed by 1920. The modern system began as a state system in the late 1940s, but had its main growth in the 1970s when the federal government entered the field. There are indications that it is in gradual decline: the number of programs has decreased with every federal survey, except in 1984 (Table 2). Its basic characteristics and financing have changed several times. Public programs are often not hospital- or medical-based (Institute of Medicine 1990; Saxe 1983). The system is often characterized as being underfunded and over-crowded; with diminishing resources it is supposed to provide treatment to the growing number of people not eligible for public or private reimbursement.

The private system, in contrast, began its main growth about fifteen years ago. Programs treat predominantly those with health insurance or who can afford to pay. Private programs are often inpatient and generally cost more than public programs (Miller and Hester 1986). Increasing numbers of clients are referred to private treatment through intervention based on job performance (employee assistance programs), or screening programs for alcohol problems in the work place. Another striking development in the past fifteen years has been the growth of a private nonprofit sector, which is beginning to blur the distinction between public and private. Many nonprofit and some for-profit agencies contract with local government to provide public services.

Thus, the overall view of alcohol treatment in the United States is one of a very large number and of many types of alcohol programs, divided into a private and a public system, with private nonprofit agencies cutting across the two. These systems are relatively new and in a short time have grown and undergone several basic organizational changes, reflecting shifts in financing.

History of Alcohol Treatment

For several decades, until the 1950s, the main provision for alcohol-specific treatment was in public mental hospitals, established in the nineteenth century as state-financed and state-run institutions. This remained the major base for inpatient treatment until the 1970s. However, alcohol treatment, broadly construed, also took place in general health, mental health, and criminal justice agencies, financed by local and state governments. In the late 1940s and early 50s, with the advent and growth of Alcoholics Anonymous (AA) and of public advocacy for alcoholism treatment, many states formed agencies to plan, coordinate, and, in some cases, run alcoholism treatment services, although funding levels were low. Initially, these often took the form of outpatient clinics under medical direction.

Halfway houses (group residences for recovering alcoholics) emerged in the 1950s; they were mostly charity-funded but sometimes partially supported by state funds (Cahn 1970). Recovering alcoholics, often AA members, began to assist in treatment services, often as volunteers. Legislation in the early 1960s providing start-up funds to community mental health centers, where alcohol treatment was an optional service, marked the beginning of direct federal funding. In the late 1960s, small amounts of federal resources, along with state and local resources, were put into treatment programs, including detoxification programs, to which public inebriates were referred from the criminal justice system.

As mental health services were deinstitutionalized in the 1960s, the use of mental hospitals for the treatment of alcoholics decreased also. By 1975 the number of patients in mental hospitals was only one-third of the 1955 figure (President's Commission on Mental Health 1978).

In 1970, after a long and arduous effort by the alcoholism movement and other interest groups, a far-reaching federal statute, the Comprehensive Alcohol Abuse and Alcoholism Treatment Act, crystalized today's system of public alcohol-specific agencies and also stimulated the growth of private treatment. It established the National Institute on Alcohol Abuse and Alcoholism (NIAAA), a federal agency that became part of the Alcohol, Drug Abuse and Mental Health Administration (ADAMHA), located within what is now the Department of Health and Human Services. Thus the legitimacy of alcohol treatment as a primary condition for treatment was recognized, separate from the scope of mental health and mainstream health care. Many constituencies within the alcoholism movement had fought hard for this separate institutional status. Alcohol problems had received inadequate attention when treated with mental health and mainstream health services. It was hoped that its separate status would increase the standing of alcoholism treatment, and that professionals and nonprofessionals in the field, including recovering alcoholics, would be able to exert more control than in the past over the manner of treatment (Wiener 1981; Cahalan 1987; Room 1980).

Although the new federal agency broadened the financial base of support for alcohol treatment by encouraging expanded health-insurance coverage and initiating demonstration projects, the legislation directly affected the structure and resources of only the public sector. During the 1970s there were a few scattered private treatment programs; there had always been a few "drying-out" clinics for the affluent. An early-1960s survey found no specialized alcohol units in private psychiatric hospitals and reported admissions of alcoholics to be about 6% of admissions to general psychiatric units (Glasscote et al. 1967).

Thus, it was only after the late 1970s that the private sector came to play an important role in the alcohol-specific treatment system.

After 1970 the influx of large amounts of federal and some state matching funds, and a mandate for a centralized government alcohol office, helped to assure the growth of public treatment systems in a very short time. Many preexisting programs were incorporated into these systems, which were supported either in whole or in part by government. New and more diverse community-based alcohol treatment programs also began as a result of the new funding. In addition, the Office of Economic Opportunity, set up as part of the Kennedy-Johnson administration's War on Poverty, had begun community-based social and health programs. When these ended, local alcoholism authorities became responsible for some of their alcohol programs. Thus, a system of care that had relied predominantly on mental hospitals shifted to local treatment, including detoxification, halfway house, other residential programs, and outpatient centers and hospitals. In this way, federal involvement led to greater diversity in types of treatment institutions and community involvement.

Contracting for services from the private nonprofit sector served as a mechanism for funding many of the preexisting programs. For some, it was a way to employ existing staff rather than having to hire civil servants. In line with the strong focus on community involvement in the early 1970s, it gave more power and administrative authority to the existing boards and to communities in which the programs were located. In addition, groups putting together new services were often considered to have alcohol-program expertise that government agencies might not have. Finally, it was argued that contracting was less expensive because it could avoid the heavy infrastructural costs and higher pay scales of most government agencies (Shonick 1981; Institute of Medicine 1990; Weisner and Room 1984; Hoffman 1989). Contracting for services has now become common: state and local governments often do so with either a new or a preexisting private nonprofit corporation. The evolution of this practice may well be responsible for the development of the public-related side of the now very large private nonprofit sector.

Financing since 1970

The Public Sector

Several financing shifts have occurred since 1970 in both the public and the private sector. On the public side, the National Institute on Alcohol Abuse and Alcoholism began formula grants to states, with categorial grants and contracts targeted to special programs and populations, and, in theory, serving as research or demonstration projects to point the way to further state and local efforts. Government funding was the predominant funding mechanism.

However, after the initial period of strong federal leadership in the 1970s and the building up of a prominent public alcohol treatment system, there came a period of decentralization and return to state leadership. This era and its policies, which came to be called the "New Federalism," affected other areas of health and social services as well. The aim was to streamline and diminish the federal role, reduce reporting requirements and related bureaucracies and give states the flexibility to make funding decisions. It was epitomized by the 1981 Omnibus Budget Reconciliation Act, which set up a system of block grants to the states and replaced the formula and categorial grants of the previous decade. The federal role became one primarily of funding and directing research and providing technical assistance. In 1989 the Anti-Drug Act, part of the "War on Drugs," was passed. It reversed some of the provisions of the 1981 legislation, such as increasing reporting requirements for the states. A new pool of public money available for the campaign against drugs may result again in substantial changes in alcohol treatment policies and services.

After 1970 the number of recorded cases of alcohol treatment increased greatly. Although very few statistics are available on alcohol treatment services before that time, it has been possible to obtain a general picture of the nature and scope of treatment during the 1940s and 70s (Table 1). Between 1942 and 1976, the caseload, relative to population, increased 22-fold, and alcoholism services became more diversified. In 1942 alcohol treatment took place almost exclusively in hospitals. By 1976 the proportion being treated in hospitals had been reduced to about half, while federally funded alcoholism programs, and programs based on community mental-health centers, represented a strong minority of services (Room 1980). The main growth of the private system had not yet begun.

Other Federal Treatment Mechanisms

In addition to the federal role through block grants, there are other sources of government funding, both direct and indirect. The U.S. military has an extensive system of alcohol programs, existing in its current form since 1980. It is under the overall jurisdiction of the Department of Defense, but the individual branches of the armed services operate their own programs. Most personnel enter them either through a method of chemical detection or by referrals from commanding officers. They include education and inpatient and outpatient modalities. One study reported 54,000 military personnel treated in drug and alcohol programs in 1985 (9,000 in 52 residential programs and 45,000 in 400 nonresidential programs) (Bray et al. 1986). Another study reported 100,000 treated in 1981 (20,000 in residential and the remainder in nonresidential programs) at a cost of $60 million (Killeen 1984).

The Veterans Administration (VA) provides alcohol treatment services for veterans of the U.S. armed services. VA hospitals had 103 direct alcohol treatment units, both inpatient and outpatient, in 1986 (Institute of Medicine

TABLE 1

Alcoholism Treatment Caseload in the U.S.A., 1942 and 1976
(partial and approximate figures)

	1942	1976	
State mental hospitals	10,461[a]	106,615[c]	
Private mental hospitals	4,754[b]	10,827[c]	
Public and other general hospitals	22,147[b]	481,000[c,d]	
Social institutions for alcoholics	6,689	308,929	
		federally funded alcoholism programs (except CMHC: and drinking driver):	
Veterans Administration hospitals	3,886	95,000	
Small numbers for Alcoholics Anonymous, outpatient programs, nonmedical institutions (missions, rehabilitation farms, etc .)		Community mental health centers (CMHC)	121,300[c]
		Drinking driver programs	49,472[c]
		Military programs	40,000
		Indian hospitals	137,000
		Halfway houses	36,000
		Alcoholics Anonymous	320,000
TOTAL:	47,937	TOTAL	1,706,143
Total US population:	133 million	214 million	

Notes:
[a] 1940

[b] incomplete returns

[c] 1975

[d] Apparently does not include 89,057 psychiatric caseloads in general hospital services.

Sources: 1942: Corwin, E.H.L. and Cunningham, E.V., "Institutional Facilities for the Treatment of Alcoholism," *Quarterly Journal of Studies on Alcohol*, vol. 5, 1944.

1976: Mental Hospitals: "President's Commission on Mental Health," Appendix, vol. 11, 1978, p. 102; all other figures "PCMH," Appendix, vol. 4, 1978, p. 2096.

1990; USNIAAA 1989). In addition, other agencies have specialized programs for veterans; in 1984 there were 579 alcohol and combined alcohol and drug units (Reed and Sanchez 1986).

The federal government operates alcohol and combined alcohol and drug treatment programs also through the Indian Health Service. Some of these are programs formerly funded through categorial grants from the National Institute on Alcohol Abuse and Alcoholism (NIAAA), and located primarily on reservations. In 1987 there were 309 programs (Institute of Medicine 1990).

As described earlier, Medicare is a federal health insurance program primarily for individuals aged sixty-five and over. It provides coverage for alcohol problems under the psychiatric health services category and reimburses the costs of inpatient care.

Medicaid, an entitlement rather than an insurance program, is financed by both federal and state governments, and supports private as well as public care. It covers predominantly inpatient care, and reimburses for alcohol treatment under a mental health rubric. Its levels of reimbursement are not sufficient to cover the cost of many private programs.

The Private Sector

During the early 1970s, one of the goals of the National Institute on Alcohol Abuse and Alcoholism was to develop a broader funding base for alcohol treatment, to include coverage by private health insurance in addition to public financing of alcohol treatment as a primary condition (Alcoholism Report 1973; Roman 1988). Together with the National Council on Alcoholism, the major voluntary association in the field, it developed a model benefit package as early as 1973 and encouraged states to accept it. Currently, 37 states, representing 85% of the population, have legislation mandating at least the option for coverage of alcohol treatment as a primary disorder. This compares with 19 states in 1978 (Institute of Medicine 1990).

Private alcohol treatment has grown considerably since the late 1970s (Table 2). The private for-profit sector may have a larger increase than the table shows. There are indications from survey nonresponse data analysis of underreporting of private programs as well as of funding levels in the private sector. The private for-profit sector is the only one not reporting a decrease in the number of programs between 1984 and 1987. A major stimulus to the development of hospital-based private treatment programs was the passage of the Hill-Burton Act of 1940, which provided for the building of new hospitals. This resulted in overbuilding and an excess of beds (Hoffman 1989; Shonick and Roemer 1983). While the private for-profit sector is largely characterized as a hospital-based and inpatient set of services because of the nature of its funding, there are indications that the number of outpatient units may continue to increase, partly because of the high costs of hospital inpatient care. Many outpatient units are now aftercare components of inpatient programs rather than independent outpatient programs.

The Private Nonprofit Sector

The private non-profit treatment sector has become the largest and most complex sector. According to the National Drug and Alcoholism Treatment

TABLE 2

Number of Alcohol Treatment Units[a] by Ownership and Year

	1979	1980	1982	1984	1987[b]	Percent change 1979–87
PRIVATE						
For-profit	199	248	295	851	879	342
Nonprofit	2,736	2,959	2,769	4,325	3,693	35
Total	2,935	3,207	3,064	5,176	4,572	56
PUBLIC						
State-local government	1,070	1,062	964	1,459	895	−18
Federal government	214	196	205	277	160	−25
Other	—	—	—	51	—	—
Total	1,284	1,258	1,169	1,787	1,055	−18
Total private and public	4,219	4,465	4,233	6,963	5,627	33

Notes:

[a] Includes both alcohol only and combined alcohol and drug treatment units.

[b] In 1987 the number of treatment units is lower than the overall sample size of 5,971 on Table 3, owing to missing fiscal data.

Sources: 1) Reed and Sanchez, 1986 (NDATUS 1979, 1980, 1982; NDAPI 1984).
        2) USNIAAA, 1989 (NDATUS 1987).

Utilization Survey (NDATUS), in 1987, 66% of treatment units were private nonprofit (Table 2), and 58% of all clients were treated in those units (Table 3). Although NDATUS presents data from this sector under the private sector because of its legal status, it cannot be characterized as completely private. Agencies in this category vary with regard to main source of funding and to whether their clients are privately or publicly funded. As described earlier, some states contract almost exclusively with such programs for their public clients. Thus, the vast majority of public alcohol-treatment agencies in California and Minnesota are run under contracts with private nonprofit agencies (Weisner and Room 1984; State of Minnesota 1987). At the same time, these programs can also be operated in hospitals and charge fees, like for-profit programs. Jacob (1985, 5) points out: "Some of the most successful non-profit programs are quite similar to the for-profit programs except for their tax and legal status." As an indication of the public/private mix of this sector, "programs operated by private nonprofit organizations reported in the 1987 NDATUS survey were receiving 34% of their funds from private third party payers (e.g., Medicare), 14% from client fees, 9% from public third party payers, and 34% from state and local government sources. The amount received from private insurance had not changed greatly since 1982, when these programs reported receiving 30 percent of their funding from private health insurance" (Institute of Medicine 1990).

Statistics on client utilization for the same period, although less complete, reflect much the same pattern (Table 3). However, they indicate that the increases in the private sector may not offset the losses in the public sector.

TABLE 3

Number of Alcohol[a] Treatment Clients by Year

	1979	1980[a]	1982[b]	1987	Percent change 1979–87
PRIVATE					
For-profit	10,924	—	—	42,328	287
Nonprofit	153,476	—	—	194,354	27
Total	164,400	—	—	236,682	44
PUBLIC					
State-local government	106,733	—	—	83,123	–22
Federal government	21,619	—	—	18,123	–92
Other	—	—	—	—	—
Total	128,352	—	—	101,246	–21
Total private and public	292,752	307,174	289,933	337,928	108

Notes:
[a] Includes both alcoholism and combined alcohol and drug treatment units.

[b] Data on client utilization were not reported from the 1980 and 1982 NDATUS Survey.

Sources: 1) USNIAAA, 1979 (NDATUS 1979).
         2) USNIAAA, 1983 (NDATUS 1980, 1982).
         3) USNIAAA, 1986 (NDATUS 1987).

Combined Alcohol and Drug Services

In addition to the shifts in financing in the public sector and the growth of the private sector, major changes have occurred during the past decade in the nature of alcohol treatment services. Perhaps the most pervasive has been the substantial increase in combined alcohol and drug units (Table 4). In contrast to the first formation of the state alcohol agencies, all but four states now have administrative agencies for combined alcohol and drug abuse, and most people in treatment are now in combined programs, often called "chemical dependency" or "substance abuse" programs.

TABLE 4

Alcohol Only and Combined Drug and Alcohol
Public and Private Treatment Units, 1979–1984

Treatment units	1979	1980	1982	1984[a]	1987	Percent change 1979–87
Alcohol Only	2,821	3,016	2,729	—	1,664	−41
Combined	1,398	1,449	1,504	—	3,963	183
Total	4,219	4,465	4,223	6,963	5,627	33

Notes:
[a] Data were not reported for alcohol only and combined alcohol and drug treatment units in the 1984 report except when prevention and treatment units were aggregated.

Sources: 1) USNIAAA, 1983 (NDATUS 1979, 1980, and 1982).
2) Reed and Sanchez, 1986 (NDAPI 1984).
3) USNIAAA, 1989 (NDATUS 1987).

The rise of these combined units in the public sector has been attributed to a simplifying of administration, partly because of the emphasis of the block grant legislation, but also it reflects the claim by treatment providers of an increased number of clients with both alcohol and drug abuse diagnoses. In the for-profit sector, alcohol-specific programs also have often widened their target population to include drug abuse. Much of the increase in combined units comes from this changing emphasis. However, there is no evidence that many units have done more than simply change their names from alcohol treatment to chemical dependency or substance abuse treatment. It is not known whether the nature of their services has changed.

Nonalcohol-Specific Treatment

Outside the alcohol-specific sector, many other types of agency that treated alcohol problems before 1970 continue to do so. Most large communities have a range of family-service counseling agencies, mental health facilities, and other health and social-service organizations handling alcohol problems. Other health and social-service agencies also provide treatment for alcohol problems, and in some cases the number of alcohol-related cases is high. It is difficult to document the scope of such treatment. With the exception of some ongoing hospital research, there has not been systematic research outside the alcohol-specific system since 1970. Studies have used different methods and not produced consistent estimates of prevalence (Weisner 1987).

Many alcohol problems continue to be treated in hospitals as part of general medical care. In the health sector, to be reimbursed for alcohol treatment, the client must fit into a reimbursable diagnostic-related group (DRG), a mechanism first adopted by Medicare in 1983 (but applied to alcohol more recently), and since expanded to other third-party insurance, for cost containment reasons. Under this system, 20,000 medical conditions were classified into 467 DRGs. Each DRG has a specific predetermined payment rate for all hospital admissions. There are five alcohol-related DRGs: alcohol/drug abuse or dependence; alcohol/drug abuse or dependence, detoxification, or other symptomatic treatment with complications or co-morbidity; alcohol/drug abuse or dependence, detoxification, or other symptomatic treatment without complications or co-morbidity; alcohol/drug dependence with rehabilitation; and alcohol/drug dependence with detoxification and rehabilitation (Alcoholism Report 1987). Hospital-based alcohol treatment services are often shaped by adherence to DRG criteria. DRGs are tending to shorten the 28-day stay most common in alcohol hospital programs.

Treatment Modalities and Institutions

Since the program type often influences the particular method, treatment methods are discussed here according to the types of institution in which they are most typically found.

Detoxification facilities are located within hospitals or as freestanding units. They are brief programs, lasting from three to ten days. Both public and private hospital programs and some independent facilities use medication, usually tranquilizers, for withdrawal symptoms. However, many communities have begun to operate ''social model'' detoxification units, which do not use medicines or medical personnel. Some of these are simply drying-out stations, where individuals are observed in order to prevent serious withdrawal reactions; others offer more extensive services (Borkman 1983).

Inpatient hospital programs are often private and frequently include a variety of methods. They often consist of alcohol education and some type of psychological therapy, usually group-based, along with Alcoholics Anonymous (AA) or some AA-based group interaction. Some involve pharmacological treatment or have a group-therapy component carried out by a nurse or other health-care practitioner. Nonmedical halfway houses or recovery homes, which are commonly found in many communities' public treatment systems, usually rely on an AA approach.

Outpatient programs exist as separate units or are attached to some residential services. Their clientele and treatment modalities then differ accordingly. Independent outpatient programs often have a mix of individual and group psychotherapy. Most are group-oriented. Until recently, many of them have been "aftercare programs", designed for clients who have had hospital inpatient care.

The treatment modalities found within the public and private treatment systems range from pharmacological to various social-model and AA twelve-step approaches. Many of the therapies cross-cut the type of environment. The particular approaches used range from psychotherapy to behavioural and family-system therapies.

The most common pharmacological method is the use of tranquilizers for the management of alcohol withdrawal. They are no longer extensively used after detoxification, however. Antipsychotic and antidepressant drugs are increasingly limited to individuals with psychiatric diagnoses in addition to alcoholism. Disulfiram (Antabuse) is prescribed as a behavioral therapy, either alone or as part of another treatment. There is great variation in its use across the United States and across different types of service. Some physicians, hospital units, and multiple-offender drinking-driver programs, and even some out-patient services, prescribe it for selected patients. Chemical aversion therapies are found in only a few programs, all in the private for-profit sector.

An increasing number of treatment methods are based on social-model approaches. The social-model modality is based primarily on an AA approach and is integrated into detoxification, outpatient, and residential recovery programs (Borkman 1983). However, AA plays an increasingly strong role in treatment across the various settings.

The treatment model that may be said to represent, in general, much of American treatment, both public and private, is the so-called Minnesota model. Treatment takes place in a hospital or independent facility and typically takes 28 days. It is based on the disease concept of alcoholism, and is oriented to abstinence. Its basic components are detoxification, education, group sessions (with a variety of approaches represented, including AA-based group interaction, confrontation, and more traditional group therapy), AA meetings, peer-level meetings, and individual recovery plans. The approach also emphasizes aftercare and continued AA attendance.

Table 5 presents a comparison of the basic types of care for 1980 and 1987, based on NDATUS point prevalence data. There have been large increases in the number of medical detoxification and rehabilitation/recovery programs, and small increases in social detoxification and outpatient programs. The custodial category is the only one in which the number of units has declined. However, except for custodial programs, numbers of clients have not been greatly affected. They decreased in all types of care despite increased numbers of units, even in medical detoxification, where the increase in units has been greatest. The only increases in client numbers have been in the outpatient and rehabilitation/recovery services.

TABLE 5

Number of Alcohol and Combined Alcohol and Drug Treatment Units[a] and Number of Clients by Type of Care, 1980 and 1987

	1980[b]		1987	
	Number of units	Number of clients	Number of units	Number of clients
Inpatient/Residential				
Medical detoxification	568	7,327	939	6,391
Social detoxification	357	4,289	390	4,015
Rehabilitation/ recovery	1,587	37,171	2,185	37,501
Custodial / domiciliary	207	4,715	182	2,688
Outpatient	3,007	253,267	3,701	287,333

Notes:

[a] The number of units may not equal the number of units presented in earlier tables, because units may offer more than one type of care.

[b] 1980 data for outpatient include "ambulatory medical detoxification," "limited care (including day care)," and outpatient services. 1987 outpatient data are reported only in the category of "outpatient."

Sources: 1) USNIAAA, 1980 (NDATUS 1980).
        2) USNIAAA, 1987 (NDATUS 1987).

Regrettably, these data are not reported separately for public and private sectors. However, other studies using the same data indicate an unevenness across public and private sectors for these different types of care. Medical detoxification and hospital-based services are more often found in the private sector, and social detoxification and outpatient services more often in the public sector (Yahr 1988).

The sex, age, and ethnicity distributions have also remained similar between 1982 and 1987 when aggregated across public and private programs (Table 6). The only noticeable difference is that the 1987 population was younger (a larger proportion under age 45). Again, 1987 data on client demographics were not reported separately for public and private programs.

However, 1984 data showed programs funded by the National Institute on Alcohol Abuse and Alcoholism to have a nonwhite clientele of 37% and private programs only 27% (Reed and Sanchez 1986). If the 1987 data underreport private programs, the proportion of minority clients in treatment in 1987 is likely to be less than in 1984.

TABLE 6

Demographic Characteristics of Clients in Alcohol Treatment Units [a] (percent)

	1982	1987
Male	78	76
Female	22	24
Age		
20 and under	11	13
21–44	59	69
45–64	27	17
65 and over	2	2
Ethnicity		
American Indian	4	2
Asian	0.3	0.5
Black	16	15
Hispanic	9	10
White	71	72
Other	—	0.4

Note:

[a] Includes both alcoholism and combined alcohol and drug treatment units.

Sources: 1) USNIAAA, 1983 (NDATUS, 1982).
          2) USNIAAA, 1989 (NDATUS, 1987).

Some statistics have been reported on public and private specialized programs, such as those for the elderly, youth, and women. According to surveys in 1982 and 1984, specialized programs are increasing. The 1984 federal survey reported the largest growth to be in programs for youth, which had increased from 892 in 1982 to 1,871 in 1984. The number reported in 1987 was 1,782. These programs are often found in the private for-profit sector; they therefore may be underrepresented in the 1987 survey (USNIAAA 1989).

Availability of Treatment

It is difficult to determine the availability of treatment programs throughout the population. The NDATUS data show, from the budgeted capacity and utilization rate of units, that, on a given day, the range of treatment modalities (inpatient/residential and outpatient/nonresidential) have utilization rates of less than 85% (Institute of Medicine 1990). However, the more important questions have to do with the overall distribution of facilities throughout the population (such as equal geographic, urban/rural, and public/private distribution) and the distribution of types of program throughout the population (such as whether people without insurance have access to only detoxification rather than rehabilitation services).

An analysis of the 1987 NDATUS data (Institute of Medicine 1990) revealed considerable variation among most of these variables. First, there is a large range across states in the rate for the total budgeted treatment capacity (from 0.34/1000 to 3.86/1000). Second, there are large differences across states in regard to the per capita rate of different types of treatment, and it does not appear that when one type of care is lower another type is higher. Third, no relationship was found between cirrhosis rates and treatment capacity or between per capita consumption rates and treatment capacity, suggesting that the density of treatment provision has little relation to levels of population need.

Again, even if there were evenness across states regarding the variables discussed above, the availability for individuals financially not eligible for private programs would still be unknown. In addition to the large differences by state in the proportion of the population covered by health insurance, there are differences in the public/private proportion of treatment units (USNIAAA 1989).

Alcohol-Treatment Target Groups

One of the dramatic changes in alcohol treatment in the past twenty years has been in the groups targeted for treatment and in methods of attracting clients. Traditionally, the predominant client has been the public chronic alcoholic. To provide quality services for this group was one of the original purposes of the 1970 legislation (Plaut 1964). In 1971 the National Conference of Commissioners on Uniform State Laws recommended all states to decriminalize public drunkenness and provide treatment alternatives; by 1985, thirty-four states had done so, at least in part (Finn 1985). As might be expected, most of these programs are in the public sector (Yahr 1988). Data for 1987 showed a drop in the number of units offering services to public inebriates to 404, compared with 537 in 1982 and 598 in 1984 (USNIAAA 1989; Reed and Sanchez 1986; USNIAAA 1983).

Since the early 1970s there has been a movement to broaden the treatment population. An increase in third-party coverage for alcohol treatment and an increased societal concern about alcohol problems have been accompanied by programs targeting a wider range of clients. Notions of the "hidden alcoholic" fit with the movement's perception that alcoholism and alcohol problems are fairly evenly distributed throughout all groups in society. There are many problem-specific programs, such as employee assistance programs and "drinking driving" programs. There is some indication that, in some areas at least, the traditional treatment groups are being replaced by these new groups (Weisner 1986; Jacob 1985; Yahr 1988).

Criminal Justice Referrals

The drinking, or driving while intoxicated (DWI), driver is increasingly found in alcohol treatment, especially in the public sector. Most states have increased the penalties for this offense and many now mandate treatment, even for first offenders. Consequently, services designed especially for drinking drivers have increased throughout the country. In 1982, for instance, NDATUS reported 1,392 DWI treatment services (USNIAAA 1983). By 1984 the same source reported 2,219 units, an increase of over 60% in only two years (Reed and Sanchez 1986). The 1987 number reported by NDATUS was 2,237 (USNIAAA 1989). The state-level data system on public programs (SADAP) reported a larger number, 2,551, with a client load of 864,000 in 1984 (Butynski et al. 1985). The range among states for the proportion of overall treatment units that provided DWI treatment, according to the 1987 NDATUS survey, was 12 to 69%, very likely reflecting variation in penalties for driving while intoxicated and therefore great variation in the proportion of DWI programs in state services (Diesenhaus 1989).

In addition to drinking drivers, individuals arrested for other offenses, such as child abuse, domestic violence, forgery, and burglary, are increasingly diverted from criminal justice to alcohol treatment (Weisner 1990). Detoxification programs for public inebriates are one kind of treatment service. In the past, local diversion programs funded by the Federal Law Enforcement Assistance Administration formally referred clients to treatment. These set a precedent for diversion, so that, even in states or counties that no longer have formal programs, there is a great deal of "informal diversion" from the criminal justice to the alcohol treatment systems. Probation officers, lawyers from the public defender's office, and private attorneys frequently make referrals to alcohol treatment for the handling of their clients outside the criminal justice system. The states of New York and Connecticut, for example, report large proportions of their alcohol treatment slots taken up by such referrals (State of Connecticut 1988; State of New York 1986).

Clients referred from the work place make up an increasing part of referrals to alcohol treatment programs. Most of these clients are covered by employment-based health insurance. These programs take several different forms, but most are described as employee assistance programs. Data on these programs are sketchy, and there are no accurate counts of the numbers of referrals. Roman (1988) estimated over 10,000 programs, and reported that the National Survey of Worksite Health Promotion Activities had found that 24% of work sites with over fifty employees had such programs. These programs are less common in the state or local government alcohol-treatment sector than in the private sector (Yahr 1988). Again, there is very uneven distribution across states in the proportion of units providing such services. The range is from 4 to 69% (Diesenhaus 1989).

Compliance and Coercion

Many of the new groups targeted for treatment often enter treatment under different forms of coercion rather than voluntarily. They include involuntary committals, criminal justice referrals, welfare referrals, "constructive coercion" work-place referrals, and family intervention programs.

Alongside more explicit coercion, there has been a push toward early case-finding and intervention, concerned particularly with those whose problems are less noticeable or pervasive than those of the chronic alcoholic. Indeed, coercive programs, such as DWI, often have been redefined as being early case-finding programs (Flores 1982; Schuerman et al. 1961). Several states now label their DWI and occupational work-place programs as "early intervention" or "prevention" programs (Butynski et al. 1987; State of Minnesota 1987). This has been the case especially in programs for special populations: minorities, youth, and women (Argeriou 1978).

Decentralization

The federal government, through the National Institute on Alcohol Abuse and Alcoholism, has played a strong leadership and policy-setting role during some periods, but there is no centralized authority and no attempt at coordination between the public and the private systems.

As described earlier, the public system is organized at the state level, and states organize their services differently. State agencies use several different arrangements for disbursing their funds. Some organize their treatment systems on a county basis and some on a regional basis, and some administer programs directly. The amount of centralization at the state level also varies greatly. Those states that run programs directly have more centralized systems. Those that organize their programs through county or regional agencies have less authority over those agencies. In states with a strong county level of government, the primary role of the state office is to approve county plans and certify public programs. However, the county decides on the types of program on which to spend its resources, and whether to operate them directly or to contract with nonprofit or for-profit institutions; also it certifies DWI programs. Some states certify alcohol counselors, and thus have a stronger voice than others regarding educational criteria for counselors.

The private system has no federal agency for setting policy or regulating programs, except for hospitals under the jurisdiction of the quasi-governmental

Joint Commission on Accreditation of Health Care Organizations. This body deals primarily with technical structures, such as staffing levels. The health insurance industry, in determining what services are reimbursable, has some indirect impact on the basic organizational consistency of programs, and on the inpatient/outpatient ratio.

Medicare policy is set at the federal level, and serves mainly as a benchmark for other health coverage. Medicaid, however, is very much affected by state policy and operates differently from state to state. There is perhaps more standardization in diagnosis and payment schemes since the initiation in the early 1980s of the reimbursement system based on diagnostic related groups.

The Division of Labor between Systems: Split and Competition

The fundamental division of labor within treatment systems is between public and private institutions, differentiated in general by financing arrangements. In most states, the public system is used by individuals receiving third-party reimbursement from the public sector, such as Medicaid, or by those without any third-party reimbursement. The private system generally is used by individuals who have health insurance coverage for alcoholism treatment or who can afford to pay for treatment. However, public providers claim that many of their clients have had prior treatment in private programs before they lost their jobs and health insurance coverage.

However, the two systems continue to compete (Jacob 1985). Although it is claimed that many people are in need of alcohol treatment, too few enter private treatment to fill the facilities profitably (Room 1980). With a general decrease in public resources during the 1980s, public programs have increasingly needed to attract fee-paying clients to remain solvent. Within the private sector also, there is a great deal of competition for clients, evidenced by an abundance of marketing techniques and advertising in the press and on television (Cahalan 1987). The result is a proliferation of marketing courses for treatment programs, which are sometimes advertised in ways commonly used for commodity marketing but foreign to a public health strategy. Also, the competition for clients has resulted in advertising of private treatment programs, which have come under scrutiny for validity of advertisements, especially undocumented claims of high success-rates (Jacobs 1981; Miller and Hester 1986).

Financing Issues

The funding of alcohol treatment in the U.S.A. is indeed complex. Preliminary data from the 1987 NDATUS sample of private and public alcohol and combined alcohol and drug programs show that over $1.7 billion was spent in the 4,949 facilities reporting budgetary information (USNIAAA 1989), compared with $1.1 billion in 1982 (Institute of Medicine 1990). The largest source was private third-party health insurance ($592 million). Other sources, in order of funds spent, were state governments (including the ADAMHA block grant), client fees, public third-party government fees for service, other federal funds, public welfare funds, private donations, and ADAMHA program support (other than the block grant). In the private sector, financing for both inpatient and outpatient services comes mostly from employer-provided or individually-purchased health insurance. Private programs do not always accept payment from the public third-party payment mechanisms, Medicare and Medicaid, because they do not reimburse adequately.

Public-sector financing is even more complicated. Since 1984, the federal government allocates funds to the states, by means of the ADAMHA block grant. A state's share of the national allocation is set by a complicated formula including the state's population (NASADAD 1987). The states then match part of these funds. The funds are then distributed according to the state administrative systems. In many cases, the local level is required to match a proportion of the state funds. According to NASADAD, 53% of those funds administered by state alcohol or drug agencies in 1985 came from the states, 19% from the federal government (mostly by means of the alcohol/drug abuse block grant), 7% from county or local governments, and 21% from other sources. These other sources include court fines, client fees, and health insurance payments. These data apply only to about 14% of the total alcohol and drug programs (Butynski et al. 1986). Proportions for 1987 are similar, with the total amounting to $1.6 billion (Butynski and Canova 1988). The figures for both years include funds for both alcohol and drugs.

Funding affects the treatment component directly. Third-party reimbursement calls for a medically-based modality, even though in some cases the medical aspect of the program exists only for the sake of reimbursement (Weisner and Room 1984). At present, financing issues are highlighted by several different constituencies. Employers and the health insurance industry are concerned about the high cost of inpatient hospital treatment and are examining alternatives (Cahalan 1987). Advocates of nonmedical-based programs are lobbying for coverage of their programs on the grounds that they are as effective as medical-based programs (Reynolds 1987; Wright 1986). This debate is beginning to focus on an examination of cost-effectiveness and outcome for different program modalities.

Concern over rising costs of health care have fueled the growth of health maintenance organizations (HMOs), which are health insurance organizations that base costs on a general rate per service or individual. In some states, such as California and Oregon, they account for a large proportion of the market share of health-care services. Compared with services paid for by other types of insurance, alcohol services in HMOs tend to be more often outpatient

(Institute of Medicine 1990). Thus, if this type of health-care option continues to grow, the basic characteristics of treatment may be affected.

Although inpatient treatment costs much more than outpatient treatment (Saxe 1983; Yahr 1988; Jacob 1985; Institute of Medicine 1990), studies have found little difference in outcome (Miller and Hester 1986; Saxe 1983; Emrick 1982). The growing concern over cost containment may affect what public and private insurers are willing to reimburse, and thus the inpatient/outpatient ratio of treatment. Already, many insurance companies have hired case managers who review for appropriateness alcohol treatment referrals to inpatient care.

Statistics on Alcohol Treatment Populations and Services

From World War II to the formation of the National Institute on Alcohol Abuse and Alcoholism, most alcohol-related statistics were collected through federal and state mental health agencies from local and state programs. These were reports of the state alcohol agencies. Information was generally limited to public inpatient facilities. Since the formation of the national institute several information collection systems have been created, and later revised. The National Alcoholism Program Information System was the federal client-oriented monitoring system used until 1982, and the State Alcoholism Profile Information System was the voluntary information-collection system that monitored state programs.

Today national data on public and private treatment programs and clients are collected by the National Drug and Alcoholism Treatment Utilization Survey (NDATUS), co-sponsored by the National Institute on Alcohol Abuse and Alcoholism and the National Institute on Drug Abuse. The National Association of State Alcohol and Drug Abuse directors contract with the federal government to report state-level data on public institutions through the State Alcohol and Drug Abuse Profile (SADAP).

NDATUS collects clinic-level point prevalence data on the nature of alcohol and drug treatment in the United States from both private and public providers. The data in this chapter are based largely on its official reports and secondary analysis. Surveys were conducted in 1979, 1982, 1984, and 1987. NDATUS is the only national-based information retrieval system that obtains public and private data on each unit's treatment capacity and utilization, staffing, and funding. These data are collected on a voluntary, self-reporting basis. Although the amount and type of data collected in each survey have varied, data have been collected on types of treatment, funding, ownership, treatment capacity, demographic characteristics, staffing and referrals.

The major limitations of the NDATUS reporting system include the irregular time-frame for gathering information, reliance on point prevalence data, the lack of data on clients, the lack of comparable data across surveys, and the need to rely on self-report data. Finally, because of the voluntary nature of the reporting system for public and private agencies, and lack of any pressure on private treatment agencies to report, there is no way to determine accurately the extensiveness and representativeness of the sample of treatment facilities.

SADAP was instituted to provide a comprehensive state-by-state overview of public alcohol and drug programs, activities, and policies. This involves the completion of a data collection workbook by each state alcohol office, asking for the following information: funds earmarked for alcohol treatment services; counts and modalities of services provided; accreditation licensure status of agency and staff; identification of prevention and special emphasis programs; health insurance coverage, etc. Because, increasingly, alcohol and drug administrations are combined at state level, recent data do not separate alcohol and drug information. In addition to state programs, approximately fifteen national data sources participate in SADAP by providing state-level accounts of their programs. These include a range of institutions from the Federal Bureau of Investigation to the National Council on Alcoholism. While the public sector seems to be well represented in SADAP reports, there is variation across states regarding which types of program are reported. Since the data-base includes data from any program that receives any block grant funds, and the states vary greatly in the proportion and type of private program with which they contract, private nonprofit programs are included differentially, by state, in the data.

Alcoholics Anonymous and Treatment

Historically, in the United States, Alcoholics Anonymous has been the major alternative to treatment. It has grown rapidly in the last ten years, at the same time as the treatment system has expanded. Since its beginning in 1935, its membership has grown to 868,171 in 1980, to 1,191,946 in 1985, and to 1,734,734 in 1988 (General Service Board 1981, 1986, 1989). This growth has occurred at several levels: numbers of groups and new meetings, increasing attendance at meetings, and diversity of membership, including more women and young people. Women accounted for 34% of the sample in 1986 (General Service Board 1987).

There is also increasing diversification in the types of meeting offered. They include, for example, meetings for women only, for men only, for young people, for gays and lesbians, and for the disabled (such as the hearing-impaired), and for professionals such as physicians and lawyers.

The popularization of AA has resulted also in an increase in AA-related groups, using the twelve steps, such as Alanon, Alateen, and Adult Children of Alcoholics. These are groups of people who do not necessarily have drinking problems themselves, but who attend meetings to cope with someone else's drinking. Along with this has been a large increase in popular literature promoting twelve-step mutual help ideology and programs for many types of lifestyle problem, such as gambling, sexual promiscuity, and overeating, in accordance with a conception of American society as an addicted or dependent one (see, for example, Schaef 1987).

Although AA is defined as being outside the official treatment sphere, it has made a striking impact on traditional alcohol treatment modalities. Most treatment models, whether medically-based or following a social model, have incorporated an AA-oriented approach and even AA meetings into their regimen. Many 28-day residential alcohol programs introduce their clients to AA. Some even carry their clients up through several of the AA steps before releasing them (Phillips 1989). Public and private treatment providers now commonly refer their clients to AA as part of, or after, the established treatment course. Thus, many individuals are referred to AA from treatment programs and counselors, rather than from more traditional sources, such as another AA member or a family. The criminal justice system also has begun to send DWI and other alcohol-involved offenders to AA meetings.

Thus, there is reason to believe that the role and perhaps even the nature of AA have undergone some changes during the past decade. Rather than being solely an alternative to treatment, it has also become an adjunct to treatment and a part of aftercare. A major role of AA members in the past was that of informal outreach workers in missions, "skid-row" streets, and jails to find new members. Now, AA members work with community treatment providers, judges, and counselors to determine with them the boundaries of AA activities. There are also indications that the mainstream AA population has changed from being older, male, less affluent, and self-referred to one with more women and young people, and of a higher socio-economic status, and not self-referred (Phillips 1989).

The almost universal incorporation of AA into treatment programs indicates the strong adherence of U.S. treatment institutions, both public and private, to the disease concept of alcoholism. Although there may be individual therapists and a few programs providing treatment based on different ideologies and with goals other than abstinence, the overarching ideology of treatment is the disease concept, and the goal of treatment is abstinence.

Conclusion

This report has been an attempt to describe and explain a large and complicated network of treatment agencies for alcohol problems in the United States of America. Rapid changes in the social handling of alcohol problems, along with shifts in funding and administration, have combined to create two systems of care: one private and one public.

It is clear that the various financing schemes and types of care do not together form a system. As the public system declines, the growing private system fails to incorporate the lost clients in its programs. It provides a different set of services and treats different clients. Indeed, the systems are so separate as to obviate the validity of any aggregate analysis of availability, utilization, or treatment capacity.

This has further implications. Since the types of care provided by the two sectors are different (the private more medical and hospital-based, and the public less medical, more nonhospital based) (Yahr 1988), and since there is a financial sorting of clients across systems, the characteristics of the clients of the two different types of care are likely to be inversely related (Miller and Hester 1986). The literature indicates strongly that those who have health insurance are healthier than those without, and that they have less severe alcohol problems (Chopra et al. 1979; Roman 1988; Jacob 1985; Reis and Davis 1979). Yet, this is the population most likely to be found in hospital inpatient programs.

Perhaps the problem of two such different systems of care, which results in uneven availability of treatment and utilization of types of care, can be attributed to the lack in the United States of a national health-care system or even a national health policy. It is certainly aggravated by the fact that several levels of government influence alcohol-treatment policy. The public and private systems of care operate from such different motives that any overall strategies are rendered impossible. The public alcohol treatment system, though fragmented, is in essence a public health system, making its decisions on the basis of need for services. However, even here, the case can be made that its use of contracting and its resultant dependence upon the private nonprofit sector have begun to erode traditional public health motives. The development and reliance on the private nonprofit sector can be argued to be the public sector's way of accommodating to the goals of the economic market and the efficiency of the private system. This has been said of public hospital contracting as well. In this case also, while efficiency has sometimes increased, indigent clients have been dropped from services (Shonick 1981; Shonick and Roemer 1983).

The private system, on the other hand, has characteristics more familiar to a business or industry than to a public health system. It has developed partially to fill a share of the empty hospital beds and is motivated primarily to keep treatment slots filled. The investor-owned hospital systems have been the hospital area of most growth (Shortell 1988). Alcohol treatment has become marketable and its institutions have prospered. With the listing of alcohol treatment corporations on the international stock exchanges, and the buy-outs and mergers of alcohol treatment by other industries, such as food chains, they cannot be expected to function differently. Leading U.S. business advice magazines, such as *Business Weekly*, suggest alcohol treatment hospital services as lucrative investments.

The alcohol treatment system in the United States had its most rapid growth in the very late stages of the postwar welfare state era, in the 1970s. It continued to grow in the 1980s, which might almost be characterized as a garrison-state era, with the rapid growth of prison populations and war in the streets over illicit drugs. The timing of the growth of the system has greatly affected its character. Public treatment grew up outside the conventional civil-service channels of government agencies, in part to save money by keeping salaries low, and in part to avoid being co-opted by health bureaucracies.

At the same time as the prison system has failed to grow as fast as the population being processed through the criminal courts, the public alcohol system has increasingly become an adjunct of the courts, a softer option for more deserving cases. It has accordingly taken on a more coercive nature. Meanwhile, the burgeoning private treatment sector has responded to, and reflects, the desires and needs of not only the affluent upper segment of the population but also the large, comfortable middle class with "good jobs." The increasing bifurcation of the alcohol treatment system reflects the increasing bifurcation of American society in the 1980s.

Note

This paper was partially sponsored by a National Center Research Grant AA05595 to the Alcohol Research Group, Institute of Epidemiology and Behavioral Medicine, Medical Research Institute of San Francisco.

References

Alcoholism Report. 1973. 1(21). Alexandria, Va.

_____. 1987. 15(17). Alexandria, Va.

Argeriou, M. 1978. Reaching problem-drinking blacks: The unheralded potential of the drinking driver programs. *International Journal of Addiction* 13:442–59.

Borkman, T. 1983. *A social-experiential model in programs for alcoholism recovery: A research report on a new treatment design.* Rockville Md.: National Institute on Alcohol Abuse and Alcoholism.

Bray, R. M., et al. 1986. *1985 Worldwide survey of alcohol and nonmedical drug use among military personnel.* Research Triangle Institute, RTI/3306/06-02FR. June.

Butynski, W., N. Record, and J. Yates. 1985. *State resources and services related to alcohol and drug abuse problems: An analysis of state alcoholism and drug abuse profile data.* Rockville, Md.: National Institute of Alcohol Abuse and Alcoholism.

_____. 1985. State resources and services related to alcohol and drug abuse problems: Fiscal year 1984. *A report for the National Institute on Alcohol Abuse and*

Alcoholism and the National Institute on Drug Abuse. Washington, D.C.: National Association of State Alcohol and Drug Abuse Directors.

_____. 1986. State resources and services related to alcohol and drug abuse problems: Fiscal year 1985. *A report for the National Institute on Alcohol Abuse and Alcoholism and the National Institute on Drug Abuse.* Washington, D.C.: National Association of State Alcohol and Drug Abuse Directors.

Butynski, W., et al. 1987. State resources and services related to alcohol and drug abuse problems: Fiscal year 1986. *A report for the National Institute on Alcohol Abuse and Alcoholism and the National Institute on Drug Abuse.* Washington, D.C.: National Association of State Alcohol and Drug Abuse Directors.

Butynski, W., and D. Canova. 1988. State resources and services related to alcohol and drug abuse problems: Fiscal year 1987. *A report for the National Institute on Alcohol Abuse and Alcoholism and the National Institute on Drug Abuse.* Washington, D.C.: National Association of State Alcohol and Drug Abuse Directors.

Cahalan, D. 1987. *Understanding America's drinking problem.* San Francisco: Jossey-Bass Publishers.

Cahn, S. 1970. *The treatment of alcoholics: An evaluative study.* New York: Oxford University Press.

Chopra, K., D. Preston, and L. Gerson. 1979. The effect of constructive coercion on the rehabilitative process. *Journal of Occupational Medicine* 21:749–61.

Diesenhaus, H. 1989. Memo and worksheets on NDATUS and SADAP data. Institute of Medicine, Committee for the Study on Alcohol Treatment, April 1989.

Emrick, C. D. 1982. Evaluation of alcoholism therapy methods. In *Encyclopedic Handbook of Alcoholism.* Ed. E. M. Pattison and E. Kaufman. New York: Gardner Press.

Finn, P. 1985. Decriminalization of public drunkenness: Response of the health care system. *Journal of Studies on Alcohol* 46(1): 7–23.

Flores, P. J. 1982. The efficacy of the use of coercion in getting DWI offenders into treatment. *Journal of Alcohol Drug Education* 28:18–27.

General Service Board, Alcoholics Anonymous. 1981. *Survey of Membership.* New York: Grand Central Station, Box 459.

_____. 1986. *Survey of Membership.* New York: Grand Central Station, Box 459.

_____. 1987. *Survey of Membership.* New York: Grand Central Station, Box 459.

_____. 1989. *Survey of Membership.* New York: Grand Central Station, Box 459.

Glasscote, R., et al. 1967. *The treatment of alcoholism: A study of programs and problems.* Washington, D.C.: Joint Information Service of the American Psychiatric Association and the National Association of Mental Health.

Hoffman, L. M. 1989. *The politics of knowledge: Activist movements in medicine and planning*. Albany, N.Y.: Suny Press.

Institute of Medicine, National Academy of Sciences. 1990. *Broadening the base of alcohol treatment*. Washington, D.C.: National Academy of Science Press.

Jacob, O. 1985. Public and private sector issues on alcohol and other drug abuse. *A special report with recommendations*. Rockville, Md.: U.S. Department of Health and Human Services, Public Health Service. October.

Jacobs, P. 1981. *Validity of alcoholism treatment ads doubted. Los Angeles Times:* December 14.

Killeen, J. E. 1984. Military Intervention Programs. In *Prevention of Alcohol Abuse*. Ed. P.M. Miller and T.D. Nirenberg, 469–503. New York: Plenum Press.

Miller, W., and R. Hester. 1986. Inpatient alcoholism treatment: Who benefits. *American Psychologist* 41(7): 794–805.

National Association of State Alcohol and Drug Abuse Directors (NASADAD). 1987. *Renewal of the federal alcohol, drug abuse and mental health services (ADMS) block grant*. Alcohol and drug abuse report. Washington, D.C., March-April 1987 monthly report.

Phillips, M. 1989. *The American criminal justice system and mandates to alcohol treatment*. Berkeley, Ca.: Alcohol Research Group.

Plaut, T. 1964. The state alcoholism program movement: A critical analysis. In *Selected Papers Presented at the Fifteenth Annual Meeting, North American Association of Alcohol Programs*, 74–93. Washington, D.C.: NAAAP.

President's Commission on Mental Health. 1978. Report of the task panel on the nature and scope of the problem. In *Task Panel reports*, vol. 2, appendix, 1–138. Washington, D.C.: U.S. Government Printing Office.

Reed, P., and D. Sanchez. June 1986. *Characteristics of alcoholism services in the United States—1984: Data from the September 1984 National Alcoholism and Drug Abuse Program Inventory (NDAPI)*. USNIAAA: Division of Biometry and Epidemiology.

Reis, R., and L. Davis. 1979. DUI client characteristics: An interim analysis of the random assignment process. In *Comprehensive Driving under the Influence of Alcohol Offender Treatment Demonstration Project*, DOT HS-805-587. Sacramento, Ca.: County of Sacramento Health Department.

Reynolds, R. 1987. Opening remarks. The alcohol piece in the health care cost containment puzzle. In *Proceedings, National Conference*. San Diego: Extension Program on Alcohol Issues, University of California.

Reynolds, R. 1988. Evaluating recovery outcomes. *Opening Remarks, at Conference of the University of California, San Diego, Program on Alcohol Issues*. San Diego: University of California.

Roman, P. 1988. Growth and transformation in the workplace. In *Recent Developments in Alcoholism.* Ed. M. Galanter, 6:135–58. New York: Plenum Press.

Room, R. 1980. Treatment seeking populations and larger realities. In *Alcoholism Treatment in Transition.* Ed. G. Edwards and M. Grant, 205–24. Longdon: Croom Helm.

Saxe, L. March 1983. *The effectiveness and costs of alcoholism treatment.* Washington, D.C.: Office of Technology Assessment.

Schaef, A. W. 1987. *When society becomes an addict.* San Francisco: Harper and Row.

Schuerman, A., E. Pearman, and L. Glass. 1961. A study of 54 compulsory referrals to a county alcoholism rehabilitation clinic. *Californian Alcoholism Revue Treat. Dig.* 4:13–15.

Shonick, W. June 1981. The state of the public sector health services in California. *Journal of Public Health Policy* 2(2): 164–75.

Shonick, W., and R. Roemer. 1983. *Public hospitals under private management.* Berkeley: Institute of Governmental Studies, University of California.

Shortell, S. 1988. *The evolution of hospital systems: Unfulfilled promises and self-fulfilling prophesies.* VII. Berkeley, Ca.: School of Public Health, University of California.

State of Connecticut. 1988. *The drug and alcohol abuse crisis within the Connecticut Criminal Justice System.* Drug and Alcohol Abuse Criminal Justice Commission, Gordon Bates Chairman: March 1.

State of Minnesota. 1987. *Biennial report, 1987.* St. Paul: Chemical Dependency Program Division, Department of Human Services.

State of New York. 1986. *Alcoholism treatment in criminal justice: Task force report to the Governor.* Governor's task force on alcoholism treatment in criminal justice.

U.S. General Accounting Office. 1986. *Health insurance: Comparison of coverage for federal and private sector employees.* Washington, D.C.: USGAO.

U.S. National Institute on Alcohol Abuse and Alcoholism (USNIAAA). 1979. *Comprehensive report: data from the April 30, 1979, national drug and alcoholism treatment utilization survey* (NDATUS). Contract No. 271-79-5802. Rockville, Md.: NIAAA.

———. 1987. *Sixth special report to the U.S. Congress on alcohol and health.* U.S. Department of Health and Human Services, Alcohol, Drug Abuse and Mental Health Administration. Rockville, Md.: NIAAA.

———. 1989. *National drug and alcoholism treatment unit survey (NDATUS): 1987 Final report.* DHHS publication no. (ADM) 89-16265. Rockville, Md.: NIDA and NIAAA.

Weisner, C., and R. Room. 1984. Financing and ideology in alcohol treatment. *Social Problems* 32(2): 167–84.

Weisner C. 1986. The transformation of alcohol treatment: Access to care and the response to drinking-driving. *Journal of Public Health Policy* 7(1): 78–92.

_____. 1987. The social ecology of alcohol treatment in the United States. In *Recent developments in alcoholism.* Ed. M. Galanter, 5:203–43. New York: Plenum Press.

_____. 1990. Coercion in alcohol treatment. In *Broadening the base of alcohol treatments.* Ed. National Academy of Science Press, 579–611. Washington, D.C.: Institute of Medicine.

Wiener, C. 1981. *The politics of alcoholism: Building an arena around a social problem.* New Brunswick, N.Y.: Transaction Books.

Wright, A. 1986. *A community model approach to alcohol-related problems.* Los Angeles, Ca.: Los Angeles County Office of Alcohol Problems, Department of Health Services.

Yahr, H. 1988. A national comparison of public- and private-sector alcoholism treatment delivery system characteristics. *Journal of Studies on Alcohol* 49(3): 233–39.

Alcoholism Treatment in Canada: History, Current Status, and Emerging Issues

Brian R. Rush and *Alan C. Ogborne*

Historical Overview of Alcohol in Canadian Society

Canada is a federalist state comprised of ten provinces and two northern territories. Confederation dates from 1867 when an Act of the British Parliament provided for the union of three British North American provinces—Canada (Ontario and Quebec), New Brunswick, and Nova Scotia. Most of the other provinces and the territories joined over the next fifty years, but Newfoundland not until 1949. Historically, the jurisdictional responsibilities across federal, provincial, and territorial governments have played a major role in shaping the development of alcoholism-treatment services.

Geographically, Canada is second in size only to the Soviet Union, but its population of about 26 million is less than half that of the United Kingdom. Most of the earliest immigrants to Canada were from Great Britain and France. The French language and culture remain predominant in the province of Quebec and in many smaller areas throughout the country. Subsequent waves of immigration came from many western and east European countries, as well as the Pacific Rim and South and Central America.

Although previously unknown to Canada's native people (Indian and Inuit), alcohol became an important commodity in trade between them and the first European traders. They soon experienced many alcohol-related problems, but attempts by both French and British authorities to ban the alcohol trade with them were largely unsuccessful. The native people continue to experience many problems with alcohol. For example, it has been estimated that although they represent only 1–2% of the population, they account for about 17% of hospital admissions for alcohol-related problems (Health and Welfare Canada 1982).

Tales of heavy drinking and of alcohol-related problems feature prominently in accounts of early colonial life in Canada. However, it was not until 1827 that concerns about alcohol found a common focus in Canada's first temperance society, which had been heavily influenced by the American Temperance Society, formed in 1807. The initial purpose of both societies was to "restrain the use of ardent spirits," but they tolerated the moderate use of beer, wine and cider. It was not until 1855 that the Canadian temperance movement became united against the use of all forms of alcohol.

From about 1850 the Canadian temperance movement began to press for prohibition in Canada and was successful in many provincial and municipal plebiscites. National prohibition was introduced as a war-time measure during World War I and had varying degrees of success around the country. Quebec, in particular, vigorously opposed it and it had little success in that province. Between 1920 and 1925 prohibition was defeated in various plebiscites in the provinces and territories, but it continued in Prince Edward Island until 1948.

After the repeal of prohibition, each province enacted a series of laws designed to regulate the production and distribution of alcoholic beverages, and all provinces eventually established government monopoly systems, which continue to this day. Since the end of World War II, Canadian drinking laws have become increasingly liberal, although not uniformly so across the country.

Trends in Consumption and Problem Indicators

Although lack of data precludes precise comparisons, it is generally acknowledged that alcohol use was considerably higher in the eighteenth and nineteenth centuries than in modern times. The temperance and prohibition years clearly coincided with a trend of declining alcohol consumption. Per capita adult consumption of absolute alcohol then increased during the postprohibition era, and especially after the end of World War II, rising from about 4.3 liters in 1945 to a high of about 11 liters in 1976 (Popham and Schmidt 1958; Addiction Research Foundation 1989). It has since leveled off and decreased moderately, to about 10.3 liters in 1986. Internationally, Canada's per capita alcohol consumption was ranked twenty-sixth in 1980, the last year for which complete data are available (Addiction Research Foundation 1989).

Per capita consumption varies considerably within the country, from a low of about 7.9 liters of absolute alcohol annually in New Brunswick to a high of 18.2 liters in the Yukon, one of the northern territories (Addiction Research Foundation 1989). Alcohol use shows many other regional differences, such as the estimated proportion of the adult population who are abstainers, which ranges from 13 to 32% (Health and Welfare Canada 1988). Since beer and ale account for about 51% of alcohol consumed, Canada is often thought of as a beer-drinking country. However, preferences for beer, spirits, and wine vary considerably.

Consistent with the rise in consumption, alcohol-related problems have increased markedly since World War II. Although there is recent evidence that some are beginning to decline (e.g., Mann et al. 1988), they still impose a very high cost on Canadian society (Addiction Research Foundation 1989).

Historical Development of Alcoholism Treatment Services

Before World War II. Throughout Canada's history up to World War II, alcoholism was viewed primarily from a moralistic standpoint. Although the early advocates of the temperance movement and prohibition were influenced by eighteenth and nineteenth-century medical research and debate concerning alcoholism as a disease (e.g., the works of Thomas Trotter and Benjamin Rush), they were concerned primarily with the social and legislative control of alcohol. They did not lobby for treatment services for individuals with alcohol problems, who were seen as victims of a powerful drug and admonished to exercise more self-control. However, temperance societies welcomed reformed drinkers, who often became convincing advocates of the temperance cause.

In the latter part of the 1800s and the early 1900s, a small number of private treatment facilities were established for "inebriety" or "narcomania." One of the earliest was the Homewood Retreat in Ontario, established in 1882, specializing in the treatment of alcohol addiction as well as other mental illnesses.

Although at the Homewood alcoholism was considered a disease amenable to treatment, the moralistic influence still predominated in treatment institutions. For example, at the Deer Park Sanatorium, established in 1891 in Toronto: "one of the main objects of the founders is to surround a patient with a Christian influence and send him out, not only cured of his appetite for alcohol and other narcotics, but a restored man" (*Quarterly Journal of Inebriety,* 1892, p. 96).

A few programs, asylums, and sanitariums specialized in the care of alcoholics before World War II, but in general this period was characterized by a lack of government attention. Alcoholism was not viewed as something requiring significant resources from the public purse. Also, it was largely ignored by the medical profession. Indeed, the primary "treatment" response in most regions during this period was a legislative one, providing for the committal of chronic alcoholics to mental institutions or imprisonment for public drunkenness. Breach of provincial liquor laws, typically public drunkenness, was the most common "crime." In some provinces the minister of health was required to provide facilities where alcoholics committed by the courts could be treated. However, this had little direct influence on the number of treatment services made available.

World War II to the mid-1960s. The Alcoholics Anonymous (AA) movement entered Canada in the 1940s and by the end of the decade a new period in the development of alcoholism services had begun. The impetus came primarily from the clear shift away from the previously dominant moralistic view of alcoholism to the view that alcoholism was a disease. Viewed in this new light, alcoholism became a legitimate concern for health professionals,

who could offer "care" in the hope of "cure." This move toward acceptance
of the disease model was heavily influenced by the work of E. M. Jellinek
and others in the United States. Jellinek's work, and its application within the
AA movement, was highly successful in providing an alternative to the
temperance, prohibitionist approaches.

In most of the Canadian provinces, members of AA, key individuals,
and other community groups exerted considerable pressure on the provincial
governments to expand treatment capabilities. Some of these people were
closely connected with the temperance movement, while others were quite
independent of it. During the late 1940s and the 1950s most provinces
established alcoholism foundations, commissions, or departments, with
responsibilities for prevention, treatment, and, in some cases, research. In some
regions (e.g., Newfoundland and the Yukon) this did not occur until the 1960s.
They evolved through various stages, and even through the 1970s and 80s their
status in the different provincial and territorial governments was still changing.
Mostly they were placed in the provincial ministries of health, in accordance
with the prevailing medicalization of the problem, and, from being quite small
at first, became gradually larger and more complex. In most of the provinces,
it was intended that the commissions would eventually fund all the treatment
services under their administrative umbrella. The extent to which this was
achieved varied from province to province and has evolved over time. In
Quebec, for example, the provincial commission was short-lived; it was
dissolved after a major reorganization of health and social services. This
reorganization resulted in a de-emphasis on specialized facilities and in
increasing integration of addiction services with general health-care services.
Each province dealt with this issue of integration versus specialized service
delivery in its own unique way, with the result that there is considerable
diversity in the planning and development of the provincial alcoholism treatment
systems. The different provinces also devoted varying levels of attention to
drugs other than alcohol, but the primary concern was, and in most cases
remains, alcohol. In British Columbia two organizations were established—
one for alcohol and the second for other drugs.

As noted above, developments in the United States after World War II
influenced significantly the Canadian response to alcoholism. Many people
associated with the provincial alcoholism commissions and local community
treatment programs attended the Yale Summer School of Alcoholic Studies,
where they were exposed to the ideas of Jellinek and other founders of the
so-called modern approach to alcoholism. Through Dr. David Archibald, a
pioneer in the Canadian addiction field, Jellinek was also directly involved
with the Ontario Alcoholism Research Foundation. This provincial foundation
was the first to be established (1949) and became a model for some of the
other regions.

It is noteworthy that the relationship with the United States in the development of treatment services became reciprocal in many important respects over the ensuing years. For example, Dr. Gordon Bell of Ontario had close connections with many influential groups in the alcoholism field in the United States during the 1950s and 60s, and his comprehensive, health-oriented approach to treatment provided the general guidelines for a treatment model still widely used in the United States (Bell and Solomon, 1989). In later years, scientists and others associated with the Ontario Addiction Research Foundation had a significant influence in the United States—for example, in the development of a non-medical, social model for detoxification.

The mid-1960s to 1980. The period between 1965 and 1980 is worthy of note in the history of alcoholism treatment in Canada, primarily because of the remarkable rate of growth in treatment capacity. Of about 340 specialized agencies operating in 1976, fully two-thirds had been established since 1970 (Reid 1981), and their costs had increased from Can.$14 million to Can.$70 million over this six-year period. Much of this growth was related to the continued expansion and evolution of the provincial commissions and the treatment services they funded. However, even in provinces that no longer had a commission, or whose commission had given up the direct funding of treatment services, there was a major expansion of treatment resources. Many types of service were established, including detoxification centers, outpatient programs, short-and long-term inpatient facilities, and aftercare services.

This period was characterized also by an increasing professionalization of treatment-service personnel. A range of medical and paramedical professions initially became involved in the provision of treatment, but this range was later extended to include psychologists, social workers, and mental health counselors. Recovered (or "recovering") alcoholics also played a significant role in developing or staffing the new treatment services, and today represent a major proportion of the treatment staff across the country.

Finally, this period saw an increase in the misuse of drugs other than alcohol and the need for appropriate prevention and treatment responses. The mandates of the provincial commissions and treatment services were, therefore, broadened to respond to problems posed by younger, multiple-drug abusing populations. To some extent this adaptation continues today.

1980 to the present. For a number of reasons, the beginning of the 1980s serves as a benchmark for the current era of alcoholism treatment in Canada. Consistent with changes in the funding of most other types of government health and social services, the expansion period of the 1970s gave way to a period of more controlled growth. Although treatment capacity continues to increase in some regions of the country, especially those that lagged behind in the development of services, growth elsewhere has become marginal or clearly stabilized. This stabilization is related in part to a large supply of treatment services in some areas. In other regions, however, a declining tax base has capped the expansion of most health and social services, including those for the treatment of alcoholism.

Two other features of this new period are evident. First, the broader perspective on the nature of addictive behaviour, which has been emerging from the research literature in the field over the past ten to fifteen years, has affected the development of new services. Rather than postulating a unitary, biomedical cause of alcoholism, this "biopsychosocial" perspective holds that the causes of alcohol problems are multidimensional, and the treatment needs quite heterogeneous. Among the native community, the three elements of the biopsychosocial perspective revolve around a fourth, a spiritual/cultural element. This provides the base for a very culturally-oriented approach to treatment in native treatment centers. In addition, a broader view of alcohol problems has developed, which sees problems as existing along a continuum of severity, ranging from alcohol dependence to less severe alcohol-related disabilities or at-risk consumption. In response to these broader perspectives about the nature of the problem, treatment services are more likely to be planned along a continuum of care, corresponding to this continuum of severity.

There is considerable variation across the country in the extent to which these perspectives have supplanted or merged with the disease concept and influenced the development of new services. These regional differences are discussed more fully in a subsequent section.

The second development in the present era has been a systems approach to the planning and delivery of treatment, influenced to a large extent by the work of such individuals as Glaser and his colleagues (1978) and Pattison (1982). Whereas the 1970s saw the development of different types of treatment facilities, the systems approach provides for a broader continuum of care with a well-defined role for detoxification, assessment, treatment, and aftercare services. A stronger emphasis is being placed on matching individual clients to treatment, on the basis of an assessment of individual needs and strengths. This has led to considerable diversification of new and existing services. The systems approach has contributed also to more integration and coordination of alcoholism services within the general health and social service system, as it has become clear that these generalist services have an important functional role within the community treatment system (case-finding, assessment, aftercare, case management). This has become especially clear in the planning of services in the rural, less populated areas of the country.

To summarize this brief historical overview of treatment in Canada, four periods of development can be distinguished: (1) from early Canadian history until the end of World War II, dominated by a moralistic view of the problem and little attention from government or the medical community; (2) the late 1940s until the mid-1960s, characterized by the view of alcoholism as a disease and a legitimate chronic health problem to be dealt with by provincially funded agencies with a mandate to develop treatment services; (3) the mid-1960s until

1980, a period best described as one of expansion and professionalization of the treatment field in Canada; and (4) the 1980s to the present, represented by a diversification of new and established services, a more modest rate of growth, a broader perspective of the nature of alcohol problems and a systems approach to planning.

Although these general periods of development can be distinguished, it is important to recognize that each province and territory had its own unique historical development, was heavily influenced by key individuals and community groups, and is still at a different point from the others along this historical continuum. In short, there is not one Canadian treatment system. What has developed is a set of largely independent provincial/territorial networks of treatment services. This is due primarily to the federalist structure of the country and the place of alcoholism treatment within the health and social jurisdictions of the provinces.

Federal Responsibilities and Initiatives

Federal/provincial jurisdictions were set in law at the time of confederation, in the British North American Act of 1867. This gave the provinces responsibility for such areas as health, education, and other social services, while the federal government retained control over such domains as defense, forests and fisheries, other natural resources, and transportation. In the case of the production and trade of alcohol, federal constitutional authority still includes the licensing of breweries and distilleries, and the regulation of interprovincial transportation of liquor. With respect to alcohol programs, federal involvement depends somewhat on the nature of the program and its target group. It is generally agreed that the provision of treatment programs lies within the provincial domain, under a provision of the British North American Act, which gave the provinces responsibility for hospitals, asylums, and charitable institutions. The federal government has more authority within the addiction field for public education, information services, and research. However, by either convention or constitutional authority, a number of groups do fall under federal responsibility for health-care services. They include status Indians, members of the armed forces, the Royal Canadian Mounted Police, and war veterans. Each of the two northern-territory governments is responsible for its own alcohol and drug services but receives partial support through federal cost-sharing arrangements. Separate funding of native alcohol services is administered federally in the Yukon and via transfer of federal health funds in the northwest territories. Treatment is also available in many federal correctional institutions, and to federal employees through their employment benefits.

In addition to these responsibilities, however, the federal government is also a significant contributor to the treatment offered at the provincial and territorial level, through cost-sharing arrangements for hospital and medical-care insurance, vocational rehabilitation services, welfare, and other social assistance. For example, in some provinces the cost-sharing formula under the Vocational Rehabilitation of Disabled Persons Act reimburses 30–40% of program costs to the provincial treasury.

It is beyond the scope of this paper to describe all the specific federal initiatives that have contributed to the development of treatment services at the provincial and territorial level. However, one initiative especially worthy of note is the National Native Alcohol and Drug Abuse Program (NNADAP), initiated in 1975. Currently, it funds forty residential treatment centers and about four hundred community health workers employed in Indian reservations, with broad responsibility for community education and health promotion. Other funding for native programs comes directly from the province or territory, or is transferred from federal sources by other means. These programs face many important issues today, such as the lack of other basic support services and the remoteness of some of the native communities.

In addition to treatment services for native people, the federal government has actively sponsored various initiatives and mechanisms to help coordinate and share information across the country. These initiatives have typically involved the heads of the various provincial/territorial commissions. In 1989 the government established the Canadian Centre for Substance Abuse, which will undoubtedly become an important national forum for policy debate, comparative studies, and information sharing.

Not all national initiatives in alcoholism treatment have been sponsored by government. Alcoholics Anonymous and other self-help groups are well represented across the country, although not formally organized at the national level. Another important organization is the Salvation Army, which was first established in Canada in the 1870s and quickly spread across the country, dealing with a wide variety of social problems, including alcoholism. It has recently reorganized its addiction services across Canada into one department, the Addictions and Rehabilitation Department, which will play an important role in the delivery of services in many communities.

Finally, there are many treatment-related voluntary, lay, and professional initiatives with a national focus. The role of many of these groups is to lobby for more effective action from government for dealing with alcohol problems. Some groups also train professionals and disseminate information to increase public awareness.

In summary, the provision of alcoholism treatment in Canada is primarily a provincial responsibility, grounded in the legislative intent and traditions of the British North America Act. The federal government has some specific areas of responsibility and uses a variety of mechanisms to help fund, promote, and coordinate the treatment programs implemented in the provinces and territories. Other national organizations and programs also play a key role.

Current Canadian Alcoholism Treatment Systems

The relative independence of the provincial/territorial alcoholism treatment networks makes it very difficult to summarize the Canadian situation. Comparisons across the various regions are made especially difficult by differences in the provincial information systems, which monitor the availabiity and utilization of alcoholism services. Further, some regions do not have such information systems, or their systems do not capture the entire network of services. Reid and Chappel (1978) provided an overview of the Canadian situation in the late 1970s, and a national survey of treatment programs was completed in 1976 (Reid 1981). The survey information is now considerably out of date.

For purposes of this chapter, structured interviews have been conducted around the country to determine how the current network of services is operating in each region and to identify important trends and issues. The intent is to highlight some of the major differences and similarities across the country in a qualitative rather than quantitative manner, while recognizing the limitations of this approach from a comparative, analytical point of view.

Major Differences across Regions

One of the major differences across the provinces and territories is the administrative arrangement within which alcoholism services are planned, funded, and implemented. While the Ministry of Health remains the predominant department of government for addiction services, in some regions services may be funded from social services, welfare, labor, or even the housing sector. In still other areas, alcoholism services are funded quite separately from any specific government ministry. Although the administrative arrangements have evolved differently in each region, and continue to evolve, there has been a clear move toward more community-based, and less institution-based, services in all areas of the country. One consequence of the diversity in administrative relationships, however, is that services are financed differently. In some of the provinces and territories all addiction services are funded directly by government; thus managers and staff of the programs are part of the civil service. In other regions, some such direct services are funded, as well as other services that are funded and operated as independent community programs. In still other regions, all programs are supported by such indirect funding. The many different funding arrangements translate into varying degrees of government control, accountability, and interagency coordination.

Across the country there are clearly divergent views about the nature of alcoholism and alcohol problems. While a broader, biopsychosocial model is emerging in some areas, there is clearly no national consensus on this issue. In some regions the traditional disease concept is still the normative view of the problem, and forms the basis of a primarily medical orientation of detoxification, anti-alcohol drug therapy, and inpatient care. In others, the disease concept has been broadened, and supports a more comprehensive approach to alcoholism treatment, including nonmedical detoxification, psychosocial interventions, and a balance of inpatient care, day treatment, and outpatient care. In still other areas, the disease concept has been giving way to a biopsychosocial perspective, emphasizing, for example, behavioral therapies, stress management, and problem-solving for alcoholic clients in nonresidential programs. Finally, in the northern regions, and specifically for the treatment of native people, the predominant perspective is cultural/spiritual in nature, consistent with the values and philosophies of native people.

The regions are also at different stages in their development of programs for special target populations. With the exception of services for native people, youth and, to a less extent, women, the general strategy has been to develop specialized programs within existing treatment facilities rather than new, independent services. This has contributed to an increased diversification of treatment settings and modalities. However, the extent to which specialized programs have been developed for different target groups depends largely upon the availability of services that are aimed at the general population in the region. In a few regions, alcoholism treatment services are only now being developed and there is little emphasis on special target groups. In many areas, however, a very diversified network of services is emerging, with considerable emphasis being placed on services for populations with special needs (e.g., multicultural populations, the physically and mentally disabled, the elderly).

Finally, a consequence of this diversity is the varying degree to which the care of alcoholics has been systematized within each region. Indeed, there are different views on the criteria that an optimally functioning treatment system should meet. One is that the degree to which alcohol treatment services are organized into a system may be assessed by the level of coordination and cooperation among the specialist addiction agencies themselves—that is, the relationship between detoxification, assessment, treatment, and aftercare services and the flow of clients through this continuum of care. At this level, there are variations across the country, reflecting in part the varying degree of administrative control over all components of the network. Another is that it can be assessed by examining the relationship among the addiction specialists and the other nonaddiction services in the community, such as those provided by physicians, hospitals, mental health clinics, and social and correctional services. Here the regions appear more similar, as all strive to involve such services more actively in case-finding, diagnosis, management, and referral of clients with alcohol problems.

Major Similarities across Regions

All regions have allocated substantial financial resources to treatment for alcohol and other drug problems. An estimate of the total annual cost of treatment in Canada would now exceed Can.$300 million, almost entirely derived from public funds. Quebec is the only province with a significant private sector (for profit) involvement (Rush and Brochu in press). Overall, there are few financial barriers to access to treatment.

One of the most striking similarities across the country is the broadening of treatment to include drugs other than alcohol. While alcohol remains the major drug of abuse, most treatment services describe themselves as "substance abuse services" for the treatment of "chemical dependence" or "addiction." Many programs have different detoxification or treatment procedures for certain drugs (e.g., tranquilizers, cocaine), but few services would describe themselves as drug-treatment programs. A reasonable national estimate of the percentage of clients that present with a "drug-only" problem would be 5–10%. Most, of both sexes and all ages, take multiple drugs.

Three other aspects are quite consistent across the country. The first is a clearly declining trend in the age of the treatment population. The average age is now in the range of 30–35 years, and many more teenagers and young adults are presenting for treatment than in the past. This decline has resulted in part from the stronger linkage between addiction programs and other types of community services, such as educational, correctional, family, and children's services. In many communities this has contributed to a call for more treatment services specifically for youth.

The second is an increasing proportion of women presenting for treatment. A reasonable estimate of the ratio of men to women in treatment is now between two and three to one, compared with nearly five to one in the 1970s, and an even higher ratio during the earliest development of services. Although specialized facilities for women are not very common, treatment programs provide more gender-specific treatment. Clearly, women now have greater access to treatment than they have had in the past.

The third is a general decline in involvement of treatment services with chronic, skid-row alcoholics. Many of the alcoholism services developed in the 1960s and early 70s, such as nonmedical detoxification centers, halfway houses, and rehabilitation farms, were aimed at this group. They still play an important role for the chronic abuser, but they form a declining proportion of the total treatment network. Also, many have become more closely integrated with the mainstream treatment network. For example, detoxification centers are increasingly viewed as gateways to assessment or treatment services rather than as simply an alternative to incarceration for public-drunkenness offenders. Also, many of the halfway houses and recovery homes originally designed to help with the long-term reintegration of the chronic abuser have now shortened and structured their programs and targeted them at a more socially stable clientele.

Although treatment services differ in many ways across the country, several aspects of program design and delivery are common to all parts. First, the emphasis that was placed on the medical aspects of alcohol abuse in the 1950s and 60s resulted in the location of many treatment services in hospitals. In most parts of the country, this medical orientation of treatment is being deemphasized and priority is being given to the development of nonmedical, community-based services. This trend has been influenced by research into the cost-effectiveness of treatment provided in different settings (e.g., medical compared with nonmedical detoxification, or hospital care compared with community-based care) and is consistent with general trends in the deinstitu-tionalization of mental health programs and with concerns about the cost-effectiveness of health and social services, generally.

In addition to the decrease, or at least stabilization, of hospital resources for the treatment of addiction, considerations of cost-effectiveness have also led to greater emphasis on outpatient care. It is recognized that a range of community settings is needed, including outpatient and day-treatment services, as well as the residential services provided by detoxification centers, and short-term and long-term facilities. Although the mix of these alternative settings varies from region to region, this continuum of care exists to some degree in all the provinces and territories. As noted previously, assessment of clients is receiving more attention, as a means of matching clients to appropriate programs. Assessment is performed in specialized community facilities (Ogborne and Rush 1990) or in multimodal treatment centers. This is all part of a trend toward a broader systems-approach to the delivery of treatment services, described earlier.

With one exception (Prince Edward Island), all regions of the country have de-emphasized coercive, mandatory treatment, relying instead on the client's voluntary participation. Of course, "voluntary" help-seeking behaviour often has a significant coercive but covert dimension, such as the seeking of treatment under the threat of job loss. Legislated or policy-driven mandatory treatment is now limited mostly to a requirement for the assessment or treatment of persons convicted once or more often of a driving-while-impaired offense. In Prince Edward Island, mandatory treatment is still viewed as a significant aspect of the treatment approach.

Alcoholics Anonymous and other self-help groups continue to play a significant role everywhere. Many of the treatment programs are grounded in the AA approach and twelve-step program, and AA is usually cited as the most frequent recommendation for referral or community support upon completion of treatment (e.g., Rush and Ekdahl 1987). The Canadian public and many community professionals view AA as the primary source of assistance for alcohol problems.

Finally, the nature and role of program evaluation is also generally similar across the country. The emphasis tends to be on process rather than outcome evaluation. The former involves an assessment of program coverage and service delivery, accomplished primarily through the use of management information systems. These computerized systems describe, for example, the characteristics of clients, services provided, waiting periods and referrals. Little outcome evaluation has been undertaken, and it has been mostly in the context of tightly controlled research studies. However, there is an increasing interest in conducting outcome evaluation, and increasing pressure from government to do so.

Emerging Issues and Trends

One of the significant challenges in Canada today is to provide services to the rural, less populated areas of the country. Considerable ingenuity in program design and implementation will be required. In some regions, services to rural communities are being provided by means of a large number of specialized outpatient services. In others, the strategy is to make maximum use of existing resources in the community, extending the role of generalist agencies beyond case-finding and referral to include assessment, case management, counseling and aftercare. This obviously requires a significant investment of human and financial resources in community training. One of the most innovative approaches to the delivery of treatment services in remote areas of the country is known as "community mobile treatment." This approach was initially developed in British Columbia and is at present being implemented in the northern regions of Saskatchewan. A team of addiction counselors and other health-care professionals move into a remote community (typically a native community or reserve) and conduct a culture-based treatment program over a four- to five-week period. Community members provide continuing support and aftercare.

With the development of the continuum of care in the provinces and territories, comprehensive assessment and matching of clients will become crucial for the cost-effective use of treatment resources. However, first, matching criteria, well-grounded in research, are needed. There is a limited research base for the matching of clients to outpatient care, day treatment, and inpatient care, and these settings vary considerably in cost and cost-effectiveness (e.g., Longabaugh et al. 1983). More research guidance is needed on these matching criteria in order to maximize the cost-effectiveness of the new community treatment systems.

Treatment is broadening its focus to provide more assistance to the families of people with alcohol/drug problems as well as more family-based treatment. Many programs are now available for family members, and more are likely to be established over the next decade. In native services, in particular, the consideration of alcohol abuse as a problem that crosses generations is having a major influence on the design and delivery of culture-based programs.

Lastly, over the past decade the population has become increasingly aware of alcohol and other drug problems in the community, and more readily accepts treatment for alcohol problems. Consistent with this trend, and the existence of basic services in most of the provinces and territories, attention is shifting toward the role of general health, social and correctional services in the addiction treatment system. Despite the hundreds of specialized addiction agencies now in place, most people with alcohol problems are unlikely to seek treatment. Also those who seek treatment often do so only after their problems have become serious and resistant to change. Those who provide generalist services such as family physicians, hospitals, and social counseling agencies, are being encouraged to screen their patients and clients for alcohol and other drug problems and to assess, treat, or refer them. The addition of such early case-finding to the present network of treatment services and other sustained health promotion activities should contribute greatly to a reduction of alcohol and other drug problems in Canada.

Note

The views expressed in this paper are those of the authors and do not necessarily represent those of the Addiction Research Foundation of the University of Western Ontario, Toronto. The authors wish to thank the many individuals across Canada who have shared their information and insight toward the development of this paper.

References

Addiction Research Foundation. 1989. *Statistics on alcohol and drug use in Canada and other countries: Statistics on alcohol use* 1. Toronto: Addiction Research Foundation.

Bell, R. G., and S. Solomon. 1989. *A special calling.* Toronto: Stoddart.

Glaser F. B., S. W. Greenberg, and M. Barrett. 1978. *A systems approach to alcohol treatment.* Toronto: Addiction Research Foundation.

Health and Welfare Canada. 1982. *Discussion paper: National Native Alcohol and Drug Abuse Program.* Ottawa: Minister of Health and Welfare Canada.

————. 1988. *Canada's health promotion survey: Technical report.* (Cat. No. H39–119/1988E). Ottawa: Minister of Supply and Services Canada.

Longabaugh, R., et al. 1983. Cost effectiveness of alcoholism treatment in partial versus inpatient settings: Six month outcomes. *Journal of Studies on Alcohol* 44:1049–71.

Mann, R., R. Smart, and L. Anglin. 1988. Reductions in liver cirrhosis mortality and morbidity in Canada: Demographic differences and possible explanations. *Alcoholism: Clinical and Experimental Research* 12(2): 290–97.

Ogborne, A., and B. Rush. 1990. Specialized addictions assessment/referral services in Ontario: A review of their characteristics and roles in the addiction treatment system. *British Journal of Addiction* 85(2): 197–204.

Pattison, E. M. 1982. A systems approach to alcoholism treatment. In *Encyclopedic handbook of alcoholism.* Ed. E. M. Pattison and E. Kaufman, 1089–108. New York: Gardner.

Popham, R. E., and W. Schmidt, ed. 1958. *Statistics of alcohol use and alcoholism in Canada 1871-1956,* 29. Toronto: University of Toronto Press.

Quarterly Journal of Inebriety. 1892. Clinical notes and comments: Deer Park Sanatorium. *Quarterly Journal of Inebriety* 14:96. Toronto.

Reid, A., and N. Chappel. 1978. Overview of alcohol and drug programs in Canada. In *Core knowledge in the drug field.* Ed. L. A. Philips et al., 1–46. (Cat.no. H45-6/1978-2). Ottawa: National Health and Welfare.

Reid, A. 1981. Alcoholism treatment in Canada: A review of current programs and policy issues. *The International Journal of the Addictions* 16(4): 647–81.

Rush, B., and S. Brochu. n.d. Treatment services for alcohol and drug abuse in Ontario and Quebec: A comparison of provincial surveys. *Journal of Drug Issues.*

Rush, B., and A. Ekdahl. 1987. *Treatment services for alcohol and drug abuse in Ontario: Results of a provincial survey.* 1986. Toronto: Addiction Research Foundation.

The Alcoholism Treatment System in China

Zhang Yanyi

The System of Treatment of Alcoholism in China: An Overview

As a country of multiple nationalities, China's situation in regard to the use of alcohol is rather complex. A nationwide epidemiological survey of alcohol abuse has shown higher prevalence in regions inhabited by some minority nationalities, such as Yunnan, Xingjiang, Inner Mongolia, Heilongjiang, and Sichuan, than elsewhere. This higher prevalence may have some relation with the natural environments of the minority nationalities, the peculiarities of their history, and their cultural background and local customs.

Since the founding of new China in 1949, a three-tier network of prevention and treatment of alcoholism has been established. Treatment is carried out at different levels. Along with economic reform in the last ten years, medical establishments have been guided by the principle of "working together at the state, collective, and individual levels." As part of the economic reform, the system of contractual responsibilities for all technical and economic enterprises has resulted in strengthening the capacity of health-care organizations for self-development. On this basis, it has been possible to set up a growing number of collective clinics and home-care sick beds, thereby expanding the scope of prevention and treatment services. Funds collected from various sources for the construction of medical facilities have supplemented capital expenditure on health-care organizations.

Recent political and economic changes have been accompanied by a marked increase in the number of alcoholics. By the end of 1985, according to a survey conducted in regions of minority nationalities, the rate of prevalence of alcohol dependence and poisoning was 35% in the areas of Simao and Xishangbanna of Yunnan Province, 6.61% in Hubei Province, and 4.55% in the city of Chongqing. These figures are evidently much higher than the rate of 0.16% based on a countrywide survey of twelve regions carried out in 1982. In view of this, research and inquiries into the cause, development, and symptoms of alcohol dependence and poisoning, and studies aimed at improvement of mental health and reduction of cases of psychosis and other mental disorders, have become a matter of common concern to the nation's psychiatrists, psychologists, and sociologists.

Before 1949, because the civil war had wreaked havoc on the political, economic, and cultural life of China, the country's mental health institutions were in a state of stagnancy. Since then, with the help of the state government, psychiatric hospitals and other alcoholism prevention and treatment centers began to be established, with a total of sixty-two set up between 1949 and 1958. In 1958 the Ministry of Public Health convened a conference on the prevention and treatment of mental illness, in the city of Nanjing. The conference adopted the guiding principles of "prevention and treatment through the participation of the masses, by the combined methods of traditional Chinese and Western medicine, by the combined use of medicine and psychiatric care, and by the combined therapy of work and recreation." After the conference, the cooperation of the general public was mobilized, and training and research in mental health strengthened. Since the 70s, community mental health work has begun to be organized in major cities throughout the country.

Since the founding of the People's Republic of China, decrees of the state government have played a definite role in the elimination of drug addiction and in the control of alcohol abuse. China being a country of multiple nationalities and with a vast territory, the regions vary greatly in their ecological and social conditions. Because of economic backwardness, the country has lacked sufficient resources to conduct nationwide surveys on the prevalence of alcoholism. Nevertheless, surveys carried out in a few regions known to have higher rates of alcohol consumption than others found a relatively low prevalence rate of alcohol dependence. This may be related to Chinese culture and history. Traditionally, people believed that a small or moderate amount of drinking was good for health and contributed to longevity. Besides, alcohol was considered as having medicinal value for the cure of certain diseases.

The beginning of the 80s saw significant economic growth, an increase in national income, population concentration caused by urbanization, and a trend toward smaller families. As a result, the regulatory control of drinking has broken down, and there has been an increase in the volume of alcohol consumed, in the number of drinkers, and in the prevalence of alcohol dependence and poisoning, particularly among males.

During the 80s, surveys of alcoholism have been carried out in four provinces, using the same methods as those of the joint epidemiological survey of mental illness in twelve regions (Table 1). They were conducted primarily among the Han nationality. The survey of Shandong Province in 1984 had the largest sampling, with a total of fifty-nine samples of population at age 15 and over, covering 19,160 in the cities and 9,662 in the countryside. It showed that the rates of prevalence of alcohol dependence and poisoning in both urban and rural areas were yet quite low, at 0.31 and 0.37% respectively. A survey conducted in 1983–1984 by Ai-Ding Hospital in Beijing, among a population group aged 60 and over, showed the prevalence rate for alcoholism at 2.29%. Similar investigations of alcoholism were undertaken in 1985 and 1986 by Chongqing Psychiatric Hospital and the Mental Health Research Institute of Beijing Medical University among inhabitants of the city of Chongqing, Sichuan Province, and of the urban and rural areas of Xiangyang, Hubei Province. The Chongqing survey showed a prevalence rate of 4.55% in an urban population group of 3,700 aged 15 and over. The Xiangyang survey showed a prevalence rate of 6.61% in an urban population group of 2,571 at the age of 15 and over, and 0.38% in a rural population group of 2,397. The urban rate was thirty times as high as the rate of alcohol dependence disclosed by the joint survey carried out in twelve regions (Table 1).

TABLE 1

Data of Incidence of
Alcoholic Dependence and Alcoholism in Diverse Regions

Investigative units	Region	Nationality	Time	Number of examples		Age	Incidence of disease	
				City	Country		City	Countryside
Cooperative investigation of all over country	12 regions	Han	1982	19,116	19,020	over 15 years	0.21%	0.16%
Psychosis hospital of Shandong Province	59 points	Han	1984	19,160	19,662	over 15 years	0.21%	0.16%
Andin Hospital	Beijing	Han	1983–1984	8,700		over 60 years	2.29%	
Psychosis Hospital Chongqing	City Chong-qing	Han	1985	3,700		over 15 years	4.35%	
Psychohealth Institute of Medical Uni. Beijing	Xiang-Yiang Hebei	Han	1986	2,571	2,397	over 15 years	6.61%	0.38•

Investigative method: sieve, door by door

Table for sieve: made cooperatively all over the country

Standard of diagnosis: ICD-9

So far, only seven surveys of alcoholism have been carried out among the minority nationalities. The method of door-to-door screening was used to collect data for the surveys (Table 2). The prevalence of alcohol dependence and slow poisoning was highest among the Orogen nationality living in Da Xinganling, Heilongjiang Province, at 43.09% (1986); next came the rate for the Dai and Bai nationalities living in Simao, Yunnan Province, at 35 and 30% respectively (1985); the third highest rate was 12.5%, for the Hezhen nationality living in Heilongjiang Province (1986) (Table 2). Those rates were three to seven times more than the highest prevalence rate among the population of Han nationality.

TABLE 2

Investigation into Incidence of Disease from Alcoholic Dependence and Alcoholism in Regions with Minority Nationalities

Investigative worker or units	Nationality	Time of Investigation	Number of examples	Occurrence	Ratio (%)	Proportion men / women
Psychohealth Hospital of Medical University Beijing Lu Jiyuan	Dai Yunnan	1985	739	26	35	20/0
Wan Peng etc. Yunnan	Bai Yunnan	1985	370	11	30	10/1
Psychosis Hospital of Helongjiang Province	Orogen	1986	1,137	49	43	46/3
Sun Mousuei etc. Helongjiang	Hezhen	1986	638	8	12.54	8/0
Li Ti etc.	Li Hainan Island	1984	662	2	3.02	2/0
He Mutao etc.	Qiang Shichuan	1984	2,852	14	4.91	12/2
Xiang Mentan etc.	Lijing Shichuan	1980– 1983	3,223	1	0.13	1/0

Cases of alcohol dependence have led to such widespread serious problems as traffic accidents, crimes, breaches of law and discipline, break-up of families, and disruption of work. The problems have become particularly acute in the last ten years with the appearance of such new social phenomena as heavy drinking by adults, wild drinking by adolescents, and alcohol dependence among old people. Those problems have received much attention from sociologists, psychiatrists, mental health specialists, and judicial organs, who have been working together to develop a comprehensive program of treatment.

The system of treatment of alcoholism in China is based on the principle of division of labor at different levels. It pools and coordinates the resources of medical care and prevention organizations to form a network of treatment and prevention. The work of medical units at each level is divided so that cases may be treated by the unit concerned, by referral to another unit, or jointly by two or more units. As well as the division of labor among medical units at each level, units at a higher level provide operational guidance to those at lower levels.

Medical organizations for the treatment and prevention of alcoholism exist at three levels. Those at the first level consist of factory health-care stations, neighborhood health-care stations, and hospital outpatient clinics, which provide general treatment and supervision, help patients under recovery with therapy by means of work or recreation, and arrange for medical care in their homes. They receive operational guidance from organizations at the second level, which comprise local hospitals, enterprise hospitals, and specialized medical institutions. While maintaining close links with the first-level organizations, those at the second level are in turn guided by third-level organizations. The third-level organizations, which are at the top of the network of treatment and prevention, include provincial or municipal general hospitals, teaching hospitals of medical colleges, and specialized hospitals. They are responsible, under the leadership of the public health bureau, for coordinating alcoholism treatment and prevention within the region under their jurisdiction, and for bringing all the concerned organizations in the region together to form an organic and interrelated structure. Their task is the early discovery and treatment of cases of alcohol dependence and assistance in the recovery of patients suffering from alcohol-related diseases.

Financial resources for medical establishments include appropriations from the state government budget, funds allocated for health care by ministries in charge of industrial or mining enterprises, medical-care premiums to supplement wages of workers of enterprises, government-workers' medical-care reserve funds, and funds for cooperative medical services contributed by the masses in the countryside. Health care in China is paid for by individuals or cooperatives or from public funds. City dwellers usually pay their own medical expenses. In the countryside, health care is either paid for privately or financed by various types of cooperative arrangements.

Since 1985, within the framework of the three-level medical-care organizations, psychiatric hospitals, mental-health research institutions, and mental-illness prevention centers have set up wards for patients suffering from alcohol dependence and poisoning. They have continued to develop various methods of treatment of alcoholism, both psychotherapeutic, such as aversion therapy, behavioral therapy, and systematic detoxification, and medicinal, often combined with Chinese herbal medicine or with *ogong* (a system of deep breathing exercises), acupuncture, and moxibustion. These methods have yielded very good results.

A national conference on alcohol dependence and poisoning, convened in October 1986, proposed strict measures for the control of alcohol use, established joint teams of investigation into the prevalence of alcohol addiction and poisoning in various communities, stressed the importance of detoxification and abstinence, and promoted public awareness of the harmful effects of alcohol use.

There are still deficiencies in the judicial sphere in dealing with alcoholics. According to the ordinance for the maintenance of public security and the penalizing of offenders, persons who commit offenses while intoxicated are liable to punishment after they have sobered up. If the behavior of intoxicated persons threatens their own well-being or the safety of surrounding areas, they must be held in restraint until they become sober and then placed in detention or fined, or warned or required to pay for damages. Under the criminal code, pathological alcoholics bear no legal liability; however, persons who voluntarily become drunk and commit acts in violation of the law are liable to punishment.

The following diagram depicts the preventive measures against alcohol abuse:

Drinkers	Public information on harmful effects of alcohol abuse	Medical organizations at the first and second levels
Heavy drinkers	Counseling and guidance	Psychiatric departments and psychological counseling departments of general hospitals
Alcoholics	Treatment	Wards for alcoholic patients in psychiatric hospitals, etc.
Persons recovering from alcoholism	Prevention of relapse	Out-of-hospital clinics; family support

To sum up, China is searching for an effective system for the treatment of cases of alcohol dependence and poisoning. Under the existing system, the work of treatment and prevention is carried out in a network composed of three levels of mental health organizations, which are jointly supported by public health authorities, the civil administration, and public security organs. It is hoped that in the future practical steps will be taken to continue the promotion of public knowledge of the subject, beginning with the education of children, to improve the qualities of the population, to enlist the support of the mass organizations and academic institutions, to make use of the information media to publicize the dangers of alcohol intoxication, to strengthen the functions and authorities of administrative organs, to improve the legal system so that drunken offenders will be liable to severe penalties according to law, to restrict the production and distribution of alcoholic drinks of high potency or poor quality, and to encourage the production of nonalcoholic beverages. It is believed that through the joint efforts and division of labor among social workers, psychological counselors, mental health workers, and legal organs, it will be possible to bring the prevalence of alcohol dependence under effective control.

References

China Psychohealth Magazine.

China Health Yearbook. 1988.

Encyclopaedia of Chinese Medicine: Book for Social Medicine and Health Management. Book for Recovered Medicine.

Proceedings of the Conference in 1986: Nationwide Alcohol Dependence and Alcoholism.

Psychohealth Activities in the Beijing Region. 1987.

Alcohol-Treatment Issues in Nigeria: Traditional Healers and Modern Psychiatry

Adebayo Olabisi Odejide, Jude Uzoma Ohaeri,
Moruff Adelekan, and *Benson Adebowale Ikuesan*

Nigeria, a West African country, has an estimated population of one hundred million and an average annual population growth rate of 3.1%, with more females than males (52% females—1963 census). Its population consists of three main ethnic groups (Hausas, Yorubas, and Igbos), each of which has several dialects. The Hausas live mainly in the north and the other two groups in the south. They mix readily and people are free to settle in any part of the country.

The country is essentially agricultural, with traditional—that is, subsistence—farming as the mainstay of most rural communities. Petroleum is the major earner of foreign exchange; until recently, the consequent affluence was evident in the cities. During the last two decades the country has seen much sociocultural change. There has been a noticeable migration of rural dwellers to the principal towns and cities. Annual per capita income is estimated at US$ 211. Development projects are under way in many parts and society in general is becoming more sophisticated.

Historical Background

Alcohol has always been used in Nigeria, as in many parts of Africa, even before colonization. There is a wide variety of African alcoholic drinks: fermented honey water, fermented fruits and juices, fermented sap of various species of palm, and beers. There are many accounts of the preparation of alcoholic drinks in Africa (Lois 1964), but, as Lord Lugard, the founder of Nigeria, is reported to have said, drunkenness in Africa during the colonial period was far less evident among the native people than among Europeans. Lynn Pan (1975) in her monograph described well the economic motives of the European colonists in bringing about a considerable increase in alcohol consumption in Africa: "Alcohol was part and parcel of the commerce which for centuries constituted the basic tie between Europe and Africa. It was an article of the barter system through which European goods were exchanged for African slaves." By 1844 one traditional ruler in the area that is now Nigeria is reported to have cried out: "Rum has ruined my country; it has ruined my people. It has made them become mad." He therefore begged "the English Queen to prevent the bringing of rum into this land...to spoil our country" (Pan 1975).

Later in colonial times, under pressure from religious bodies and aware of the damaging effect of the liquor traffic on their economic interests, the colonial powers sought to limit the sale of alcohol by means of international treaties: one in 1889, after the Brussels Conference (on the control and sale of liquor) of that year, and another in 1919 at St Germain-en-Laye. The League of Nations adopted a resolution on the matter in 1922. In 1925, in Geneva, an international conference on alcoholism adopted a number of resolutions on the liquor question in the colonies. After World War II, alcohol control ceased to be formally included in the terms of Trusteeship for Mandated Territories. However, in April 1947 the United Nations requested answers to several questions on alcohol control (among 247 questions relating to other issues) from colonial administrations. Two of these questions were: "What types and quantities of alcoholic and other spirituous beverages were imported, manufactured, and consumed?" and "What measures in the interests of the inhabitants have been taken to regulate the import, production, and consumption of such beverages?" In July 1956 the first Inter-African Conference on the Alcohol Problem, held in Abidjan, Ivory Coast, adopted a number of proposals aimed at the control of the use of alcohol in Africa (Pan 1975). However, none of these laudable measures of the colonial powers had any significant effect in controlling the supply or use of alcohol.

Little was known about the prevalence of alcohol consumption and its associated pathologies in Africa in the earlier part of this century, but several reports from Nigeria have indicated a remarkable increase in the last decade. If increased production and availability of alcohol is taken as an indirect measure of alcohol consumption, per capita consumption of alcohol must have increased sharply: the number of breweries increased from 15 in 1979 to 34 in 1985, and there are also now four distilleries and nine wineries (FOS 1985).

Epidemiological studies have shown an increased prevalence of alcoholism and alcohol-related problems (Odejide and Olatawura 1977; Odejide 1979; Anumonye 1980; Ebie and Pela 1981; Nevadomsky 1981a, 1981b, 1982, 1985; Oshodin 1981a, 1981b). These studies have found that both sexes (with males predominating) and all age groups, especially the young and the middle-aged, are involved; and that they include people from all educational and socioeconomic backgrounds. Thus, alcohol consumption and its associated medico-social pathologies constitute a major health hazard in Nigeria.

Hospital data indicate an increase in alcohol-related problems seen in hospitals. In the past two decades, the number of alcoholics treated at the Neuropsychiatric Hospital at Abeokuta, one of the country's principal psychiatric hospitals, has increased (Asuni 1975; Adelekan et al. 1986). Cases of alcohol-related problems have also been reported from general hospitals, in particular the University College Hospital at Ibadan (Odejide 1978).

The Approach of Traditional Healers

Traditional African society treats the alcoholic first by informal social sanctions; for example, he is socially isolated, in the sense of losing respect. If this fails, he is taken to a traditional healer. The traditional healers believe that alcoholism, like mental disorders, is caused by external agents, usually evil spirits (Abimbola 1975). This belief is in line with the tendency of the African to blame external factors for his problems. Accordingly, the traditional healer regards alcoholism as a curse, and treats it by performing certain rituals designed to remove the curse. The patient is admitted into the healer's home, his head is shaved and scalp scarified, and powder is rubbed into the scarifications to circulate in the bloodstream and there act as an antidote to the curse. Sacrifices are then made to the evil spirits that the healer has determined to be responsible for the condition in the particular patient, after which the patient is taken to a stream and his head washed into it; the evil spirits are supposed to flow away in the stream. The patient while staying in the healer's home, usually for several months, remains abstinent, and this prolonged abstinence is believed to be an effective element in the traditional healers' armamentarium.

The healers believe that anyone who completes this course of treatment is completely cured of his drug habit, but it is known that many relapse (Odejide et al. 1978a, 1978b). The healers do not follow up their patients. A positive feature of the system is the element of rehabilitation it provides, in that the patient during the period of six months to one year in the healer's home is encouraged to engage in such rural creative activities as farming and building. However, there is no liaison between the traditional healers and hospital treatment, although there have been popular appeals for some form of cooperation.

The Approach of the Main Religions and Sects

Lynn Pan (1975) has described how the Muslim and Christian leaders in colonial Africa tried to win converts by preaching abstinence from alcohol. It is to the credit of the early missionaries that they lent their moral weight to the campaign for international control of the liquor trade in Africa in the late nineteenth and early twentieth centuries. In Nigeria today, Christian and Islamic fundamentalism is rife. Every day on television and radio, and at revival meetings, the fundamentalists wage an indirect campaign against alcoholism as part of their efforts to win souls. Alcoholics may be admitted to church buildings, where they stay for months at a time. Prayers are offered for them and they are sprinkled with holy water in an attempt to cast out the evil spirits supposed to possess them. Also, the church provides them with some economic and moral support, and looks into their social problems.

The Penal Code and Public Disgrace

Under the penal legislation of northern Nigeria a Muslim who takes alcohol in any form other than for medicinal purposes is liable to be punished by imprisonment for up to one month or a fine, or both. In addition he may be caned in public, which serves to deter by public disgrace. Asuni (1975) observed, however, that these deterrents have not totally prevented people in northern Nigeria from taking alcohol, and that it is well known that alcohol is served in restaurants, in teacups as a disguise. Nevertheless, alcohol is much less likely to be used and abused in predominantly Muslim areas than elsewhere.

Northern Nigeria has no known organized treatment system for alcohol-related problems, apart from the psychiatric services of various general hospitals. The south has no penal legislation against drinking, but the few treatment systems in the country are to be found there. This reflects the general cultural attitude to drinking, where alcoholism is regarded as a social problem and not a disease.

Modern Methods of Treatment

In Nigeria, medical and social methods of treatment comparable to those in use in Western countries are practiced, mostly by government medical and social welfare institutions, with a minimal contribution from lay self-help groups.

Primary Preventive Measures

Some of the state governments (e.g., Oyo State) have established drug-abuse committees at the state capitals and local government headquarters, and have made them responsible for educating the public about the adverse effects of drug abuse. They are composed of health-care staff, teachers, religious heads, village heads, and other community leaders.

For the past five years, the International Council on Alcohol and Addictions has been running an annual two-week intensive training program on drug abuse, at Benin, Bendel State, for workers from various disciplines, such as law-enforcement agents, customs officials, teachers, and health personnel. It is designed to inform them about drugs that are commonly abused in Nigeria, and train them in the recognition and treatment of drug dependence. They are then expected to spread information on the abuse of drugs, including alcohol, to their local communities in various parts of Nigeria.

Hospital-Based Treatment

Alcoholic patients are treated in general and psychiatric hospitals. There are two specialized treatment units for alcohol and drug-abuse problems, one at the Neuro-Psychiatric Hospital at Aro, Abeokuta, which is a World Health Organization Collaborating Center for Research and Training, and the other at University College Hospital at Ibadan. Each has at least thirty-two beds. The mental health legislation makes no provision for the compulsory committal of alcholics to these centers or any other treatment facility.

Only a few attempts have been made to study the hospital patients being treated for alcoholism and alcohol-related problems in Nigeria. Asuni (1975) reviewed sixty cases of alcoholic complications admitted to the Neuro-Psychiatric Hospital at Aro over a ten-year period. Only three were females. Most were middle-aged and were either semiskilled or unskilled workers. The sociodemographic variables of groups described by other workers were essentially similar to Asuni's (Odejide 1978; Adelekan and Adeniran 1986).

Most of the patients present late and usually with psychiatric, physical, or social complications. The alcohol-related problems with which patients present at the Aro Neuro-Psychiatric Hospital (Asuni 1975) and University College Hospital, Ibadan (Odejide 1978), are quite diverse. They include alcohol dependence symptoms, occasional drunkenness, delirium, and dementia. The physical complications include liver malfunctioning, polyneuropathy, and impotence. Some of the associated social problems include loss of employment, marital disharmony, and financial problems.

Odejide (1985) conducted a one-year prospective study in three general hospitals in Ibadan to ascertain the role of alcohol in emergency cases. Of 29,354 subjects who attended at casualty departments during the period of study, 57 (0.2%) had alcohol-related problems. The commonest were alcohol-related road-traffic accidents (33.3%), duodenal ulcer (26.3%), and intoxication (17.5%). This strikingly low number of patients with alcohol-related problems probably reflects the general national insensitivity to alcoholism.

Treatment Methods

The hospital treatment of alcoholics follows the traditional Western approach: full physical, psychiatric, and social assessment; admission for detoxification, treatment of diagnosed conditions, maintenance of abstinence (by psychotherapy, behavior therapy, etc.) and rehabilitation. The rehabilitation effort begins on admission, by liaison with relations, who invariably bring the patient to the hospital. The supportive role of the extended-family system is highly evident. In hospital, patients take part in occupational therapy, group psychotherapy, and sporting and social activities. Chemical deterrents (disulfiram, abstem, etc.) are not used.

Outcome and Follow-Up

Systematic outcome and follow-up studies of hospital-treated alcoholics have been very few in Nigeria. Of the sixty patients reviewed by Asuni (1975), eight absconded from hospital and never returned, two died a few months after discharge, thirteen were readmitted, and thirty-seven (62%) defaulted on follow-up appointments. Adelekan and Adeniran (1986) noted that 70% of their patients were lost to follow-up within six months. Some of the factors that militate against proper rehabilitation and follow-up include the severe nature of their illness, their poor socioeconomic and educational standing, and distance of the treatment unit from their normal abode.

In these circumstances, primary preventive measures and follow-up of treated patients in the community would be likely to be more effective than hospital treatment alone. Such measures would depend on the organization of a uniform information system on alcohol morbidity and mortality throughout the country, which would be difficult, as each state in the federation has its own health system.

Alternative Treatment Resources

Lay self-help groups such as Alcoholics Anonymous (AA) have a negligible presence. A small AA group was established in Lagos about 1982 by Gilbert (a Nigerian), and by 1985 consisted of twenty-five members from Lagos, Ibadan, Benin, and Port Harcourt; however, it is only in Lagos that members gather to discuss their problems. Another voluntary group, the Good Samaritans, maintains a small, poorly publicized, group at Ibadan.

Future Developments

The fact that law-enforcement agencies and social philanthropic organizations recognize the enormity of Nigeria's alcohol-related traffic casualties is attested to by the many signposts on the highways warning road users about the dangers of drinking while driving, and by the many newspaper articles and lay-organized seminars on this problem.

Yet there is a paucity of scientific data regarding alcohol-related problems and treatment systems in Nigeria in particular and Africa in general. The various social and cultural factors mentioned earlier may be partly responsible for this, but there has been little serious research into these problems in Africa. This situation can be remedied in the following ways:

1. Intensification of the public enlightenment campaigns so that people will come to realize that alcohol is a drug that can lead to physical, emotional, and social disabilities, that cultural denial of this disease will thus be lessened, and that cases will be diagnosed or recognized earlier.

2. Financial support for well-planned research relating to alcohol-related problems and treatment systems.
3. A study of the methods used by the religious healing homes. The popularity of these homes with patients and their acceptability cannot be ignored. They are closer to the people, more acceptable to most of them, more accessible, and cheaper than hospital services. Consideration might be given to integrating them into the general medical system as it relates to alcoholism in particular and mental disorders in general.
4. The involvement of lay self-help groups concerned with alcohol in a national effort to develop a program for alcoholism. They do not have to function like Alcoholics Anonymous in the Western world. Rather, concerned philanthropic social organizations, such as the Lions and Rotary Clubs and the Red Cross, have antidrug-abuse sections, the efforts of which could be effectively coordinated, since they have national coverage.
5. As a means of integrating statistics on alcohol-related problems into the general health information systems, first-line duty doctors and nurses in emergency units of general hospitals can be trained to apply such simple screening instruments as the CAGE test, in a way that will not overburden the staff. However, the feasibility of this idea will have to be tested in a well-planned study; and the quality of hospital record-keeping must be improved. To improve early case finding among offenders, the police will need to add the "breath-alyzer" to their equipment.

Conclusion

In conclusion, though issues relating to the control of alcohol-related problems have received scant attention, numerous potential resources in the public and private sectors can be harnessed for effective national action. Action at the primary, secondary, and tertiary levels of prevention should be backed by longitudinal research, surveillance, and funding.

References

Abimbola, W. 1975. *Ifa: An exposition of Ifa Literary Corpus.* Ibadan: Oxford University Press.

Adelekan, M. L., and R. A. Adeniran. 1986. Rehabilitation and follow-up issues in the management of drug abusers in Nigeria. *Proceedings of the 16th Annual Scientific Conference of the Association of Psychiatrists in Nigeria,* December 3–5.

Anumonye, A. 1980. Drug use among people in Lagos, Nigeria. *Bulletin on Narcotics* 32(4): 39–45.

Asuni, T. 1975. Nature of alcoholic and drug dependence problems in Africa with special reference to Nigeria. *Proceedings of the 31st International Congress on Alcoholism and Drug dependence,* February 23–28.

Ebie, J. C., and O. A. Pela. 1981. Some aspects of drug abuse among students in Benin City, Nigeria. *Drug and Alcohol Dependence* 8:265–70.

F.O.S. (Federal Office of Statistics). 1985. *Industry Profile.* Lagos.

Lois, P. E. 1964. Palm oil, illicit gin and the moral order of the Ijaw. *American Anthropology* 66:828–38.

Nevadomsky, J. J. 1981. Drug experimentation and social use among secondary school students in Bendel State—some recent findings. *Nigerian Journal of Economic and Social Research.*

———. 1981b. Patterns of self-reported drug use among secondary school students in Bendel State. *Bulletin on Narcotics* 33(1): 9–19.

———. 1982. Self-reported drug use among secondary school students in Bendel State. *Bulletin on Narcotics* 34:21–32.

———. 1985. Drug use among Nigerian university students: prevalence of self-reported use and attitudes to use. *Bulletin on Narcotics* 37:31–42.

Odejide, A. O., and M. O. Olatawura. 1977. Alcohol use in a Nigerian rural community. *African Journal of Psychiatry* 1(1): 69–74.

Odejide, A. O. 1978. Alcoholism. A major health hazard in Nigeria? *Nigerian Medical Journal* 8(3): 230–32.

———. 1979. Alcohol use in a sub-group of Nigerian literates. *African Journal of Psychiatry* 1(2): 15–20.

———. 1985. Alcohol-related casualties: the Nigerian experience. *Paper presented at the WHO International Conference on Alcohol-Related Problems.* Ontario, Canada.

Odejide, A. O. et al. 1978a. Some socio-psychiatric attributes of patients who utilize the facilities of traditional healers in the city of Ibadan. *Tropical and Geographical Medicine* 30:115–19.

———. 1978b. Traditional healers and mental illness in the city of Ibadan. *Journal of Black Studies* 9(2): 195–205.

Oshodin, G. O. 1981a. Alcohol abuse—a case study of secondary school students in a rural area of Benin district, Nigeria. *Drug and Alcohol Dependence* 8:207–13.

———. 1981b. Alcohol use among high-school students in Benin City, Nigeria. *Drug and Alcohol Dependence* 7:141–47.

Pan, L. 1975. Alcohol in Colonial Africa. *The Finnish Foundation for Alcohol Studies* 22. Aurasen Kirjapaino Forssa.

Afterword: Common Directions and Remaining Divergences

Jukka-Pekka Takala, Harald Klingemann,
and *Geoffrey Hunt*

In the chapters of this book, the authors have related the stories of their countries' alcohol-treatment systems. In doing so they have suggested a variety of factors that had influenced that evolution—factors determined largely by each country's unique history and culture, but to some extent also shared with others. In this afterword the editors undertake three tasks. First, they discuss, in general and "qualitative" terms, the commonalities among the countries and the ways in which they diverge. Second, they use the data provided by the authors on the extent of alcohol treatment systems (with some additional information) to construct a tentative order of the "size" of alcoholism treatment systems, and seek in other societal elements possible explanations of the differences in size. Finally, they look more closely at the formerly designated "socialist" countries, to take some account of the dramatic political changes that took place during the preparation of this book.

While large differences remain in the ways in which different countries regard alcohol and tackle alcohol problems, most of the countries represented here have much in common. Most obviously, almost all have seen a large growth in alcoholism treatment. However, there have also been parallel shifts in the way in which alcohol problems are conceptualized and treatment administered, and in the clients of treatment services.

From "Badness" to "Illness" to "Alcohol-Related Problems"

The title of this book, *Cure, Care, or Control: Alcoholism Treatment in Sixteen Countries,* points to three possible basic models of problem comprehension: alcoholism as a disease, alcoholism as a social problem, and alcoholism as a problem of public order and security. The relative significance of these conceptions corresponds to the institutional reactions of health care systems, social welfare facilities, and the criminal justice systems.

Most of the chapters report a shift in the image of alcoholism—roughly, from "badness" to "illness"—and a related change in the social division of labor in the handling of alcohol problems: much of the responsibility for dealing with deviant drinking has shifted from the police and the judiciary to the social and medical authorities. However, the changes have been different and their timing diverse, with the result that the roles of social as distinct from medical authorities vary greatly.

The concept of alcoholism as a disease has gained some ground, but it is still far from being universally regarded as a discrete, irreversible disease (cf. Miller 1986). In Nigeria traditional healers hold the view that it is a curse of evil spirits—that is, something caused externally—and that it can be permanently cured by the use of proper rituals. Even when a disease concept is central, it takes varying forms. In the U.S.S.R. and Hungary, much more than elsewhere, the concept is strongly influenced by biological psychiatry. In the U.S.A. particularly, the concept of alcoholism as a discrete, irreversible disease, rather as Alcoholics Anonymous regards it, seems to prevail, officially at least. In other countries, the concept is less clear-cut or central, and alcohol problems are often seen as complex sociopsycho-medical issues.

Similar variance is to be found in the accepted goals and methods of treatment. More and more, the classic requirement of abstinence as the only acceptable goal of treatment is being relativized. In New Zealand, after some controversies in the mid-1970s, many treatment institutions consider controlled drinking and a holistic-treatment approach legitimate, and the requirement that the staff of treatment units be abstinent has been largely dropped. To the extent that survey data on treatment ideology are available, they show a dwindling influence of the abstinence dogma in treatment practice: in Switzerland, about half of the alcohol counselors are no longer abstinent, and for only 19% of the counselors was abstinence found to be of significance for obtaining employment in the alcohol treatment system. Hunt's survey among British counseling facilities demonstrates a similar shift in the organizational goals pursued.

In the "socialist" countries a change in the way of thinking has also taken hold after a phase in which deviant behavior was considered alien to the political system and the individual was held responsible. In Hungary, for example, the traditional influence of psychiatry and neurology has diminished in favor of sociotherapeutic approaches.

Officially in the U.S.S.R. and Yugoslavia individual abstinence has been the main goal of treatment, but in practice treatment is "more tolerant" and the attainment of unharmful drinking habits is also registered as a success. Yugoslavia can be characterized in particular by the use of group therapy in the widest sense. Some of the countries may eventually draw upon alternative traditions, such as psychoanalytic thinking in Hungary, the Hudolin model in Yugoslavia, and the combination of Western and traditional medicine in China.

All in all, it seems not only that many countries have moved from the "moral" to an "illness" model but also that the concept of alcoholism as a disease is being replaced by that of "alcohol-related problems," as Morawski states regarding Poland (Morawski in this book). It is also true of these countries, as of Poland, that the "disease" model has not fully replaced the "moral" model, nor the "problems-approach" the "disease" model: "all three are practiced today in the treatment system, although in different proportions."

Diversification and Smaller Treatment Packages

In most countries, the general increase in alcohol treatment resources has been associated with increasing deinstitutionalization, decentralization, and a differentiation of available treatment. This has favored endeavors toward privatization and the abandoning of the classic alcoholic by the treatment system. Almost everywhere, alcohol-specific treatment has been absorbed by the health care system.

Outpatient treatment has become relatively more significant than inpatient treatment in practically all the countries. While the early specific-treatment offers for alcoholism often included only inpatient institutions intended for long-term treatment—if indeed there were any offers apart from those in general and psychiatric hospitals—outpatient treatment has now become more prominent. In Sweden, for example, the number of outpatient facilities increased by 60% (from 100 to 160) between 1970 and 1987; during the same period the number of outpatient alcohol clinics ("A-clinics") in Finland rose from twelve to about fifty-six. However, despite the growth of outpatient treatment, some countries, such as Hungary and the Soviet Union, still rely greatly on compulsory inpatient treatment.

Alcoholism treatment has become more diversified. Instead of only one or two types of treatment services, many countries have diversified services, which better meet the needs of patients. Day-centers, short-term residential facilities, and other kinds of facilities have emerged as forms intermediate between classic outpatient and classic inpatient treatment. The average length of stay for inpatient cures has also decreased. The classic one-year cure has become an exception, and not only in Switzerland.

There are many reasons for the increase in outpatient care and the diversification of treatment. For one, outpatient treatment is cheaper. Also, the results of evaluation of inpatient therapy are hardly convincing. Moreover, considerations of civil liberty have lent support to outpatient treatment, particularly over compulsory inpatient "cures." The role of reform in psychiatry can be cited also, particularly in Italy, as parallel to, or sometimes a forerunner of, the rise of outpatient care. The expanding treatment system has in many countries also reached younger clients, who are "less likely than older patients to have serious medical or chronic-abuse problems requiring hospitalization or inpatient treatment," as the New Zealand chapter states.

Mutual-support groups, such as Alcoholics Anonymous, the largest and best known, have gained a foothold particularly in the Nordic and anglophone countries, while Italy, Poland and particularly Yugoslavia have set up similar groups, clubs of treated alcoholics, which employ trained therapists and have a formal link with the official treatment system. Alcoholics Anonymous often has a close de facto, but informal, presence in many organizations of the official treatment system. In the U.S.A., Alcoholics Anonymous, "rather than being solely an alternative to treatment, . . . has also become an adjunct to treatment and a part of aftercare."

Alcohol treatment has become more decentralized in many countries, often as part of a general shift of health policy implementation to the local level: the Italian mental health centers operate at a community level; the tendency to create autonomous chains of treatment at a cantonal level dominates in Switzerland; the new conservatism in the U.S.A. has shifted the burden of social problems to local communities; and in Sweden the new Social Services Act of 1982 transferred all alcohol-treatment affairs to communities.

Demographic Characteristics of Clients

Although few chapters cite specific studies about the demographic characteristics of treatment clients, it is plausible to assume that the client profile now tends to resemble the general population more closely than formerly. Yet it remains highly biased. Men still form the great majority of the patients, although the proportion of women has increased, according to every chapter that mentions the issue. The clients still tend to be much worse off socio-economically than the population at large, but, as many chapters report, the classic, truly down-and-out, unemployed, single male alcoholic is no longer common in many alcohol treatment agencies. The client profile of alcohol treatment services seems to have shifted from heavy overrepresentation of the lowest social strata to increasing proportions of the middle strata, particularly in the more modern outpatient and short-term inpatient facilities.

Differentiation of available treatment can also imply new inequalities. In some countries, two classes may be distinguished in the treatment system. Thus, in the U.S.A. the "public alcohol system has increasingly become an adjunct of the courts, a softer option for more deserving cases; it has accordingly taken on a more coercive nature. Meanwhile, the burgeoning private treatment sector has responded to, and reflects, the desires and needs of not only the affluent upper segment of the population, but also the large comfortable middle class with 'good jobs' " (Weisner and Morgan in this volume). Austria is seen to have a two-class system: treatment-reluctant alcoholics are compulsorily admitted to general psychiatric services, and treatment-seeking alcoholics can enter special inpatient and outpatient institutions, which are separated physically and administratively from general psychiatry and are better staffed and equipped.

Differentiation has also accompanied increasing privatization. In some cases, 'classic' alcoholics are being eliminated from the treatment system, not because there are none or that they do not need help, but because treatment providers reach out for other kinds of clients.

The change in the client profile is probably closely linked with changes in the ways in which clients approach and end up in treatment. These are influenced by the opportunities that prospective clients have to seek treatment voluntarily and the sorts of pressure or coercion that may be applied to persuade them to accept treatment. Civil committals to institutions have become less common almost everywhere, while some other forms of compulsory treatment may have increased, at least in some countries. In the anglophone countries, a growing share of clients has been referred by the criminal courts, while some other countries have no provision for such referrals. Also, there are various forms of indirect legal compulsion, such as those provisions of employee assistance programs that compel employees to choose between being dismissed and entering treatment.

The initial phase of the International Studies in the Development of Alcohol Treatment Systems—the project upon which this book is based—on the legal framework of alcohol treatment in six countries, led to the following conclusion: "There has been a definite tendency to reform this sort of legislation so that civil liberties are given better legal protection than earlier" (Klingemann and Takala 1987,78) and "the recent laws on alcohol treatment tend to emphasize voluntary treatment relatively more than earlier laws used to do" (ibid., 9). By and large, the country studies contained in this book confirm this finding. In New Zealand, for instance, although the 1966 Drug Addiction Act varied little from the earlier in its provisions for involuntary committal, it shifted official responsibility for the custodial care of alcoholic patients from the Justice Department to the Health Department. The symbolism was important: in the first fifteen years of operation, voluntary admissions exceeded custodial committals. In 1983 only 11% of all alcohol-related admissions to psychiatric hospitals and other official treatment centers came under the act. In Italy, the legislation on the reform of psychiatry abolished the regulations (obviously rarely applied) on the committal of patients to "judiciary asylums" for "chronic intoxication."

To what extent this trend to more voluntariness in treatment has been replaced by covert or indirect forms of coercion remains an open question. Recent developments in some countries seem to point to a renewed delegation of control functions to the treatment system: public participation in the drama "drunk driving—dying too young" has increased remarkably in the U.S.A., New Zealand, and also recently in France, as well as in Switzerland and Italy. The drinking-driving programs in the U.S.A. increased by 60% between 1982 and 1984, and in New Zealand, in 1986, 31% of the new clients in outpatient

care were referred by the Justice Department. The element of social control
again plays an important role in early detection, particularly at the work place.

The differentiation in the treatment offered in many countries may be
regarded as an adaptation of treatment systems to changes in national
environment. Changing referral practices in other sectors have already been
mentioned as an important influence in the cases of the U.S.A. and New
Zealand. Three other factors also are significant: the explicit recognition of
alcohol treatment by both national and private health-insurance companies;
the increasing use of preventive medicine, including early detection, at the
work place especially; and the integration of alcohol-specific care into national
public health systems. These factors, combined with deep cuts in social-welfare
budgets, have opened up a lucrative therapy market in Western countries, and
east European countries may soon follow suit.

The Size of Alcohol Treatment Systems

The rapid growth that characterized alcoholism treatment systems in
almost all the countries, particularly during the 1970s, started off from various
levels and proceeded in different ways across the countries. Great differences
persist in the relative density of alcoholism treatment. Even among the
developed countries some seem—from admittedly imperfect data—to have
alcoholism-specific treatment services that are tens of times denser than those
of others.

Ideally, data would refer to the numbers of people needing alcoholism
treatment, the count of inpatient beds and outpatient visits available for them,
and the numbers of patients treated in a year, together with information on
such topics as the professional levels of treatment providers, and the length
and intensity of treatment. The ideal data set would contain alcoholism-specific
treatment events in all contexts: in a general practitioner's consulting room,
at a general or psychiatric hospital, in a unit specialized in alcoholism and
other addictions, and in mutual support groups. Regrettably, however, efforts
to obtain comparable data about the extent of alcoholism treatment organizations
have been unsuccessful; there is no reliable and suitable quantitative measure
that all the countries could use.

It was decided to use the available data, and to fill with estimates the
remaining gaps, in order to rank the countries with respect to "density of
alcoholism treatment." Almost all the chapters contain data on the numbers
of alcoholism treatment units. For nine countries, there are data on numbers
of beds in inpatient institutions, for five on the yearly count of clients in inpatient
treatment units, and for four on the total of outpatient clients. These four
measures are presented in Table 1, and with one exception they date from
around the year 1985. The "density of alcoholism treatment" is a constructed

ordinal variable based mainly on a combination of the ranks of the countries on these four dimensions.

Admittedly, this is not a very robust basis for comparing the relative size of different alcoholism treatment systems, and it is hoped that the reader will be aware of its limitations. Besides the large gaps in the dimensions presented, the data do not take into account alcoholism treatment outside addiction-specific treatment organizations—they do not cover alcohol-related admissions to general or psychiatric hospitals or alcohol-related visits to general medical practitioners; nor do they take into account other formal or informal organizations or social processes that may be fulfilling similar functions in society. Also, it must be remembered that the large federal states and the small jurisdictionally uniform countries are rather different units of comparison (cf. Kohn 1987). The countries represented range from such small and culturally homogeneous countries as Austria and Finland to large federal or multinational and heterogeneous countries such as Canada, U.S.A., U.S.S.R., and China. Even in smaller federal countries such as Switzerland and Yugoslavia, treatment systems vary considerably from one jurisdiction to another. In their chapter, Weisner and Morgan state that the U.S.A. has a "large range across states in the rate for the total budgeted treatment capacity (from 0.34/1000 to 3.86/1000)." In Canada, Ontario indicates much more concern about alcohol treatment than the other large provinces. The chapter on Yugoslavia relies heavily on data for one republic, Croatia.

Despite these shortcomings it was considered worthwhile to use the data to examine—tentatively, at least—the relationship between the amount of alcoholism treatment and other societal variables that might account for the differences in size. It is more instructive to investigate even fragmentary data than not to investigate them, and the editors believe that a conceivable perfect rank-list would look rather similar to that provided here. That the rank-list is based on data from units that are specialized in alcoholism treatment, and thus labeled, is certainly a limitation but also germane to the subject, since the focus of interest is on what societies call alcoholism treatment as much as, or rather more than, on what alcoholism treatment is in practice. In part, the figures are an artefact of the ways in which organizations are labeled and statistics kept, but extensive record-keeping on alcohol treatment reflects systematic attention to the matter.

The rank of the "density of alcoholism treatment" of different countries is included in Table 1. It was reached by ordering most of the countries on the basis of a combination of the number of treatment units, beds, inpatients and outpatients: lowest rank (that farthest from the top) was used as a basis for the final rank. Where countries were equal, a common dimension was given precedence over disjunctive dimensions, and of similar ranks the rank derived from the longer list was decisive. Countries for which no figures were provided were ranked on the basis of other considerations: Canada's largest province,

TABLE 1

Extent of Alcoholism Treatment per 100,000 Population in the mid-1980s.
Numbers of Alcoholism Treatment Units, Beds, Annual Inpatients and
Annual Outpatients in Facilities for Alcoholism Treatment and Care

Rank of size[1] of treatment	Units	Beds	Inpatients	Outpatients
1 Finland	4.9	97	477	755
2 Sweden	5.0	62	213	
3 U.S.S.R.		47		
4 Switzerland	2.6	15		308
5 New Zealand	1.8	23	33	270
6 Canada				
7 U.S.A.	1.5		21	119
8 Yugoslavia				
9 Hungary	1.0		217	
10 Poland	1.0	9		
11 U.K.	.4			
12 Austria		6		
13 Italy	.26			
14 France[2]	.03	1		
15 China				
16 Nigeria	.00	.06		

Notes:
[1] Final rank is based on ranking the countries' lowest ranks on single dimensions. Where countries were equal, a common dimension was given precedence over disjunctive dimensions, and of similar ranks the rank derived from the longer list was decisive.
[2] Data from 1977.

Sources: the chapters of this book.

Ontario, which has more than a third of Canada's population, has about 350 alcohol-treatment clients per 100,000 population (Mann et al. 1988). Yugoslavia has approximately four clubs of treated alcoholics per 100,000 population (Lang and Srdar in this volume); unlike "pure" self-help support groups, such as Alcoholics Anonymous, these clubs have trained therapists and they are explicitly part of the official alcohol-treatment system. Although both China and Nigeria have only scattered alcohol-specific treatment units, the indications are that China is the more concerned about providing treatment of alcoholism on a national scale.

Ranking France, with data from 1977 only, is open to question. In the 1980s, concern about alcohol problems increased in France (Dubois et al. 1990; Sulkunen 1988). In 1980 French private practitioners made 1,640 (total) and

309 (first-time) diagnoses of alcoholism per 100,000 population (Fig. 1 in Mossé's chapter)—a huge number compared with the mere 1.25 beds per 100,000 in specific alcohol-treatment units. Nevertheless, the mounting concern has not yet led to any notable changes in the offers of specific alcohol-treatment, and since the subject-matter, in the main, is treatment specifically labeled as alcohol treatment any error in ranking is unlikely to be serious.

Next, the relationships between treatment density and other societal variables are examined. In many cases, the analysis is restricted to member states of the Organization for Economic Cooperation and Development (OECD), on which data are more readily available than on the developing and the east European countries.

First, there is an inverse relationship between alcohol consumption and treatment density rank (Table 2). The countries with a high consumption of alcohol tend to have smaller alcoholism-treatment systems (Spearman's rho = -0.7 for both fourteen countries with 1972 consumption data and ten countries with 1980 data). The countries low on treatment density are also traditional wine countries, and the treatment rank correlates positively and significantly with the share, but not the absolute amount, of spirits in the total alcohol consumption.

TABLE 2

Density Rank of Alcoholism Treatment and
Alcohol Consumption (with the share of spirits)

Country	Treatment extent rank	Alcohol consumption liters of pure ethanol		Share of spirits 1980 (%)
		1972	1980	
Finland	1	5.1	6.3	44
Sweden	2	5.8	5.4	44
U.S.S.R.	3	6.3		
Switzerland	4	10.8	11.5	20
New Zealand	5	8.2	8.6	22
Canada	6	7.6	8.8	38
U.S.A.	7	6.8	10.5	35
Yugoslavia	8	7.7		
Hungary	9	9.5		
Poland	10	.6		
U.K.	11	6.9	7.3	23
Austria	12	12.4	11	15
Italy	12	13.6	13	15
France	14	16.8	16.3	21
China	15			
Nigeria	16			

Secondly, those countries with low treatment density also have high cirrhosis mortality, which is not surprising, given the consumption data. Table 3 indicates the direction of change in mortality from liver cirrhosis. It reveals no clear pattern, although the growth countries (Finland, Yugoslavia, Hungary, and England and Wales) average a little higher in the extent-of-treatment rank than do countries with diminished rates of cirrhosis.

TABLE 3

Extent of Alcohol Treatment Rank and Liver Cirrhosis Mortality per 100,000

	Size of treatment rank	1976		1987		Change 1976–1987
		Male	Female	Male	Female	
Finland	1	7.4	4.1	11.8	5.5	growth
Sweden	2	17.5	8.3	9.5	5.1	decline
U.S.S.R.	3					na
Switzerland	4	19.8	6.1	16.9	6.4	decline/stable
New Zealand	5	6.4	3.2	4.4	2.5	decline
Canada	6	17	7.4	11.2	5.7	decline
U.S.A.	7	19.8	9.8	14.4	7.3	decline
Yugoslavia	8	18.9	7.8	25.2	11	growth
Hungary	9	25.3	13.4	62.7	26.3	growth
Poland	10	14	7.8	13	7.2	stable
U.K.	11	4.3	3.4	6.4	5.2	growth
Austria	12	46.5	16.8	38.3	14.6	decline
Italy	13	49.5	19.5	42	19.7	decline/stable
France	14	47.6	18.9	29.2	11.5	decline
China	15			17.8[a]	9.4[a]	na
Nigeria	16					

Note:
[a] Selected cities

The negative correlations between extent of treatment, on the one hand, and, on the other, alcohol-consumption and cirrhosis rates do not mean that a large alcohol-treatment system has been able to keep drinking and cirrhosis in check. Rather, high consumption has tended to go with both high risk of liver cirrhosis and relatively little political concern about drinking, while the "spirits countries" have had lower total consumption combined with much political concern about drinking—a concern that has inter alia favored measures for providing specific treatment for alcohol problems. Certainly, alcohol treatment may marginally reduce the incidence of liver cirrhosis (cf. Mann et al. 1988), although it is more likely that both increase in alcohol treatment and decrease in liver cirrhosis reflect growing cultural and political concern about alcohol problems.

There is, then, no simple relation between alcohol problems and alcohol treatment efforts. One might guess that, if there is any alcohol-problem indicator that would have a clear positive correlation with the extent of an alcohol-treatment system in a multicountry comparison, it would be the number of arrests for drunkenness. This figure is very high in Finland and probably the U.S.S.R., rather high also in Sweden, and rather low in the central and southern European countries. However, unlike the rate of liver cirrhosis, the count of arrests for drunkenness is rather an indicator of problem management than one of a mere condition; alcoholism treatment and arrests for drunkenness may be two expressions of one concern.

Thirdly, there is little correlation between wealth and the extent of alcohol treatment. Empirical evidence from the OECD countries suggests that economic factors play a major role and demographic factors a rather minor role in explaining differences in health-care spending among countries (Pfaff 1990). The rank order of the extent of alcoholism-treatment systems indeed shows a positive correlation with per capita gross domestic product, but the relationship is weak (Spearman's rho $= 0.53$ and $p = 0.4$) and mostly owing to China and Nigeria (without which rho $= 0.31$ and $p = 0.27$). Thus, a certain minimum wealth is a prerequisite for any sizeable specialized alcoholism treatment but, given this minimum, the size of the alcohol-treatment system depends more on factors other than wealth. This corresponds to Mäkelä's findings on the presence and extent of Alcoholics Anonymous in different countries (Mäkelä 1990). Like general wealth, a country's total spending on health care fails to explain the size of its alcoholism-treatment system, as OECD statistics of health expenditure have indicated (OECD 1987).

Fourthly, there are hints that some structural aspects of the general health care system bear a relation to the size of a particular alcohol-treatment system. One is the weight of inpatient treatment and outpatient consultations in health care. It would be plausible to expect that countries that offer many health services would offer many kinds of such services. However, Mäkelä (1980) for one draws attention to the intriguing fact that the annual number of inpatient days per capita seem to correlate negatively with the number of outpatient consultations. This was true also for the OECD countries in our sample, for data from 1980 (OECD 1987). Also, the rank on the number of outpatient consultations (in general health care) shows a negative, but nonsignificant, correlation with rank on alcohol treatment, and there is as well a weak positive correlation between treatment-extent rank and inpatient days per capita. Analogous relationships exist with regard to the share of institutional and ambulatory treatment in total expenditure on public health: the OECD countries with high spending on institutional treatment tend to have much alcoholism treatment—both inpatient and outpatient—while countries with higher spending on ambulatory care tend to have less alcohol-specific treatment of either kind.

Perhaps inpatient treatment can be more readily specialized than ambulatory treatment, or there may be some deeper reasons for countries that have emphasized institutional over ambulatory treatment to be also the more concerned about alcoholism.

Another pertinent aspect of the general health-care structure is the relative importance of the market mechanism and government intervention in the provision of health services. Roemer (1989, 74) offers the following fourfold typology of health system policies: *entrepreneurial and permissive, welfare-oriented, universal and comprehensive, and socialist and centrally planned.* With an "entrepreneurial and permissive" health system policy (e.g., U.S.A.) "most of the health system, as reflected in overall expenditures, operates through a private market. Government's role in the system is relatively weak." In "welfare-oriented" countries (e.g., Canada), "market intervention has been substantial with respect to the financing of the system. Health care for most, nearly all, of the people is a public responsibility. A private medical market continues, however, and much government money is spent on payments to private providers." In countries with "universal and comprehensive" health system policies (e.g., Great Britain, New Zealand), "government has intervened in the market even more extensively. Both the financing and the provision of health services have become highly organized. The total population has become entitled to virtually complete health service as a civic right—at least to the extent of available resources." "Socialist and centrally planned" health systems (e.g., the Soviet Union, Czechoslovakia, China), "have been almost completely removed from market dynamics. Government has become responsible for all health services; all health resources, physical and human, have come under government control. Private buying and selling of health care has not been prohibited, and it exists, but to a very small degree."

In Table 4 the countries represented in this book are classified according to Roemer's four types of national health systems. It shows also, for the OECD countries, the percentage share of public health expenditure in total expenditure on health services, 1984. We have taken 75% as the cut-off point between "welfare-oriented" and "universal and comprehensive." Of course, classifying Nigeria is difficult, as is, particularly after the political changes of 1989, the labeling of four of the European countries as socialist.

The "universal and comprehensive" health system policies seem to go with a larger alcohol-treatment system than the "welfare-oriented," but the association is weak.

Here we leave the discussion of the relationship of the extent of alcoholism-treatment with the structure of health care: the suggestion is that outpatient vs. inpatient orientation, and market mechanism vs. government intervention, may have something to do with it.

TABLE 4

Extent of Alcohol Treatment Rank and Health System Policies

Size of treatment rank	Health policy type	Public share of health spending 1984 (%)
1 Finland	Universal and comprehensive	78.8
2 Sweden	Universal and comprehensive	91.4
3 U.S.S.R.	Socialist and centrally planned	
4 Switzerland	Welfare-oriented	65.4[a]
5 New Zealand	Universal and comprehensive	78.4
6 Canada	Welfare-oriented	74.4
7 U.S.A.	Entrepreneurial and permissive	41.4
8 Yugoslavia	Socialist and centrally planned	
9 Hungary	Socialist and centrally planned	
10 Poland	Socialist and centrally planned	
11 U.K.	Universal and comprehensive	88.9
12 Austria	Welfare-oriented	60.9
13 Italy	Universal and comprehensive	84.1
14 France	Welfare-oriented	71.2
15 China	Socialist and centrally planned	
16 Nigeria	Entrepreneurial and permissive (?)	

Note:
[a] 1980

Sources: Roemer 1989, OECD 1987

Fifthly, the size, expansion, and character of alcohol treatment seem to depend less on the amount of, or changes in, alcohol consumption, or on any well-defined treatment needs, or even on economic resources, than on the ways in which societies perceive alcohol and alcoholism. Temperance movements are one factor that has expressed and molded the perception of alcoholism in different countries (Levine 1990). Countries with a strong temperance history tend also to be countries with strict alcohol control policies and well-established research into alcohol problems. Table 5 shows two—admittedly anecdotal—indicators of such interest: the number of contributors from the countries to recent conferences of the International Council on Alcoholism and Addictions (ICAA) and membership counts of temperance associations one hundred years ago. ICAA participants are seen to rank high also on extent of treatment. It may be that in a country in a specific political and cultural situation, "the expansion of the treatment system may be seen as a kind of cultural alibi for the normalization of drinking and the relaxation of controls," as Mäkelä et al. (1981, 65) have suggested, but the normal finding in an inter-country

Takala, Klingemann, and Hunt

TABLE 5

Importance of Alcohol Treatment and Selected Indicators in Temperance History

Rank of size treatment	Contributors to selected ICAA meetings			Members of temperance organizations 1885[2]
	absolute number	population weighted no.	pop. weighted rank	
1 Finland	59	12.0	1	8,933[3]
2 Sweden	56	6.7	2	70,750
3 U.S.S.R.	25	0.1	14	1,200[4]
4 Switzerland	16	2.7	3	6,009
5 New Zealand	5	1.6	8	
6 Canada	51	2.0	6	
7 United States	308	1.3	10	552,596
8 Yugoslavia	52	2.3	4	
9 Hungary	29	2.7	3	
10 Poland	37	1.0	11	
11 U.K.	82	1.8	7	1,689,432
12 Austria	6	0.8	12	870
13 Italy	98	2.1	5	
14 France	80	1.5	9	3,269
15 China				
16 Nigeria	14	0.2	13	

Notes:
[1] Oslo 1988, Budapest 1986, Rome 1985, Zagreb 1983, Vienna 1981, Tours 1979. Host countries are attributed the average contribution for non host years; multiple authors count.
[2] Meeting international d'Anvers contre l'abus des boissons alcooliques, 11, 12, et 13 septembre 1885. Brussels 1886.
[3] Finnish associations in Russia proper (874 members) included
[4] Russia; Finnish associations in Russia proper excluded

comparison is that alcohol political restrictions go hand in hand with extensive alcoholism-treatment facilities.

In sum, the attention paid to alcoholism treatment seems to depend more on alcohol cultural and political traditions than on any clearly defined treatment needs or total economic resources. Of course, this is no surprise to students of alcohol issues. Moreover, "much treatment" is not necessarily better, and evaluation of different ways of organizing alcoholism treatment efforts is beyond the scope of this book. In general, variations in treatment offers are acceptable when "they result from uncertainties in medical science regarding appropriate treatment" (Smits 1986), and certainly there is room for doubt as to whether there is or will ever be an appropriate (medical or multidisciplinary) treatment

TABLE 6

Importance of Alcohol-Treatment System and Selected Dimensions of
Government Alcohol Control Policy (1987/1988)

Size of treatment/ rank[a]	Country	State monopoly[b]	Advertisement regulations[c]	DrDrLim[d]	T%B[e]	T%L[e]	T%W[e]	LibIn[f]
1.	Finland	m	3	.5	41	66	66	2
2.	Sweden	m	3	.5	34	92	69	2
3.	U.S.S.R.	m	0	.0	—	—	—	1
4.	New Zealand	m	9	.8	30	53	20	4
5.	Canada	m	9	.8	53	82	69	3
6.	U.S.A.	m(18states)	9	1.0	34	56	31	5
7.	Hungary	nm(1982)	0	.0	58	86	28	2
8.	Switzerland	pm	3	.8	14	31	5	4
9.	Poland	pm	0	.2	80	90	80	1
10.	U.K.	nm	8	.8	31	51	29	5
11.	Austria	pm	9	.8	36	40	31	4
12.	Italy	pm	9	.8	20	27	8	6
13.	France	pm	6	.8	16	45	18	5

Notes:

[a] 1 = best developed

[b] State monopoly (comprehensive monopoly m = 0, partial monopoly pm = 1, no monopoly nm = 2) # of advertisement outlets from 0 -9/BAC levels indicative of drunk driving higher than 0.8 or no regulation (0 = 0; 0-0.8 =1; above 0.8 = 2)/the sum of the tax percentages for home consumption of the three beverage types (0-100 = 2; 101-150 = 1; 151 and more = 0).

[c] Number of possibilities for advertisement according to media and beverage type; 0= no advertisement; 9= advertisement for beer, liquor, and wine in print, radio, and TV. Source: *Brewers Handbook*, p. 443, Table 31.

[d] BAC levels indicative of drunk driving.

[e] Tax burden on beer, spirits, wine: percentage of price for home consumption.

[f] Liberalization/Index ranging from 0 to 8.

for alcoholism. However, whether differences in the amounts of alcoholism treatment and in the ways of offering it make any difference to the average alcoholic, they do make a difference to society.

Changes in the Former "Socialist" Countries

During the preparation of this book, far-reaching changes took place in China (the steady increase of markets since 1978), the U.S.S.R. (*perestroika*), Poland (from martial law to the victory of *Solidarnosc*), Hungary (free elections), and Yugoslavia (the redefinition of central power after the death of Tito). The respective chapters in this book deal mostly with the time before these changes could have any impact on these countries' alcohol treatment systems. How have these changes influenced alcohol treatment?

Private economy and a pluralization of social life gained ground in most East European countries as well as in China during the last decade. Democratization and decentralization made alternative ways of meeting health needs more acceptable. Inside the official health-care systems, medical cooperatives were formed and private medical practice was permitted; outside the systems, self-help groups, healers, and church groups (especially in Poland) became more important (Sokolowska and Rychard 1989). Similar tendencies can be seen in the alcohol treatment system in Poland. The number of clubs of alcohol patients has quadrupled since 1984 and Alcoholics Anonymous groups are spreading, after attempts to involve professionals have been given up. In the U.S.S.R. the network of anonymous treatment services for paying patients has been expanding since 1985. In Yugoslavia, since the 1960s, the sociotherapeutic model of the Zagreb School of Alcoholology, which emphasizes family therapy and includes an aftercare network of patient clubs, has become an influential arm of the alcohol treatment system. In Hungary, concern about the ineffectiveness of alcohol-treatment methods under the official system led to a greater acceptance of psychotherapy and sociotherapy by the end of the 1970s.

Since the death of Mao Zedong a more individualistic, Western-medicine perspective has gained ground in China, and local practices vary even more (Waitzkin and Britt 1989). Along with a movement toward a more market-oriented economy, treatment responsibilities, including partial financing, were shifted to neighborhood and factory health-care stations, supported and supervised by hospital personnel. A ''strengthening of the capacity of health care organizations for self-development'' was propagated. Although it fits into the picture, the reader may be surprised to learn that in China it is part of health policy that individuals pay part of the cost of treatment.

Changes in the public health-care systems of the socialist countries were paralleled by changes in official definitions of the nature of social problems, corresponding to the ways in which alcohol problems were dealt with. It became progressively untenable to claim that such phenomena as alcoholism, crime, and suicide ''compromised'' the socialist society, were only remnants of capitalism, and had to be hidden from the public view (Pataki 1989).

Official recognition of alcohol problems as an important topic on the public agenda led in some of these countries to the adoption of stringent alcohol policy measures. Even though the U.S.S.R. had already rather severe alcohol laws (see Table 6) and a record of failed experiments, bold alcohol-policy measures were undertaken: the decree of 1985 was the most stringent alcohol-policy package since prohibition times, and provided for a strengthening of treatment efforts. Less spectacular but still impressive is the list of indicators of ideological change in the other formerly socialist countries: in Hungary political rejection of psychoanalysis, and the subordination of psychiatry to neurology, were typical of the alcohol-treatment field for the period 1950–65. In the mid-1960s, however, interdisciplinary welfare centers for alcoholics were set up and the low status of alcohology on the periphery of the public health system was subjected to growing criticism. By the end of the 70s the government even approved a complex research program in order to study deviant phenomena and to institute a preventive service. In Yugoslavia after 1964, the political climate favored the integration of the twelve-step approach of Alcoholics Anonymous into the Hudolin program (the law until then had forbidden the anonymity of group members). In Poland, after a long period of compulsory treatment measures, the 1982 Act, *Upbringing in Sobriety and Counteraction of Alcoholism,* introduced a new long-term alcohol policy, influenced by ideas of community psychiatry. Indicators of a new sensitivity toward alcohol problems in China are the organization, since 1985, of special treatment units for patients suffering from "alcohol dependence and poisoning," the national conference on alcohol dependence and poisoning in 1986, and the conduct of several epidemiological surveys in the 1980s.

The recognition of alcoholism as an important political issue in China especially is surprising in view of the traditionally minor role of problem drinking in the Chinese culture. Confucianism and Taoism emphasized moderation, order, and harmony, and also had a powerful influence upon Chinese attitudes toward alcohol consumption (Heok 1987). These values have been decisively undermined with the onset of rapid economic growth, the dramatic transition from a redistributive and collective economy to a marketlike economy (Nee 1989), and urbanization, which in turn has led to a breakdown of the regulatory control of drinking in smaller families, especially in the case of males (Zhang, in this book).

How have these new official attitudes in the "socialist" countries toward ways of handling social problems affected the treatment of alcohol problems? Have ideological changes been accompanied by specific action in the treatment field to establish new institutions and apply new therapies?

In the U.S.S.R. the ambitious 1985 policy did not lead to a lasting reduction in consumption, and the restrictions on the availability of alcohol had to be moderated; nevertheless, the growth of alcohol-specific treatment is apparently an enduring effect, even though the allocation of funds may change again in the future. In Poland, however, the number of treatment units has hardly increased, and the new institutions envisioned in the new alcohol policy of the 1980s have not materialized. In Hungary, although the number of registered alcoholics and welfare centers almost doubled between 1965 and 1985, the idea of treatment coordination meets with many difficulties.

The formerly socialist countries being discussed here are faced with enormous economic problems and their gross domestic product may well fall temporarily below the minimum level of wealth that seems essential if a country is to have a sizeable specialized alcohol treatment system. Once such basic commodities as soap and bread become scarce, the staffing of after-care alcohol institutions with specialists and the training and employment of staff for new institutions will end up last in national priorities. However, with gradual liberalization and an improving economy, public opinion on social problems is likely to become increasingly influential for policy makers responsible for the allocation of resources to such a specific domain as alcohol treatment. Public opinion seems ambivalent about the management of alcohol problems. Any type of state intervention has been discredited, and alcohol-treatment systems in particular are still "tainted with the stigma of compulsion" (Morawski, in this book), which in the public mind may be hard to distinguish from control of political deviance in the past. Hence, the public may opt for the opening up of new treatment markets as alternative ways of meeting treatment needs. The public health system may resist this course, however. In the specific case of alcohol treatment, the problem is compounded. Hungary is probably typical: alcohol treatment attracts no "gratitude money"; neurologists, an influential professional subgroup, hold out for aversion therapy; and a planning mentality that favors large centralized institutions prevails. However, there may be cause for optimism: in Yugoslavia "the period of program and theory evolution is coming. . .our society is going to develop in the sense of efficiency, responsibility, and freedom." It remains to be seen whether after a couple of decades we shall come full circle to the discussion of problems of the welfare state and the reprivatization of health care, which today dominates the debate in Western countries.

Spring 1990

References

Dubois, G. et al. 1990. *Honneur pour notre démocratie.* Le Monde 29. March.

Heok, K. E. 1987. Drinking in Chinese culture: old stereotypes re-examined. *British Journal of Addiction* 82(3): 224–25.

Klingemann, H., and J.-P. Takala. 1987. International studies of the development of alcohol treatment systems—a research agenda for the future. *Contemporary Drug Problems* 14(1): 1–13.

Kohn, M. L. 1987. Cross-national research as an analytic strategy. *American Sociological Review* 52(6): 713–31.

Levine, H. G. 1990. Temperance cultures. Paper presented at the Society for the Study of Addiction Seminar on "Substance misuse—what makes problems," April 25–27. Windsor, England.

Mäkelä, K. 1990. Social and cultural preconditions of AA and factors associated with the strength of AA. Paper presented at the 16th Annual Alcohol Epidemiology Symposium of the Kettil Bruun Society for Social and Epidemiological Research on Alcohol. Budapest.

Mäkelä, K. 1980. What can medicine properly take on? In *Alcoholism treatment in transition.* Ed. G. Edwards and M. Grant, 225-33. London: Croom Helm.

Mäkelä, K. et al. 1981. Alcohol, society and the state. *A comparative study of alcohol control* 1. Toronto: Addiction Research Foundation.

Mäkelä, K., and S.-L. Säilä. 1987. The distribution of alcohol-related overnight stays among different authorities in Finland, 1960—1980. *Contemporary Drug Problems* 14(1): 125-36.

Mann, R. et al. 1988. Are decreases in liver cirrhosis rates a result of increased treatment for alcoholism? *British Journal of Addiction* 83:683-88.

Miller, W. R. 1986. Haunted by the Zeitgeist: reflections on contrasting treatment goals and concepts of alcoholism in Europe and the United States. In *Alcohol and culture.* Ed. T. Babor. New York: Academy of Sciences.

Nee, V. 1989. A theory of market transition: from distribution to markets in state socialism. *American Sociological Review* 54(5): 663-81.

OECD. 1987. Financing and Delivering Health Care. A comparative analysis of OECD countries. *OECD Social Policy Studies* no. 4. Paris: Organisation for Economic Cooperation and Development.

Pataki, F. 1989. The study of deviant behaviour in Hungary. In *Complex analysis of deviant behaviour in Hungary*—Project no. 4, ed. I. Münnich, and B. Kolozi, 9-14. Budapest: Institute for Social Sciences of the Central Committee of the HSWP.

Pfaff, M. 1990. Differences in health care spending across countries: statistical evidence. *Journal of Health Politics, Policy and Law* 15(1): 1-29.

Roemer, M. I. 1989. National health systems as market interventions. *Journal of Public Health Policy* 10:62-77.

Smits, H. L. 1986. Medical practice variations revisited. *Health Affairs.* Fall.

Sokolowska, M., and A. Rychard. 1989. Alternatives in the health area: Poland in comparative perspective. In *Cross-national research in sociology.* Ed. M. L. Kohn, 263-78. London: SAGE Publications.

Sparrow, M. et al. 1989. Alcoholic beverage taxation and control policies. *Brewers Association of Canada,* 7th ed. Ontario, Canada.

Sulkunen, P. 1976. Drinking patterns and the level of alcohol consumption: an international overview. *Alcohol 3.* New York: John Wiley.

————. 1988. A la recherche de la modernité. Boissons et buveurs en France aujourd'hui. Interprétation par un étranger. *Reports from the Social Research Institute of Alcohol Studies* 178. Helsinki.

Waitzkin, H., and T. Britt. 1989. Changing the structure of medical discourse: implications of cross-national comparisons. *American Sociological Review* 30(4): 436–49.

GLOSSARY

A-clinic/A-klinikka (*Finland*)—Units offering outpatient services for alcohol problems, usually staffed by one or more social workers, a nurse, and a part-time physician, and led by a social worker. Began as experimental private units in 1953. In the mid-1980s there were some 75 clinics, most owned by communes (local government). A-clinics also administer withdrawal facilities and other services.

1982 Act "on upbringing in sobriety and counteracting alcoholism" (*Poland*)—An act passed in 1982 by the Polish Parliament. It defines principles of alcohol policy and treatment, and specifies a number of preventive steps concerning demand and supply. It regulates various issues related to alcohol. It provides for a system of commissions for counteracting alcoholism at central, county and local level, a separate enterprise responsible for sales of alcohol (except beer), and other control measures. It obliges the government to introduce education about alcohol in schools. Since its introduction in 1983, the act has been amended frequently.

ADAMHA, Alcohol, Drug Abuse and Mental Health Administration (*U.S.A.*)—A federal agency that incorporates the National Institute on Alcohol Abuse and Alcoholism (NIAAA), the National Institute on Drug Abuse (NIDA), and the National Institute of Mental Health (NIMH). It is located within the National Institutes of Health.

ALAC (*New Zealand*)—Alcoholic Liquor Advisory Council

Alcohol Advisory Services (*England and Wales*)—These services, originally called Councils on Alcoholism, are information and referral agencies offering individual and group counseling and coordinating local prevention activities.

Alcohol Concern (*England and Wales*)—A government organization bringing together the Federation of Alcoholic Residential Establishments and the Medical Council on Alcoholism under one grouping.

Alcohology (*France*)—A medical speciality, but not yet recognized as such by the universities. It encompasses the whole field of alcohol-related problems from a multidisciplinary and multiprofessional point of view.

Alcohol tithe/Alkoholzehntel (*Switzerland*)—According to the Swiss Constitution and the law, the net income of the Alcohol Administration is set aside for social purposes. It is divided equally between the Swiss Government, for the Old Age and Widows and Orphans Pension Scheme and the Invalid Insurance, and the cantons, according to their resident population. This provision (Swiss Constitution art. 32, paragraph 9) is unique in the world. The cantons receive 10% of the net income of the Alcohol Administration (17.9 million francs for the budget year 1989/1990) to combat the causes and effects of alcoholism, drug dependency, and the abuse of generic drugs.

ALKO/Oy Alko Ab *(Finland)*—The Finnish Alcohol Company, Finland's alcohol monopoly. Founded after prohibition in 1932. Its retail shops have the monopoly of off-premises sale of alcoholic beverages stronger than "medium beer" (4.7 percent ethanol by volume). Alko licenses off-premises sale of medium beer and on-premises sale of all alcoholic beverages. It is the sole importer of alcoholic beverages. Alcohol may be manufactured only by Alko or under its license.

All-Union Research Center on Medico-Biological Problems of Narcology *(U.S.S.R)*—Founded in 1985 under the U.S.S.R. Ministry of Health, it coordinates the medico-biological research of all the institutes and agencies of the U.S.S.R. as well as all international collaboration on the problems of alcohol abuse, alcoholism, and drug abuse. Its areas of research are: methods of preventing alcoholism, biological mechanisms, diagnosis, and treatment.

All-Union Voluntary Temperance Promotion Society (TPS) *(U.S.S.R)*— Founded in 1985, the main task of the society is prevention, through the promotion of total abstinence and the creation of a negative opinion about alcohol. In addition to its main responsibilities of stopping drunkenness and alcoholism, and promoting an alcohol-free lifestyle, the society is responsible for the social control of alcohol consumption. Owing to its strong support from the trade unions (which are its co-founders), it has grown fast and counted about 14 million members (65% total abstainers) in 1988.

Area Commissions for Counteracting Alcoholism *(Poland)*—Commissions created by the act of 1982 "on upbringing in sobriety and counteracting alcoholism." They consist of officials, representatives of temperance societies, and private specialists. The central commission was attached to the prime minister's office in 1983, and transferred to the Ministry of Health in 1987. It acts as an advisory body, reviews programs for promotion of sobriety and control of alcoholism, advises on proposed legislation, and cooperates with private organizations. Every county *(voivodship)* has its own commission (49 in all). Its responsibilities are the planning, initiation, coordination, and review of action in the field of control of alcoholism. The responsibilities of about two thousand local (area) commissions include cooperating with other state administration bodies and voluntary organizations in the prevention of alcoholism and initiating action to treat and reform alcohol-dependent persons, granting assistance to such persons and to their families, and ordering, in the manner specified by the law, tests to determine alcohol dependence.

ARF (*Canada*)—The Addiction Research Foundation, an agency of the province of Ontario, responsible for research, development, and dissemination of programs and services for the prevention and treatment of substance abuse.

ATU (*England and Wales*)—Alcohol Treatment Unit. Usually within hospital premises.

Blue Cross/Blaues Kreuz (*Switzerland*)—Founded in 1877 in Geneva originally as the Swiss Temperance Association by the Swiss theologian Louis Rochat. Its foundation was closely linked with the Protestant awakening movement at the end of the eighteenth and throughout the nineteenth century, which, spreading from England, gained influence in Geneva as the *Réveil*. The Blue Cross played a key role in the development of professional treatment of alcoholism (1890 first Blue Cross agency in Zurich). The minister Arnold Bovet set up the first local chapter in the German-speaking part of Switzerland, in Bern in 1880. By 1915 membership figures had reached 31,302, and they soon surpassed those of the Swiss unions. Since the 1930s the Blue Cross has lost its broad backup as a social movement (1984: 6,743 abstinent and 990 nonabstinent members) but is still the most important Swiss temperance organization.

British North American Act (*Canada*)—Passed by the British Parliament in 1867, providing for the union of the British provinces in North America (New Brunswick, Nova Scotia, Quebec, and Ontario). The act, which became effective July 1, 1867, provided for the institutions of government for Canada and the distribution of power.

Canadian Centre on Substance Abuse (*Canada*)—A national agency established by an act of Parliament in 1988, with a mandate to provide leadership and a national focus for programs and community services contributing to the reduction of harm associated with licit and illicit drugs.

Care of alcoholics and drug abusers Act/Lagen om vård av missbrukare i vissa fall, LVM (*Sweden*)—In effect since 1982, it specifies the prerequisites for involuntary treatment of alcoholics and addicts.

Care of young persons Act/Lagen om vård av unga, LVU (*Sweden*)—In force since 1982, it specifies the prerequisites for treatment of young persons under twenty who are heavily using alcohol or drugs.

Caritas (*Austria*)—An organization of the Catholic Church founded in 1900 for the care of marginalized groups and outsiders—for instance, mentally disabled. In the 1920s undertook also the care of alcoholics.

CHA/Centre d'Hygiène Alimentaire (*France*)—A unit of a decentralized nationwide system of centers established between 1965 and 1976 to screen for early alcoholism, now often called. "Centre d'Alcoologie."

Chemical dependency programs (*U.S.A.*)—Residential treatment programs, often in the private sector and hospital-based. They usually borrow from the Minnesota model of treatment, are based on the disease concept, oriented toward abstinence, and rely heavily on AA ideology. Originally they were alcohol-specific programs, but they now admit also drug-treatment clients and those with combined problems. In the private sector they account for a large number of the combined alcohol and drug programs.

Clubs of Patients and Abstainers (*Poland*)—Clubs that create an alcohol-free environment for persons under and after alcohol treatment, as well as for their families. They were established by alcohol treatment facilities (patient clubs) or in local communities, parishes, work places, etc. (abstainer clubs). Their legal position varies; some are independent registered associations. Most belong to the National Federation of Abstainers Clubs. Some clubs organize meetings of AA groups.

Clubs of treated alcoholics (*Yugoslavia*)—Aftercare therapeutic groups, which include family members and are led by professional therapists. The first clubs were established in the late 1960s. Later they became the treatment system of choice and were very often used instead of inpatient of institutional treatment.

CNDCA/Comit National de Défense contre l'Alcoolisme (*France*)—National Committee of Defense against Alcoholism. A private association financed by the state, carrying out mainly national information campaigns. It also runs the *centres d'Alcoologie* and other kinds of treatment units.

Community Alcohol Teams (*England and Wales*)—Interdisciplinary teams that work with social services and community groups.

Community Mental Health Center/Centro di Igiene Mentale, CIM (*Italy*)—Refers to a unit of the system of centers organized since 1978 in the public sector and at a district level, for the prevention and treatment of psychiatric disorders.

Community Mobile Treatment (*Canada*)—A method of delivering prevention and treatment services to remote areas of the country, whereby a trained team of addiction specialists flies into a community to deliver treatment and prevention programs for a specified time.

Dalrymple House (*England and Wales*)—The first private retreat for patients suffering from problems related to alcoholism.

Detoxication (*Hungary*)—At most, twenty-four hours stay in a detoxification center.

DHSS *(England and Wales)*—Department of Health and Social Security. Now separated into two departments: the Department of Health and the Department of Social Security.

Dispensary *(Italy)*—A unit providing psychosocial therapy without the need of hospitalization. It offers the advantages of not disrupting the everyday life of alcohol patients, and freedom from the bureaucracy of hospital organization. Treatment is intensive, comprising group therapy three times a week for three months.

DRG, Diagnostic Related Group *(U.S.A.)*—DRGs are the categories under which reimbursement schedules are fixed for private health insurance and Medicare. The system covers 20,000 medical conditions classified into 467 DRGs. Each DRG has a specific predetermined payment rate for all hospital admissions. There are five alcohol-related DRGs. They are considered to have resulted in decreasing the length of stay and types of charges reimbursable under the private alcohol-treatment system.

Drinkwatchers *(England and Wales)*—Self-help group (rather similar to weight watchers) that helps members control drinking.

"Dryers" *(Sweden)*—A popular term for traditional asylums for alcoholics.

"Drying-out Clinics" *(U.S.A.)*—An informal term for medical detoxification programs instituted for paying clients in the 1950s. The term is sometimes used also for nonmedical detoxification centers.

DWI treatment programs *(U.S.A.)*—Driving While Intoxicated, also known as DUI, "driving under the influence." Most states have programs of alcohol education and treatment for convicted drinking drivers. In some states and counties the treatment is instead of other criminal justice sanctions; in others it takes place in addition to them. The number of individuals in such programs is very large.

Economic reform *(China)*—The economic reform in the People's Republic of China began after the Cultural Revolution and the death of Chairman Mao Zedong (1976), at the initiative mainly of Deng Xiaoping and other reformist leaders. It was a bold and large-scale reform in a Marxist country, involving all strata of Chinese society. For the peasantry (70–80% of the population) it meant access to private property and the possibility of selling part of their goods on the free market. In industry and business it meant that some companies could be run in an almost capitalist way, and could reinvest part of their profits. Foreigners were encouraged to invest in China through the creation of so-called "special economic zones" and of various joint ventures all over the country. The development of tourism was an important part of the reform. At first, the reform was quite successful, but since 1983-1985, it has been beset by considerably difficulties: inflation, inequality, unemployment, corruption, and lately, the homelessness of millions of people. These problems, and the fact that the economic reform was not accompanied by any political reform, gave rise to general dissatisfaction, of which the events in Tian'anmen Square in 1989 were a tragic expression.

Emerging drinkers (*Italy*)—Refers to the recent spread of young drinkers, male and female, meeting in discotheques, "pubs," or fast-food places. Beer is the preferred drink. Cultural values attributed to drinking are not only the traditional, related to socialization (in this case as a means of facilitating communication between the sexes), but also those related to fashion and to the symbols of a consumer society. Episodes of excessive drinking are fairly frequent. At the group level, drug abuse and addiction may be associated with ethanol abuse and excessive drinking. Drug abuse may represent a form of transgression against social norms.

Feldsher (*U.S.S.R.*)—A German word used in the U.S.S.R. to designate a health worker who corresponds fairly closely to "medical assistant," Health extension officer, "medox," "nurse-practitioner," etc.

Forel, Auguste (*Switzerland*)—(1848–1931) Born in the French speaking canton of Vaud, he was raised in a strict Calvinistic home. He gained a worldwide reputation as psychiatrist and brain researcher, as an ants specialist, and alcohol opponent, as well as a hypnotist and the author of *The Sexual Question*. Professor of psychiatry from 1879 to 1898 at the university of Zurich and director of the Burghoelzli clinic. He is considered to be the father of Swiss psychiatry and introduced modern work therapy for the mentally ill. He founded the Swiss Good Templars in 1892.

Grille de Le Go (*France*)—A set of clinical screening tests invented by Professor Le Go during the 1960s designed to classify individuals on a scale of physical and behavioral consequences of alcohol consumption.

Hassela communities (*Sweden*)—A group of treatment homes founded in 1969 for young abusers (under the age of 20) who have been subjected to compulsory treatment under the Care of Young Persons Act (LVU). According to the Hassela treatment ideology, the reeducation of the client, including the transformation of the abuser identity, is a necessary part of resocialization.

Hazelden Minnesota model (*Sweden*)—Treatment units—mostly inpatient— that base their therapy on AA ideology and rely on ex-alcoholics (alcohol counselors) as staff members.

HCEIA (*France*)—High Committee of Studies and Information on Alcoholism; created in 1954 by P. Mendes France, it is now related to the Ministry of Health.

HMO, Health Maintenance Organization (*U.S.A.*)—HMOs are a health insurance system developed as a response to rising health-care costs in the U.S.A. They are health insurance organizations that admit those insured to medical care only within a designated provider group. In some states, such as California and Oregon, they account for a large market share of the health-care system.

Hudolin model (*Yugoslavia*)—The Zagreb School of Alcohology system of treatment and prevention of alcoholism is known also, after its founder, as the Hudolin model. It is based on principles of social psychiatry.

IDREM/Institut de Documentation et de Recherche sur les Maladies (*France*)—Institute for Documentation and Research on Diseases. A research institute that analyzes and provides data about patients treated by physicians.

Incapacitation law/Entmündigungsordnung (*Austria*)—The law regulating the incapacitation of the mentally ill and of alcohol and drug addicts. It was introduced in 1916 and abolished in 1983. In 1984 a new law was enacted ("Sachwalterschaft für behinderte Personen"), which does not any longer distinguish between mentally ill and alcohol and drug addicts.

INSERM/Institut National d'Etudes et de Recherches Medicales (*France*)—National Institute for Medical Studies and Research.

Inuit (*Canada*)—People who, with the closely related Aleut, constitute the chief element of the native people of the Arctic and sub-Arctic regions of Canada, Greenland, Alaska, and Siberia. Inuit were earlier known by Europeans as Eskimos.

Involuntary Medical Committal/Trattamento Sanitario Obbligatorio, TSO (*Italy*)—Refers to mandatory treatment for acute mental disturbances. It lasts for sevem days (renewable) and is proposed by two doctors with the co-authorization of the municipal and legal authorities. It was introduced in 1978 with the Mental Health Act.

Järvenpää, Järvenpää Social Hospital/Järvenpään sosiaalisairaala (*Finland*)—Founded in 1951 as the Reception Unit for Alcoholics, and renamed in 1962. Outstanding for a long time as Finland's only public alcoholism institution headed by a physician.

Juice bars (*Austria*)—Alcohol-free restaurants and meeting places for recovering alcoholics and for those who prefer to abstain, founded by social workers in the early 1980s. Since it is difficult to raise funds for juice bars, only two have survived: one in Salzburg and one in Vienna.

Kanninen, Volmari (*Finland*)—(1860–1942) Kanninen was a little-known forerunner of voluntary outpatient treatment in Finland. "Cured of dipsomania" at Professor Bechterev's clinic in St. Petersburg, Kanninen started, with the help of some physicians, informal outpatient counseling for alcoholics in Helsinki in the 1920s. He criticized the dominance of involuntary inpatient institutions in official alcoholism treatment.

Local Health Unit/Unità Sanitaria Locale (USL) (*Italy*)—The local level of the National Health Care Service. Each district, for one or more municipalities of 50,000 to 200,000 inhabitants, has a local health unit. It is responsible for the administration and provision of health-care services, including prevention, diagnosis, treatment, and rehabilitation. It offers consultive services for legal, familial, and psychological problems. Its organization is established according to the norms of each region.

Maori (*New Zealand*)—The indigenous people of New Zealand.

Medical Centers of Social Assistance/Centri Medici di Assistenza Sociale (CMAS) (*Italy*)—A nationwide system of centers created by the 1975 Act on Drug Abuse, for the prevention, treatment, and rehabilitation of drug, including alcohol addicts. They may have inpatient and outpatient services, with a wide spectrum ranging from a minimum of methadone maintenance to several psychotherapeutic and rehabilitative activities, including assisted working programs. Alcohol problems are rarely handled except in cases of alcohol abuse in young polydrug abusers.

Medical Statistics of Diagnoses—Swiss Hospital Association/Medizinische Statistik, Diagnosestatistik—Vereinigung Schweizerischer Krankenhäuser (VESKA) (*Switzerland*)—The Medical Statistics-VESKA system is a service of the private Swiss Hospital Association, enabling Swiss hospitals to collect and analyze diagnoses and operations, with computer support, according to uniform standards, since 1970. The numbers of units included, and of registered cases, have increased continuously. In 1987, 139 hospitals contributed data from the diagnosis statistics for 520,000 patients, based upon the German translation of the Ninth Revision of the International Classification of Diseases (ICD9). VESKA publishes a comprehensive annual statistical report.

Medicare (*U.S.A.*)—A national social insurance system providing third party coverage for health care for many individuals over age 65, some categories of the disabled, and a few of their dependents. It reimburses primarily for inpatient treatment.

Modern drinkers (*Italy*)—Found in large industrial areas of northern Italy. They drink "new" alcoholic beverages, imported distilled spirits (whisky, vodka, or cocktails), and beer at any time of the day in "bars," which are premises meeting the demand of a short pause in a dynamic working life and of private alcohol consumption. Heavy alcohol consumption, mostly as a mechanism of coping with dissatisfaction, is also extended to women and younger subjects. Because of its relative new appearance, its social implications have gone almost unnoticed.

Narcology (hence **Narcological**) (*U.S.S.R.*)—The anglicized version of the Russian term for the medical specialty dealing with alcohol and drug abuse. In English it is used only in English-language publications and reports from the Soviet Union. Recently the term "addiction" is being used instead.

National Health Care Service/Servizio Sanitario Nazionale (SSN) (*Italy*)— Refers to the health care system, which was nationalized in 1978. By the obligatory payment of health insurance, every Italian citizen is entitled to health assistance in any part of the Italian territory, and for any kind of disease, at no additional cost. The act states: "the maintenance and the recovery of the physical and psychological health of all the population must be promoted without social and individual distinctions, and according to ways that assure the equality of the citizens in relation to the services."

NDATUS, National Drug and Alcohol Treatment Utilization Survey (*U.S.A.*)—NDATUS is co-sponsored by NIDA and NIAAA, and represents the only national data system on public and private alcohol and drug programs in the U.S.A. Point prevalence surveys have been conducted six times between 1979 and 1990. The data refer to agencies rather than clients.

New Federalism (*U.S.A.*)—An era of politics and policies beginning in the 1980s, which lessened the role of the federal government by decentralizing many of its former functions and increasing the responsibilities of state governments. This followed a period of strong federal leadership in the 1970s.

NIAAA, National Institute on Alcohol Abuse and Alcoholism (*U.S.A.*)— The federal-level agency mandated by the U.S. Congress to fund alcohol research and provide policy direction.

NNADAP (*Canada*)—The National Native Alcohol and Drug Abuse Program, the federal government program that funds direct services and training for native prevention and treatment programs.

NSAD (*New Zealand*)—National Society on Alcohol and Drugs.

Occupational therapy (*Hungary*)—Part of both voluntary and obligatory treatment in health institutions; it complements somato-, psycho-, and socio-therapy.

Occupational therapy in institute (*Hungary*)—Refers to institutional care of which occupational therapy is the main therapy. It may be complemented by other therapies. It takes place in open institutions for voluntary and obligatory treatment, and in closed institutions for obligatory occupational therapy and forced cure.

Outdoor pursuits programmes (*New Zealand*)—Programs that include a substantial proportion of physical activities such as canoeing, tramping, or abseiling. The purpose is to help clients become more self-aware, and gain self-confidence and self-esteem when tackling such activities with others. The programs are usually aimed at younger clients, and include counseling and group discussion.

Passbook system (*Sweden*)—Also called the Swedish restrictive system, or the Bratt system. An alternative to the prohibition laws of the U.S.A. and some Nordic countries. The purchase of spirits was restricted and controlled by "ration books." The system was in effect between 1919 and 1955.

Pathological drunkenness (*China*)—Acute psychotic episodes induced by relatively small amounts of alcohol. These are regarded as individual idiosyncratic reactions to alcohol, not due to excessive consumption and without conspicuous neurological signs of intoxication. [International Classification of Diseases, Fifth revision (291.4)].

Pavlov's reflexology (*Hungary*)—Treatment limited to reflex conditioning with apomorphine, used as an emetic.

Preporod (*Yugoslavia*)—Was Yugoslavia's first self-help group of alcoholics. Owing to the very restrictive political system of those days, the twelve-step appraoch of AA was not officially incorporated into the program, and the law forbade the anonymity of the members of such a group.

Pub (*England and Wales*)—Public house: a licensed tavern permitted to sell all alcohol beverages on the premises. Often a meeting place for local residents.

Reformatories for men/Männerheime (*Switzerland*)—One type of "multipurpose restitutive institution" besides halfway houses and retreats. They admit, in addition to addicts, persons who are socially deviant in other respects, except for delinquents. Their particular characteristic is that they admit alcoholics who are given little or no chance of being successfully treated.

Rejected drinkers (*Italy*)—Men who drink heavily (mainly cheap wine and distilled spirits) in unconventional ways, such as drinking alone or during the morning hours. Because of their disruptive familial and working situation, they live on social welfare. They usually cause public order disturbances, have high rates of suicide, and mental disturbances. They correspond to "skid row" alcoholics.

Resolution on actions taken to overcome drunkenness and alcoholism (*U.S.S.R*)—This resolution came into force on June 1, 1985, together with a corresponding resolution of the Council of Ministers of the Soviet Union, and the edict of the Presidium of the Supreme Soviet of the U.S.S.R. on the intensification of the struggle against drunkenness. The resulting program included antialcohol media campaigns, the creation of a nationwide volunteer temperance society, changes in the legal system to make some types of abuse offenses, greater controls on sale and availability of alcohol, and more rigid enforcement of existing laws.

SADAP, State Alcohol and Drug Abuse Profile (*U.S.A.*)—A data base on publicly operated and contracted alcohol and drug treatment programs in the U.S.A. The National Association of SADAP directors contracts with NIAAA to provide aggregate data on program-level data on program and client characteristics.

Samogon (*U.S.S.R*)—The generic name "self-distilled" covers a variety of illegally distilled beverages, such as chacha, tutovaia, vodka, and araka. Illegal home distillation has traditionally contributed a major share of the total alcohol consumed in the country. While the alcoholic strength of *samogon* varies between 25 and 75%, most often it matches that of standard vodkas. Impurities may affect the odor and taste of *samogon*. There are frequent cases of poisoning. Since the 1960s, sugar is the main raw material from which *samogon* is produced.

Sans Souci (*Sweden*)—The first private asylum for alcoholics, established in 1891 by the Uppsala county temperance association. Treatment was directed at both physical condition and moral state.

Sectorisation (*France*)—Organization of mental health services introduced in 1960. It allocates to every mental hospital service the care of a defined geographical area. Its effect has been to develop outpatient activities and decrease the importance of "classic" hospital care.

Sober (*Italy*)—Refers to people with drinking patterns that are popularly believed to have no harmful consequences, owing to the drinkers' capacity to tolerate alcohol and consequently moderate and control its effects, because of its use by Italians from historical times.

Socialist Workers Abstainers Union (*Austria*)—The largest and most important temperance movement in Austria, founded in 1905 as part of the Social Democratic Party. Like the other Austrian temperance organizations, it lost its importance after World War II.

Social Medical Commissions for Compulsory Treatment of Alcoholics (*Poland*)—The commissions were attached to local administrations between 1956 and 1982, under laws "on fighting alcoholism." Members were volunteers. A commission consisted of a chairman, secretary, medical doctor, and three representatives of temperance societies. The commissions decided on outpatient compulsory treatment of alcoholics, and supervised inpatient compulsory treatment imposed by a court.

Social pathology (*Poland*)—In Poland the term is often used for demoralization of juveniles, evasion of employment ("social parachutism"), alcoholism, and drug use: the subjects of four laws enacted during martial law in Poland.

Social Services Act/Socialtjänstlagen, SOL (*Sweden*)—Legislation to regulate social welfare and public assistance, introduced in 1982.

Société Française d'Alcoologie (*France*)—A scientific society created in 1978 for professionals (physicians, social workers, scientists, etc.) involved in alcohol related studies.

Society for support of free treatment of alcoholics/Vapaan Alkoholisti-huollon Kannatusyhdistys (*Finland*)—A voluntary organization founded in 1948 to establish small-scale (24 beds) retreats for alcoholics who voluntarily seek treatment. It was founded mainly to supplement the official homes for inebriates, which admitted mainly involuntary patients and were large institutions.

Sociopsychiatric service centers (*Austria*)—Outpatient treatment centers for mentally ill persons. Their task is to replace inpatient treatment and provide aftercare for those treated in psychiatric hospitals.

Stalinist science policy (*Hungary*)—This policy was founded on the ideology that poverty, alcoholism, insanity, and other social problems were the remnants of capitalism, and would disappear automatically with socialism. For this reason their existence was denied.

Swiss Alcohol Law/Eidgenössisches Alkoholgesetz (*Switzerland*)—In 1887 the Swiss voted to accept the first federal alcohol legislation, granting the government a monopoly for producing and importing spirits. In 1930 a new article (32) of the federal constitution was accepted by the Swiss people in a general vote. It was designed in the interests of public health to reduce the consumption of potable spirits and accordingly their import and production. It promoted the cultivation of dessert fruit and the use of raw materials for domestic distillery such as food and fodder. The 1932 federal law on spirits (revised in 1949, 1967, 1969, and 1974) was based on this constitutional foundation. Fermented beverages do not come under its jurisdiction.

Swiss Alcohol Monopoly and Federal Alcohol Administration/Eidgenössische Alkoholverwaltung (*Switzerland*)—For the discharge of the public health and fiscal functions of the Alcohol Administration, a monopoly of the federal government was found necessary. The Alcohol Monopoly, which comprises production, import, rectification, sales, and taxation of spirits, is the basic element of the success of the measures in the sector of the nonalcoholic use of fruit and potatoes, and also of the other measures taken to reduce the consumption of spirits.

"Talk dryers" (*Sweden*)—A popular term for asylums for alcoholics; they were established in the 1960s and employed psychodynamically oriented therapy.

Temperance Act (*Sweden*)—Legislation enacted in 1954, in effect until 1981, which regulated both voluntary and involuntary treatment of alcoholics, as well as temperance work carried out by municipal authorities.

Temperance office (*Sweden*)—The agency of a (municipal) temperance board.

Therapeutic community/Comunità terapeutica, CT (*Italy*)—Refers to private organizations offering treatment for drug addicts. Although at first voluntary self-supporting organizations, since 1975 they have been subsidized, in accordance with the Act on Drug Abuse. They do not necessarily adopt the "therapeutic community" treatment model. They were organized to decentralize assistance. Their number has remained limited, as drug abusers continue to attend general hospitals and the medical centers for social assistance for their medical needs (among them methadone maintenance).

Ticket modérateur (*France*)—Co-payment. A percentage of medical expenses (varying from one type of care to another) paid by the patient and not reimbursed by the French national health insurance.

Traditional Chinese medicine (*China*)—The study of the physiology and pathology of the human body and the diagnosis and control of diseases. It has its unique theory system and rich clinical experience. The theory system of traditional Chinese medicine was deeply influenced by ancient materialism and dialectic thought—the theory of yin and yang (the two opposing, yet uniting forces in nature)—and the five elements (five evolutive phases)—wood, fire, earth, metal, and water. Its medical theory system is characterized by taking the concept of the human body as a whole as the dominant idea, the physiology and pathology of the organs, bowels, channels, and collaterals as the basis, and the determination of treatment on the basis of the differentiation of symptoms and signs as the main method of diagnosis and treatment.

Traditional drinkers (*Italy*)—Male heavy wine-drinkers (sometimes with grappa) who drink in social contexts, whether at family meals or at work, in taverns (*osterie*), where men meet from the early afternoon to play cards or bowls, or during family or religious celebrations. The social group exerts informal control of alcohol consumption and of alcohol-related behavior. Hence alcohol-related problems go unnoticed until the manifestation of intolerance toward ethanol and hepatic or mental disturbances.

Treatment and cure (*Hungary*)—Somatic treatment followed by different kinds of therapy at least officially.

Treatment penalty (*Austria*)—Imprisonment combined with compulsory treatment. This type of penalty was introduced in 1975 and is carried out in special prisons. One of these special prisons was founded exclusively for alcohol and drug addicted offenders, in Vienna.

T-sprii (*Finland*)—A brand of denatured alcohol for domestic and industrial purposes, at one time popular among "skid row" alcoholics, and thought responsible for many deaths before it was removed from the market in 1972.

Turva (*Finland*)—Finland's first home for inebriates (1888-1938), founded by temperance activists on a farm. It admitted voluntary patients, who were expected to stay for one year at least, but usually did not.

Venngarn (*Sweden*)—The first public asylum for alcoholics. It was opened in 1916 with the coming into law of the Alcoholics Act of 1913. Venngarn received involuntary committed alcoholics.

Vinodol Law (*Yugoslavia*)—From January 6, 1288; a compilation of regulations and laws written in Croat. It regulated the position and rights of the princes of Krk (feudal order), the production, sale, and consumption of alcoholic beverages, and the cultivation of vineyards.

Vocational Rehabilitation of Disabled Persons Act (*Canada*)—An act of the federal government concerned with the vocational rehabilitation of disabled persons and the coordination of rehabilitation services.

Weiler Committee (*England and Wales*)—A government committee set up in 1967, to investigate the treatment of habitual drunkards within the criminal justice system.

Withdrawing cure (*Hungary*)—Somatic treatment, mostly aversion and reflex conditioning, and usually of two to three weeks duration.

White Paper on Alcoholism (*England and Wales*)—A White Paper puts forward government proposals on which legislation is to be based.

Zagreb's School of Alcohology (*Yugoslavia*)—was founded in 1964 at the initiative of Professor Dr. Vladimir Hudolin at the University Department of Neurology, Psychiatry, Alcoholism, and other Dependencies, which is part of University Hospital "Dr. Mladen Stojanovic," Vinogradska cesta, in Zagreb. It enables many scientific and medical workers, from Yugoslavia and other countries, to carry out joint research work and collaborate on projects concerning professional problems, rehabilitation, and prevention in the field of alcohology. The basis of treatment is the family therapy of alcoholics and clubs of treated alcoholics.

CONTRIBUTORS

Moruff Adelekan, NIGERIA, is a lecturer and consultant psychiatrist at the University of Ilorin Faculty of Medicine. While working as a resident doctor at the Aro Neuropsychiatric Hospital at Abeokuta, he joined Professor Odejide's research team at Ibadan University and contributed to a number of projects on alcohol- and drug-related issues.

Irina Petrovna Anokhina, U.S.S.R., is Professor and deputy scientific director at the All-Union Research Center on Medico-Biological Problems of Addiction, U.S.S.R. Ministry of Health. She is also a corresponding member of the U.S.S.R. Academy of Medical Sciences. Her research activities are in the fields of the neurobiological basis of alcohol and drug abuse, the biological mechanisms of predisposition to alcoholism, and the development of new methods of treatment of alcoholism and drug addiction.

Sally Casswell, NEW ZEALAND, is director of the Alcohol Research Unit. Her major area of interest is research that contributes to the development and evaluation of policies and programs designed to prevent alcohol-related problems. Recent publications include several on the evaluation of a major community project on alcohol, studies of alcohol advertising and alcohol taxation, and a framework for evaluating health promotion programs.

Vladimir Feodorovich Egorov, U.S.S.R., is a psychiatrist. He was scientific secretary of the U.S.S.R. Ministry of Health for eight years and is now chief of the Department of Narcology and Psychiatry in the Ministry of Health.

Irmgard Eisenbach-Stangl, AUSTRIA, is a researcher at the Ludwig-Boltzmann Institute for Addiction Research in Vienna and a lecturer at the University of Vienna. She is co-editor of the *Wiener Zeitschrift für Suchtforschung,* member of the Austrian Advisory Board for Alcohol and Drug Problems, and member of the WHO Expert Advisory Panel on Drug Dependence and Alcohol Problems. Her main research interests are alcohol and drug policies, social history of alcohol and illegal drugs, and cultural studies.

Zsuzsanna Elekes, HUNGARY, is a first assistant at the department of sociology of the Budapest University of Economic Sciences, Budapest. She contributed to the International Project of Adolescent Drinking Habits, and does research on deviant behavior, in particular on alcohol and drug epidemiology, alcohol and drug treatment and suicide frequency.

Geoffrey Hunt, GREAT BRITAIN, is a research and evaluation consultant working with the County of Santa Clara in California. He has carried out research and evaluation in the areas of health, social policy and addiction. He has written extensively on various aspects of alcohol consumption, and drug and alcohol treatment. His published work includes *Cohesion and Division: Drinking in an English Village; Darts, Drink and the Pub: The Culture of Female Drinking; Thinking about Drinking; Prayers and Piecework: Inebriate Reformatories in England at the End of the Nineteenth Century;* and *Wretched, Hatless and Miserably Clad: Women and the Inebriate Reformatories.*

Benson Adebowale Ikuesan, NIGERIA, is a research fellow in the department of psychiatry at the College of Medicine, University of Ibadan. He holds a master's degree in clinical psychology and is currently following a doctoral program. As a member of Professor Odejide's research team he has co-authored a number of papers on alcohol- and drug-related issues.

Nikolai Nikolayevich Ivanets, U.S.S.R., is director of the All-Union Research Center on Medico-Biological Problems of Addiction of the U.S.S.R. Ministry of Health. He does clinical research on the pathogenetic classification of alcoholism and the development of individual therapy methods.

Harald Klingemann, SWITZERLAND, studied at Cologne University (Germany), where he received the degree of Doctor of Economics and Social Science. He has taught at the Univeristy of Bonn, where he was a senior researcher in criminology and at the Fachhochschule of Cologne. He is director of research at the Swiss Institute for the Prevention of Alcohol and Drug Problems (Lausanne). His main research interests include the crosscultural analysis of treatment systems and self-help groups, and the study of everyday definitions of deviant behavior with regard to alcohol, drugs, crime, and youth problems. Recent articles: *From controlling a wayward life to controlled therapeutic measures? Changes in Swiss commitment laws* (Contemporary Drug Problems 1987); *Supply and demand-oriented measures of alcohol policy in Switzerland - current trends and drawbacks* (Health Promotion 1989), and *The movtivation for change from problem alcohol and heroin use* (British Journal of Addiction 1991).

Noriko Kurube, SWEDEN, is a doctoral student and a research project leader at the department of social work, University of Stockholm. Her current research project is a social historical study on the emergence of treatment in Sweden for alcoholics, which is financed by the Commission of Social Research (Social Department). The chapter on the Swedish system is based on this work. She also plans to investigate a client organization of alcoholics—Länkarna, which is a Swedish alternative to Alcoholics Anonymous.

Branko Lang, YUGOSLAVIA, is head of the Clinic for Neurology, Psychiatry, Alcohology, and other Addictions at the Dr. Mladen Stojanovic Hospital, Zagreb. He is a professor of neurology, psychiatry, and diseases of addiction at Zagreb University, a neuro-psychiatrist and psychotherapist. He is concerned mainly with the treatment and rehabilitation of alcoholics.

Juhani Lehto, FINLAND, is Head of Social Work Research and Development at the National Agency for Welfare and Health. He has also worked as a researcher at the Finnish Foundation for Alcohol Studies. His Ph.D. (soc) dissertation analyses the work of physicians, social workers and police officers with problem drinkers. His early experience in the field includes a period as junior physician in the alcohol ward of a Helsinki hospital.

Jenny Mellor, GREAT BRITAIN, is Head of the School of Social Work at the Polytechnic of North London. In addition to her teaching duties she has conducted research on Alcohol Advice Agencies, girls in Borstal, race relations in Britain, and the national health service. Her published work includes *Thinking about Drinking; Prayers and Piecework: Inebriate Reformatories in England at the End of the Nineteenth Century;* and *Wretched, Hatless and Miserably Clad: Women and the Inebriate Reformatories.*

Jacek Morawski, POLAND, is assistant professor at the Institute of Psychiatry and Neurology, department of studies on alcoholism and drug dependence, Warsaw. He is the scientific secretary of an expert group of a government council on counteracting alcoholism and has served as a WHO temporary advisor. His special fields of interest are criminology, social pathology, and alcohol treatment policies.

Patricia Morgan, U.S.A., is associate professor of public health at the University of California at Berkeley. She has conducted research on drug, alcohol, and mental health policy for the past fifteen years and participated in several international research projects under the sponsorship of the World Health Organization. These include the international study of alcohol control policies and the study of international trade in alcohol beverages. In 1982 she was awarded a Fulbright Fellowship to Italy where she conducted research on alcohol drinking patterns and problems, which resulted in several major publications.

Philippe Mossé, FRANCE, is a researcher in health economics at the Laboratoire d'Economie et Sociologie du Travail (LEST-CNRS), Aix-en-Provence. His publications deal mainly with hospital economics, medical care, and alcoholism. In 1987 he completed a thesis on the subject, ''The Logic of the Health Care System: The Case of Alcoholism,'' for which he was awarded the 2nd Robert Debré Prize in 1987 by the haut comité d'étude et d'information sur l'alcoolisme.

Adebayo Olabisi Odejide, NIGERIA, is professor of psychiatry at the College of Medicine, University of Ibadan, and dean of the faculty of clinical sciences and dentistry. Although he has carried out research in diverse areas of psychiatry, his predominant interests have been in psychopharmacology and drug- and alcohol-related problems. Recently he has pioneered the founding of the African Network of Alcohol and Drug Abuse (ANADA), of which he is secretary-general.

Alan C. Ogborne, CANADA, is a senior scientist at the Community Programs Evaluation Centre of the Addiction Research Foundation of Ontario and an associate professor in the department of psychology at the University of Western Ontario. His current research interests include alcoholism treatment systems and especially the role of specialized assessment/referral services. Other interests include the use of computers in substance abuse and treatment and the value of self-help methods for the control of substance use. He is co-author (with Reginald G. Smart) of *Northern Spirits: Drinking in Canada Then and Now* (1986).

Jude Uzoma Ohaeri, NIGERIA, is a lecturer at the College of Medicine, University of Ibadan, and consultant psychiatrist at the teaching hospital of Ibadan. Since 1980 he has been involved in a number of research projects on alcohol- and drug-related problems. He has a strong interest in the phenomenology of psychiatric disorders and rehabilitation issues.

Flavio Poldrugo, ITALY, is associate professor of psychiatry at the University of Trieste School of Medicine and coordinator of the Alcohol Research Center. He is also one of the founding members of the Association of the Clubs of Treated Alcoholics (1979). He is particularly interested in family therapy for alcoholics and evaluation of alcohol treatment programs.

Pia Rosenqvist, SWEDEN, is a sociologist at the Nordic Council for Alcohol and Drug Research, Helsinki. She is a co-author with Kettil Bruun and others of *Den svenska supen,* a historical study of Swedish drinking practices and alcohol control. At the Nordic Council she is responsible for the functioning of the secretariat, including joint Scandinavian research projects. Her current research interests include informal control of drinking and the management of alcohol problems and narcotics control systems in the Scandinavian countries.

Brian R. Rush, CANADA, is a scientist at the Community Programs Evaluation Centre of the Addiction Research Foundation of Ontario. His current research concerns the longitudinal study of the addiction treatment system in Ontario and the relationship between research and program development. Other research interests include forecasting models for assessing the need for treatment services and programs/procedures for screening and intervention with early-stage problem drinkers.

Sophia B. Shesterneva, U.S.S.R., is chief of the department of alcohol and drug dependency outpatient treatment at the All-Union Research Center on Medico-Biological Problems of Addiction, U.S.S.R. Ministry of Health. From 1981 to 1986, she was chief of the laboratory at the Ministry of Civil Aviation, State Research Institute of Civil Aviation. Her research has been focused on the rehabilitation of psychiatrically disabled offenders, psychophysiological methods of selecting aviation personnel, aviation psychology, and the clinical and social aspects of alcoholism.

Jasna Srdar, YUGOSLAVIA, is chief of the department of psychology at the Dr. M. Stojanovic Hospital in Zagreb and director of the Center for Education in Cybernetics, Transactional, and other Humanistic Approaches in Psychotherapy. She combines epidemiologic research on alcoholism and other addictions with treatment of alcoholics and drug addicts. She is responsible for the epidemiologic research program of the Center for Social Work of Zagreb and involved in nationwide programs for the protection and promotion of mental health.

Liz Stewart, NEW ZEALAND, is a researcher in the alcohol research unit, department of community health, University of Auckland, New Zealand. Her major area of interest is the development and implementation of alcohol control policies in New Zealand, focusing on the new liquor licensing system. Recent publications include articles on the lobbying of New Zealand parliamentarians on alcohol-related issues, and developments in the regulation of alcohol advertising in New Zealand.

Jukka-Pekka Takala, FINLAND, is a researcher at the National Research Institute of Legal Policy. He has published papers on conceptual issues of "alcoholism" and the development of the Finnish alcohol treatment system. Mr. Takala was coordinator of the international studies on the Development of Alcohol Treatment Systems in 1984–1986. Also, he has done research at the Finnish Foundation for Alcohol Studies and has been project secretary at the Nordic Council for Alcohol and Drug Research.

Janet Turner, GREAT BRITAIN, was a member of the alcohol research team at the Polytechnic of North London. Since then she has worked as a researcher on a race relations project for the Department of Sociology at the University of Aberdeen. She is now a Research Officer in the Medical Department of the International Planned Parenthood Federation in London. Her published work includes *Prayers and Piecework: Inebriate Reformatories in England at the End of the Nineteenth Century;* and *Wretched, Hatless and Miserably Clad: Women and the Inebriate Reformatories.*

Roberto Urizzi, ITALY, is resident in psychiatry in the department of psychiatry of the University of Trieste, and coordinator in the Alcohol Unit of Gorizia (Italy).

Yuriy Vladimirovich Valentik, U.S.S.R., is chief of the department of psycho-therapy at the All-Union Research Center on Medico-Biological Problems of Addiction, U.S.S.R. Ministry of Health. He is also scientific secretary of the commission of the U.S.S.R. Academy of Medical Sciences on "Clinic diagnostics and therapy of alcoholism, drug addiction, and toxicomania." His research interests are the dynamics of pathological craving for alcohol in alcoholic patients, the methods of pharmacotherapy and psychotherapy in alcoholism treatment, and the development of new methods and means of alcoholism treatment.

Constance Weisner, U.S.A., is senior scientist at the Alcohol Research Group of the Institute of Epidemiology and Behavioral Medicine, Medical Research Institute of San Francisco, and lecturer at the School of Public Health, University of California at Berkeley. She is director of the Alcohol Research Group's Community Epidemiology Laboratory, a series of studies measuring the prevalence and characteristics of alcohol problems in a variety of health and social service institutions.

Zhang Yanyi, CHINA, finished his studies at the Beijing Chinese Medicine College (six years), and works in the psychiatric branch of the Red Cross Chao Yang Hospital, with three years of clinical experience. He is now vice-secretary of the Beijing Mental Health Association and a member of the China Mental Health Society. He is an investigation and research worker for epidemic disease in a cooperative project of the United Nations Development Program in Beijing. In clinical work he has practiced Chinese medicine (acupuncture, Qigong, and the practice and pharmacy of Chinese medicine), Western meditation, and psychology as therapy methods.

INDEX